A Publication Sponsored by
the Society for Industrial and Organizational Psychology, Inc.,
a Division of the American Psychological Association

PERSONNEL
SELECTION
IN
ORGANIZATIONS

PERSONNEL SELECTION IN ORGANIZATIONS

Neal Schmitt
Walter C. Borman
and Associates

Foreword by Irwin L. Goldstein

 Jossey-Bass Publishers
San Francisco

For sales outside the United States, please contact your local Simon & Schuster
International Office.

Jossey-Bass Web address: http://www.josseybass.com

Manufactured in the United States of America on Lyons Falls
Turin Book. This paper is acid-free and 100 percent totally
chlorine-free.

Library of Congress Cataloging-in-Publication Data

Schmitt, Neal.
    Personnel selection in organizations / Neal Schmitt, Walter C.
Borman, and associates ; foreword by Irwin L. Goldstein. — 1st ed.
       p.   cm. — (A joint publication in the Jossey-Bass management
series and the Jossey-Bass social and behavioral science series)
    "A publication sponsored by the Society for Industrial and
Organizational Psychology, Inc., a division of the American
Psychological Association"—1st printed p.
    Includes bibliographical references and indexes.
    ISBN 1-55542-475-9
    1. Employee selection. I. Borman, Walter C. II. Society for
Industrial and Organizational Psychology (U.S.) III. Title.
IV. Series: Jossey-Bass management series. V. Series: Jossey-Bass
social and behavioral science series.
HF5549.5.S38S35   1993
658.3'112—dc20   92-23346
                                                      CIP

FIRST EDITION
HB Printing   10 9 8 7 6 5 4 3   *Code 9274*

CONTENTS

ix

Contents

Contents

FOREWORD

One of the principal objectives of the Society for Industrial and Organizational Psychology is, according to its bylaws, to "advance the scientific status of the field." In 1982, Richard J. Campbell, then the president of the society, asked Raymond A. Katzell to assume the chair of the Committee on Scientific Affairs, with the express charge of intensifying the society's pursuit of that objective.

One result of those efforts was a plan to publish a series of volumes entitled *Frontiers of Industrial and Organizational Psychology*. Each volume would deal with a single topic considered to be of major contemporary significance in the field, presenting cutting-edge theory, research, and practice in chapters contributed by individuals doing pioneering work on the topic.

The society wisely chose Katzell to serve as the first series editor. Under his guidance, the editorial board specified a number of objectives. First, the volumes are to be aimed at members of the Society for Industrial and Organizational Psychology, in the hope and expectation that scholars, professionals, and advanced students will all find them of value. Second, each volume is to be prepared by an editor who is a leading contributor to the topic it covers and who will take responsibility for the development of the volume. Third, the choice of topics and editors is made by the editorial board, which consults with the volume editors in planning each book. The chairperson of the editorial board serves as series editor and also coordinates the relationships and responsibilities of the volume editors, the editorial board, the series publisher, and the executive committee of the society. Fourth, volumes are issued when timely, rather than on a fixed schedule, but at a projected rate of approximately one a year.

Under Katzell's leadership, three significant volumes were developed and published: *Career Development in Organizations,* edited by Douglas T. Hall (1986); *Productivity in Organizations,* edited by John P. Campbell and Richard J. Campbell (1988); and *Training and Development in Organizations,* edited by Irwin L. Goldstein (1989). That these volumes achieved our objectives is evidenced by the number of sales, the laudatory book reviews, and the requests for rights to translate the books into other languages. I know that all the editors and authors of these first three volumes consider their success to be directly related to Katzell's thoughtfulness and energy during the entire six years that he served as series editor. With the completion of the third volume, I was chosen as series editor; since then, the fourth and fifth volumes, *Organizational Climate and Culture* , edited by Benjamin Schneider (1990) and *Work, Families, and Organizations,* edited by Sheldon Zedeck (1992) have been published and are already showing clear signs of the same success achieved by the first three.

As with earlier volumes in the series, *Personnel Selection in Organizations* was chosen because of its theoretical and empirical significance. Again, we were fortunate that two leading scholars, Neal Schmitt and Walter C. Borman, were willing to serve as coeditors. The society again owes a deep debt of gratitude both to Neal and Walter and to the authors who have contributed their thoughts for this volume. As Neal, Walter, and the authors clearly describe, there have been significant theoretical and empirical developments in the way that we approach many personnel selection topics, such as job analysis, criterion development, biographical and personality measures, and the concept of validity itself. In addition, there are significant societal changes, such as the development of small organizations, the changing demographics of work populations, the decline of the manufacturing economy, and the effects of technology, that significantly influence the way we think and perform research on personnel selection issues. Thus, this volume will explore a dynamically changing area of research; we hope the volume will be an important stimulus to growing theoretical and empirical interests.

This entire undertaking requires the cooperation and efforts of many dedicated people. In particular, I want to thank the volume editors, the authors, and the members of the editorial board. They have all contributed their wisdom and efforts to make this series a success. I also want to thank William Hicks, senior editor of the Management Series, and his colleagues at Jossey-Bass who have worked with us in making the goals of this series a publishing reality. Finally, I want to express my appreciation to Raymond Katzell for standards he set as the first series editor. I hope that the series, over the term of my editorship and beyond, can meet those standards.

September 1992   IRWIN L. GOLDSTEIN
                                                        University of Maryland
                                                        Series Editor

PREFACE

Personnel Selection in Organizations is an attempt to fill a gap between the broad, summary textbook treatment of selection issues and the relatively specific journal pieces that typically develop a technical point or present empirical evidence on a particular topic. The chapters in the book reflect cutting-edge thinking and research both in traditional areas of personnel selection (such as job analysis and criterion development) and in areas not usually covered in texts and journals (such as selection as a corporate strategy and selection out of the organization—downsizing, layoffs, and retirement).

Recent Developments in Selection Research

The timing of *Personnel Selection in Organizations* is excellent. Several new concepts and analytical procedures have significantly influenced the science of personnel selection. For example, meta-analysis and validity generalization work have been influential in addressing situation and site specificity in test validation. An important outcome of this research is that predictor measures appear to have more lawful relations with criteria than previously thought, which has made a more systematic study of predictor-criterion linkages possible. Path analysis and latent variable models have helped us regard predictors and criterion measures as partial indicators of underlying constructs. Accordingly, we, the principal authors of the book, believe that the relationships among predictors, among criteria, and between predictors and criteria can provide information about relations between these theoretical constructs as well as promote the scientific study of personnel selection.

Besides being the starting point in sound personnel selection practice, job analysis is increasingly enhancing our understanding of the constructs underlying performance and ability domains. Job analysis can, and should, help provide linkages between task and performance requirements and knowledge, skill, and ability requirements. Taxonomic developments in both domains have expanded the role of job analysis more effectively toward a scientific study of job performance and "person" requirements.

Efforts to develop models of job performance and models of criteria first help us to understand better what our traditional criterion measures are gauging. The models can also provide multiconstruct, multimethod depictions of criteria, in turn allowing a more differentiated view of criterion constructs and better understanding of relations between predictors and these constructs. In addition, various researchers have challenged us to broaden the set of performance outcomes we consider. While traditional concerns with productivity, turnover, and absenteeism continue to be important, there has been increased interest in considering the role selection plays in promoting job and life satisfaction, organizational citizenship behaviors, organizational commitment, and so forth.

Emphasis on identifying and measuring predictor and criterion constructs has also had an impact on some traditional predictor measures. Researchers who pay attention to a framework focusing on the notion of behavioral consistency across time and situation have found that framework helpful in developing more useful interview procedures and biographical and personality measures for selection. Recent emphasis on the process of interviewing will undoubtedly yield richer understanding of which constructs are, or can be, effectively measured in interviews. We continue to be concerned with fairness and have become increasingly aware of the impact of public and examinee perceptions of our selection procedures. This impact certainly affects what can be used, but it may also influence the meaning of the measures we do obtain. Finally, technology has broadened the possibilities we have available to present test stimuli and likely also has broadened the types of predictor constructs that we can measure efficiently.

During the last decade, there has been a great deal of discussion about the meaning of validity. The question arises as to which evidence adequately supports the inferences about job behavior we draw from our selection procedures. The issue is discussed in scientific publications, professional standards (the Society for Industrial and Organizational Psychology's *Principles* [1987] and the American Educational Research Association's *Standards* [1985], and major research programs (for example, the U.S. Army's Project A). Also, meta-analysis and validity generalization have afforded researchers another means of supporting inferences about test scores.

Applied psychologists have always realized that evidence of the validity of personnel selection procedures must be accompanied by evidence that those procedures are practically useful and that the constructs we measure have practical relevance to the organizations in which we work. Nothing is so practical as demonstrating to users of selection tests the cost savings or incremental levels of productivity to be realized from successful personnel selection programs. Recently, researchers have made considerable progress in estimating utility gains from selection, and work on utility formulations and utility measurement has generated new issues concerning constructs.

Thus, advancements in the science of personnel selection have been seen recently on several fronts. *Personnel Selection in Organizations* describes these exciting developments. Chapters on the construct of performance, alternative dimensions that expand the criterion domain, job analysis, predictor constructs, the selection interview, changes in testing technology, the concept of validity, and the practical usefulness of selection procedures all focus on these and related scientific developments.

Internal and External
Influences on Selection Research

We also believe that several significant societal and internal organizational changes influence the outcome and implementation of this research model. One of these is the growing realization that selection can help further organizational goals and strategy. Increases in the number and importance (to our national economy) of small organizations have led to consideration of appropriate selection procedures in small organizations and the way in which the research paradigm outlined in Figure P.1 (p. xxii) "fits" these applications: the changing demographic composition of our workforce and changes in technology may have considerable impact on the performance and predictor constructs we attempt to measure and on the recruitment, selection, and promotion of organization members. Finally, the decline in parts of our manufacturing sector has forced organizations to downsize and to implement voluntary and involuntary layoffs and retirement. This is selection in reverse, or selection out of an organization. Viewed within the context of the criterion-related research paradigm, this problem poses new and challenging questions about predictor and criterion constructs.

Audience

In recent years (and perhaps always), research and practice in human resource (HR) management, and particularly in selection, have been heavily influenced by a variety of internal and external forces. As researchers, psychologists, and organizational behavior specialists, we are aware of the impact of meta-analysis and validity generalization, the emphasis on construct validity and theory, and the role of cognitive science on personnel selection. As practitioners, we must be cognizant of changing demographics, the role of our legal system and society, the need to justify the expenditure of scarce organizational resources, and the need to articulate how selection influences (and is influenced by) various other organizational and HR interventions and efforts. As such, this book should be of interest to researchers and practitioners engaged in the study and implementation of selection systems (or HR interventions in general). Each chapter describes a variety of advances about which all involved in practice and research should be informed. Questions are raised that can and should be addressed by graduate students, researchers, and practitioners so that they can be aware of these issues and plan for their examination.

Overview of the Contents

In developing the content of *Personnel Selection in Organizations,* we asked the chapter authors to consider how researchers have treated construct validity issues either implicitly or explicitly. We also asked them to think about, whenever applicable, how consideration (or lack thereof) of construct issues has influenced development in an area. Finally, we asked them to explain how recent research in the areas they address has contributed to the science of I/O psychology and which additional scientific issues should receive our attention.

To organize the book, we adapted the traditional citerion-related validation paradigm (Figure P.1). A study based on this paradigm includes a job analysis, which serves as the basis for developing job performance measures, selecting or developing predictors, and developing a recruitment strategy. Our validity evidence comprises documentation of the inferences we draw from our predictors as accurate reflections of job performance measures. Validity, plus the practical constraints of the situation in which selection procedures are to be implemented and the individual differences in productivity, determines the utility of a procedure. As the outline of the book suggests, we believe there have been significant scientific advances in each of the components of this research model.

The chapters in Part One discuss various aspects of the paradigm of personnel selection. In Chapter One, Irwin L. Goldstein, Sheldon Zedeck, and Benjamin Schneider describe a model of the job analysis process as it applies to content-valid test construction. They point to many areas in which research should continue to assess the appropriateness of judgments made by subject matter experts and selection researchers during the test development process.

Figure P.1. Outline of *Personnel Selection in Organizations*.

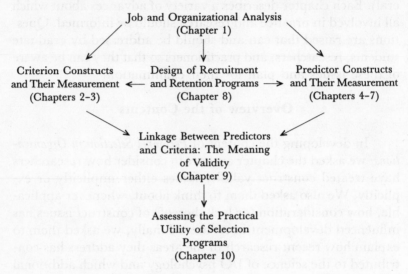

Job and Organizational Analysis
(Chapter 1)

Criterion Constructs
and Their Measurement
(Chapters 2–3)

Design of Recruitment
and Retention Programs
(Chapter 8)

Predictor Constructs
and Their Measurement
(Chapters 4–7)

Linkage Between Predictors
and Criteria: The Meaning
of Validity
(Chapter 9)

Assessing the Practical
Utility of Selection
Programs
(Chapter 10)

Internal and External Influences on the Implementation and Outcomes of This Criterion-Related Research Paradigm:

   Downsizing and Retirement: Selection Out of the Organization (Chapter 11)
   Changing Demographics and Technology (Chapter 12)
   Selection in Small Organizations (Chapter 13)
   Selection as Corporate Strategy (Chapter 14)

In Chapter Two, John P. Campbell, Rodney A. McCloy, Scott H. Oppler, and Christopher E. Sager provide a coherent theory of performance that should provide needed direction in generating hypotheses about exactly which measures of individual difference constructs ought and ought not to predict. In Chapter Three, Walter C. Borman and Stephan J. Motowidlo describe ways of assessing individuals' work behavior that go beyond the traditional definition of job responsibilities.

Richard J. Klimoski looks at the research that examines the constructs assessed in personality tests, selection interviews, assessment centers, and biodata. In Chapter Four, he explores the degree to which each of these selection instruments assesses similar individual difference constructs. The cognitive and behavioral processes that influence behavior, decisions, and, ultimately, measurement of job-relevant knowledge and ability are discussed by Robert L. Dipboye and Barbara B. Gaugler in Chapter Five. Moving beyond traditional concerns for psychometric fairness, Richard D. Arvey and Paul R. Sackett discuss the factors that affect the perceived fairness of selection procedures in Chapter Six. In Chapter Seven, Michael J. Burke examines the ways in which the computerized presentation of test stimuli affects the inferences we make about predictor constructs and future job behavior.

The attention of selection researchers (and most of the chapters in this book) typically focuses on promoting good decision making regarding the ability of job applicants. In Chapter Eight, Sara L. Rynes provides an interesting look at the selection process from the applicant's perspective.

Chapter Nine, by Neal Schmitt and Frank J. Landy, includes a discussion of the ways in which psychologists have examined and supported the inferences they draw from the scores generated by selection procedures. Beyond the concern for correctness, working in an applied situation for organizations demands that human resource practitioners and researchers examine the practical costs and benefits of the procedures they recommend.

In Chapter Ten, Wayne F. Cascio provides a description of recent advances in the assessment of utility.

With declines in the size of our workforce in certain segments of our economy and changes in retirement policies, employers have been forced to make painful decisions about who remains with an organization and who leaves. In Chapter Eleven, Stephen M. Colarelli and Terry A. Beehr discuss the impact this selection out of an organization might have on selection practices and the types of questions that selection researchers must address. In Chapter Twelve, Lynn R. Offermann and Marilyn K. Gowing provide a useful perspective on how the changing demographics of our workforce may influence selection research and practice in the future. While most of our selection research is based on the assumption that large numbers of incumbents and applicants are available, most organizations and jobs involve relatively small numbers of people. In Chapter Thirteen,

Paul R. Sackett and Richard D. Arvey explore the ways in which procedures developed for jobs with many incumbents can be applied to situations in which there are small numbers of people. In Chapter Fourteen, Charles C. Snow and Scott A. Snell look at the relationship between organizational objectives and selection strategy and argue that selection is often central to establishing and maintaining the organization's competitive advantage.

The chapters in Part Two offer commentaries on the chapters in Part One. In Chapter Fifteen, Robert M. Guion outlines six themes that point to the need for change in the practice of personnel selection; in Chapter Sixteen, Frank L. Schmidt discusses innovations in the field of personnel psychology.

In sum, we are enthusiastic about both the advances made recently in the science of personnel selection and the contributions made toward enhancing selection practices. We hope that the chapters in the book provide a worthy showcase for these advancements and contributions.

Acknowledgments

Several people and groups contributed to the creation of *Personnel Selection in Organizations*. First, the authors of the chapters in this volume contributed their time, effort, and creative thought. The diversity of ideas represented in these chapters and the authors' cooperation in reacting to our comments on various versions of their chapters made this project an extremely rewarding one. Second, we appreciate the confidence placed in us by the board of the Frontiers Series of the Society for Industrial and Organizational Psychology (SIOP) in inviting us to edit this book. In particular, Irwin L. Goldstein guided the project in its early stages, read initial drafts, and provided comments on all chapters. Third, we want to thank the staff and our colleagues at our respective universities for their help in producing this book and for "taking up the slack" when we neglected other duties to work on this project.

We also acknowledge the continuing efforts of Bill Hicks, senior editor of the Management Series, and the management team (especially Marcella Friel, our production editor) at Jossey-Bass. More than any other editor with whom we have worked, Bill understands the field of industrial and organizational psychology and confronts the various hurdles involved in producing an edited book. We believe SIOP's association with Jossey-Bass and Bill Hicks has been a very productive one and hope that future books in the series can be produced as smoothly as was ours.

September 1992   NEAL SCHMITT
East Lansing, Michigan

WALTER C. BORMAN
Tampa, Florida

References

American Educational Research Association, American Psychological Association, and National Council on Measurement in Education. (1985). *Standards for educational and psychological testing.* Washington, DC: American Psychological Association.
Society for Industrial and Organizational Psychology (1987). *Principles for the validation and use of selection procedures.* College Park, MD: Author.

THE AUTHORS

NEAL SCHMITT is professor of psychology and management at Michigan State University, where he has taught and conducted research on personnel selection and decision making since 1974. He received his B.A. degree (1966) from Loras College and his M.S. (1969) and Ph.D. (1972) degrees from Purdue University in industrial and social psychology. He is past president of the Society for Industrial and Organizational Psychology and current editor of the *Journal of Applied Psychology*. He is coauthor of *Staffing Organizations* (1986, with B. Schneider) and *Research Methods in Human Resource Management* (1991, with R. Klimoski).

WALTER C. BORMAN is professor of psychology at the University of South Florida and president of Personnel Decisions Research Institute in Minneapolis, Minnesota. He received his B.A. degree (1964) from Miami University in Ohio in psychology and his Ph.D. degree (1972) from the University of California, Berkeley, in industrial psychology. Borman is currently a consulting editor with *Personnel Psychology* and has extensive consulting experience in criterion development and employee selection with both public- and private-sector clients.

Richard D. Arvey is Curtis L. Carlson professor of industrial relations and adjunct professor of psychology at the University of Minnesota. He received his B.A. degree (1966) from Occidental College and his M.A. (1968) and Ph.D. (1970) degrees from the University of Minnesota, all in psychology. Arvey's areas of interest and research include employee selection and placement, motivation and job satisfaction, and training and development. Arvey's best-known work is his book *Fairness in Selecting Employees* (1979).

Terry A. Beehr is professor of psychology at Central Michigan University. He received his B.S. degree (1968) from Central Michigan University and his M.A. (1973) and Ph.D. (1974) degrees from the University of Michigan, all in psychology. Beehr was research investigator at the Survey Research Center of the Institute for Social Research from 1974 to 1975 and assistant professor of psychology at Illinois State University from 1975 to 1978. He is coauthor of *Human Stress and Cognition in Organizations* (1985) and *Psychological Stress in the Workplace* (in press). His primary professional interests are job stress, retirement, careers, and work-related attitudes.

Michael J. Burke is associate professor of psychology and business at Tulane University. He received his B.A. degree (1977) from the University of Notre Dame, his M.S. degree (1980) from Purdue University, Indianapolis, and his Ph.D. degree (1982) from the Illinois Institute of Technology, all in psychology. His primary research interests are prediction models, selection and classification, and utility analysis.

John P. Campbell is professor of psychology and industrial relations at the University of Minnesota. He received his B.S. (1959) and M.S. (1960) degrees from Iowa State University and his Ph.D. degree (1964) from the University of Minnesota, all in psychology. From 1964 to 1966 Campbell taught in the Department of Psychology at the University of California, Berkeley, and has been at Minnesota from 1967 to the present. From 1974 to 1982 he served as associate editor and then editor of the *Journal of Applied Psychology.* Campbell's current research interests include human performance measurement and selection and placement. He is author of *Measurement Theory for the Behavioral Sciences* (1978) and coauthor of *What to Study: Generating and Developing Research Questions* (1984, with R. Daft and C. Hulin) and *Productivity in Organizations* (1988, with R. Campbell).

Wayne F. Cascio is professor of management at the University of Colorado, Denver, and is president of the Society for Industrial and Organizational Psychology. He received his B.A. degree (1968) from Holy Cross College in psychology, his M.A. degree (1969) from Emory University in experimental psychology, and his Ph.D. degree (1973) from the University of Rochester in industrial and organizational psychology. In 1988 he received the Distinguished Faculty award from the Personnel/Human Resources Division of the Academy of Management. He is author of *Applied Psychology in Personnel Management* (1987) and *Costing Human Resources: The Financial Impact of Behavior in Organizations* (1987). His research on personnel selection, training, performance appraisal, and the economic impact of human resource management activities has appeared in several scholarly journals.

Stephen M. Colarelli is associate professor of psychology at Central Michigan University. He received his B.A. degree (1973) from Northwestern University in political science, his M.A. degree (1979) from the University of Chicago in social and organizational psychology, and his Ph.D. degree (1982) from New York University in industrial and organizational psychology. He is interested in the social psychology of personnel programs and the effects of organizational structures and values on the use of personnel programs.

Robert L. Dipboye is professor of psychology and administrative science at Rice University. He received his B.A. degree (1968) from Baylor University and his M.A. (1970) and Ph.D. (1973) degrees from Purdue University, all in psychology. Dipboye's research interests include staffing and selection, training, job analysis, and organizational behavior. He is on the editorial boards of the *Journal of Applied Psychology* and the *Academy of Management Review* and is a consulting editor for the *Journal of Organizational Behavior*. He is the author of *Selection Interviews: Process Perspectives* (1992) and coauthor of *Essentials of Industrial/Organizational Psychology* (1986, with W. C. Howell).

Barbara B. Gaugler is assistant professor of psychology at Rice University. She received her B.S. degree (1978) from St. Lawrence University in psychology, her M.S. degree (1981) from Ohio University in clinical psychology, and her Ph.D. degree (1987) from Colorado State University in industrial and organizational psychology. Her primary professional interests are personnel decision making and psychological assessment.

Irwin L. Goldstein is professor and dean of the College of Behavioral and Social Sciences at the University of Maryland, College Park. He received his B.B.A. degree (1959) from City College of New York and his M.A. (1962) and Ph.D. (1964) degrees from the University of Maryland, all in psychology. His research interests have focused on needs assessment and job analysis, evaluation models, and personnel systems, including selection and training systems. He has served as president of the Society for Industrial and Organizational Psychology and as associate editor of both the *Journal of Applied Psychology* and *Human Factors*. In 1988, he became the second series editor of the Frontiers of Industrial and Organizational Psychology Series.

Marilyn K. Gowing is assistant director for personnel research and development, a senior executive service position with the Office of Personnel Management in Washington, D.C. The office conducts basic, applied, and innovative research in every area of human resource management. Gowing received her B.A. degree (1970) from the College of William and Mary in psychology, her M.A. degree (1975) from George Washington University in industrial and organizational psychology, and her Ph.D. degree (1981) from George Washington University in psychology. In 1990, the university honored her with a Distinguished Alumni Award. She has also received awards for her achievements from the Internal Revenue Service, the U.S. Department of Housing and Urban Development, and the American Society of Association Executives.

Robert M. Guion is distinguished university professor emeritus in the Department of Psychology at Bowling Green State University. He received his B.A. degree (1948) from the State University of Iowa in psychology and his M.S. (1950) and Ph.D. (1952) degrees from Purdue University in psychology. Guion has been at Bowling Green since 1952 except for visiting positions elsewhere. He has consulted on selection and equal employment opportunity issues with many government agencies and private businesses. He is past president of the Society for Industrial and Organizational Psychology (SIOP) and of the Division on Evaluation and Measurement of the American Psychological Association. Honors from SIOP include twice receiving the James McKeen Cattell Award for excellence in research design and the Distinguished Scientific Contribution Award.

Richard J. Klimoski is professor of psychology and vice chair of the Department of Psychology at the Ohio State University, Columbus. He received his B.S. degree (1965) from the University of Massachusetts in psychology, his M.S. degree from Purdue University in industrial and organizational psychology and measurement, and his Ph.D. degree (1970) from Purdue University in psychology and management. Klimoski's teaching and research interests revolve around the areas of organizational control systems in the form of performance appraisal and performance feedback programs. He is coauthor of *Research Methods in Human Resource Management* (1991, with N. Schmitt) and editor of the *Academy of Management Review*. In 1990, Klimoski was elected president of the Society for Industrial and Organizational Psychology.

Frank J. Landy is professor of psychology and director of the Center for Applied Behavioral Sciences at Penn State University. He received his B.A. degree (1964) from Villanova University and his M.A. (1967) and Ph.D. (1969) degrees from

Bowling Green State University, all in psychology. He is author of an introductory psychology textbook, *The Psychology of Work Behavior* (1989), and a general psychology text, *The Science of Human Behavior* (1987). Landy is also coauthor of *The Measurement of Work Performance* (1983, with J. Farr). Landy served as president of the Society for Industrial and Organizational Psychology from 1990 to 1991.

Rodney A. McCloy is a research scientist at the Human Resources Resource Organization in Alexandria, Virginia. He received his B.S. degree (1985) from Duke University in psychology and his Ph.D. degree (1990) from the University of Minnesota in industrial and organizational psychology. His main research activities have involved test validation and performance modeling. In 1991, McCloy received the S. Rains Wallace Dissertation Award from the Society for Industrial and Organizational Psychology.

Stephan J. Motowidlo is associate professor of management at the University of Florida. He received his B.A. degree (1969) from Yale University in psychology and his Ph.D. degree (1976) from the University of Minnesota in industrial and organizational psychology. His research interests include work attitudes, employee selection, and simulations as selection procedures.

Lynn R. Offermann is associate professor of industrial and organizational psychology at George Washington University and is consulting on executive training programs with the World Bank. She received her B.A. degree (1975) from the State University of New York, Oswego, her M.A. degree (1978) from Syracuse University, and her Ph.D. degree (1981) from Syracuse University in psychology. Her major area of research is in organizational leadership, and her current interests include the implications of workforce diversity for leadership theory and executive development. She was coeditor of the 1990 issue of the *American Psychologist,* which focused on future trends and issues in organizational psychology.

Scott H. Oppler is a research scientist at the American Institutes for Research in Washington, D.C. He received his B.S. degree

(1985) from Duke University in psychology and his Ph.D. degree (1990) from the University of Minnesota in industrial and organizational psychology, with a focus on the investigation of subgroup bias in performance measurement. Oppler's work has been published in the *Journal of Applied Psychology*.

Sara L. Rynes is professor of management and organizations in the College of Business Administration at the University of Iowa. She received her B.S. degree (1974) from the University of Wisconsin in social work and her M.S. (1977) and Ph.D. (1981) degrees from the University of Wisconsin, Madison, in industrial relations. Rynes's primary research interests include total quality management and continuous improvement, applicant attraction and selection, human resource strategies and decision making, and compensation.

Paul R. Sackett is professor of industrial relations at the University of Minnesota. He received his B.A. degree (1975) from Marquette University in psychology and his M.A. (1977) and Ph.D. (1979) degrees from the Ohio State University in industrial and organizational psychology. Sackett's research interests include the assessment of managerial potential, job analysis, honesty in the workplace, and methodological issues in employee selection. He served as editor of *Personnel Psychology* from 1984 to 1990, and is coauthor of *Perspectives on Employee Staffing and Selection* (1983, with G. Dreher).

Christopher E. Sager is assistant professor of psychology at George Washington University. He received his A.B. degree (1985) from San Diego State University and his Ph.D. degree (1990) from the University of Minnesota, both in psychology. His research interests include the modeling and measurement of job performance and cognitive processes in performance appraisal.

Frank L. Schmidt is Ralph L. Sheets Professor of Human Resources at the University of Iowa. He received his Ph.D. degree (1971) from Purdue University in industrial and organizational psychology and has served on the faculties of Michigan State and George Washington Universities. From 1974 to 1985, Schmidt directed a research program in personnel selection at the U.S. Office of Personnel Management, during which time he published numerous studies in personnel psychology. Research on the generalizability of employment test validities led to the publication of *Methods of Meta-Analysis* (1990, with J. Hunter). Schmidt is on the editorial board of the *Journal of Applied Psychology*.

Benjamin Schneider is professor of psychology and business management at the University of Maryland, College Park. He is also vice president of Organizational and Personnel Research, a consulting firm that specializes in designing and implementing strategically focused human resource approaches to organizational effectiveness. He received his B.A. degree (1960) from Alfred University in psychology and business administration, his M.B.A. degree (1962) from the City University of New York, and his Ph.D. degree (1967) from the University of Maryland in industrial and social psychology. Schneider's most recent work has been on the assessment of service climate and culture, the design of human resource systems to enhance service organization effectiveness, and research on how "the people make the place." His five published books include *Staffing Organizations* (1986, with N. Schmitt), *Facilitating Work Effectiveness* (1988, with D. Schoorman), and *Organizational Climate and Culture* (1990). Schneider serves on the editorial board of the *Journal of Applied Psychology*.

Scott A. Snell is assistant professor of management and organization at the Pennsylvania State University. He received his B.A. degree (1981) from Miami University in psychology, his M.B.A. degree (1985) from Michigan State University in management, and his Ph.D. degree (1988) from Michigan State University in business administration. Snell's area of research includes the strategic determinants of human resource practices, and he has worked with both manufacturing and service organizations redesigning human resource systems to adapt to changes in the competitive environment. He is on the editorial review board of the *Journal of Managerial Issues* and has published articles in numerous journals.

Charles C. Snow is professor of business administration at the Pennsylvania State University. He received his B.S. degree (1967) from San Diego State University in business management and his Ph.D. degree (1972) from the University of California, Berkeley, in business administration. His research on business strategy serves as the basis for the senior human resource professional certification program offered by the Society of Human Resource Management. Snow's books include *Organizational Strategy, Structure, and Process* (1978, with R. E. Miles), *Strategies for Competitive Success* (1986, with R. A. Pitts), and *Strategy, Organization Design, and Human Resource Management* (1989, editor).

Sheldon Zedeck is professor of psychology and director of the Institute of Industrial Relations at the University of California, Berkeley. He received his B.A. degree (1965) from Brooklyn College and his M.A. (1967) and Ph.D. (1969) degrees from Bowling Green State University, all in psychology. He is past president of SIOP and is on the editorial board for the Frontiers of Industrial and Organizational Psychology Series. Among Zedeck's research interests are moderator variables, selection and validation, performance appraisal, assessment centers, stress, and work and family issues. His books include *Performance Measurement and Theory* (1983, with F. Landy and J. Cleveland) and *Data Analysis for Research Designs* (1989, with G. Keppel). He is also editor of *Work, Families, and Organizations* (1992) and of the book series *People and Organizations*.

PERSONNEL
SELECTION
IN
ORGANIZATIONS

Part One

EXPANDING
THE PARADIGM
OF
PERSONNEL
SELECTION

1

An Exploration of the
Job Analysis–Content Validity Process

Irwin L. Goldstein, Sheldon Zedeck,
Benjamin Schneider

In this chapter we explore the processes involved in job analysis as a prerequisite for establishing the validity of personnel selection devices. Specifically, we focus on a particular job analysis strategy and how it contributes to establishing content validity, or as it is more recently discussed, the "content-oriented strategy for test development" (Tenopyr, 1977). We focus on content validity for several reasons. First, we accept the view that validity is not a characteristic of a test but, instead, of inferences from test information (Guion, 1980). For us, however, content validity is the most illustrative of all the strategies in that it demonstrates the need to overtly link knowledge, skills, and abilities (KSAs) and tasks; KSAs and tests; and tasks and tests.

The second reason we focus on content validity, which follows from the first, is that we agree with Schmitt and Landy (see Chapter Nine) that the central interest in the selection context is demonstration of the linkage between the construct underlying test measurement and the construct underlying performance measurement. Here again, the job analysis–content validity process described in this chapter illustrates the above-stated linkages. As Schmitt and Landy state, if it can be shown that a test measures a specific construct that has been determined to be critically linked to the job performance domain, the inferences about job performance based on the test are justified. Although they label this linkage "construct validity," they also indicate that the above-stated linkages can be demonstrated by showing that the test and performance domains are interchangeable. This latter demonstration they label "content validity."

A third reason for focusing on content validity is that even though its underlying concern is for better understanding of constructs, it causes us to attend to observables, that is, to focus on the overlap or similarity between test content and the performance domain. The issues and definition of constructs within the testing context have been argued elsewhere (compare Cronbach & Meehl, 1955; Messick, 1981), with the general consensus being that a construct is a trait or characteristic *underlying* behavior. But this description is vague. Perhaps a more useful definition of a construct is the one offered by Binning and Barrett (1989), who state that "a construct is merely a hypothesis about which behaviors will reliably covary" (p. 479). Again, we indicate in this chapter how the job analysis–content validity process described allows us to understand behaviors on the test and the performance domain, and does so in behavioral terms. The process is one that generates hypotheses about test–performance linkages.

Finally, we focus on content validity because the contexts in which we have found ourselves most recently are ones in which content validity is the only strategy for developing information to support inferences about test scores. We are not alone in this experience, and it is clear that content strategies are becoming increasingly utilized. They are often used in settings where it is not possible to conduct criterion-related validity studies. Many times this occurs because the sample size is not large enough for a criterion-related validity study, for example, when testing small samples of persons in the public sector for promotion purposes. In other instances, reliable criterion information cannot be obtained for a variety of reasons, such as the adversarial conditions that often occur as a result of lawsuits alleging unfair employment practices.

Of course, in industrial and organizational psychology, it is not unusual for practice issues, such as the legal arena in which validity studies are conducted, to stimulate the research agenda. Unfortunately, the research literature concerning topics such as the use of job analysis as a foundation for content validity, as well as the research literature concerning content validation strategies themselves, is remarkably lean. Accordingly, in this chapter we explore some of the concerns that need to be addressed when one wishes to support inferences about content validity and, consequently, inferences about test scores in general. We say this in full recognition of the unitarian view of validity; but, given the test development strategies we outline, a test based on content validity should also have construct- and criterion-related validity. We are not certain that tests based on construct- or criterion-related validation strategies necessarily have content validity.

Content Validity of Selection Procedures

Content validity as a process for establishing the appropriateness of tests for selection decision making has received considerable attention in the last few years (Guion, 1977, 1978; Landy, 1986; Tenopyr, 1977). Perhaps one way of defining the concept is to refer to the *Principles for the Validation and Use of Personnel Selection Procedures* (Society for Industrial and Organizational Psychology, 1987), which state, "In content oriented strategies, any inferences about the usefulness of a score must be preceded by inferences based on the content and method of construction of the measurement instruments" (p. 18). The *Principles* state further that the content-oriented strategy can be restricted to situations in which a job domain is defined through job analysis by identifying important tasks, behaviors, or knowledge and the test is a representative sample of tasks, behaviors, or knowledge drawn from that domain. The *Principles* also offer a second perspective on content-oriented validity by applying the term to selection procedures in which the ability to be assessed is defined in a context-specific way. It is when there is a reference to more general abilities, such as spatial ability, that other strategies, such as criterion-related validity, are necessary to establish the construct.

It is clear that a major ingredient in establishing the content validity of a selection procedure is job analysis, about which much has also been written (for example, Gael, 1983; Levine, 1983; McCormick, 1979). Although many procedures are described under the rubric "job analysis," in this chapter we propose a particular strategy that needs to be part and parcel of content-oriented strategies so that content validity and job analysis are inextricably linked.

Content validity has received attention recently in both the training (for instance, Ford & Wroten, 1984; Goldstein, 1986) and selection literatures (for example, Sackett, 1987; Schmitt & Noe, 1983). However, most efforts to establish inferences about the validity of selection and promotion devices have focused on whether the term *content validity* is appropriate, rather than on what issues need to be resolved to support inferences about the degree of content validity achieved. For example, Guion (1978) has expressed concerns about even using the term *validity* in this context. Since one view of content validity refers to the degree to which testing instruments are representative of the KSAs, he suggests that the term *content relevance* be used.

Certainly, even supporters of a content validity strategy would not argue that a poorly designed content validity study provides compelling evidence concerning inferences about validity. On the other hand, our view is that some industrial and organizational (I/O) psychologists are more comfortable in being able to assess the quality of a criterion-related validity study, at least partially because the associated statistical techniques allow for more confidence in inferences about test scores, which are based on empirical predictor-criterion relationships. Judgments about content validity are qualitative ones, and the rules for establishing qualitative judgments are not a traditional I/O psychology subject. As a result, there has been little discussion in the literature about the appropriate methods and rules required to generate confidence concerning inferences based on a content validity strategy.

For example, as noted previously, the *Principles for the Validation and Use of Personnel Selection Procedures* (Society for Industrial and Organizational Psychology, 1987) states that content-oriented strategies may be sufficient when the knowledge or skill is defined in a specific way but offers no further advice on the elements of a meaningful content validity strategy. Several of us present when that language was drafted agreed there was a serious need to begin to explore the issues in making inferences about content validity with the understanding that those inferences concern the degree to which we can infer that the KSAs in the job domain are represented in the testing instrument. Whether or not the term *validity* should be used seems to be a moot point, since the word does not seem likely to go away.

Psychological Fidelity and Content Validity

As noted, a primary focus in this chapter is on the issues involved in making inferences concerning the content validity of a testing instrument with the understanding that the inferences concern the degree to which the critical job KSAs are represented in the selection or promotion device. It is not our intention to ignore the tasks performed on the job. Tasks describe what a worker actually does on the job; the closer the test approximates the tasks, the greater the physical fidelity of the test. Often, the example used to illustrate a content validity test is the example of a typing test for a secretary, with the emphasis on the equipment. However, the example results in the misleading impression that the emphasis in content validity is on the tasks and the reason we use the typewriter is because typing is the critical task.

What is of greater importance from the standpoint of content validity is that the test calls forth important KSAs stemming from a job analysis, such as "knowledge of spelling, grammar, punctuation, and letter composition when typing business correspondence," or "ability to construct a finished, typed document from a handwritten draft." For some, even these latter concepts are "constructs." Yet, returning to the Binning and Barrett (1989) view, a behavioral domain is inherent in these definitions and can be defined, measured, and linked. When a test or assessment device is being designed, it is not usually the case that the actual physical fidelity that constitutes the job tasks is being replicated. Rather, a test is a simulation of the physical components of the job in which the KSAs required to perform the job tasks are called forward. When these KSAs are called forward, the test has psychological fidelity. Figure 1.1 represents this relationship. In Figure 1.1, the test is content valid to the extent that it is designed so that the appropriate critical tasks are simulated, providing candidates the opportunity to display the relevant KSAs. The section of the figure that models that relationship is shaded, and to the degree to which a test represents that shaded area, it has psychological fidelity. Thus, a typing test would be content valid for a typing job if it properly simulated the required tasks, thereby providing the appropriate opportunity for assessing the KSAs necessary to perform the job. In addition, the caveat offered here is that the test *format* as well as the test content needs to offer opportunities for displaying job-relevant KSAs.

**Figure 1.1. A Model of Psychological
Fidelity as a Foundation for Content Validity.**

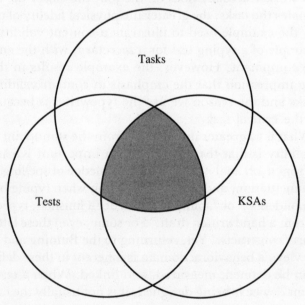

Thus, three important issues contribute to the psychological fidelity and, thereby, the content validity of a test. One concerns the degree to which KSAs required by a job are tapped in the test, regardless of the testing mode. The second concerns whether the testing mode is representative of the way tasks are accomplished on the job. Finally, there is the issue of the degree to which the test is scored for KSAs *not* even required by the job in question. An illustration of this last point is candidates for a promotion exam who are asked to memorize huge amounts of material for a knowledge test when they will never be expected to know that material or do not have to memorize it for their job.

A multiple-choice test that calls forth the knowledge required may not appear to have as much physical fidelity as an airplane simulator where pilots are assessed on their capabilities to fly and land an aircraft. The principles involved in establishing content validity, however, are the same. The test must be designed so that it calls forth the required KSAs (psychological fidelity) for the job regardless of whether physical fidelity is present. Interestingly, problems with the use of multiple-choice exams often have nothing to do with whether they are designed to tap job-relevant KSAs; rather, the problem is whether the tests measure KSAs that are *not* job relevant. Often, the testing mode results in assessing KSAs that are not job relevant.

For example, when a lieutenant in a fire department arrives at a fire scene, he or she gives short orders indicating where the fire fighters should place themselves, what equipment to take into the fire, and so forth. If in the testing situation the testees are required to respond to a fire scene by writing an essay concerning what they would do, it is questionable whether that form of test is content valid; the physical fidelity is missing, and the psychological fidelity may be missing, too. If the candidates are required to write the essay in perfect English, and the exams are scored for spelling and the quality of the written essay, then there are even more serious concerns about content validity. If in the fire department under study, the lieutenant does not perform any writing of essays or reports, then there is the further question of whether the examination format requires KSAs

not required by the job. As a solution for these problems, examinees could be given a tape recorder and told to respond to
the fire scene situations by speaking the directions and orders
they would give. Now the testing situation more reasonably
simulates what is required on the job. The point is, the test format itself, as well as the KSAs being measured, enters into the
question of psychological fidelity and, thus, content validity.
These issues are examined further later in the chapter.

Next, we discuss briefly a job analysis procedure that accommodates a content-oriented strategy. Throughout we note
where research is needed as well as many instances where assumptions are being made on the basis of the best strategy available, but without compelling research evidence.

Job Analysis Within a Content-Oriented Strategy

Since inferences about content validity are based on the
degree to which a test reflects the critical job domains, clearly
the job analysis itself is the most critical component. Two facets
define the essence of an appropriate job analysis procedure for
deriving test content and format: the detailed task and KSA
statements needed to approach physical, and thus psychological, fidelity and the judgmental process whereby individual KSAs
are linked to tasks and task clusters and tests are linked back
to the KSAs. Our view focuses on inferences about content validity based on the psychological fidelity of the KSAs, but it is
clear that in order to develop detailed KSAs, we need explicit
tasks describing the job. Brief discussions of the issues pertinent to task and KSA development follow.

Development of Tasks and Task Clusters

Tasks are statements of the critical activities or work operations performed on the job and the conditions under which the
job is performed. Task specification is critical because the tasks
are used as input to obtain specific KSAs from subject matter
experts, and they also are the bases for developing the test simulations used to call forth the KSAs in the assessment instruments.

The rules for development of tasks have been evolving for
several years, but they are all still based on having the speci-

ficity necessary for a content validity strategy. Many of the ideas expressed here are a synthesis of the work of others (including Goldstein, Macey, & Prien, 1981; Prien, 1977; Prien, Goldstein, & Macey, 1987). A much more complete discussion of task, task cluster, and KSA characteristics can be found in Goldstein, Braverman, and Goldstein (1991). A summary of the guidelines most relevant to a job analysis–test development strategy follows.

- Each task should begin with a functional verb that identifies the primary job operation. For example, a task statement that says "presents information for the use of a supervisor in . . . " does not indicate whether a report has been written or whether a conversation is occurring or whether a speech is being made. This is a serious problem because the KSAs involved in writing a report for the use of supervisors are different from those needed in giving a speech.
- The statement should describe *what* the worker does and *how,* to *whom* or *what,* and *why* the worker does it. The *why* aspect often becomes a critical part of the task because it forms the foundation for understanding what KSAs may be required. Thus, if a manager has the task of conducting a performance appraisal to provide information for advising the job incumbent on needed improvement, KSAs called for may include the ability to assess job performance and the ability to provide feedback to the individual. However, if the purpose of the performance appraisal is to provide information for a complete career progression analysis within the organization, other KSAs may be required to perform those tasks.

After a full task set is developed from the job analysis, it is useful to develop task clusters. An example of a task cluster and specific tasks for the job of customer service representative follows:

A Task Cluster for a
Customer Service Representative

Task cluster title and definition: Interaction with the customer—
the tasks involving communication by telephone between the
customer service representative and the customer to determine
what service difficulties have occurred.

1. Determine what difficulties the customer is hav-
    ing in order to complete a service report.
2. Ask the customer for relevant information in
    order to provide all the information needed by
    the vendor to service the customer.
3. Call the customer to determine whether the prob-
    lem has been resolved by the promised date and
    time.
4. Provide the customer with information so that he
    or she can follow up the call to obtain status in-
    formation.
5. Provide instructions to the customer concerning
    basic self-checks that can be used to resolve the
    difficulty.
6. Provide information to the customer about ser-
    vices available to resolve the problem.
7. Inform the customer about possible service charges
    that may be billed to the customer in order to ser-
    vice the customer's equipment.

The purpose of clustering is to help organize the individual task statements, to help edit them, to provide insight into
the job-specific constructs represented in the job, and to facilitate specification of the KSAs required to do the tasks. These
KSAs serve as the foundation for the design of tests being developed with content strategies.

A rational clustering procedure whereby subject matter experts (SMEs) make independent judgments is often used to organize the clusters. Other procedures for clustering use statistical techniques. Cranny and Doherty (1988) have discovered,

however, that the clusters that emerge from such statistical (factor) analyses are frequently not interpretable by SMEs as representing important job dimensions. Such results suggest ambiguous constructs are being framed. At this point, there are no definitive answers as to why this ambiguity occurs, leading many researchers (for example, Schmitt, 1987) to strongly urge research on these issues.

In the meantime, our preference for rational clustering of task statements is based on several considerations. First, having to cluster tasks rationally forces the test developer to write unambiguous task statements. Second, presenting task statements by clusters in a job analysis survey facilitates the respondents' mind-set, which is especially important when the list of tasks is very long. Third, rational clusters presented to SMEs as a basis for KSA specification have a similarly facilitative effect. SMEs appear to generate more *comprehensive* sets of KSAs when asked to respond with regard to tasks listed within clusters than they do when confronted with long lists of individual tasks. Research on this issue would be useful.

Development of Knowledge, Skill, and Ability Statements

Whereas task analysis specifies the required job operations, the key concern for test development is determining the competencies necessary to effectively perform the job tasks. Several different systems for specifying human capabilities exist. One system (Goldstein, Macey, & Prien, 1981; Prien, 1977; Prien, Goldstein, & Macey, 1987) emphasizes constructing specific KSAs necessary to effectively perform the tasks that were identified in the task analysis; we adopt this system here.

The critical aspect in developing KSAs within a content validity strategy is to generate KSA statements specific enough to build assessment exercises and tests that reflect the KSAs required for the job domain. A KSA statement should indicate *what* the KSA is, to *what effect* or in *what context* it operates, and to *what degree of accuracy or level* it is used. For example, the ability "to write" is too broad, as is the ability "to communicate orally." The ability "to write" can mean any of the following:

- Ability to record information without a standardized form so it can be understood by others
- Ability to compose clear and concise sentences and
  paragraphs in preparing a written report
- Ability to spell sufficiently well to complete citations and department forms
- Ability to take notes describing an event that can
  be interpreted later
- Ability to transcribe alpha-numeric data accurately

In a content validity strategy, an exercise would be constructed very differently for a KSA statement that required
the "ability to take notes describing an event" and one that required the "ability to transcribe alphanumeric data accurately."
Also, if the KSA is described in the broad sense of "ability to
write," any exam, whether it be taking notes or transcribing
alphanumerics, would end up being judged by SMEs as testing the ability to write. Yet, such exams would all be testing
very different KSAs if a content validity strategy were being
used. It is possible to argue that some of these KSAs may covary
together and are part of a general construct involving writing.
However, that cannot be determined when using a content validity strategy; thus, the investigator bears the burden of writing KSAs that are specific enough to not only facilitate the design of a proper exam but also enable SMEs to independently
determine whether the exam is indeed measuring the specific
KSA construct.

Some investigators use a "KSAO" format for collecting information, where the O stands for "other" dimensions, such as
personal characteristics. For us, the same principles apply. If
the characteristic is written in a specific way so that it is observable and can be judged by raters, then it is possible to assess
the behavior in a content-oriented strategy. Examples of such
"O" items are "ability to accept criticism of one's views and decisions and not respond with threats, hostility, or by being defensive," or "ability to not let irate and rude customers affect how
one delivers service." We have built simulations where such behaviors had the opportunity to occur and were reliably judged.

On the other hand, if the "O" characteristic refers to a broad dimension, such as self-esteem or self-confidence, then a construct-oriented methodology is necessary.

Evaluating the Relevance of Tasks and KSAs

Task and KSA specification is comprehensive. Methods for identifying the *critical* tasks and KSAs are required, and this is usually accomplished through a survey format, which permits the collection of quantitative rating information. The survey format makes it possible to collect rating data from experienced job incumbents and supervisors across large samples to ensure confidence in indicators, such as the average importance of the task. Also, by gathering information on such characteristics as different geographical locations or different units in the organization, the investigator can determine whether the job is viewed the same way across the organization. The survey, because of administrative convenience, may have the added benefit of involving more participants, an important issue when job analysis is conceptualized as an organizational intervention (discussed below).

Unfortunately, analyses of differences in how tasks and KSAs are rated as a function of various demographic characteristics are scarce and inconsistent (Harvey, 1991; Schmitt & Landy, 1992). Thus, there is little consistent information about the ways tasks and KSAs are viewed as a function of gender, race, job effectiveness, or job level within the organization. Much more information about the correlates of job analysis ratings needs to be obtained.

Which rating scales respondents use in completing surveys depends on the purpose of the survey. For rating tasks, it is typically necessary to have information concerning the importance of the task and the frequency with which it is performed. (In our analysis procedure, we tend to give more weight to the importance of the tasks than the frequency with which they are performed because importance provides a better understanding of the job domain.) It seems that, for some occupations, using different scales is likely to produce different views of the job; but research exploring different approaches across different occupations is not available. For example, in some occupations critical job functions occur very infrequently, yet in others the most important tasks occur most often. In the former instance, emphasizing frequency would not provide a solid foundation for developing the task base.

For KSAs, it is typically necessary to have information regarding the importance of the KSA and to determine whether the KSA is needed at entry into the job position ("needed day one") or can be learned in training or on the job. Here, for the purpose of test development, we emphasize important KSAs needed at entry. For the knowledge component, it is also critical to determine whether the information needs to be memorized with full recall or can be looked up when needed. Too many selection instruments (especially for promotion exams) consist of tests requiring the memorization of large amounts of material that do not have to be stored in memory to perform the job and thus cannot be supported by a content-oriented procedure.

The survey data collected can be analyzed to determine average responses, variability, and degree of agreement between those providing the job analysis information (for example, between supervisor and incumbent or across different geographical locations). The analyst establishes cutoffs for determining which tasks and KSAs would be retained in further analyses. The important aspect of setting rules for selecting tasks and KSAs is to set a standard high enough to ensure that only the truly important tasks and KSAs (those KSAs needed at entry) are identified and retained for further use.

Linking KSAs to Tasks

After determining which KSAs and tasks are needed for the job and which are important, as well as which KSAs are needed at entry, the analyst must link the KSAs to the tasks to create a basis for establishing which tasks to simulate in a test exercise (which would be those providing opportunities for demonstrating the KSAs). This linkage becomes the basis for establishing the psychological fidelity of the testing instruments. Thus, it is critical to develop information about which KSAs are important to perform the critical job tasks. We believe that the specificity of the KSA statements and their linkage to a task provide the foundation for establishing content validity *and* are critical in establishing constructs. Following is an example of a set of instructions for performing the linking process between KSAs and tasks.

2 = Essential	This knowledge or ability is essential to the performance of this task. Without this knowledge or ability, you would not be able to perform this task.
1 = Helpful	This knowledge or ability is helpful in performing this task. This task could be performed without this knowledge or ability, although it would be more difficult or time-consuming.
0 = Not Relevant	This knowledge or ability is not needed to perform this task. Having this knowledge or ability would make no difference in the performance of this task.

Using this set of instructions, a group of subject matter experts links each individual KSA to each individual task independently. Even though only the tasks and KSAs that have survived a priori criteria are being linked, sometimes the number of remaining KSAs and tasks turns out to be quite large. In those cases, an alternative procedure is to first link the individual KSAs to task clusters and then to individual tasks.

To illustrate this process, we take as an example the job of state police radio operator. The person in this particular job serves as the radio link for state troopers patrolling the roads, receiving and relaying information from other state troopers and the public. For this job, the "ability to organize incoming information for verbal transmission on the radio or telephone" is linked to the following tasks, among others:

1. Receives information from the public by telephone concerning items such as speeders or accidents to relay to the trooper responsible for that geographical area.

2. Logs trooper activities in direct response to ra-
    dio communications for purposes of record keep-
    ing and ensuring trooper safety.
3. Obtains information by radio on the status of
    troopers who are on stops in order to ensure safety
    of troopers.

In an actual analysis this ability was linked to a total of
ten tasks. Further examination of this data set indicated other
abilities that were linked to many of the same tasks and to additional tasks as well. For example, the following abilities were
also linked to many of the same tasks: "ability to remain attentive to radio traffic throughout the shift," "ability to give directions in terms of compass points in the post area," and "ability
to record information onto proper places on forms." Thus, a
matrix began to form that revealed the set of KSAs linked to
the set of tasks. This matrix of information formed the foundation for the design of a content-valid simulation by revealing
the tasks that could be used to assess the important KSAs. It
was possible to design a simulated transmission of radio and
telephone calls with varying kinds of information, such as license
plate numbers, to which the candidate had to respond by recording them in appropriate places on a form.

Thus, precise task and KSA specification followed by task
and KSA linkage provides job-specific cues to the design of tests
with psychological fidelity. This procedure avoids the frequent occurrence of generic abilities in job analyses, which yield ambiguity
and the design of generic, non–content valid assessment procedures. For example, most analysts would agree that the data set
from the police radio operator case, in a content-oriented strategy,
would not support a geography test that requires the candidate to
answer questions about the capitals of various states in the nation.
Research on the *processes* involved in linking strategies is needed.

Content-Construct Dilemma

KSA–task cluster linkages do raise the question of the
content-construct dilemma (Tenopyr, 1977). A point raised by

Tenopyr is that inferences from content-based tests are also based on constructs; there must be common constructs underlying both test performance and job behaviors. She concludes that any interpretation of a content-based employment test strictly in terms of tasks is inadequate. We agree, and propose that the job analysis process described here, based on the psychological fidelity of KSAs tied to tasks, ensures that common constructs are measured. Certainly, a set of KSAs linked to the same tasks provides the opportunity to consider whether a construct is involved.

For example, in a job analysis of a fire fighter, several abilities involve decision making under speed and stress, such as "ability to decide quickly how to rescue victims," "ability to quickly decide course of action in response to fire characteristics," and "ability to determine which equipment should be used in fire-fighting activities." Many of these and other similar abilities are linked to the same tasks. Thus, the job analysis process suggests that there is a decision-making construct and, furthermore, that there should be a test to examine the ability to make decisions of the kind specified. Indeed, if a job analysis were being done as part of a criterion-related validity model, identifying such a construct would be one purpose of the analysis. In that instance, it would be possible to make the inference that there is a decision-making construct (perhaps under stress) and that it is possible to select a paper-and-pencil test that is known to test that construct. Then, the investigator would determine the degree of relationship of the test with a criterion measure (hopefully also established from the job analysis!), thereby potentially strengthening inferences concerning the relevance of the construct for job performance.

Of course, statistically establishing this relationship between predictor and criterion measure is the key point in criterion-related validity. In the traditional content validity model, even if the psychologist in most of us suspects a construct, the procedure to assess the construct's explanatory power can be very complex (see Chapter Nine). We believe, however, that a process that provides for the description of both job-specific tasks *and* job-specific KSAs, and calls for independent SMEs to judge whether the test reflects the KSAs in the job domain, is a major step toward incorporation of the construct concept directly into test development. Such a process is, in particular, a way of establishing the link between test and performance in construct terms. If such a careful specification is achieved, it is then more likely that, in addition, a criterion-related validity study also would provide some evidence for the relationship between the test and the performance, thus beginning the chain of evidence for establishing the construct. Whether strong evidence for content validity, based on careful and detailed job analysis and test development procedure as described, results in a stronger indicant of criterion-related validity is not a topic that has been systematically explored and deserves research attention.

Establishment of Content Validity

From the KSA–task linkage process described above, test exercises are designed to assess job candidates. Design of tests and answer keys, establishment of reliability, and so on, are beyond the scope of this chapter, but the issues are the same (and are just as critical) as for tests designed in a criterion-related format. Once the test is developed, it is necessary to have SMEs establish the degree to which content validity has been achieved, that is, the degree to which the test does represent a measure of intended KSAs. In this instance, an independent group of subject matter experts (for example, experienced job incumbents, supervisors, or trainers) who have not been involved in the actual design of the test serve as the panel. They take the actual test and then use a scale to judge the degree to which the KSAs are needed to answer the questions. An example of a test-KSA content validity linkage instruction might read as follows:

> To what extent are each of the following knowledge, skills, and abilities needed to answer these questions (or perform these exercises)?

The scale could be 4 = to a great extent, 3 = to a moderate extent, 2 = to a slight extent, 1 = not at all.

At this time it is also important to have the SMEs judge whether the test questions are at the appropriate level for the

KSAs needed on the job at entry. In one study (Maye & Gold-stein, 1989) involving the state trooper radio operator, we collected data for the radio performance test described previously from SMEs who listened to a radio tape and responded by placing important information on forms. Seventy-two SMEs independently assessed the questions, and a criterion was established a priori that if 70 percent of the SMEs independently agreed that a simulation assessed a KSA, then the linkage between the KSA and the test had been established. For the state trooper radio operator performance tests, the SMEs agreed that the following KSAs (as well as some others) were needed to perform on the test: the ability to remain attentive to radio traffic throughout the shift and the ability to record information in proper places on the form.

Interestingly, the SMEs were able to make judgments indicating a real understanding of the difference between the KSAs required for the actual job and the simulation. For instance, one KSA required for the job is the "ability to remember where one was in the performance of a task after an interruption," but the test did not have interruptions and the SMEs judged it appropriately. Similarly, the "ability to organize incoming information for verbal transmission on the radio or telephone" is required but was not tested, and the SMEs judged that the KSA was not required to perform on the test. Our experience generally indicates that SMEs are very astute at making judgments about test components when the KSAs being linked are specific.

Moreover, these types of analyses, which use the specific KSAs from the job analyses as input, can be used to examine old test batteries currently in use. In this instance, the analysis of the old test battery indicated there were several components where inferences concerning content validity could not be supported. That evidence, in part, resulted in the organization's making a decision to develop a new test.

From the KSA–task linkage analysis described in the preceding section, it is possible to determine the number of tasks or task cluster links for each content-validated KSA. With this type of analysis, it is possible to give weights to each KSA depending on the degree to which it represents either tasks or task clusters. This permits differential weighting of examination com-

ponents because test components that are related to KSAs that
are also linked more to aspects of the job (as represented by tasks
or task clusters) are given more weight.

An important question is how much of the job needs to
be covered in order to support inferences that a test is content
valid. Clearly, in a content validation scheme, if a very small
percentage of the job is being measured, say less than 10 percent or 20 percent, there is cause for concern. One guide we
have employed is that the KSAs tested should approach being
linked to 50 percent or more of the coherent task clusters. In
some situations, this criterion would be difficult to achieve. In
tests developed for entry levels into various jobs, this problem
sometimes becomes more difficult because of feasibility issues
connected with often having to examine very large numbers of
people. Too often, this has resulted in tests where the applicants
are given a large number of books to study, are told to memorize the information, and then are asked to respond on paper-
and-pencil multiple-choice tests. That strategy is very difficult
to defend in a content-oriented strategy when KSAs "to memorize large amounts of information" are either not required at
all or are linked to a very small part of the job. In that instance,
in order to strengthen inferences concerning validity, a criterion-
oriented strategy would be required. From a content validity
model, it behooves us to become more ingenious at finding ways
to construct simulations that permit testing of specific required
KSAs that reflect reasonable amounts of the job.

Issues Concerning the
Job Analysis–Content Validity Process

In addition to the job analysis strategy and its relationship
to content and construct validity, the focus of this chapter thus
far, several other related research issues involving job analysis
and content validity need to be explored.

Job Analysis as an Intervention

Our view is that job analysis should be thought of as a type
of organizational intervention. An intervention is a procedure

that interrupts organizational members' daily routines and patterns of work behavior. Often, because of the very nature of the climate in which validation studies are conducted (especially content validation), this intervention is extremely critical to the lives of members of the organization. It is not unusual for a content validity study to be conducted in an organization where issues of employment discrimination are a fact of life, and where litigation has resulted in no promotions for a dozen or more years. In this atmosphere, failure to gain the cooperation of all parties and to set realistic expectations concerning issues such as the eventual use of test scores can be damaging. The potential for such problems has led the authors of this chapter to consider very carefully who should provide the requisite job analysis information and how it should be collected. Thus, in forming job analysis panels to generate the basic task and KSA information, time for the participants to discuss their various concerns is built into our procedures. If we do not plan time for this to occur very early in the session, it happens anyway at other points throughout the entire job analysis discussion panel and disrupts attempts to collect information.

Again, the mere undertaking of a job analysis is an intervention that must be recognized as such and accordingly planned. In most situations where content validity studies are likely to be conducted, it is important to agree on expectations concerning the outcome of the process, including the following: how test scores will be used; what happens if there is adverse impact; which parties share which information, such as viewing the test components before the examination; rules for selection of panel members; the timing for the phases of the project; and the confidentiality of individual information.

Interestingly, research does not exist on how the organizational setting in which the job analysis is conducted affects the quality of job analysis information generated. For us, answers to many of the questions raised above emerged by happenstance. Thus, in many projects with which we have been associated, we have found instances where the quality of the job analysis information might have been compromised. These include occasions where data indicated that more women or minorities completed the job analysis panel than actually existed in the organization, or a case in which various groups were suspected of conspiring to raise the difficulty level of the job (for example, enhancing the physical requirements of the fire fighter job to keep females out of the organization).

The potential for compromise has led us to adopt various procedures to attempt to determine whether the data generated are reliable. These include presenting in our job analysis surveys a number of task items that come from the same job category (for example, from the next level up in the organization), but which are not performed by the particular incumbents completing the job analysis survey. Individuals who respond to those "extraneous" items, beyond a certain preset criterion level, are excluded from the data analysis. In addition, response patterns are examined for irregularities.

Unfortunately, beyond anecdotal reports, precious few data exist to help us understand these phenomena. Research on job analysis and the introduction of a testing system as interventions in volatile atmospheres would be extremely valuable. For example, it would be useful to know whether the number of persons completing extraneous job task items varies with the volatility of the situation or whether persons responding to such items deviate from the remaining sample on other indicators. In any case, it is highly improbable that participants who mistrust the process will go out of their way to facilitate the needs assessment procedure. Thus, gaining the trust of organization members is an important first step for the job analyst. Goldstein, Braverman, and Goldstein (1991) describe some of the procedures, such as establishing liaison teams, that they think can be used to establish organizational support. Some data on their suggestions would also be helpful. This is yet another instance where there are many strategies being adopted on the basis of researchers' and practitioners' judgments without any empirical support.

Many investigators believe that the more methods used and the more persons involved in the job analysis process, the more accepting the organization will be of the outcomes; that is, more is better. This is a complicated issue. Our experience concerning whether organizations in *adversarial* situations will be more accepting of results based on more participation is inconclusive. In one sense, various parties want to participate because they do not trust others' input as well and want to learn as much as possible about what is occurring in the situation. However, in the end, the question for the organization is not the job analysis or the test, but rather the distribution of test scores among participating groups. If the test produces serious adverse impact, members of minority groups are going to be disturbed regardless of whether they participated in the process. Whether there is more acceptance as a result of participation is yet another research question that deserves attention; perceptions of justice in these cases are difficult to predict.

From the perspective of the I/O psychologist, however, use of more individuals and more methods does increase confidence in inferences about the results. Yet a factor to consider is that the job analyst (often the I/O psychologist) is usually the facilitator of the process. Thus, a question can be raised as to whether independent job analysts or researchers would end up with significant overlap on critical tasks, KSAs, and even test items if they conducted independent but parallel processes from beginning to end. The real question, of course, is whether they would end up testing the same job domain. Since content validity methods typically have not been used to address the issue of constructs, the relevant question is how large a role is played by the job analyst with his or her perceptions and interpretations in the job analysis–content validity process. At present, there is no definitive research on this issue.

Qualitative Judgments

A prime area for research is the means by which the actual job analysis data collected provide a reliable data set useful for establishing content validity. A key factor to recognize is that the entire job analysis–content validity process is built on human judgments, and, as such, many of the lessons of qualitative research and case studies (Eisenhardt, 1989) may be useful. We offer the two following principles:

1.   The entire job analysis–content validity process should be based on the idea that if differences truly exist, the procedures should be designed to uncover them. This is discussed further later, but it includes potential differences between individuals and their view of their job, and it also includes critical ways in which the target job varies.

2.   Collecting one of anything is probably not very useful. Replication is a critical aspect of qualitative data collection. In qualitative judgments, the power of the design is directly related to using replications to make up for small sample sizes. This principle can be applied to both the collection of information across individuals and the use of multiple methods in the collection of information.

These principles suggest several research areas that need attention, which are discussed next.

Determination of Participants. Who should be the SMEs and what are the rules for selecting participants? We have found that persons who directly supervise the job being analyzed serve as effective SMEs to provide KSA information, while job incumbents are effective in providing task information. This may be because supervisors often are concerned about and responsible for what job incumbents need to know or what skills and abilities they need to have to perform the tasks. In contrast, job incumbents appear to be more adept at focusing on what they do and are more effective in describing the exact tasks they perform on the job. Data on this issue are needed.

Several methods for selecting participants can be employed. One is to select the individuals by using a consistent strategy, such as random stratified sampling of all individuals who have a reasonable amount of previous job experience. Logically, this appears to make it more likely that the sample will be truly representative. Another approach is to have the analyst select the individuals according to a set of criteria, such as individuals who are considered good job performers. Data on whether these selection criteria produce consistent differences in job analysis information are not available. As to a third possible approach, it is not usually a good idea to have supervisors or members of the organization select the individuals for participation, because they may tend to select particular kinds of individuals, which would result in a nonrepresentative sample, such as job incumbents who might not be scheduled for important assignments that day. It appears that if the organization does the actual selection of the individuals, it should do so according to criteria established by the analyst; but data on the differences stemming from these approaches are lacking.

In addition to selecting a representative sample across job strata, the organization or the analyst should select individuals in a way that is sensitive to differences in the work population. This is especially the case if there are groups of individuals within the organization that are small in number (perhaps ethnic minorities or women) and thus might not be represented in the usual SME selection process. In that instance, it usually makes sense to overrepresent those groups to ensure that the sample size is large enough to be representative of their views of the job and to provide an opportunity to collect sufficient data to determine whether there are differences in the way the job is viewed by members of these groups.

Again, only a few studies concerning such differences are readily available in the research literature. In one such study, Schmitt and Cohen (1989) examined middle-level managers and found few differences. However, where there were ethnic differences in job perception, they were most often due to nonwhite job incumbents' reporting that they did not perform a task as compared to their white colleagues. Landy and Vasey (1991) also found few racial differences concerning judgments on police officer tasks, but did find that more experienced individuals (more than eleven years in the position) reported performing different tasks from those reported by less experienced individuals. The more experienced officers spent more time in noncriminal police activities such as answering questions for the public, whereas those with less experience spent more time in traffic activities. Anderson, Warner, and Spencer (1984) found higher estimates of experience on bogus tasks for minority respondents than for nonminority ones for two of thirteen jobs. Studies concerning gender are also not conclusive, with some finding differences between males and females (for example, Arvey, Passino, & Lounsbury, 1977) and others not (for instance, Arvey, Davis, McGowen, & Dipboye, 1982). Clearly, more of these types of studies are needed, especially those that focus on exploring the conditions under which differences are likely or not likely to occur.

Qualitative Judgments and Replication. The way data are collected from participants often determines whether the analyst gains the advantages of replication. For example, using *individual* data judgments rather than *consensus* panels achieves replication across persons. At present, there is no research data on whether group consensus data give the same results as individual independent responses. Until data suggest otherwise, we think it is more beneficial to collect independent responses. This holds whether analysts are collecting information about the importance of tasks or KSAs or whether they are linking KSAs to tasks. It is also clear that research on the dynamics of group versus individual data collection methods would be very useful.

In addition, using different methods for job analysis data collection (panels to generate task and KSA statements, observations, interviews, and so on) helps take advantage of the principles concerning replication and also allows for the particular advantages of the different techniques. It is also possible to increase the size of the participant sample by including some participants in the job observations, with others partaking in individual interviews, yet others participating in panels, and finally a larger sample completing a job analysis questionnaire. How a method is used, however, will often determine whether the analyst achieves the benefits that stem from replication across individuals or methods. No one maintains that all the methods created by job analysts must be used, but clearly it is possible to have more confidence using a variety of approaches than a single one. Research on how to determine when enough information has been collected to stop the process and what differences occur when different persons conduct panels is also lacking and would be useful.

Content Validity Analyses Across Jobs

Also of interest is the degree to which a content validity strategy can be used to document the degree to which the same testing instruments for jobs with different titles can be supported. This type of question often arises in the public sector, where job titles proliferate. What we really want to know is, Does a particular title subsume just one job or several jobs? For example, in one instance the job title "engineering technician" was held by individuals who either performed surveying work, inspected construction sites, or did laboratory investigations of materials used in road products, such as cement. This suggested at least three different jobs. A job analysis was designed so that it contained the tasks and KSAs for all these jobs, and a combined job analysis survey was completed by job incumbents and supervisors from all the jobs. Then the task and KSA data were analyzed separately for each of the groups of persons in the hypothesized jobs and the results compared across jobs. Virtually no tasks cut across all the jobs. However, nine KSAs cut across all the different jobs, and eventually they did form the basis for an examination that tested for significant portions of each of the jobs.

The experience in this particular project has been repeated elsewhere, leading to the assumption that KSAs are more likely than tasks to generalize across jobs. In a content-oriented strategy, this causes some difficulties in test development because the goal is to simulate the tasks in order to call forth the appropriate KSAs, thus achieving psychological fidelity. It probably means that the simulated tasks in the test have to be designed at a somewhat greater level of abstraction. Certainly it becomes increasingly important to collect SME judgments about the degree to which the KSAs are needed to perform on the test in order to have any confidence in inferences about validity based on content evidence.

In several other cases, neither tasks nor KSAs generalized, thereby requiring totally different examinations. One study in which this occurred investigated the job of sergeant in a police department. It turned out that the job classification included inspectors concerned with evidence evaluation and analysis and other officers in charge of directing subordinates on the street. There were virtually no similar KSAs, and the tests designed were very different for the two jobs. Previous job analyses that used tasks and KSAs at a broad level of abstraction had erroneously concluded that the same test could be given and justified based on a content-oriented strategy.

Transportability of Content Validity Findings

The degree of similarity across job components and the physical and psychological fidelity necessary in the testing situation deserve much more research attention. Of particular concern is the question of transportability, or validity generalization, and its relationship to content validity. The job analysis procedure described in this chapter can be used to support a content-oriented strategy and to help determine the degree to which the job in question is similar to the jobs from which the validity generalization evidence was developed. Of course, other criteria for the use of validity generalization need to be addressed, such as the degree to which the job incumbents are similar, the work performance criteria are similar, and so forth.

An important issue related to validity generalization is the transportability of a test that has been developed only on the basis of content evidence. It is clear that no matter how many content validity studies are run on the same test in different jurisdictions, the evidence still refers only to the degree to which the important KSAs in the job domain are represented in the test. Thus, finding the test content valid in many different jurisdictions still does not provide evidence concerning the predictorcriterion relationship. It seems that as the data base concerning inferences about validity is being built, it is important to develop a network of construct evidence that includes not only content validity but also criterion-related validity. On the other hand, if a test is to be transported from one jurisdiction to another on the basis of content validity evidence, then the investigator has at least the responsibility to conduct a contentoriented job analysis in the second jurisdiction to ensure that the jobs contain highly overlapping task and KSA linkages. In addition, as noted in the *Principles for the Validation and Use of Personnel Selection Procedures* (Society for Industrial and Organizational Psychology, 1987), the investigators must provide other supporting evidence for transportability, such as demonstrating that the incumbents are similar on relevant dimensions, that work performance criteria are similar, and so on.

Job Analysis for Jobs That Do Not Exist

In a rapidly changing environment it may be useful to design selection and promotion procedures for placing people in new jobs or to design procedures for hiring people with the KSAs that will be required for a future job. It also appears that because of the specific nature of the tasks and KSAs, it is easier for SMEs to provide judgments about jobs that do not exist at the time (Schneider & Konz, 1989). In general, the procedure involves the following steps:

1. Conducting a job analysis using the procedures outlined earlier.
2. Conducting a panel of internal SMEs who have the expertise to comment about what the nonexisting or future job is likely to require in the way of task performance and KSAs.
3. Compiling new tasks and KSAs identified in a revised survey and administering it to the SMEs.
4. Analyzing differences in the tasks and KSAs identified as critical for selection, promotion, and training for the nonexisting jobs.

A procedure like this has been used for clerical jobs, for first-line supervisory jobs, and for identifying middle and upper management KSAs that will be required in the future. Certainly, as organizations select employees to perform jobs that may change significantly, or do not even exist in the organization at the time, such procedures will be needed. Research in this area would undoubtedly prove useful.

Conclusion

In this chapter we have explored the job analysis–content validity process and closely related issues, ranging from psychological fidelity and organizational intervention to writing task statements and conducting task and KSA linkages. Unless these issues are simultaneously entertained, the outcomes of the job analysis–content validity process may be questionable.

The content validity process rests on a series of processes and judgments. Attention to these issues is critical for a content validity approach to the design and use of tests. In addition, concern for the processes and judgments does not alleviate the necessity to pay excruciating attention to detail in activities involved in collecting and writing task and KSA statements that contain the survey data that will in turn serve as the foundation for test development. To analogize: a weak set of framing studs on a strong foundation will be blown away!

The process is made more difficult because there is little research on many key questions. We have presented principles and strategies that we have evolved along with some of our groping and conclusions, for two reasons. First, we hope that others confronted with the same problems we have faced will profit from our experiences. Second, we hope that additional research in the areas noted will be stimulated by this chapter.

References

Anderson, C. D., Warner, J. L., & Spencer, C. C. (1984). Inflation bias in self-assessment examinations: Implications for valid employee selection. *Journal of Applied Psychology, 69,* 574–580.

Arvey, R. D., Davis, G. A., McGowen, S. L., & Dipboye, R. L. (1982). Potential sources of bias in job analytic processes. *Academy of Management Journal, 25,* 618–629.

Arvey, R. D., Passino, E. M., & Lounsbury, J. W. (1977). Job analysis results as influenced by sex of incumbent and sex of analyst. *Journal of Applied Psychology, 62,* 411–416.

Binning, J. F., & Barrett, G. V. (1989). Validity of personnel decisions: A conceptual analysis of the inferential and evidential bases. *Journal of Applied Psychology, 74,* 478–494.

Cranny, C. J., & Doherty, M. E. (1988). Importance ratings in job analysis: Notes on the misinterpretation of factor analysis. *Journal of Applied Psychology, 73,* 320–322.

Cronbach, L. J., & Meehl, P. E. (1955). Construct validity in psychological tests. *Psychological Bulletin, 52,* 281–302.

Eisenhardt, K. M. (1989). Building theories from case study research. *Academy of Management Review, 14,* 532–550.

Ford, J. K., & Wroten, S. P. (1984). Introducing new methods for conducting training evaluation and linking training evaluation to program redesign. *Personnel Psychology, 37,* 651–666.

Gael, S. (1983). *Job analysis: A guide to assessing work activities.* San Francisco: Jossey-Bass.

Goldstein, I. L. (1986). *Training in work organizations: Needs assessment, development and evaluation.* Pacific Grove, CA: Brooks-Cole.

Goldstein, I. L., Braverman, E. P., & Goldstein, H. W. (1991). Needs assessment. in K. Wexley (Ed.), *Developing human resources.* Washington, D.C.: Bureau of National Affairs.

Goldstein, I. L., Macey, W. H., & Prien, E. P. (1981). Needs assessment approaches for training development. In H. Meltzer & W. R. Nord (Eds.), *Making organizations human and productive.* New York: Wiley.

Guion, R. M. (1977). Content validity — The source of my discontent. *Applied Psychological Measurement, 1,* 1–10.

Guion, R. M. (1978). Content validity in moderation. *Personnel Psychology, 31,* 205–213.

Guion, R. M. (1980). On trinitarian doctrines of validity. *Professional Psychology, 11,* 385–398.

Harvey, R. J. (1991). Job analysis. In M. D. Dunnette & L. M. Hough (Eds.), *Handbook of industrial and organizational psychology.* Palo Alto, CA: Consulting Psychologists Press.

Landy, F. J. (1986). Stamp collecting versus science: Validation as hypothesis testing. *American Psychologist, 41,* 1183–1192.

Landy, F. J., & Vasey, J. (1991). Job analysis: The composition of SME samples. *Personnel Psychology, 44,* 27–50.

Levine, E. L. (1983). *Everything you always wanted to know about job analysis.* Tampa, FL: Mariner Publishing Co.

Maye, D. M., & Goldstein, I. L. (1989, June). *Content validity with the consent of justice: A collaborative methodology.* Paper presented at the International Personnel Management Association Conference, Orlando, FL.

McCormick, E. J. (1979). *Job analysis: Methods and applications.* New York: AMACOM.

Messick, S. (1981). Constructs and their vicissitudes in educational and psychological measurement. *American Psychologist, 89,* 575–588.

Prien, E. P. (1977). The function of job analysis in content validation. *Personnel Psychology, 30,* 167–174.

Prien, E. P., Goldstein, I. L., & Macey, W. H. (1987, August). Multi-domain job analysis: Procedures and applications in human resource management and development. *Training and Development Journal,* pp. 66–72.

Sackett, P. R. (1987). Assessment centers and content validity: Some neglected issues. *Personnel Psychology, 40,* 13–25.

Schmitt, N. (1987, April). *Areas of Continued Debate in Personnel Selection: Principles III.* Symposium conducted at the meeting of the Society for Industrial and Organizational Psychology, Atlanta, GA.

Schmitt, N., & Cohen, S. A. (1989). Internal analyses of task ratings by job incumbents. *Journal of Applied Psychology, 74,* 96–104.

Schmitt, N., & Landy, F. (1992). Internal analyses of task ratings by job incumbents. In N. Schmitt & W. Borman (Eds.), *Personnel selection.* San Francisco: Jossey-Bass.

Schmitt, N., & Noe, R. A. (1983). Demonstration of content validity: Assessment center example. *Journal of Assessment Center Technology, 6,* 5–11.

Schneider, B., & Konz, A. M. (1989). Strategic job analysis. *Human Resource Management, 28,* 51–63.

Society for Industrial and Organizational Psychology. (1987). *Principles for the validation and use of personnel selection procedures* (3rd ed.). College Park, MD: Author.

Tenopyr, M. L. (1977). Content-construct confusion. *Personnel Psychology, 30,* 47–54.

2

A Theory of Performance

John P. Campbell, Rodney A. McCloy, Scott H. Oppler, Christopher E. Sager

In this chapter we examine alternative models for the substantive content and latent structure of job performance as a construct and also consider their critical measurement and research implications. The discussion is based on two premises: first, that individual performance on a "task," virtually any task that the culture views as having value, is one of the most important dependent variables in psychology, basic or applied; and second, that the word *performance* is misused and exploited to the extreme in society at large, and is frequently butchered beyond recognition in psychology. If the dependent variable is the variable of *real* interest and if performance is perhaps our most important dependent variable, then more often than not we simply may not know what our real interest is. If we want to accumulate knowledge about how to measure, predict, explain, and change performance but have no common understanding of what it is, then building a cumulative research record is difficult to impossible and industrial and organizational (I/O) psychology is in for continued unfavorable comparisons with other sciences.

Even a brief examination of applied research illustrates the diversity of measurement operations that have been labeled, explicitly or implicitly, as measures of performance. Consider just the following:

- Time to complete a training course
- Grades or achievement test scores earned in training
- Number of errors made in a simulator
- Number of Tinkertoy figures assembled in a forty-five-minute experimental session
- Number of one-minute marketing interviews completed outside a shopping center in one day
- Number of pieces produced
- Number of defective pieces produced
- The total or average cost of the pieces produced
- Number of proposals written
- Total value of contracts won
- Total value of sales
- Number of grievances or complaints incurred
- Length of tenure in the organization
- Total days absent
- Salary level
- Promotion rate within an organization
- Percentage over budget
- Supervisor, peer, subordinate, or self ratings of "overall" performance
- Scores on a paper-and-pencil job knowledge test
- Scores on a professional certification test
- Number of citations in the citation index over a three-year period
- Number of refereed journal articles published in a six-year period

Even this brief list encompasses a wide variety of phenomena under one label. For any researcher faced with such helter-skelter in any domain, a reasonable response would be to reach for the available theory for guidance as to which things are important and which are not, how the important variables should be defined and what they are good for, and what the general operations of measurement may be. For example, if our concern is with the nature of cognitive abilities (Horn, 1989), personality (Hough, Eaton, Dunnette, Kamp, & McCloy, 1990), motivation (Kanfer, 1990), or even leadership (Bass, 1990), there are literally decades of research and theory to consult. With regard to performance itself, however, there is virtually none. Performance as a construct has received very little research or theoretical attention.

Two possible reasons for the deficit come to mind. The first is that it always seems to be the independent variable that generates the most professional or scientific interest. People can get goose bumps over a new treatment (such as empowered work groups) or a new ability variable (for example, tacit knowledge), but spending a lot of time or resources to understand performance itself seems to be not very exciting or fundable. A second possibility is that most of us hold a strong stereotypical assumption that the definition of performance and the designation of its indicators are things that get taken care of by somebody else, that they are really out of our hands.

We think the latter point of view supports the one model of performance that has dominated applied research during most of the last eighty to ninety years, at least in the world of work. Be it explicit or implicit, a theory is always there (Campbell, 1990b).

The Classic Model as Villain

The classic theory, or default position, that has dominated applied research for much of the last century says simply that performance is one thing; that is, the general factor will account for almost all the relevant true-score covariances among observed measures. Covariance matrices that appear otherwise do so because of differential reliabilities, the influence of method-specific variance, or other kinds of contamination. Thus the goal of measurement is to obtain the best possible measure of the general factor. For job performance, the classic view specifies that the best possible measure is an "objective" indicator of individual accomplishment that is maintained by the organization itself, such as number of pieces produced or dollar volume of sales.

The reasons for the above characterization are as follows. First, for most of this century the single-criterion measure has dominated in personnel research. Further, in the scientific and professional literature the term *job performance* is virtually always used in the singular, with no explicit or implicit conditionals. When we discuss whether or not job performance can be changed by this or that treatment, predicted by a particular ability, or measured better or worse by a particular method, the implication is clearly that there is one general thing to be changed, predicted, or measured. This certainly seemed to be what Thorndike (1949) had in mind when he coined "immediate," "intermediate," and "ultimate" criteria relative to the validation of aptitude tests in occupational or educational settings. This was a very unfortunate and counterproductive characterization of the goals of performance measurement, but it is incorporated in virtually every I/O psychology textbook written between 1950 and 1990.

This point of view is also the major source of the hated "criterion problem," which laments that if the best way to measure individual job performance is with objective indicators of individual accomplishments that organizations keep in their archives, then we indeed have a problem, because the search for reliable, uncontaminated, objective indicators that significantly reflect the ultimate criterion has been a failure. Good ones are never found, and this holds up progress. If only we had a good criterion, *then* you would really see something. The fallback position that is forced on us is to use supervisory ratings, which are "subjective," contaminated with halo error, and full of information processing errors. Consequently, the field must bear a major burden of guilt for being unable to find, or appropriately transform, the objective archival record that surely must be there.

The gist of this chapter is that (1) the general factor cannot possibly represent the best fit, (2) the notion of an ultimate criterion has no meaning, (3) the subjective versus objective distinction is a false issue, and (4) there is a critically important distinction to be made between performance and the results of performance.

We are certainly not the only ones to complain about the classic model creating a lot of trouble (for example, Dunnette,

1963; Wallace, 1965). Upwards of fifty years ago, there were numerous calls to spend as much time and energy developing, studying, and theorizing about criteria as were spent on the predictor (Jenkins, 1946; Nagle, 1953; Patterson, 1946; Toops, 1944). Toops (1944) typified this sentiment: "The criterion . . . seldom receives half the time or attention it requires or deserves. If the criterion is slighted, the time spent on the tests is, by so much, largely wasted" (p. 290). Often, criteria were taken as given, an action that "overcame the problem of criterion development by ignoring it" (Nagle, 1953, p. 271). Wallace (1965) urged that construct validation be used to understand criteria better, and James (1973) described how construct validation could be applied to criteria as easily as to predictors.

However, such pronouncements by a few respected figures seem to have had very little impact, so why go through the same exercise again? The principal reason is that we think the cumulative record now makes it possible to offer much more substantive alternatives to the one-factor model. Also, recent developments in restricted factor models, confirmatory analysis, and the like provide a better language for talking about the latent structure of the performance domain and provide a clearer way of analyzing relevant data. It is our firm conviction that unless I/O psychology begins to argue energetically about the substantive characteristics of performance, the most critical dependent variable in the entire field will forever remain unspecified. Consequently, we propose a substantive model that specifies the content of performance, its direct determinants, and its critical dynamic properties. The implications of the model for measurement and research are also discussed. The description of the model itself is an expanded version of that presented by Campbell (1990a).

A Proposed Theory of Performance

Although our focus is on job performance, we think the basic implications are much broader and illustrate this point as we go along.

Performance Defined

A full understanding of job performance depends on having some understanding of the organizational goals to which the individual is supposed to contribute. For example, the issues surrounding the instruction versus research goal in universities are familiar to most of us. If this sounds too ho-hum, then get a bit closer to life and death and consider, for air traffic controllers, the two goals of maximizing air traffic safety and maximizing efficiency of air traffic movement *at the same time.* Even closer to home, what are, or should be, the goals of one's family? Family members are always judging each other in terms of their contribution to the family's goals. Some families consider them explicitly, others do not; but goals are always there, if only by default. In the job setting, both confusion and trouble can result if either the formal employment contract or the informal psychological contract incorporates goals different from those against which performance is actually judged (Rousseau, 1989; Schein, 1970).

Performance is herein defined as synonymous with behavior. It is something that people actually do and can be observed. By definition, it includes only those actions or behaviors that are relevant to the organization's goals and that can be scaled (measured) in terms of each individual's proficiency (that is, level of contribution). Performance is what the organization hires one to do, and do well. Performance is *not* the consequence or result of action, it is the action itself. Admittedly, this distinction is troublesome in at least one major respect — behavior is not always observable (for example, cognitive behavior, as in solving a math problem) and can be known only by its effects (for instance, producing a solution after much "thought"). However, "solutions," "statements," or "answers" produced as a result of covert cognitive behavior and totally under the control of the individual are included as actions that can be defined as performance. In general, a strict definition of "observable behavior" is epistemologically difficult. Let us simply argue that performance consists of goal-relevant actions that are under the control of the individual, regardless of whether they are cognitive, motor, psychomotor, or interpersonal. Consequently, writing a job-relevant memo falls within the definition, if the availability of a word processor is a constant, whereas the number of pieces produced does not, unless such an outcome is under the complete control of the individual.

For the model espoused here, it is axiomatic that job performance is not just one thing. A job, *any* job, is a very complex activity; and, for *any* job there are a number of major performance components that are distinguishable in terms of their determinants and covariation patterns with other variables. Some examples of performance components are giving emergency first aid (police officer), planning and designing undergraduate courses (university faculty), driving safely under hazardous conditions (truck operator), rewarding sales personnel for appropriate actions (sales supervisor), and using rules of separation efficiently (air traffic controller).

Performance is to be distinguished from *effectiveness* and from *productivity*. *Effectiveness* refers to the evaluation of the results of performance. By definition, the variance in a measure of effectiveness is controlled by more than the actions of the individual. Dollar amount of sales is an obvious example. An implication of this distinction is that rewarding or punishing individuals on the basis of effectiveness may be unfair and counterproductive. As an indicator of performance, effectiveness is by definition contaminated. This is not to argue that results are not important. They most certainly are. Ultimately, the organization needs to know the sources of variation in performance *and* the sources of variation in effectiveness. Effectiveness is the bottom line, and organizations cannot exist without it. By defining performance this way we are simply arguing the point that if the research questions deal with predictor validities, or training effects, or any other strategy focused on the individual, then the dependent variable should not be something that the individual cannot influence. Further, it would be maximally informative to know the relationship of performance to effectiveness, and not to confound them.

The usually agreed upon definition of productivity (Mahoney, 1988) is the ratio of effectiveness (output) to the cost of achieving that level of effectiveness (input). Its primary use is as a relative index of how well a group, organization, or industry is functioning. Depending on which inputs (costs) are used in the denominator, it is possible to talk about the productivity of capital, the productivity of technology, or the productivity of labor. That is, total productivity has its subcomponents.

For the sake of completeness, *utility* is defined as the value of a particular level of performance, effectiveness, or productivity. That is, we can talk about the utility of performance, the utility of effectiveness, or the utility of productivity. For example, for a board of directors the utility of particular levels of profit (an effectiveness measure by our definition) may bear no resemblance to its dollar amount. At least under the federal tax laws existing in the late 1980s, a high level of profit may have negative utility because it invites takeover attempts and ultimately leads to a heavy burden of corporate debt. In the school system, what is the relative value of high student proficiency in algebra versus high proficiency in English? For individual job holders, what is the value of a top performer versus an average one? All of these "utilities" may or may not be expressed in dollar terms. In certain kinds of organizations it may make little sense to use a dollar metric (Sadacca, Campbell, DiFazio, Schultz, & White, 1990). Also, the regression of utility on performance or effectiveness may not be linear (Pritchard & Roth, 1991).

Determinants of Individual Differences in Performance

We next must distinguish among performance *components* (performance *factor* and performance *construct* are regarded as synonymous terms), performance *determinants*, and the *antecedents* or *predictors* of performance determinants. After making these general distinctions, we propose a substantive taxonomy of performance components. The variables and relationships to be examined are summarized in Table 2.1.

The performance components, or factors, are the distinguishable categories of things people are expected to do in a job. They are the latent variables. Although their true-score inter-

Table 2.1. Determinants of Job Performance Components.

$$PC_i \; {}^a = f \begin{bmatrix} \text{Declarative} & & \text{Procedural Knowledge} & & \\ \text{Knowledge (DK)} & \times & \text{and Skill (PKS)} & \times & \text{Motivation (M)} \end{bmatrix}$$

Declarative Knowledge (DK)	Procedural Knowledge and Skill (PKS)	Motivation (M)
Facts	Cognitive skill	Choice to perform
Principles	Psychomotor skill	Level of effort
Goals	Physical skill	Persistence of effort
Self-knowledge	Self-management skill	
	Interpersonal skill	

$i = 1, 2, \ldots, k$ performance components

Predictors of Performance Determinants[b]

$DK = f$[(ability, personality, interests), (education, training, experience), (aptitude/treatment interactions)]

$PKS = f$[(ability, personality, interests), (education, training, practice, experience), (aptitude/treatment interactions)]

$M = f$(whatever independent variables are stipulated by your favorite motivation theory)

Note: This entire schema can be repeated for educational performance, training performance, and laboratory task performance.

[a]Obviously, performance differences can also be produced by situational effects such as the quality of equipment, degree of staff support, or nature of the working conditions. For purposes of this model of performance, these conditionals are assumed to be held constant (experimentally, statistically, or judgmentally).

[b]Individual differences, learning, and motivational manipulations can only influence performance by increasing declarative knowledge or procedural skill or by influencing the three choices (that is, influencing motivation).

correlations are not zero, they are low enough to yield a significantly different rank ordering of people depending on the performance component being talked about.

Individual differences on *each* specific performance component are viewed as a function of three, and only three, major determinants — declarative knowledge, procedural knowledge and skill, and motivation. Declarative knowledge is simply knowledge about facts and things. Specifically, it represents an understanding of a given task's requirements, such as general principles for equipment operation (Anderson, 1985; Kanfer

& Ackerman, 1989). Procedural knowledge and skill are attained when declarative knowledge (knowing what to do) has been successfully combined with knowing how to do it (modified from Anderson, 1985, and Kanfer & Ackerman, 1989).

As a direct determinant of performance, *motivation* is herein defined as a combined effect from three choice behaviors: (1) choice to expend effort, (2) choice of level of effort to expend, and (3) choice to persist in the expenditure of that level of effort. These are the traditional representations for the direction, amplitude, and duration of volitional behavior. The important point is that the most meaningful way to talk about motivation as a direct determinant of behavior is as one or more of these three choices.

Antecedents of the Performance Determinants

Accounting for individual differences in knowledge, skill, and choice behavior encompasses a very large number of research topics that are not to be discussed here. From the trait perspective, almost a century of research has produced taxonomic models of abilities, personality, interests, and personal histories. Another major research tradition has focused on instructional treatment. At least three major types of such treatments are relevant in the job performance content—formal education, job-relevant training (formal and informal), and previous experience. The possible antecedents of motivation, or choice behavior, are specified by the various theories of motivation. For example, an operant model stipulates that the reinforcement contingency is the most important determinant of the choices people make. Cognitive expectancy models say that certain specific thoughts (for example, self-efficacy, instrumentality, valence) govern these three choices. Other models see such choices as a function of certain stable predispositions, such as the need for achievement. For example, perhaps certain kinds of people virtually always go to work on time and always work hard.

A few general points are important. First, the precise functional form of the $PC = f(DK, PKS, M)$ equation (Table 2.1) is obviously not known and perhaps not even knowable. Further, spending years of research looking for it would probably not be of much use. Instead, consider the following. Performance will not occur unless there is a choice to perform at some level of effort for some specified time. Consequently, motivation is *always* a determinant of performance, and a relevant question for virtually any personnel selection problem is how much of the variance in choice behavior can be accounted for by stable predispositions measurable at the time of hire and how much is a function of the motivating properties of the situation or the interaction. Performance that is not simply trial and error also cannot occur unless there is some threshold level of procedural skill, and there may indeed be a very complex interaction between *PKS* and *M*. For example, the higher the skill level, the greater the tendency to choose to perform, but skill level may have no relationship with the choice of effort level. That is, the three choices may be controlled by different antecedents.

Another reasonable assumption is that declarative knowledge is a prerequisite for procedural skill (Anderson, 1985). That is, before being able to use the procedural skills that are necessary for task performance, one must know what should be done. However, this point is not without controversy (Nissen & Bullmer, 1987), and it may indeed be possible to master a skill without first acquiring the requisite declarative knowledge. Two examples that come to mind are modeling the social skills of your parents and modeling the "final form" of an expert skier without really "knowing" what you are trying to do. Nevertheless, given the current findings in cognitive research, the distinction is a meaningful one. Performance could suffer because procedural skill was never developed or because declarative knowledge was never acquired or because one or the other has decayed. Also, some data suggest that the abilities that account for individual differences in declarative knowledge are different from those that account for individual differences in procedural skills (Ackerman, 1988). At this point, the major implication is still that performance is directly determined only by some combination of these three elements.

Again, the functional relationships between individual differences on the three determinants and individual differences on a component of performance are not constrained to any particular form. That is, they could be linear or nonlinear, and even exhibit strong asymptotes. The functional relationships for declarative knowledge and procedural skill are most likely monotonically increasing, although the same may not be true for the choice determinants.

A Taxonomy of Major Performance Components

If performance is more than one thing, then what are the major parts? Across the entire occupational spectrum how many parts are there? Thousands? Hundreds? A few dozen? Is the latent structure hierarchical, such that there are a small number of general factors at the highest level and increasing specificity as one goes down the hierarchy? What is the variation in the form of the latent structure across jobs? Can a "population" of jobs be defined by a common performance structure? Is there a general performance factor? For some jobs but not for others? A sampling of such questions raises the problem of whether the inherent complexity of performance makes investigating its latent structure counterproductive. The assumption here is no.

The model described is a factor model, but it invokes no general factor. Instead, a hierarchy is proposed that has eight factors at the most general level. The eight factors are intended to be sufficient to describe the top of the latent hierarchy in all jobs in the *Dictionary of Occupational Titles*. However, the eight factors are not of the same form. They have different patterns of subsidiary general factors, and their content varies differentially across jobs. The critical constant is that the manifest representation of each factor must be in terms of things people do, not the "bottom line" or the "results" of what they do. A brief explication of each of the eight factors is given below.

1. *Job-specific task proficiency.* The first factor reflects the degree to which the individual can perform the core substantive or technical tasks that are central to the job. They are the job-specific performance behaviors that distinguish the substan-

tive content of one job from another. Constructing custom
kitchens, doing word processing, designing computer architec-
ture, driving a city bus through Chicago traffic, and directing
air traffic are all categories of job-specific task content. Individual differences in how well such tasks are executed are the focus
of this performance component.

2. *Non-job-specific task proficiency.* This factor reflects the
situation that in virtually every organization, but perhaps not
all, individuals are required to perform tasks or execute performance behaviors that are not specific to their particular job. For
example, in research universities with Ph.D. programs, the
faculty must "teach classes," "advise students," "make admission
decisions," and "serve on committees." All faculty must do these
things, in addition to doing chemistry, psychology, economics,
or electrical engineering. In the military services this factor is
institutionalized as a set of common tasks (for example, first aid,
basic navigation, using NBC equipment) for which everyone
is responsible.

3. *Written and oral communication task proficiency.* Many jobs
in the workforce require the individual to make formal oral or
written presentations to audiences that may vary from one to
tens of thousands. For those jobs the proficiency with which one
can write or speak, independent of the correctness of the subject matter, is a critical component of performance.

4. *Demonstrating effort.* The fourth factor is meant to be
a direct reflection of the consistency of an individual's effort day
by day, the frequency with which people will expend extra effort
when required, and the willingness to keep working under adverse conditions. It is a reflection of the degree to which individuals commit themselves to all job tasks, work at a high level
of intensity, and keep working when it is cold, wet, or late.

5. *Maintaining personal discipline.* The fifth component is
characterized by the degree to which negative behavior such as
alcohol and substance abuse at work, law or rules infractions,
and excessive absenteeism are avoided.

6. *Facilitating peer and team performance.* Factor six is defined
as the degree to which the individual supports his or her peers,
helps them with job problems, and acts as a de facto trainer.

It also encompasses how well an individual facilitates group functioning by being a good model, keeping the group goal-directed, and reinforcing participation by the other group members. Obviously, if the individual works alone, this component will have little importance. However, in many jobs, high performance on this factor would be a major contribution toward the goals of the organization.

7. *Supervision/leadership.* Proficiency in the supervisory component includes all the behaviors directed at influencing the performance of subordinates through face-to-face interpersonal interaction and influence. Supervisors set goals for subordinates, they teach them more effective methods, they model the appropriate behaviors, and they reward or punish in appropriate ways. The distinction between this factor and the previous one is a distinction between peer leadership and supervisory leadership. Although modeling, goal setting, coaching, and providing reinforcement are elements in both factors, the belief here is that peer versus supervisor leadership implies significantly different determinants.

8. *Management/administration.* The eighth and last factor is intended to include the major elements in management that are distinct from direct supervision. It includes the performance behaviors directed at articulating goals for the unit or enterprise, organizing people and resources to work on them, monitoring progress, helping to solve problems or overcome crises that stand in the way of goal accomplishment, controlling expenditures, obtaining additional resources, and representing the unit in dealings with other units.

These eight factors are meant to be the highest-order factors that can be useful. To reduce them further would cover up too much. However, it is also acknowledged that not all the factors are relevant for all jobs. For example, not all jobs have a supervisory or management component. Not all jobs involve formal communication tasks. Some job holders have no peers or work group. What the model asserts is that the eight components, or some subset of them, can describe the highest-order latent variables for every job in the occupational domain. Further, three of the factors—core task proficiency, demonstrated effort, and maintenance of personal discipline—are major performance components of *every* job.

Direct evidence for this taxonomy is admittedly sparse. We have been most influenced by the long-term Selection and Classification Project (Project A) sponsored by the U.S. Army (Campbell & Zook, 1990), which settled on a five-component model of performance (Campbell, McHenry, & Wise, 1990) for a population of 275 entry-level skilled jobs. The model received confirmation in a follow-up of this same sample three years later, after reenlistment (Campbell, 1991), and will be tested again on another large sample of entry-level personnel from a different cohort.

Supporting evidence comes from studies of performance using the Behaviorally Anchored Rating Scales (BARS) technique (for example, Campbell, Dunnette, Arvey, & Hellervik, 1973), which generally seem to produce factors that can be fit into the taxonomy, and from a recent study by Hedberg (1989) that used extensive interview and critical incident methodology to describe various parameters of feedback as it occurs in an ongoing job environment. A content analysis of performance feedback episodes for a sample of financial analysts and project managers tended to mirror the eight-factor solution quite closely. Also, a great deal of evidence for some of the factors comes from descriptive research on what supervisors, leaders, and managers do (for example, Yukl, 1987; Bass, 1990).

In general, however, research on the criterion problem has tended to avoid any formal investigation of the latent structure of performance. A type of study that is *not* appropriate for this purpose is a factor analysis of some mixture of performance measures, indices of effectiveness, and perhaps even measures of performance determinants in the same matrix.

If the eight-factor representation is an appropriate one, then it should receive support from future construct validation efforts, as against alternatives; and it should show consistent differential correlations with other variables. For example, the prediction equations for each factor should be recognizably different.

Implications of the Eight-Factor Latent Structure

The nature of the lower-order factors within each of the eight major components has been the subject of considerable research for some of them and is a matter of speculation for others. If we generalized from the classic situation-specificity hypothesis in personnel psychology, then we might expect the number of subfactors for component 1 (job-specific task proficiency) to equal the number of jobs. That is, the prediction equation for component 1 would be different for each job. Obviously, we already know from lots of data that this would be a very poor description of the latent structure. However, virtually no one would expect the prediction equation for component 1 to be the same for jazz musicians, graphic artists, PGA tour golfers, NFL defensive linemen, theoretical economists, Protestant clergy, farm managers, long-haul truck operators, stockbrokers, and air traffic controllers. Where between these two extremes is a more appropriate description of the latent structure of factor 1? The model proposed here assumes that the number of discriminable subfactors for component 1 is a manageable number, and that it would be quite possible to build up a systematic body of knowledge around the major differences in the correlates for the subfactors.

Also, it is interesting to speculate about the subfactors that might be found in factor 4. In particular, should there be a distinction between physical effort and cognitive effort? A possible confusion here is the distinction between effort behaviors as a component of performance and the three choices as a determinant of performance. As a component of performance, demonstrated effort consists of a set of behaviors that represent mental or physical effort expenditure that contributes to the organization's goals. As with any other performance component, demonstrated effort is a function of declarative knowledge, procedural knowledge and skill, and motivation. For example, someone may not have worked overtime because they did not "know it was an option."

To the limited extent possible, the eight basic components have been defined so as to remove causal relations among them.

However, the true structure is probably not so static. For example, it is most likely the case that being very accomplished on the core tasks of the job or being a very proficient writer or speaker enhances peer or supervisory leadership performance. This is not the same as saying that task performance and supervisory performance have common determinants (such as certain procedural skills). Instead, the supervisor's manifest task performance itself may change the perceptions of the subordinate and thereby alter the influence process.

Finally, we emphasize again that performance and the direct determinants of performance are independent constructs. Because we are just in the beginning stages, future work will most certainly show that this initial taxonomy of performance components is not the "best" description of the latent structure. However, that by itself will not change our view of how to think about the three determinants, which have a much richer history in psychological theory and research.

Critical Performance Parameters

The experimental literature on task performance identifies several performance parameters that may have particular relevance for this kind of model.

Speed Versus Accuracy. One such parameter is speed versus accuracy or quantity versus quality. The speed-accuracy distinction is important because it has been shown that speed and level scores for the same task load on independent factors (for example, Kyllonen, 1985) and speed of problem solving may not correlate with accuracy of problem solving in the same content domain (Lohman, 1989). As a consequence, it seems reasonable to expect that predicting quantity (speed) and predicting quality (accuracy) would require different equations and that more specific abilities may be more appropriate for the former than the latter. The issue in the job performance context encompasses two major questions. First, what kind of trade-off between the two does the organization value? Second, what trade-off is the individual actually making?

Automatic Versus Controlled Processing and the Performance Asymptote. A second parameter of interest is a recognizable phenomenon that can occur during cognitive, psychomotor, or motor skill acquisition and is now referred to as the development of "automaticity" regarding skills or components of skills (Shiffrin & Schneider, 1977). Automaticity means that a skill or a skill component can be performed automatically without investing very much, if any, conscious attentional effort. The individual literally does not have to "think about" performing the task. Most of us experience such a shift to automaticity when learning to read, ride a bicycle, or type. A controlled process is task performance that requires a significant investment of continuous attention. Performance moves from controlled to automatic processing as a function of learning, experience, and practice, and individuals differ in terms of the speed with which they make the transition. Tasks with the potential for being performed automatically are known as consistent tasks. At least in theory, consistent tasks have a performance asymptote, whereas controlled tasks do not.

Ackerman (1987) and Kanfer and Ackerman (1989) have used these notions to help explain the differential relationship of abilities to technical task performance at different stages of training or experience. For example, Ackerman (1987) has modified the basic Fleishman (1972) hypothesis that specific abilities become more important predictors of performance (relative to general ability) as training progresses by showing this to be true only for consistent tasks. That is, general abilities are what count when a great deal of controlled processing is necessary, but under conditions of automaticity it is the more specific abilities that predict individual differences in task performance. For inconsistent tasks, general abilities will always be major predictors. Similarly, the increase or decrease in performance variance as a function of training is seen as dependent on the degree of task consistency. Consistent tasks should show decreasing variance as a function of additional training or experience, and variability between persons on inconsistent tasks should become greater (Ackerman, 1987).

Peak Versus Typical Performance. Another major parameter is peak versus typical performance. In a very illustrative study using supermarket checkout personnel, Sackett, Zedeck, and Fogli (1988) obtained the correlation between a standardized work sample measure, administered by the researchers, and an on-line computerized record of actual performance on the very same job tasks. Both measures were highly reliable, but the correlation between the two was surprisingly low. The authors called this a distinction between maximum and typical performance and reasoned that the cause of the lowered correlation was the uniformly high motivation generated by the standardized situation versus the differential motivation across individuals in the actual work setting. If such an explanation is accurate, then attempts to model performance must face the issue of what to do with the distinction. The proposed model stipulates that both measures address the content of factor 1 (core technical performance), but the standardized job sample tries to hold the motivation determinants constant for all individuals (at a high level), whereas the archival records do not.

Measurement Considerations

In terms of consistency between the measurement operations and the definition of performance, the proposed model allows only three, or possibly four, primary measurement methods.

Ratings. First, the model strongly implies that ratings (expert judgments) should remain as an important method since they can be constructed to conform directly to the specified definition. The principal worry about ratings has always been that no matter how they are constructed, there may still be significant contamination by systematic variance unrelated to the performance of the person being assessed. Thinking of performance rating as a sequence of observation, sampling, encoding, storage, retrieval, evaluation, differential weighting, and composite scoring allows it to be a very complex cognitive process that allows many opportunities for entry of both unsystematic variance and contamination (Cooper, 1981a; DeNisi, Cafferty, & Meglino, 1984; Ilgen & Feldman, 1983).

As with any criterion measure, the overall problem is to estimate the proportion of observed variance accounted for by (1) the latent variable, (2) general method variance, (3) measure-specific method variance, (4) other systematic contamination, and (5) unreliability. It has been difficult, however, to assess the effect of nonrelevant sources of variation on the accuracy of job performance ratings. For example, the model clearly implies that it is inappropriate to infer that the variance in ratings that does not overlap with the variance in other measures of performance (say, job samples) is "error variance." As an alternative, some researchers have created videotapes in which the true level of job performance on the dimensions to be rated is scripted (Borman, 1978; Murphy & Balzer, 1989). Accuracy is then assessed by comparing the script to ratings made by raters who view the videotape. However, rating a stranger immediately after viewing a five- to fifteen-minute videotape is a very reduced construction of the situation the rater faces in an organizational setting (for example, Cooper, 1981b; Nathan & Tippins, 1990).

A complete partitioning of the total variance in job performance ratings would require *identifying sources of variance attributable to the rater* that are (1) idiosyncratic (unique to the individual rater), (2) subgroup-specific (unique to raters of the same type), or (3) shared with all raters and *identifying all the significant variables that influence each perspective,* including true score differences on performance. The optimal situation for addressing these requirements would be one in which (1) all raters from all relevant perspectives would rate all incumbents on all dimensions of job performance (Saal, Downey, & Lahey, 1980) and (2) all the variables hypothesized to influence each rater perspective would be assessed. Although this situation is generally not feasible, some partitioning of variance is often possible. For instance, partitioning the contributions due to rater subgroups requires only that each ratee be rated by at least two raters from each subgroup (Sager, 1990). However, partitioning the variance due to idiosyncratic sources requires that each rater also rate the same group of ratees.

Although ratings generally have bad press, the overall picture is not as bleak as might be expected, given all the ways the true-score variance can be contaminated. One advantage of ratings, assuming they share at least some variance with the latent variable, is that their content can be directly linked to the measurement objectives by straightforward content validation methods (for example, critical incident sampling combined with retranslation procedures). Also, *if* used with care, their reliabilities are usually respectable (.50–.60) and can be improved considerably by using more than one rater; and they are as predictable as objective effectiveness measures (Schmitt, Gooding, Noe, & Kirsch, 1984; Nathan & Alexander, 1988). Faith is added by the more thorough attempts to use the method, which have produced credible results (C. Campbell et al., 1990); and over a number of studies, the largest source of variance in ratings is in fact the performance of the ratee (Landy & Farr, 1980). Also, recent studies by McCloy (1990) and Oppler (1990) provide strong evidence that individual differences in performance ratings, when the rating content is carefully defined and raters are trained in their use, are a function of all three performance determinants. The qualifiers are important. Any procedure can be made to look bad by poor implementation, and no method should be made a victim of its most inexpert users. However, it is also true that we still have much to learn about the determinants of ratings.

Standardized Job Samples. The second measurement method allowed by the proposed model is the standardized job sample in which the task content of the job is simulated, or actually sampled intact, and presented to the assessee in a standardized format under standardized conditions. The content validity of the method can also be determined directly, but for the reasons just discussed it may not reflect the influence of all three determinants. That is, individual performance differences on the standardized job sample would be a function of individual differences in declarative knowledge and procedural knowledge and skill, but not motivation. Also, there is always a question about whether the knowledge and skills required by the standardized sample are different in any major respect from that required in the actual job setting.

Direct Task Observation. The third primary measurement method consists of direct task observation and measurement as it occurs in the job setting. This is what Sackett, Zedeck, and Fogli (1988) were fortunate enough to have for the supermarket checkout personnel. Except in rare instances, this method usually requires rather expensive observational or recording techniques; and for complex work positions the difficulties in observation may be insurmountable.

Alternative Method. In general, a fourth measurement method is dangerous because it equates performance and effectiveness, which is generally forbidden. However, it may sometimes be possible to specify outcomes of performance that are virtually under the complete control of the individual. College grade point average may be such an example; however, saying that could start an argument.

In addition to whether or not the measurement method reflects performance as defined—and not something else—the proposed model identifies two additional critical issues.

First, to avoid criterion content deficiency, the model specifies the population of performance behaviors, along with a procedure for identifying an appropriate sample of content for measurement. Traditionally, this is the domain of job analysis, and a very large literature is available. For example, Project A (C. Campbell et al., 1990) used two principal methods— extensive critical incident descriptions with subsequent retranslation and a series of task analyses that attempted to enumerate every task (that is, the population of tasks) in each job.

The critical incident method is particularly useful because it can sample from the entire population of performance content at the same time that each action is scaled in terms of its contribution to the organization's goals and the major performance components are identified. Also, by changing instructions to the experts providing the incidents, the method can be used to capture performance content for people at various levels of experience, which is a critical parameter. For example, it can be used to contrast "novice" and "expert" performance. Other job analysis methods, such as task analysis, usually cannot provide as much information. Using the critical incident method in this way does not necessarily imply the use of ratings as measurement operations. The critical incident content could be used just as well to specify the content for job observations or simulations.

The second major issue the proposed model addresses is whether the measurement method allows the appropriate determinants (declarative knowledge, procedural knowledge and skill, or motivation) to influence an individual's score. A measurement procedure (for instance, supervisor ratings or scores from a simulator) could choose to control or not control for one or more of them. For example, the measurement objective could stipulate that individual differences in motivation (the three volitional choices) should *not* contribute to individual differences in performance scores, as when evaluating the effects of a skills training program. In such an instance, the measurement goal is to determine whether the specified technical skills have in fact been mastered, not whether the individual chooses to use them in the actual job setting. If the appropriate determinants cannot influence the score on the criterion measure, then the measure is "determinant deficient," which is to be distinguished from the usual use of the term as a label for content deficiency.

Perhaps another example would help illustrate this very fundamental point. It is generally agreed that most commercial airline accidents are the results of faulty "cockpit management." That is, at the critical time there is a breakdown in task delegation, communication, or teamwork. These specific variables seem to represent factors 7 and 8 in the performance component taxonomy. If a simulator is used as a performance measure, then, given that the simulator allows performance on factors 7 and 8 to be observed, a critical question concerns which performance determinants should be allowed to operate and which should be controlled. For example, a critical determinant may be the hesitation of a junior crew member to question the actions of the senior pilot if he or she appears to be in error. To bring this determinant into the simulator, the simulator "crew" should reflect the established air crew hierarchy. To serve a different objective, the measurement procedure could control for the motivational determinants so as to evaluate the effects of knowledge or skill differentials without being confounded with motivational differences.

In general, the specifications for the measurement method are very dependent on the measurement objectives. The objectives must stipulate the performance factors to be assessed and the determinants that should be controlled and those that should be allowed to influence scores. A confirmatory test of such specifications for the set of performance measures used in Project A is provided by McCloy (1990).

Some Alternative Theories of Performance

Before summarizing the principal implications of the proposed model, we consider the major alternatives that exist in the literature.

One is described in a National Academy of Sciences report produced by the Committee on Performance Measurement in the Military Services (Green & Wigdor, 1988). It suggests that performance should be defined as some combination of the proficiency levels on each substantive task encompassed by the job, as identified in a detailed job analysis. Whether the rules for combining scores on each task are to be compensatory (for instance, a simple or weighted sum of task scores) or noncompensatory (for example, the total score is the proportion of task scores that are above some standard) is not clear. Ideally, given this model, one would enumerate the total population of tasks in each job and measure performance on each. Since that would be too expensive, the specific recommendation is to use stratified random sampling to obtain a representative task sample and then construct a work sample or simulator that includes those tasks. All other measures are viewed as "surrogates" of this one best measure. Such a model is not unlike the model of instructional design espoused by Robert Gagne and his colleagues (Gagne, Briggs, & Wager, 1988), which makes the detailed description of posttraining performance objectives the first, and most important, step in any design effort. Training is deemed successful to the extent the trainee can demonstrate mastery of the specified objectives. Although such a model is extremely valuable in a training context where mastering specific procedural skills is the overriding concern, it does not allow the motivation determinant to operate and tends to concentrate measurement almost entirely on factors 1 and 2.

A second model says that performance is the achievement of outcomes largely under the control of the individual. That is, the distinction between performance and effectiveness should be designed away. In I/O psychology the primary current proponent of such a view is Robert Pritchard (Pritchard, Jones, Roth, Stuebing, & Ekeberg, 1988), who has developed a measurement system known as the Productivity (really performance) Measurement and Enhancement System (ProMES). The general procedure is for the organization to form a special task force whose primary goal is to find or create outcome indicators (that is, measures) that are both highly relevant for the organization's bottom line and under the direct control of the individual or work group to be evaluated. The task force also creates what amounts to a marginal utility function for each indicator. For example, for the job of electronics repair, the percent return rate for components that had been repaired was chosen as a performance indicator. Direct magnitude estimation techniques were then used to scale the relative value of various return rates, including the establishment of a zero point (where the utility of performance becomes negative), below which strong remedial action had to be taken. (The high correspondence between performance and outcome is obtained by using measures that make it so.)

McLagan (1988) subscribes to the same basic conceptualization of performance but says that the entire job hierarchy in an organization must be redesigned to ensure that the outcomes for which people are to be held accountable are in fact under their direct control and that the outcomes are in fact the products the organization requires. This is a gargantuan task but one she has helped a number of organizations struggle through. As approaches to defining the specific goals for a job, or unit, these two procedures are of great value. However, although performance is assessed in an appropriate way, there is some risk that measurement will be content deficient in the context of the proposed taxonomy. That is, not all of the content factors that are relevant components of performance in a particular job may be included.

A third area of performance theory is concerned with the functional form of the relationship between performance and its antecedents. In several studies (Hunter, 1983, 1986; Vance, MacCallum, Coovert, & Hedge, 1988; Borman, Hanson, Oppler, Pulakos, & White, 1991) alternative path models have been used to construct the causal relationships among such independent variables as abilities, personality, experience, and job knowledge in terms of their collective effect on performance. For example, Hunter (1983) presented a path model examining the disattenuated correlations (that is, corrected for unreliability) among measures of cognitive ability, job knowledge, performance on a job sample measure, and supervisor ratings.

Path analysis of disattenuated correlations provides estimates of direct and indirect effects among true scores (scores without unsystematic error). Such estimates, however, do not take into account Campbell and Fiske's (1959) notion that reliable variance is a function of both construct variance and method variance. To the extent that measures are differentially affected by method variance, the path coefficients may not represent the "true" causal relationships among the latent constructs. Also, to the extent that the observed measures are "deficient" as representations of the content of the latent variable, better measurement could change the degree of fit for a specific causal model. In addition, the path coefficients will be different to the extent that alternative measures for a particular variable control differentially for the three performance determinants. For example, a job sample measure that is primarily a function of declarative knowledge should yield different results from a job sample measure that is primarily a function of procedural skill. These problems are not unique to studies of causal models; they just become more explicit, which is a virtue of using such models.

However, although the investigation of alternative path models will yield valuable information about the antecedents of performance, if the critical variables are not underdetermined, they do not speak to the substantive nature of performance itself. Consequently, we do not view them as "competing" with the model proposed here.

Potential Misunderstandings

The proposed model of performance might be misinterpreted in the following ways. We would like to preempt such misunderstandings at the outset.

1. The intent of this discussion is to describe a theory of performance where the individual is the unit of analysis. That is our specific interest and we think it is an important one. We do not wish to downplay other units of analysis. It should go without saying that there is also great interest in the performance of groups, complex organizations of multiple groups, entire industries, and even nation-states. The moral is that in attempting to better understand all such phenomena, the units of analyses should not be confused or confounded (Ostroff & Ford, 1989).

2. The proposed model is, in fact, intended to be comprehensive regarding the determinants of individual differences in performance. For example, it is obviously true that differences in the quality of management or supervision, differences in compensation, differences in perceptions of distributive or procedural justice, differences in socialization rituals, or differences in the "corporate culture" can produce differences in individual performance, as shown previously. However, our fundamental point is that all such determinants should be thought of in terms of two levels—direct determinants and their antecedents. The antecedents, or indirect determinants, can only influence performance through their effects on one or more of the direct determinants. That is, compensation practices, corporate culture, perceptions of justice, training programs, and supervision can only affect performance by changing an individual's

declarative knowledge, procedural knowledge and skill, and/or motivation. For example, even though improvements in the quality of supervision can certainly improve individual performance, the mechanisms for the change must be some combination of changes in the individual's declarative knowledge, procedural skill, and choice behavior. The supervisor can "teach" the individual new knowledge or new skills or "motivate" changes in one or more of the three choices. If we do not pay attention to what is happening with regard to the direct determinants, then we may totally misunderstand why better supervision has an effect on individual performance.

3.   The proposed model is not a prescription for the best techniques organizations can use to promote higher individual performance. Its intent is to provide a reasonable way of thinking about such issues systematically. Also, even though this book deals with personnel selection, the proposed model is not an advocate for better selection as the preferred strategy for performance improvement.

4.   The model does not "ignore" the fact that individual performance can be influenced by better tools, equipment, software, and so on. For example, the performance of air traffic controllers on a job-specific task factor called "using rules of separation efficiently" may be greatly influenced by technological changes in computerized radar displays. In fact, the change in technology may change the declarative knowledge, procedural knowledge and skill, and/or motivation requirements, which may in turn require different abilities or training courses. However, for purposes of measurement, the model simply stipulates that performance differences produced by differences in technology (for example, some job holders having better software than others) should not be confounded with performance differences produced by individual differences in declarative knowledge, procedural knowledge and skill, and motivation. That is, such external causes should be held constant; otherwise, the results of selection procedure validation, training program evaluation, or the results of evaluating any other such human resource intervention will be contaminated and misleading.

5.   A similar argument can be made about effects of "constraints" on performance (Bernardin, 1989; O'Conner, Peters,

Weekley, Frank, & Erenkrantz, 1984). Constraints exert their influence on performance through their influence on motivation. If the constraints are changed, performance and the antecedents of the performance determinants may change. However, for purposes of selection research or training evaluation, the constraints must not be allowed to operate differentially within the research sample. Also, if the constraints on the research sample are not the same as those that will operate in the future population of incumbents, then corrections for the restriction must be used when population validity is estimated (Campbell, 1990a).

6. If performance really is multidimensional, then it is also true that we must face the issue of how to combine factor scores for purposes of making specific decisions. For example, academic departments seem to select faculty almost exclusively on the basis of factor 1, with some consideration for factor 3. Perhaps it is no wonder that they are often such contentious and strangely managed places. In general, individuals have different patterns of strengths and weaknesses. How are they to be compared? The specification of the combinational rules is again an expert judgment regarding how the goals of the organization can best be served. The appropriate procedure for estimating the parameter values is a research question.

7. This chapter is not about doing performance appraisal. There is a fundamental difference between measuring performance for purposes of evaluating a personnel management strategy (for example, selection or training) and making an operational decision about an individual (terminate, promote, grant a salary increase, and so on). For quite legitimate reasons, the same method can produce a very different distribution of scores for the same sample of people as a function of the two different objectives. Performance appraisal is certainly no less important than training evaluation or criterion-related test validation, but it is not the topic of this chapter. However, the model described here does imply that using operational performance appraisals as criteria in selection research is a dangerous thing to do. For similar reasons, such methods as management by objectives (MBO) and the conceptual frameworks of McGregor (1960), Odiorne (1965), and Deming (1986) are not discussed here.

Rather than ruminating over false arguments such as the above, readers would benefit more by taking issue with the content taxonomy, the characterization of the measurement issues, or the basic definition of performance itself. Our basic hope is that I/O psychology can come to some agreement about the meaning of performance so that future research can be designed, implemented, and interpreted within a common framework, broad though it may be.

Conclusion

Let us close by arguing that the greatest benefit of a model like the one proposed here is its value for guiding the choice of the dependent variable in a wide variety of research efforts, for structuring the reporting of research, and for organizing the accumulation of research results. Although black box correlations may be useful in some operational sense, it does very little for our collective understanding to say that general mental ability predicts promotion rate in most organizations, or that training in self-management lowers labor costs, or that the average correlation of assessment center evaluations with supervisor ratings of overall performance is .40. What will have far more value is to attach research results to a known latent structure for the dependent variable. Then we will no longer ask general questions such as How valid is this test? or How good is this or that type of training program? which is the way research results have historically been summarized and which focuses on the independent variable with no reference to its purpose. If the dependent variable is the variable of real interest, then the research questions should be of the form, What are the best strategies for improving peer leadership and support in organizations? or What must new entrants to the high-technology workplace know and be able to do to be successful on factors 1 and 5 in a particular population of jobs?

Finally, the mismatch of supply and demand for declarative knowledge, procedural knowledge and skill, and motivation in the labor force that will loom ever larger as we move into the twenty-first century (Johnston & Packer, 1987) is a problem of enormous if not catastrophic magnitude, and is very much in the domain of applied psychology. Without a better conceptual structure for performance itself, we will attenuate our contributions to solving this problem. It would be better if that did not happen.

References

Ackerman, P. L. (1987). Individual differences in skill learning: An integration of psychometric and information processing perspectives. *Psychological Bulletin, 102,* 3–27.

Ackerman, P. L. (1988). Determinants of individual differences during skill acquisition: Cognitive abilities and information processing. *Journal of Experimental Psychology: General, 117,* 288–318.

Anderson, J. R. (1985). *Cognitive psychology and its implications* (2nd ed.). New York: W. H. Freeman.

Bass, B. M. (1990). *Bass and Stogdill's handbook of leadership: Theory, research, and managerial applications* (3rd ed.). New York: Free Press.

Bernardin, H. J. (1989). Increasing the accuracy of performance measurement: A proposed solution to erroneous attributions. *Human Resource Planning, 12*(3), 239–250.

Borman, W. C. (1978). Exploring upper limits of reliability and validity in job performance ratings. *Journal of Applied Psychology, 40,* 135–144.

Borman, W. C., Hanson, M. A., Oppler, S. H., Pulakos, E. D., & White, L. A. (1991, April). *The role of early supervisory experience in supervisory performance.* Paper presented at the meeting of the Society for Industrial and Organizational Psychology, St. Louis, MO.

Campbell, C. H., Ford, P., Rumsey, M. G., Pulakos, E. D., Borman, W. C., Felker, D. B., de Vera, M. V., & Riegelhaupt, B. J. (1990). Development of multiple job performance measures in a representative sample of jobs. *Personnel Psychology, 43*(2), 277–300.

Campbell, D. T., & Fiske, D. W. (1959). Convergent and discriminant validation by the multitrait-multimethod matrix. *Psychological Bulletin, 56,* 81–105.

Campbell, J. P. (1990a). Modeling the performance prediction problem in industrial and organizational psychology. In M. D. Dunnette & L. M. Hough (Eds.), *Handbook of industrial and organizational psychology* (Vol. 1, 2nd ed.). Palo Alto, CA: Consulting Psychologists Press.

Campbell, J. P. (1990b). The role of theory in industrial and organizational psychology. In M. D. Dunnette & L. M. Hough (Eds.), *Handbook of industrial and organizational psychology* (Vol. 1, 2nd ed.). Palo Alto, CA: Consulting Psychologists Press.

Campbell, J. P. (Ed.). (1991). *Building the career force — First annual report.* Alexandria, VA: U.S. Army Research Institute for the Behavioral and Social Sciences.

Campbell, J. P., Dunnette, M. D., Arvey, R. D., & Hellervik, L. V. (1973). The development and evaluation of behaviorally based rating scales. *Journal of Applied Psychology, 57,* 15–22.

Campbell, J. P., McHenry, J. J., & Wise, L. L. (1990). Modeling job performance in a population of jobs. *Personnel Psychology, 43*(2), 313–333.

Campbell, J. P., & Zook, L. M. (Eds.). (1990). *Improving the selection, classification, and utilization of army enlisted personnel: Final report on Project A.* Alexandria, VA: U.S. Army Research Institute for the Behavioral and Social Sciences.

Cooper, W. H. (1981a). Ubiquitous halo. *Psychological Bulletin, 49,* 499–520.

Cooper, W. H. (1981b). Conceptual similarity as a source of illusory halo in job performance ratings. *Journal of Applied Psychology, 66,* 302–307.

Deming, W. E. (1986). *Out of the crisis.* Cambridge, MA: Massachusetts Institute of Technology Center for Advanced Engineering Studies (MIT-CAES).

DeNisi, A. S., Cafferty, T. P., & Meglino, B. M. (1984). A cognitive view of the performance appraisal process: A model and research propositions. *Organizational Behavior and Human Performance, 33,* 360–396.

Dunnette, M. D. (1963). A note on *the* criterion. *Journal of Applied Psychology, 47,* 251–254.

Fleishman, E. A. (1972). On the relationship between abilities, learning, and human performance. *American Psychologist, 27,* 1017–1032.

Gagne, R. M., Briggs, L. J., & Wager, W. W. (1988). *Principles of instructional design* (3rd ed.). New York: Holt, Rinehart & Winston.

Green, B. F., & Wigdor, A. K. (Eds.). (1988). *Measuring job competency: Report of the Committee on the Performance of Military Personnel. National Research Council.* Washington, DC: National Academy Press.

Hedberg, P. R. (1989). *Individual perceptions of performance feedback in a work setting.* Unpublished doctoral dissertation, University of Minnesota, Minneapolis.

Horn, J. L. (1989). Cognitive diversity: A framework of learning. In P. Ackerman, R. Sternberg, & R. Glaser (Eds.), *Learning and individual differences.* New York: Freeman.

Hough, L. M., Eaton, N. K., Dunnette, M. D., Kamp, J. P., & McCloy, R. A. (1990). Criterion-related validities of personality constructs and the effect of response distortion on those validities. *Journal of Applied Psychology, 75,* 581–595.

Hunter, J. E. (1983). A causal analysis of cognitive ability, job knowledge, job performance, and supervisory ratings. In F. Landy, S. Zedeck, & J. Cleveland (Eds.), *Performance measurement and theory.* Hillsdale, NJ: Erlbaum.

Hunter, J. E. (1986). Cognitive ability, cognitive aptitudes, job knowledge, and job performance. *Journal of Vocational Behavior, 29,* 340–362.

Ilgen, D. R., & Feldman, J. M. (1983). Performance appraisal: A process focus. In B. M. Staw & L. L. Cummings (Eds.), *Research in Organizational Behavior* (Vol. 5, pp. 141–197). Greenwich, CT: JAI Press.

James, L. R. (1973). Criterion models and construct validity for criteria. *Psychological Bulletin, 80,* 75–83.

Jenkins, J. G. (1946). Validity for what? *Journal of Consulting Psychology, 10,* 93–98.

Johnston, W. B., & Packer, A. E. (1987). *Workforce 2000 (The "executive" summary).* Indianapolis, IN: Hudson Institute.

Kanfer, R. (1990). Motivation theory and industrial/organizational psychology. In M. D. Dunnette (Ed.), *Handbook of industrial and organizational psychology* (2nd ed. Vol. 1). Palo Alto, CA: Consulting Psychologists Press.

Kanfer, R., & Ackerman, P. L. (1989). Motivation and cognitive abilities: An integrative-aptitude-treatment interaction approach to skill acquisition. *Journal of Applied Psychology, 74,* 657–690.

Kyllonen, P. C. (1985). *Dimensions of information processing speed* (Report No. AFT-TP-84-56). Brooks AFB, TX: Air Force Human Resource Laboratory, Manpower & Personnel Division.

Landy, F. J., & Farr, J. L. (1980). Performance rating. *Psychological Bulletin, 87,* 72–107.

Lohman, D. F. (1989). Estimating individual differences in information processing using speed-accuracy models. In R. Kanfer, P. Ackerman, & R. Cudeck (Eds.), *Abilities, motivation, and methodology: The Minnesota symposium on learning and individual differences.* Hillsdale, NJ: Erlbaum.

Mahoney, T. A. (1988). Productivity defined: The relativity of efficiency, effectiveness, and change. In J. P. Campbell & R. J. Campbell (Eds.), *Productivity in organizations.* San Francisco: Jossey-Bass.

McCloy, R. A. (1990). *A new model of job performance: An integration of measurement, prediction, and theory.* Unpublished doctoral dissertation, University of Minnesota, Minneapolis.

McGregor, D. (1960). *The human side of enterprise.* New York: McGraw-Hill.

McLagan, P. A. (1988). Flexible job models: A productivity strategy for the information age. In J. P. Campbell & R. J. Campbell (Eds.), *Productivity in organizations.* San Francisco: Jossey-Bass.

Murphy, K., & Balzer, W. (1989). Rating errors and rating accuracy. *Journal of Applied Psychology, 74,* 619–624.

Nagle, B. F. (1953). Criterion development. *Personnel Psychology, 6,* 271–289.

Nathan, B. R., & Alexander, R. A. (1988). A comparison of criteria for test validation: A meta analytic investigation. *Personnel Psychology, 41,* 517–536.

Nathan, B. R., & Tippins, N. (1990). The consequences of halo "error" in performance ratings: A field study of the moderating effect of halo on test validation results. *Journal of Applied Psychology, 75,* 290–296.

Nissen, M. J., & Bullmer, P. (1987). Attentional requirements of learning: Evidence from performance measures. *Cognitive Psychology, 19,* 1–32.

O'Conner, E. J., Peters, L. H., Weekley, J., Frank, B., & Erenkrantz, B. (1984). Situational constraints and effects on performance, affective reactions, and turnover: A field replication and extension. *Journal of Applied Psychology, 69,* 663–672.

Odiorne, G. S. (1965). *Management decision by objectives.* Englewood Cliffs, NJ: Prentice-Hall.

Oppler, S. H. (1990). *Three methodological approaches to the investigation of subgroup bias in performance measurement.* Unpublished doctoral dissertation, University of Minnesota, Minneapolis.

Ostroff, C., & Ford, J. K. (1989). Assessing training needs: Critical levels of analysis. In I. L. Goldstein (Ed.), *Training and development in organizations.* San Francisco: Jossey-Bass.

Patterson, C. H. (1946). On the problem of the criterion in prediction studies. *Journal of Consulting Psychology, 10,* 277–280.

Pritchard, R. D., Jones, S. D., Roth, P. L., Steubing, K. K., & Ekeberg, S. E. (1988). Effects of group feedback, goal setting, and incentives on organizational productivity. [Monograph]. *Journal of Applied Psychology, 73,* 337–358.

Pritchard, R. D., & Roth, P. G. (1991). Accounting for nonlinear utility functions in composite measures of utility and performance. *Organizational Behavior and Human Decision Processes, 50,* 341–359.

Rousseau, D. M. (1989). *Psychological contracts in recruitment.* Paper presented at the meeting of the Society for Industrial and Organizational Psychology, Boston.

Saal, F. E., Downey, R. G., & Lahey, M. A. (1980). Rating the ratings: Assessing the psychometric quality of rating data. *Psychological Bulletin, 88,* 413–428.

Sackett, P. R., Zedeck, S., & Fogli, L. (1988). Relations between measures of typical and maximum job performance. *Journal of Applied Psychology, 73,* 482–486.

Sadacca, R., Campbell, J. P., DiFazio, A. S., Schultz, S. R.,

& White, L. A. (1990). Scaling performance utility to enhance selection/classification decisions. *Personnel Psychology, 43,* 367–378.

Sager, C. E. (1990). *A component model of halo: Peer and supervisory ratings of job performance.* Unpublished doctoral dissertation, University of Minnesota, Minneapolis.

Schein, E. H. (1970). *Organizational psychology* (2nd ed.). Englewood Cliffs, NJ: Prentice-Hall.

Schmitt, N., Gooding, R. Z., Noe, R. A., & Kirsch, M. (1984). Meta analyses of validity studies published between 1964 and 1982 and the investigation of study characteristics. *Personnel Psychology, 37,* 407–422.

Shiffrin, R. M., & Schneider, W. (1977). Controlled and automatic human information processing: 2. Perceptual learning, automatic attending, and a general theory. *Psychological Review, 84,* 127–190.

Thorndike, R. L. (1949). *Personnel selection: Test and measurement techniques.* New York: Wiley.

Toops, H. A. (1944). The criterion. *Educational and Psychological Measurement, 4,* 271–297.

Vance, R. J., MacCallum, R. C., Coovert, M. D., & Hedge, J. W. (1988). Construct validity of multiple job performance measures using confirmatory factor analysis. *Journal of Applied Psychology, 73,* 74–80.

Wallace, S. R. (1965). Criteria for what? *American Psychologist, 20,* 411–417.

Yukl, G. (1987, August). *A new taxonomy for integrating diverse perspectives on managerial behavior.* Paper presented at the meeting of the American Academy of Management, New Orleans, LA.

3

Expanding the Criterion Domain to Include Elements of Contextual Performance

Walter C. Borman, Stephan J. Motowidlo

Individuals contribute to organizational effectiveness in ways that go beyond the activities that comprise their "jobs." They can either help or hinder efforts to accomplish organizational goals by doing many things that are not directly related to their main task functions but are important because they shape the organizational, social, and psychological context that serves as the critical catalyst for task activities and processes. These contextual activities are sometimes represented in criterion dimensions of individual job performance, and they are sometimes implicitly recognized as important for organizational effectiveness. They are frequently ignored, however, and as a result, are not included, explicitly or implicitly, in assessments of individual job performance to be used as criteria.

In this chapter we argue that selection criteria should embrace a domain of organizational behavior broader than just task activities; they should also include contextual activities. First, we discuss contextual performance in general and show how it differs from task performance. Then we discuss four streams of research that illustrate aspects of contextual perfor-

Note: The Authors thank Irv Goldstein, Neal Schmitt, Ben Schneider, and Dennis Organ for commenting on an earlier draft of this chapter.

mance. Finally, we speculate about individual difference variables that may be useful in predicting contextual performance.

Task Performance and Contextual Performance

Work organizations absorb environmental resources, use them to create or transform products, and exchange those products for more environmental resources to continue the cycle. The heart of this cycle is the organization's technical core, in which raw materials are processed and transformed into the organization's products. Several theorists have written extensively about technology and how it shapes organizational structure (for example, Perrow, 1965; Thompson, 1967; Woodward, 1965). The most interesting thing about organizational technology for our purposes, however, is its effect on the structure of individuals' jobs.

Many jobs directly involve implementing parts of the technical core and actually transforming raw materials as a step toward creating organizational products. Assembly line workers in factories attach pieces to manufactured products, tellers in banks physically transfer money to and from bank customers, and physicians in hospitals make decisions and take actions to heal patients. Activities like these that contribute directly to the technical core illustrate a portion of what we mean by task performance.

Other jobs contribute to the technical core less directly. At the input end, for example, some jobs are dedicated to replenishing the supply of raw materials, and at the output end, other jobs are dedicated to distributing finished products and exchanging them for necessary raw resources. Still other jobs contribute to the technical core even less directly, although their organizational significance still derives from servicing it in various ways. Managers, for instance, do not contribute to the technical core directly, but they do plan, organize, coordinate, supervise, and perform other functions to make sure the multiple activities that do contribute directly are performed effectively and efficiently. Neither do staff jobs such as accounting, personnel, legal, or public relations contribute directly, but, like management jobs, they too are important because they provide services that enable the technical core to function effectively and efficiently. Such activities illustrate another portion of what we mean by task performance.

Formal descriptions of jobs emphasize activities that either contribute to the technical core directly or service it indirectly. These are typically the kinds of activities identified by job analyses that focus on tasks and estimate their importance, frequency, time spent, and similar task characteristics. Thus, task performance is the proficiency with which job incumbents perform activities that are formally recognized as part of their jobs (and, usually, are not a part of at least some other jobs in the organization), activities that contribute to the organization's technical core either directly by implementing a part of its technological process, or indirectly by providing it with needed materials or services.

Many other activities do not fall under the category of task performance but are still important for organizational effectiveness; we call them contextual activities. They include activities like these:

- Volunteering to carry out task activities that are not formally a part of the job
- Persisting with extra enthusiasm or effort when necessary to complete own task activities successfully
- Helping and cooperating with others
- Following organizational rules and procedures even when personally inconvenient
- Endorsing, supporting, and defending organizational objectives

Contextual activities differ from task activities in at least four important ways. First, task activities contribute either directly or indirectly to the technical core. Contextual activities, on the other hand, do not support the technical core itself as much as they support the organizational, social, and psychological environment in which the technical core must function.

Even when contextual activities do seem directed toward the technical core because they involve task activities that are a part of others' jobs or an incumbent's own job, the emphasis is not on the proficiency with which those tasks are carried out, but on the initiative taken to volunteer to carry them out or on the extra effort shown in carrying them out with unusual persistence or enthusiasm.

Second, task activities usually vary between different jobs in the same organization. In fact, when one job is considered different from another, it is precisely because its task activities are different. Contextual activities, however, are common to many or all jobs. Their peripheral details vary because they are performed in environments that change from job to job, but their central features are the same. Volunteering, persisting, helping, cooperating, following rules, staying with the organization, and endorsing its objectives are probably important for all jobs.

Third, because the source of variation in task performance is the proficiency with which task activities are carried out, the important human characteristics are knowledge, skills, and abilities that covary with task proficiency. The major source of variation in contextual performance, however, is not proficiency, but volition and predisposition. Differences in proficiency or in underlying knowledge, skills, and abilities are probably not the strongest determinants of behaviors such as volunteering, persisting, helping, cooperating, and so forth. Instead, such behaviors are probably better predicted by volitional variables related to individual differences in motivational characteristics and predispositional variables represented by personality characteristics.

And fourth, task activities are role-prescribed. They are formally recognized as part of the job — as behaviors that incumbents must perform in exchange for rewards that accrue from organizational membership. Contextual behaviors are not as likely to be role-prescribed. Of course, in some jobs certain of the contextual dimensions may be required and emerge from job analyses. As an example, engaging in self-development often appears as a task activity in job analysis results for patrol officers. However, in general, although contextual behaviors contribute to organizational effectiveness and incumbents are sometimes rewarded for performing them, they are less likely to be included explicitly in lists of incumbents' formal responsibilities and obligations to the organization.

Before discussing domains of contextual performance in detail, we emphasize that task performance is clearly important and must be attended to in criterion development efforts for personnel selection. As examples, for production jobs, quantity and quality of output are obvious criteria of performance. For sales jobs, measures of sales volume might be usefully included in the set of criterion variables. Managerial performance in the functional areas of planning, supervising, delegating, and coordinating will usually be very relevant and important to represent in criterion development for management jobs. Criteria such as these are clearly job-related and linked to organizational effectiveness. The point of our chapter is that *in addition to* the task proficiency domain, contextual performance criteria should be considered in developing criteria for personnel selection.

Organizational Citizenship Behavior

The concept of organizational citizenship behavior includes several elements of contextual performance. Smith, Organ, and Near (1983) and Bateman and Organ (1983) define organizational citizenship behavior essentially as extra-role, discretionary behavior that helps other organization members perform their jobs or that shows support for and conscientiousness toward the organization. This builds on earlier notions introduced by Barnard (1938), Katz (1964), and Katz and Kahn (1978). Barnard notes the importance of the "informal organization," cooperative efforts in organizations, and the need for organization members to be willing to contribute in these cooperative efforts. Katz emphasizes that spontaneous, cooperative, helpful, and altruistic behaviors beyond formal role prescriptions are important for organizational functioning. Similarly, Katz and Kahn distinguish prescribed role performance from "spontaneous behavior," which includes cooperative gestures, actions protecting the organization, and behavior that enhances the external image of the organization. Such actions go beyond prescribed role behavior.

Thus, organizational citizenship involves such activities as making suggestions to supervisors to improve the organization's functioning, helping co-workers with a heavy workload, speaking positively about the organization to outsiders, arriving early to work, and the like. An important aspect of the definition of these citizenship behaviors is that they contribute to organizational effectiveness (Organ, 1988).

Smith, Organ, and Near (1983) developed and refined a sixteen-item questionnaire that can be used by raters to evaluate individuals' performance in this domain. Raters are presented with such statements as "Volunteers for things that are not required" and "Takes undeserved breaks"; they evaluate an organization member by indicating how characteristic of him or her each statement is. Factor analyses of correlations between the items have generally yielded two factors: (1) altruism—spontaneous prosocial gestures toward others in the organization, such as orienting new people and helping co-workers or supervisors with their work, and (2) conscientiousness—generalized compliance with organizational rules and procedures, such as being on time to work and not spending time on personal phone calls. The first factor can be characterized as citizenship behavior toward individuals, the second as citizenship behavior in relation to the organization.

Prosocial Organizational Behavior

Prosocial organizational behavior is closely related to organizational citizenship and also includes several elements of contextual performance. Brief and Motowidlo (1986) define prosocial organizational behavior as behavior that is "(a) performed by a member of an organization, (b) directed toward an individual, group, or organization with whom he or she interacts while carrying out his or her organizational role, and (c) performed with the intention of promoting the welfare of the individual, group, or organization to whom it is directed" (p. 711). Brief and Motowidlo make several distinctions between different types of prosocial organizational behavior. The most important for our purposes is that such behavior can be functional or dysfunctional to the organization; we consider only functional forms of prosocial behavior in this chapter. A second important distinction here is that this kind of behavior can be role-prescribed by the organization or can be extrarole. We consider both.

The functional prosocial organizational behaviors identified by Brief and Motowidlo (1986) are assisting co-workers with job-related or personal matters, providing services or products to consumers, helping consumers with personal matters (for example, giving road directions or supplying change for telephones), complying with organizational values and policies, suggesting organizational improvements, putting forth extra effort on the job, volunteering for additional assignments, staying with the organization during hard times, and representing the organization favorably to outsiders.

Others have suggested somewhat different dimensions of prosocial organizational behavior. Organ (1988) describes a class of prosocial behavior that is actually the *absence* of certain behaviors — complaints to superiors, grievances filed or stated, and "railing against real or imagined slights." He also introduces the concept of courtesy as a prosocial behavior — touching base with the boss to forewarn him or her about an upcoming situation or event, preparing secretaries in advance of a significant work load, and so on. As Organ points out, this is similar to the organizational citizenship dimension of altruism, but deals with preventing problems rather than helping with or alleviating a problem.

Graham (1986) identifies two other prosocial constructs. One, civic virtue, refers to responsible participation in the political life of the organization. Attending meetings and reading internal organization memos are examples of this concept. The second one, loyalty, involves promoting and defending the organization.

Katz and Kahn (1978) list several extrarole categories that are also closely related conceptually to prosocial organizational behavior. In fact, some of these categories overlap with prosocial behaviors already discussed. They include helping other organization members with problems, taking on extra responsibility, making suggestions for organizational improvements, engaging in self-development related to the job, meeting deadlines, and displaying initiative, work involvement, and dedication.

A Model of Soldier Effectiveness

Another perspective on contextual performance is provided by results of efforts to define the criterion domain for Project A, a large project to improve selection and placement systems for all entry-level jobs in the U.S. Army (Campbell, 1990). One of the first steps toward defining the criteria for these jobs was to develop a conceptual model of soldier effectiveness (Borman, Motowidlo, & Hanser, 1983). The model sought to describe aspects of soldier effectiveness that cut across all the different kinds of jobs that soldiers may perform. It assumed that soldier effectiveness involves more than just performing assigned job duties effectively and that other elements contributing to soldier effectiveness are common to all or nearly all soldiering jobs in the army. The model also assumed that these common soldier performance elements have close ties to the constructs of organizational commitment, organizational socialization, and morale.

"Organizational commitment" (Porter, Steers, Mowday, & Boulian, 1974; Steers, 1977) refers to the strength of a person's identification with and involvement in the organization. It incorporates three kinds of attitudinal and cognitive elements: acceptance and internalization of organizational values and goals; motivation to exert effort toward accomplishing organizational objectives; and firm intentions of staying in the organization. The concept transcends job involvement and motivation to perform the specific tasks that comprise the job. It connotes a sense of loyalty to the organization as a whole and a desire to fulfill more general role requirements that come with organizational membership. Thus, behavioral manifestations of organizational commitment were thought to reflect one aspect of soldier effectiveness.

"Organizational socialization," according to Van Maanen and Schein (1979), is "the process by which an individual acquires the social knowledge and skills necessary to assume an organizational role" (p. 211). Some part of this knowledge and skill is, of course, job-specific. For example, training programs designed to improve the effectiveness with which a person performs job-related tasks are part of the process of organizational socialization. But there are also many other knowledge and skill requirements for effective functioning as an organizational member that are not job-specific. When the socialization process is successful, a person will acquire not only job-related skills but also new patterns of behavior with subordinates, peers, and superiors in the organization, and new attitudes, beliefs, and values in line with organizational norms.

Such individual changes are frequently crucial for ensuring that the behaviors of different individual organization members will be smoothly coordinated toward accomplishing the organization's mission. As a result, soldier effectiveness might reasonably be regarded as partly a reflection of successful socialization; that is, people whose behavior and attitudes more closely coincide with army norms might be regarded as more effective soldiers and considered of greater value to the army.

The concept of military "morale" is multifaceted. It includes feelings of determination to overcome obstacles, confidence about the likelihood of success, exaltation of ideals, optimism even in the face of severe adversity, courage, discipline, and group cohesiveness (Motowidlo et al., 1976). Motowidlo and Borman (1977) report results of a study designed in part to identify behavioral dimensions of morale in the U.S. Army. They found that the following dimensions efficiently describe behavioral expressions of morale among soldiers: community relations; teamwork and cooperation; reactions to adversity; superior-subordinate relations; performance and effort on the job; bearing, appearance, and military courtesy; pride in unit, army, and country; and self-development during off-duty hours. Because morale seems to figure so prominently as a determinant of unit effectiveness, behavioral dimensions like these should also represent important elements of individual soldier effectiveness.

From the combination of morale and commitment emerges a general category of effectiveness that can be labeled "determination." It is a motivational and affective category that reflects the spirit, strength of character, or "will do" aspects of good soldiering. The combination of morale and socialization yields "teamwork," behaviors that have to do with effective relationships with peers and the unit. The combination of commitment and socialization yields "allegiance." This taps into acceptance of army norms with respect to authority, faithful adherence to orders, regulations, and the army life-style, and being adjusted and socialized to the point of wanting to continue in the soldiering role and stay in the army.

Each of these three general categories of soldier effectiveness — determination, teamwork, and allegiance — subsumes five other dimensions that describe specific behavioral patterns of effectiveness, as shown below.

Determination

- Perseverance: struggling tenaciously to reach objectives; sustaining maximum effort over long periods.
- Reaction to adversity: shrugging off uncomfortable or unpleasant conditions; adapting to and making the best of hardship conditions; refusing to become demoralized by troubles.
- Conscientiousness: spending extra time and effort to finish the job; completing assignments on or ahead of schedule; carrying out assignments thoroughly and with close attention to detail.
- Initiative: volunteering for assignments; anticipating problems and taking action to prevent them; performing extra necessary tasks without explicit orders.
- Discipline: concentrating on the job without yielding to the temptation of distractions; controlling self-indulgent appetites; keeping emotions in check.

Teamwork

- Cooperation: voluntarily pitching in to help others with their job assignments; accepting personal inconvenience to help others with important problems; listening and supporting others with personal difficulties.

- Camaraderie: forming close friendships with others in the unit; spending off-duty time with other unit members.
- Concern for unit goals: putting unit goals before personal interests; making personal sacrifices for the unit as a whole; striving to meet unit goals even when they conflict with personal interests.
- Boosting unit morale: helping the unit stick together through hard times; encouraging others to keep going when things seem bleak and hopeless; cheering others up in unpleasant situations.
- Leadership: showing good judgment in suggesting ideas for unit action; persuading others to accept own ideas.

Allegiance

- Following orders: responding willingly and without hesitation to orders; carrying out orders promptly and thoroughly.
- Following regulations: complying with rules and regulations; conforming to standard procedures; trying to correct nonstandard conditions.
- Respect for authority: deferring to superiors; showing military courtesy; speaking respectfully about superiors to others.
- Military bearing: maintaining a crisp military appearance; standing, walking, and marching with erect military posture; showing pride in the uniform and military insignia.
- Adjustment to the army: adjusting successfully to military life; showing pride in being a soldier; showing an interest in staying in the army.

These three domains are summarized below. The summary shows the organizational citizenship, prosocial organizational behavior, and model of soldier effectiveness concepts grouped into five major areas. These five areas appear to capture the sense of the individual concepts from the three domains.

1. *Persisting with enthusiasm and extra effort as necessary to complete own task activities successfully*

   Perseverance and conscientiousness (Borman, Motowidlo, & Hanser, 1983)

   Extra effort on the job (Brief & Motowidlo, 1986; Katz & Kahn, 1978)

2. *Volunteering to carry out task activities that are not formally part of own job*

   Suggesting organizational improvements (Brief & Motowidlo, 1986; Katz & Kahn, 1978)

   Initiative and taking on extra responsibility (Borman, Motowidlo, & Hanser, 1983; Brief & Motowidlo, 1986; Katz & Kahn, 1978)

3. *Helping and cooperating with others*

   Assisting/helping co-workers (Borman, Motowidlo, & Hanser, 1983; Brief & Motowidlo, 1986; Katz & Kahn, 1978)

   Assisting/helping customers (Brief & Motowidlo, 1986)

   Organizational courtesy and not complaining (Organ, 1988)

   Altruism (Smith, Organ, & Near, 1983)

4. *Following organizational rules and procedures*

   Following orders and regulations and respect for authority (Borman, Motowidlo, & Hanser, 1983)

   Complying with organizational values and policies (Brief & Motowidlo, 1986)

   Conscientiousness (Smith, Organ, & Near, 1983)

   Meeting deadlines (Katz & Kahn, 1978)

   Civic virtue (Graham, 1986)

5. *Endorsing, supporting, and defending organizational objectives*

   Organizational loyalty (Graham, 1986)

Concern for unit objectives (Borman, Motowidlo, & Hanser, 1983)
Staying with the organization during hard
times and representing the organization favorably to outsiders (Brief & Motowidlo,
1986)

Dimensions of Management Performance

The three topics discussed so far — organizational citizenship, prosocial organizational behavior, and the model of soldier effectiveness — identify elements of contextual performance
deductively. They define contextual work activities from conceptual frameworks that describe domains of organizational behavior thought to be important for organizational effectiveness.
Now we turn to an approach that helps define contextual work
activities inductively.

As mentioned, job analyses that focus on task statements
rated for characteristics such as importance, time spent, frequency, and so on typically define the task performance part
of the criterion domain. Job analyses that focus on critical incidents, however, stand a better chance of defining at least some
portions of the contextual performance domain. In this section,
we discuss an effort to combine results of several analyses of
management jobs and define a comprehensive set of management performance dimensions. Because most of the job analyses considered here are based on critical incidents, at least some
of the performance dimensions they identify may reflect aspects
of contextual performance in management jobs.

Borman and Brush (in press) collected twenty-six sets of
performance dimensions developed from empirical studies of
managerial performance requirements. Many different kinds
of organizations were represented in these studies (including insurance, computer, financial, manufacturing, service, and communications companies). A variety of managerial levels was included, but middle to general managers composed most of the
groups studied. Twenty of the twenty-six studies were critical
incident analyses. Five studies derived dimension sets from factor

analyses of task survey responses. One study generated a set of dimensions from incumbent interviews and job observation.

Thus, this array of managerial performance dimensions was derived inductively, mostly from analyses of critical incidents. The dimensions are based not on theoretical formulations or a focus on some particular part of the managers' jobs, but on their actual performance requirements. Consequently, the dimensions reflect a representative sample of the manager performance domain.

The twenty-six sets of dimensions included a total of 187 nonredundant performance dimensions. Borman and Brush (in press) had twenty-five experienced industrial and organizational psychologists independently sort them into megadimensions according to similarities in content.

From the independent sortings, a 187×187 similarity matrix was generated by pooling data across sorters. This was done using a method attributed to Rosenberg and Sedlak (1972). Basically, the proportion of judges sorting each pair of performance categories into the same megadimension was computed, and this pooled 187×187 similarity matrix was transformed into what Rosenberg and Sedlak call an indirect similarity matrix. Factor analysis of this matrix produced eighteen orthogonal factors that summarized the matrix well and were reasonably interpretable. They are listed below in descending order of the amount of common variance they explain according to results of the factor analysis:

- Planning and organizing
- Guiding, directing, and motivating subordinates and providing feedback
- Training, coaching, and developing subordinates
- Communicating effectively and keeping others informed
- Representing the organization to customers and the public
- Technical proficiency
- Administration and paperwork
- Maintaining good working relationships

- Coordinating subordinates and other resources to get the job done
- Decision making and problem solving
- Staffing
- Persisting to reach goals
- Handling crises and stress
- Organizational commitment
- Monitoring and controlling resources
- Delegating
- Selling and influencing
- Collecting and interpreting data

Because management positions do not contribute directly to the technical core of an organization, differences between their task and contextual components are not as straightforward as in other jobs that do contribute directly to the technical core. It is still possible, however, to identify some management performance factors that are relatively saturated with contextual performance elements.

In particular, there are six megadimension factors that noticeably contain elements of contextual performance, according to our analysis of the megadimension content. Other matches between contextual dimension and Borman and Brush (in press) megadimension content might be argued, but we have attempted to be conservative in identifying these content matches. The management megadimensions that appear wholly or in part highly similar to the contextual dimensions listed earlier in the summary are organizational commitment, representing the organization to customers and the public, maintaining good working relationships, persisting to reach goals, training, coaching, and developing subordinates, and communicating effectively and keeping others informed. These megadimension factors are defined in more detail in Table 3.1 according to the definitions of the dimensions loading substantially on them.

The organizational commitment factor is highly similar to elements of the organizational rules and procedures contextual dimension in the summary presented earlier. Representing the organization is most closely aligned with the endorsing, supporting,

Table 3.1. Definitions of Managerial Megadimensions
with Elements of Citizenship, Prosocial,
or Model of Soldier Effectiveness Content.

Percentage of Variance Accounted for	
2	*Organizational commitment:* working effectively within the framework of organizational policies, procedures, rules, and so forth; carrying out orders and directives; supporting reasonable policies of higher authorities in organizations.
10	*Representing the organization to customers and the public:* representing the organization to those not in the organization; maintaining good organizational image to customers, the public, stockholders, the government, and so on (as appropriate); dealing with customer/client problems.
5	*Maintaining good working relationships:* developing and maintaining smooth and effective working relationships with superiors, peers, and subordinates; displaying personal concern for subordinates; backing up and supporting subordinates as appropriate; encouraging and fostering cooperation between subordinates.
2	*Persisting to reach goals:* persisting with extra effort to attain objectives; overcoming obstacles to get the job done.
13	*Training, coaching, and developing subordinates:* identifying staff training needs and developing responsive training programs and materials, or ensuring that such programs/materials get developed; training, teaching, and coaching subordinates; assisting subordinates in improving their job skills.
10	*Communicating effectively and keeping others informed:* communicating orally and in written form; keeping subordinates, superiors, and others informed; obtaining and then passing on information to those who should know.

and defending dimension and the assisting/helping customers element of the helping and cooperating with others dimension. Maintaining good working relationships relates closely to aspects of the helping and cooperating contextual dimensions, and persisting to reach goals reflects elements of the contextual dimension that we labeled persistence.

The other two factors have only some of their content related to contextual dimension content. The training, coaching, and developing subordinates factor has a component related to the contextual dimension labeled assisting and helping subordinates in the summary, and the communicating factor has aspects quite similar to Organ's (1988) organizational courtesy concept, that is, preventing potential problems by keeping others informed about upcoming events.

Taking into account the common variance accounted for by individual factors in the factor analysis of the managerial performance dimensions (see Table 3.1), we estimate that about 30 percent of this performance domain identified in our broad sampling of management dimensions reflects contextual performance. That is, the first four factors in Table 3.1 account for a total of 19 percent of the common variance in the factor analysis. About one-half of the fourth and one-third of the fifth factor are matched with contextual dimensions, accounting for an additional 10 percent of the common variance. Thus, inductive analysis of managerial performance requirements suggests that the contextual part of management jobs is substantial and important.

Links Between Organizational Effectiveness and Individual Contextual Performance

We know of little *empirical* research demonstrating correlations between organizational effectiveness and performance at the individual level in terms of organizational citizenship behavior, prosocial organizational behavior, or other contextual activities mentioned in connection with the model of soldier effectiveness or the study of management dimensions. A recent study (George & Bettenhausen, 1990) did examine relationships between objective sales performance in thirty-three stores and pooled unit-level ratings of prosocial behavior. The prosocial behavior measure focused on interactions with customers in this service-oriented organization. The correlation was .33 ($p < .05$), indicating a moderate relationship between one type of prosocial behavior and a measure of organizational effectiveness. Also, although not directly related to contextual performance–organizational effectiveness linkages, MacKenzie, Podsakoff, and Fetter (1991) demonstrate that sales managers' ratings of their insurance agent subordinates' overall performance were influenced substantially by these agents' organizational citizenship behavior in addition to their actual sales performance.

Arguments offered for a link between organizational effectiveness and performance in these contextual domains are typically logical and conceptual rather than empirical. Organ (1988),
for example, argues that organizational citizenship behavior sub-
stitutes for resources the organization would otherwise have to
expend on maintenance activities and thus increases organizational efficiency. Citizenship behavior in organizations "lubri-
cates the social machinery of the organization" and "provides
the flexibility needed to work through many unforeseen contingencies" (Smith, Organ, & Near, 1983, p. 654). Following
the analogy, this lubrication reduces friction in the organization and, accordingly, increases efficiency. More concretely, if
organization members help co-workers with work-related and
personal problems, orient new employees, volunteer suggestions
for improvements, and so on, then more organizational resources
are freed for other uses.

The conscientiousness dimension of organizational citizenship is also linked logically to organizational effectiveness. Organ
(1988) pointed out that when employees come to work with conscientious regularity, organizations save money that would otherwise be used to hire other employees to compensate for absent
ones. When organization members are highly conscientious, the
organization essentially has available a larger resource pool at
no additional cost — in other words, it can get more work from
the same number of employees. Interestingly, in a recent meta-
analysis of personality *predictors* of job performance criteria, Barrick and Mount (1991) found that conscientiousness, defined
in part as dependability and conformity, was consistently related
to performance.

Citizenship and prosocial dimensions related to working
with customers or clients also have reasonably clear links with
organizational effectiveness. Being helpful and responding above
and beyond the call toward customers or clients should increase
the likelihood of retaining their business. Referrals of business
on the basis of satisfied customers reporting these prosocial behaviors to other potential customers are also possible outcomes.
These outcomes may be most likely when the client base is small,
potential clients tend to talk to each other, and referrals are an
important source of business.

Recent research and discussion about service organizations are relevant here (Schneider, 1990). As an example, Schneider, Parkington, and Buxton (1980) found an association between employee perceptions of organizational climate regarding service and customer reports of service quality. The important point for our purposes is that organizational climate focused on service is very similar to some of the contextual dimensions we have been discussing. In particular, Parasuraman, Zeithaml, and Berry (1985) identified ten dimensions of service quality from research in a variety of service-oriented industries. Several of these dimensions, such as responsiveness (the willingness of employees to provide service), courtesy (the politeness, consideration, and friendliness of contact employees), communication (keeping customers informed and listening to their problems), and understanding (making the effort to understand customer needs) are all closely associated with one or another of the contextual dimensions discussed so far. Thus, organizational climate for service consists at least in part of contextual behaviors performed by organization members, and these behaviors appear linked to organizational effectiveness.

Another criterion area discussed recently is also relevant here. Hogan and Hogan (1989) describe "employee reliability" as a set of productive job behaviors, presumably strongly related to organizational effectiveness. Organization members who are ineffective in this criterion domain tend to defy rules, ignore social expectations, avoid commitments to others, be insubordinate to bosses, and may even commit theft, sabotage, or arson. The employee reliability criterion concept appears highly similar to certain elements of the contextual performance domain.

Finally, Grubb and Elder (1991) present a model they call the Organizational Adaptation Paradigm, which includes a criterion domain strikingly similar to the domain we are discussing. They argue that effective performance in an organization is a function of both organization members' performing their jobs *and* these individuals' fitting into the organization's culture, responding appropriately to supervisors' initiatives, getting along well with other organization members, and generally doing what the organization needs beyond performing their own job.

Some dimensions of contextual performance are probably more appropriate and important for certain types of organizations than for others. Service companies have special requirements on dimensions related to dealing with customers and representing the organization to outsiders; team-oriented organizations especially require helping, cooperating, and displaying courtesy to team members; and conservative, more bureaucratic organizations may consider as more important some of the compliance or following orders and regulations and respect for authority dimensions. Other contextual dimensions, however, such as conscientiousness, extra effort and responsibility, and involvement in work, are probably quite widely appropriate for all work organizations.

Antecedents of Contextual Performance

If we can agree that contextual performance dimensions are important performance criteria for many jobs in many types of organizations because they are likely to be important for organizational effectiveness, the next issue to address is the importance of individual difference variables for predicting contextual performance. Provided contextual performance is reasonably stable across specific organizational situations, then individual difference variables are very useful in selecting organization members according to the likelihood that they will function effectively in the domain of contextual performance.

Empathy (sensitivity to the feelings and perspectives of others) is a top candidate for predicting behavior in several areas of contextual performance, such as altruism and dimensions related to helping other organization members. Several studies from social psychology have shown that measures of empathy predict helping behavior (for example, Barnett, Howard, King, & Dino, 1981). Other correlates of altruism and related citizenship and prosocial behavior are extroversion (Krebs, 1970), "belief in a just world" (Zuckerman, 1975), educational level (Gergen, Gergen, & Meter, 1972), neuroticism (negative correlation: Smith, Organ, & Near, 1983), and cognitive aspects of job satisfaction (Organ & Konovsky, 1989).

Regarding these potential predictors, Krebs (1970) reasons that outgoing, extroverted organization members are more likely than their introverted counterparts to engage in prosocial acts. Zuckerman (1975) found that persons with a strong belief in a just world are more likely than others to exhibit prosocial behavior. Educational level predicts organizational citizenship behavior (Organ, 1988). Organization members who are burdened with neurotic anxieties are presumably often too caught up in their own personal problems to be concerned about helping other organization members with their work-related or personal problems (Smith, Organ, & Near, 1983). Finally, positive and negative affect have proved to be reasonably stable individual differences, and positive affect appears linked to prosocial behavior in the social psychology literature (for instance, Isen & Levin, 1972); negative affect does not show this link quite so clearly.

Regarding other aspects of contextual behavior, organizational commitment has been related to achievement motivation (Puffer, 1987), autonomy needs (negative correlation: Puffer, 1987), feelings of self-competence (Mowday, Porter, & Steers, 1982), and belief in a strong work ethic (Mowday, Porter, & Steers, 1982). Compliance with organizational rules and procedures correlates with achievement motivation (Puffer, 1987). Hogan and Hogan (1989) developed a personality scale that successfully predicts the employee reliability–organizational delinquency criterion behavior discussed previously. In correlations with other variables, high scorers on their scale tend to be "mature, thoughtful, responsible, and somewhat inhibited" (p. 278); low scorers are "hostile, impulsive, insensitive, self-absorbed, and unhappy" (p. 278).

Thus, it appears that personality predictors are dominant in their relationships with organizational citizenship and prosocial organizational behavior. Organization members performing effectively in one or another of these domains are likely to be empathic, extroverted, nonneurotic, reasonably cheerful and "up," and achievement- but not autonomy-oriented and to have relatively strong beliefs in a "just world" and in a hard-work ethic.

An example of how a contextual performance criterion might be predicted compared with a task performance criterion in the same set of jobs is provided by Project A, the large-scale test validation research program mentioned previously (Campbell, 1990). In attempts to define a criterion model to reflect the performance requirements of all U.S. Army jobs, confirmatory factor analyses identified one performance factor that clearly represents a task performance dimension, Core Technical Proficiency, and one factor that is a good example of a contextual performance dimension, Personal Discipline (Campbell, McHenry, & Wise, 1990). Core Technical Proficiency was defined as proficiency in performing the technical tasks central to the job. Work sample and job knowledge test scores, reflecting performance on the core job tasks, loaded most highly on this performance factor. Personal Discipline was defined as adhering to army rules and regulations, exercising personal self-control, and not creating disciplinary problems. Supervisor and peer ratings on the rating scales, Following Regulations and Orders, Self-Control, and Integrity, and counts of the number of disciplinary cases loaded most highly on this performance factor.

A broad array of general cognitive ability, aptitude, temperament, and vocational interest measures was administered to more than eight thousand early-career soldiers (Peterson et al., 1990), and the performance of these same soldiers was assessed. Of this predictor array, measures of general cognitive ability correlated highest with Core Technical Proficiency, whereas the temperament factor Dependability correlated most highly with Personal Discipline. The ability and aptitude predictors correlated minimally with Personal Discipline, and the temperament measures showed low correlation with Core Technical Proficiency. The example is from a study of U.S. Army soldiers, but these results are likely to generalize to other jobs and organizational settings.

We know from validity generalization work that ability has strong links to job performance (for instance, Schmidt & Hunter, 1981). However, if contextual dimensions become more explicitly recognized as legitimate criteria in selection research, our review of the antecedents of citizenship, prosocial, and other dimensions of contextual performance suggests that personality measures may be most successful in predicting performance in these criterion domains. Accordingly, if we are serious about expanding the criterion space to include the contextual performance dimensions discussed in this chapter, then personality predictors are likely to be more useful in selection.

Pitfalls in Using Contextual Criteria in Personnel Selection

One potential problem with the use of contextual dimensions as performance criteria involves *expecting* and including as *performance requirements* such behaviors as volunteering for additional assignments outside one's own job, expending beyond-the-call extra effort on job tasks, and altruistic helping of coworkers and supervisors. This is a potential problem for two reasons. First, it is somewhat paradoxical to *require* that employees do more than their jobs specifically call for. In practice, of course, employees who perform beyond normal requirements and expectations are frequently rewarded for this. But it is difficult to imagine how sanctions might be applied to employees for *not* doing more than required.

Second, explicit expectations in these areas could upset the natural occurrence of this kind of behavior in organizations. For example, Organ (1988) argues that organizational citizenship behavior, with technically elaborate behavior-based scales to evaluate it or with merit pay plans that emphasize differentiation among employees, should not be explicitly required. Detailing organizational citizenship behavior requirements on behavioral scales may well leave out *other* expressions of such behavior, in turn leading to a focus on only the activities listed as targets for future performance at the expense of many other possible ones. The zealous differentiating of employees in certain merit pay systems may breed jealousies, competitiveness, and a sharp decrease in cooperation and altruistic helping of others because of the perception that "every man for himself" is the appropriate strategy under such systems.

Another way to view this potential problem is to recognize that if these kinds of contextual dimensions are to be valued and rewarded in an organization, then organization members will usually want to know this. Thus, to be fair to employees in providing them with information about the values and expectations relevant to their success in the organization, it seems quite important to inform them about these contextual criteria and how they relate to their own job.

A second potential pitfall arises from the fourth and fifth contextual dimensions in the summary presented earlier. If an organization expects all its members to be highly "successful" in following organizational rules and procedures and in endorsing, supporting, and defending organizational objectives, then there is little room for healthy dissent and for new ideas to be expressed if they run counter to the prevailing organizational views. At the extreme, strict, across-the-board requirements for "effectiveness" in these two contextual criteria clearly could lead to a severely homogeneous, inbred organization and inhibit its ability to be flexible and to change when market or other external factors require a sharp departure from the status quo.

Our reaction to this possible problem is to encourage a broad perspective when considering performance on these kinds of criteria. A balanced approach may be to consider these criteria in making judgments about individual organization members' performance, while at the same time recognizing that some employees may choose not to be very supportive of organizational policies, procedures, and objectives, but instead to contribute to the organization in other ways, such as technical expertise. Thus, it seems prudent not to demand that all employees stand high on these two contextual dimensions.

On the other hand, it is clear that organizational behavior at the low end of these dimensions can be very troublesome for organizations. Employees who ignore standard procedures when personally inconvenient, rebel against reasonable organizational rules, consistently question supervisors' judgment, or deride the organization to fellow employees and persons outside the organization definitely contribute to problems and can seriously undermine organizational effectiveness. Again, a balance should probably be maintained here between demanding that all employee behavior be at the high end of these dimensions and ignoring the fact that these criterion areas legitimately influence organizational effectiveness.

Conclusion

We argued that more attention should be paid to criteria beyond core task performance. The term *contextual performance* was introduced, and we showed what contextual activities are and how they differ from core task activities. The topics of organizational citizenship behavior and prosocial organizational behavior were reviewed, along with a model of soldier effectiveness, as areas that reflect this contextual criterion domain. From an analysis of managerial performance requirements, we estimated that about 30 percent of the managerial performance domain may involve contextual performance. In addition, antecedents and predictors of organizational citizenship behavior, prosocial organizational behavior, and related contextual activity areas were identified to provide ideas about the types of predictors that might be useful if contextual criteria are more often employed in personnel selection research and practice. Finally, we identified and discussed two potential pitfalls associated with using these contextual criteria in personnel selection practice and provided some ideas about how these criteria might be viewed in perspective as contributors to organizational effectiveness.

References

Barnard, C. I. (1938). *The functions of the executive.* Cambridge, MA: Harvard University Press.

Barnett, M. A., Howard, J. A., King, L. M., & Dino, G. A. (1981). Helping behavior and the transfer of empathy. *Journal of Social Psychology, 115,* 125–132.

Barrick, M. R., & Mount, M. K. (1991). The big five personality dimensions and job performance: A meta-analysis. *Personnel Psychology, 44,* 1–26.

Bateman, T. S., & Organ, D. W. (1983). Job satisfaction and the good soldier: The relationship between affect and employee "citizenship." *Academy of Management Journal, 26,* 587–595.

Borman, W. C., & Brush, D. H. (in press). More progress toward a taxonomy of managerial performance requirements. *Human Performance.*

Borman, W. C., Motowidlo, S. J., & Hanser, L. M. (1983, August). A model of individual performance effectiveness: Thoughts about expanding the criterion space. In N. K. Eaton & J. P. Campbell (Chairs), *Integrated criterion measurement for large scale computerized selection and classification.* Symposium conducted at the meeting of the American Psychological Association, Anaheim, CA.

Brief, A. P., & Motowidlo, S. J. (1986). Prosocial organizational behaviors. *Academy of Management Review, 11,* 710–725.

Campbell, J. P. (1990). An overview of the army selection and classification project (Project A). *Personnel Psychology, 43,* 231–239.

Campbell, J. P., McHenry, J. J., & Wise, L. L. (1990). Modeling job performance in a population of jobs. *Personnel Psychology, 43,* 313–333.

George, J. M., & Bettenhausen, K. (1990). Understanding prosocial behavior, sales performance, and turnover: A group level analysis in a service context. *Journal of Applied Psychology, 75,* 698–709.

Gergen, K., Gergen, M., & Meter, K. (1972). Individual orientations to prosocial behavior. *Journal of Social Issues, 28*(3), 105–130.

Graham, J. W. (1986, August). *Organizational citizenship informed by political theory.* Paper presented at the meeting of the Academy of Management, Chicago.

Grubb, P. D., & Elder, E. D. (1991, August). *Selection based on the structural and procedural dimensions of organizations.* Paper presented at the meeting of the American Psychological Association, San Francisco.

Hogan, J., & Hogan, R. (1989). How to measure employee reliability. *Journal of Applied Psychology, 74,* 273–279.

Isen, A. M., & Levin, A. F. (1972). Effect of feeling good on helping: Cookies and kindness. *Journal of Personality and Social Psychology, 21,* 384–388.

Katz, D. (1964). The motivational basis of organizational behavior. *Behavioral Science, 9,* 131–146.

Katz, D., & Kahn, R. L. (1978). *The social psychology of organizations.* New York: Wiley.

Krebs, D. L. (1970). Altruism—an examination of the concept and a review of the literature. *Psychological Bulletin, 73,* 258–302.

MacKenzie, S. B., Podsakoff, P. M., & Fetter, R. (1991). Organizational citizenship behavior and objective productivity as determinants of managerial evaluations of salespersons' performance. *Organizational Behavior and Human Decision Processes, 50,* 123–150.

Motowidlo, S. J., & Borman, W. C. (1977). Behaviorally anchored scales for measuring morale in military units. *Journal of Applied Psychology, 62,* 177–184.

Motowidlo, S. J., Dowell, B. E., Hopp, M. A., Borman, W. C., Johnson, P. D., & Dunnette, M. D. (1976). *Motivation, satisfaction, and morale in army careers: A review of theory and measurement* (Army Research Institute Technical Report TR-76-A7).

Mowday, R. T., Porter, L. W., & Steers, R. M. (1982). *Employee-organization linkages.* New York: Academic Press.

Organ, D. W. (1988). *Organizational citizenship behavior: The good soldier syndrome.* Lexington, MA: Lexington Books.

Organ, D. W., & Konovsky, M. A. (1989). Cognitive versus affective determinants of organizational citizenship behavior. *Journal of Applied Psychology, 74,* 157–164.

Parasuraman, A., Zeithaml, V. A., & Berry, L. L. (1985). A conceptual model of service quality and its implications for future research. *Journal of Marketing, 49,* 41–50.

Perrow, C. (1965). Hospitals: Technology, structure, and goals. In J. G. March (Ed.), *Handbook of Organizations.* Skokie, IL: Rand McNally.

Peterson, N. G., Hough, L. M., Dunnette, M. D., Rosse, R. L., Houston, J. S., Toquam, J. L., & Wing, H. (1990). Project A: Specification of the predictor domain and development of new selection/classification tests. *Personnel Psychology, 43,* 247–276.

Porter, L. W., Steers, R. M., Mowday, R. T., & Boulian, P. V. (1974). Organization commitment, job satisfaction, and turnover among psychiatric technicians. *Journal of Applied Psychology, 59,* 603–609.

Puffer, S. M. (1987). Prosocial behavior, noncompliant behavior, and work performance among commission people. *Journal of Applied Psychology, 72,* 615–621.

Rosenberg, S., & Sedlak, A. (1972). Structural representations
of perceived personality trait relationships. In A. K. Rom-
ney, R. J. Shepard, & S. B. Nerlave (Eds.), *Multidimensional
scaling.* New York: Seminar Press.

Schmidt, F. L., & Hunter, J. E. (1981). Employment testing:
Old theories and new research findings. *American Psychologist,
36,* 1128–1137.

Schneider, B. (1990). The climate for service: An application
of the climate construct. In B. Schneider (Ed.), *Organizational
climate and culture.* San Francisco: Jossey-Bass.

Schneider, B., Parkington, J. J., & Buxton, V. M. (1980). Employee and customer perceptions of service in banks. *Administrative Science Quarterly, 25,* 252–267.

Smith, C. A., Organ, D. W., & Near, J. P. (1983). Organizational citizenship behavior: Its nature and antecedents. *Journal of Applied Psychology, 68,* 653–663.

Steers, R. M. (1977). Antecedents and outcomes of organizational commitment. *Administrative Science Quarterly, 22,* 46–56.

Thompson, J. D. (1967). *Organizations in action.* New York:
McGraw-Hill.

Van Maanen, J., & Schein, E. H. (1979). Toward a theory of
organizational commitment. In B. M. Staw (Ed.), *Research
in organizational behavior* (Vol. 1). Greenwich, CT: JAI Press.

Woodward, J. (1965). *Industrial organization: Theory and practice.*
London: Oxford University Press.

Zuckerman, M. (1975). Belief in a just world and altruistic behavior. *Journal of Personality and Social Psychology, 31,* 972–976.

4

Predictor Constructs and Their Measurement

Richard J. Klimoski

Investigators in the field of industrial and organizational (I/O) psychology have from its earliest days been interested in understanding and modeling individual effectiveness in work organizations (Schmitt & Klimoski, 1991). Traditionally, human variability and individual differences in personal qualities or traits have played a central role in these investigations. Indeed, many of those active in the then "new" field that has its focus on worker behavior thought of themselves as differential psychologists (Ackerman & Humphreys, 1991). Moreover, although interested in developing and testing basic theories of individual effectiveness, many researchers sought to identify key individual differences in order to apply this knowledge to the task of selecting personnel for employment.

As highlighted in other chapters, this interest in a construct approach to selection is augmented by both practical and scientific considerations. On the practical side, personnel specialists are regularly challenged to be efficient in their approach to developing selection devices and systems. Understanding in advance *where* and *when* predictor constructs (and their measures) would be relevant goes a long way toward narrowing the possibilities. Understanding *what* a selection device measures also allows personnel specialists to know when and where it should not be used and what to do if the device is modified. Moreover, practitioners are under increased accountability as "stakeholders" to the personnel selection function (for example, unions, federal agencies) seek to be reassured that there is indeed a rationale for selection practices and outcomes. The traditional retort — "We use it because it works" — is no longer viable. Selection specialists must be prepared to explain why it works. Thus, contemporary pressures serve to reaffirm the observation made years ago that "there is nothing as practical as a good theory" (Lewin, 1945, p. 127).

As part of this effort to develop theory, writers are weaving the extensive data base of predictive studies that use selection devices into theories of individual effectiveness (for example, Hunter, 1986). Similarly, investigators seeking a better understanding of both the predictor and criterion domains are examining combinations of traditional selection devices (Borman, Rosse, & Abrahams, 1980; Pulakos, Borman, & Hough, 1988; Peterson et al., 1990). Finally, there is increased realization that to really be able to create at least a middle-range theory of individual effectiveness (Blalock, 1969), we will have to transcend the notion that answers lie in the development of better predictor devices. Far more likely is that scientific advances lie in seeing what these devices have in common (Ackerman & Humphreys, 1991). That is exactly what this chapter is about.

In the next section we review the nature of constructs in the context of prediction devices and personnel selection. The research literature (personality tests, selection interviews) on assessment centers and biographical data is used to illustrate the points made. Some key issues involved in establishing the nature of useful predictor constructs in theory building and applied research are highlighted as well. The last section in the chapter emphasizes the problems of maintaining the integrity of predictor constructs in personnel practice or in future research.

The Nature of Predictor Constructs

A construct can be thought of as a concept that has been deliberately created or adopted for a scientific (or in our case, applied) purpose. The term *predictor construct* has come to mean some aspect of a person which, if assessed, has relevance to predicting (or understanding) future behavior or performance. Thus, although the phrase implies an attribute of a device or measure (an interview or a test), it usually reduces to a factor thought to be useful for distinguishing among individuals; in other words, a trait. Predictor construct categories that come up frequently in this chapter include ability, skill, and motivation. In fact, these particular concepts are the basis of one theory of employee performance offered in Chapter Two.

In their treatment of the nature of individual difference constructs, Ackerman and Humphreys (1991) emphasize three dimensions along which constructs differ: general-specific, permanent-transitory, and continuous-discrete. The issue of how *general* a construct should be is a complex one. In this chapter, we present arguments for conceptualizing predictor constructs at different levels of generality. The appropriate level of specificity of a predictor construct depends on the nature of the criteria of interest.

On the other hand, applied psychologists usually seek to uncover individual difference constructs that imply some *permanence* (Ackerman & Humphreys, 1991). We seek to measure attributes that reflect enduring aspects of individuals and that are transsituational. In contrast, although measuring transitory "states" may be interesting, it is felt to be far less useful for selection.

It is not uncommon for investigators to confuse the first two dimensions, whereby more general constructs are considered to be more permanent. However, Ackerman and Humphreys (1991) argue that there are degrees of relative permanence. "Thus one *central concern* of an applied psychology of individual differences must lie with an evaluation of the permanence, and by indirect implication, the malleability of the attributes of interest" (p. 6). A highly malleable attribute, to the degree that it is related to performance, implies training and development rather than selection as a strategy of choice (see Chapter Fourteen).

On the last dimension, Ackerman and Humphreys (1991) are unequivocal. They think that important and useful individual difference constructs are inherently *continuous* along a dimension of interest. Thus, they discount one-dimensional or multidimensional typologies or classification systems as "inherently flawed."

Holding or sharing a trait implies exhibiting particular patterns of behavior or performance (Funder, 1991). It does so by influencing such things as the perception of situations, the capacity to do things, the habits likely to be invoked, or the effort expended. Simultaneously, behavior or performance will be affected (in most settings) by several traits at once. Thus, some writers (for example, Digman, 1990; Funder, 1991) think that it is unrealistic to expect a great deal of predictive power vis-à-vis performance from knowing of the existence of a single trait for an individual.

Predictor constructs as traits also imply behavior or performance in relation to particular contexts. Such contexts may involve social, task, or physical features (or demands). To put it another way, we would expect a trait to affect behavior, depending on such features. But traits may *interact* with the situation in several ways. For example, Funder (1991) notes that most psychologists acknowledge that the situation can serve to elicit the manifestation of a given trait. But he also points out that it is just as likely that traits predispose people to select situations. Finally, the person/situation linkage implies the potential for changes imposed *on* the situation by virtue of an individual with a given trait being there. The impact of a gregarious, outgoing guest on the dynamics of a party is a case in point (Pervin, 1989).

Predictor Constructs as Personal Constructs

The goal in this chapter is to summarize developments regarding predictor constructs as they affect, or imply better models for, personnel selection. To appreciate which constructs and what measurement approaches are useful requires an understanding of the role of human judgment in interpersonal relations. With the possible exception of paper-and-pencil tests, human judgment is part of the measurement of predictor constructs in most personnel selection contexts.

Research and theories from person perception and social cognition have stressed that individuals are actively involved in the interpretation of interpersonal events. As part of life (and work) they must attend to, encode, store, integrate, and retrieve social information (Cooper, 1981; Lord, 1985). To facilitate this activity, individuals are thought to develop techniques or systems for coping with all the information potentially available to them. In particular, over time people develop and use cognitive structures to categorize, simplify, and give meaning to interpersonal information (Cantor & Mischel, 1979; Kenny & Albright, 1987). These include *schemata* (cognitive structures that allow us to categorize people and events), *implicit personality theories* (a type of schema that we hold with regard to other people), and *prototypes* (mental models that capture the essential features of a category, as in the case of a "good worker").

Operationally, Borman (1987) suggests that personal construct theory (Kelly, 1955; Mancuso & Adams-Webber, 1982) and related tools — for example, the repertory (rep grid) — can be used to establish the content of mental structures. He successfully demonstrated the existence and nature of personal work theories (prototypes) held by a sample of army officers. In doing so he found that such soldier qualities as "hard work/initiative," "maturity/responsibility," and "technical proficiency" were consistently used by the officers as benchmarks for effectiveness, *apart from any of the dimensions stressed by the formal appraisal program.* They were, in effect, part of the "folk theories" operating in that context. These would logically constrain the universe of potential constructs that could be used to think about or judge effectiveness.

The ubiquity and the power of mental models to affect assessments of candidates for employment is well documented in the personnel selection literature. Nowhere is this more of an issue than in the selection interview (see Chapter Five). For example, from the early work by Webster (1962) to recent summaries (for example, Harris, 1990), writers have addressed the role of implicit theories and prototypes. Fortunately, recent research has given us some insights as to their nature and dynamics.

The work of Jackson and his associates (Seiss & Jackson, 1970; Jackson, Peacock, & Smith, 1980; Rothstein & Jackson,

1980; Jackson, Peacock, & Holden, 1982) illustrates some discoveries regarding the nature and impact of schemes and personal constructs in selection interviewing.

Seiss and Jackson (1970) found that untrained subjects had a very differentiated view (for example, complex mental models) regarding the worker requirements of thirty-seven occupations. They could actually classify these occupations according to the salience of twenty-two personality dimensions in a manner consistent with empirically based analyses. Similarly, Rothstein and Jackson (1980) reported that what they call the inferential accuracy of subjects (their capacity to judge the pertinent characteristics of job incumbents and to identify behavioral exemplars, given limited information) is high. In fact, having subjects refer to mere job labels produces greater accuracy than having them read job descriptions.

These and other studies demonstrate that people do have reasonable mental models of worker requirements. But the studies also point out that candidates in the selection interview are evaluated with regard to more than one type of model. Specifically, Seiss and Jackson (1970) argue that a favorable impression in the interview may be a function of a person's matchup with *three* "models" of suitability: the "good person" (an applicant revealing attributes found attractive in people in general), the "good employee" (one meeting companywide worker requirements), and the "good candidate" (an applicant possessing those traits or qualities believed to be necessary for the successful performance of interest).

Beyond articulating the nature of this complex template-matching process, Jackson's research provides some reassurance that decision makers in selection contexts can distinguish (and rate differentially) perceived general suitability for employment from a hiring recommendation for the position in question. Raza and Carpenter (1987) also support this conclusion. They found hirability ratings (implying a job fit) were distinct from employability ratings (reflecting the general suitability of a candidate for the company). Moreover, their causal analysis revealed that skill assessments (but not personal liking) were the primary determinants of the former (as theoretically they should be).

Creating a Theory of Personnel Selection

Theory building involves a variety of activities, most of which require personal knowledge or insight on the part of the investigator with regard to the phenomenon of interest. It is an iterative and recursive process with each stage of development providing additional wisdom (Weick, 1989). Further, as pointed out in Chapter Nine, the line between theory development and theory testing is often blurred. Thus, theory guides data acquisition, and data inform theory. In the end, however, the goal (at least for most individuals reading this book) is to be able to make broad yet accurate statements about the nature and causes of individual effectiveness in work organizations. Usually, as implied above, this involves making statements about the role of personal traits or qualities.

The three antecedents of performance described in Chapter Two (declarative and procedural knowledge and motivation) are thought to be the proximal causes of performance. As such, they constitute a form of theory. Thus, in some respects, theory development regarding *the* key constructs involved in understanding and predicting performance is well known. But these three factors are what might be considered "open concepts" (Osigweh, 1989). They are universal in nature, defined by their systemic meaning. More to the point, although they inform us at some level, they really do not go far enough as to specifying exactly which knowledge, skill, and so on is involved. Similarly, these concepts are not tied to operational definitions (Schmitt & Klimoski, 1991).

What is needed in personnel selection theory is a set of "empirical concepts" (Osigweh, 1989). These would have meanings that could be used in both concrete and abstract contexts. Empirical concepts, then, would be based on observations and derived from inferences made from such observations. Such concepts would then become the building blocks of a truly practical theory of individual effectiveness.

To illustrate, Peterson et al. (1990) describe the process by which the team of investigators working on Project A came to identify the predictor domain for research aimed at understanding individual effectiveness in the U.S. Army. They used subject matter experts to establish a pool of potential predictor constructs (there were forty-five of these). In effect, the researchers were using the "folk theories" of these individuals as a starting point. A review of the psychological literature was then conducted to identify a list of variables and potential measures. Ultimately, eight predictor constructs, such as social skills and cognitive abilities, emerged from empirical analysis.

With few exceptions, the theory and practice of personnel selection start with the desire to be able to predict and understand performance of individuals employed in particular roles or in particular organizations. Thus, most efforts to build models or theories of effectiveness are done with regard to some context. This implies that the value of a given predictor construct (and the validity of particular combinations of constructs) must be reestablished as we move across contexts. Thus, although some generalizations regarding the usefulness of one predictor construct over another can be made, the construct's relative explanatory power in a given case is problematic. A generally relevant construct (for example, cognitive ability) is useful to a point. In most cases, particular predictor construct combinations appropriate to the situation yield more information. What is implied here is that investigators need to come to grips with and articulate the target or criterion variable of interest.

A second factor likely to have a major impact on uncovering and establishing the importance of a predictor construct is the type of measures used in the inductive phase of research. It seems fair to say that currently we only have a few instances where there is convergence between construct conceptualization (like human abilities) and construct measurement (in this case, cognitive ability tests and physical ability measures). For the most part, there are usually a number of defensible ways to operationalize a given predictor construct. Although there are sometimes benefits to multioperationalism (Runkle & McGrath, 1972), in the present case it leaves us with a handicap. When investigations are compared, different patterns of results regarding the role of particular constructs may be a function of the specific measurement choices made.

Most investigators take an inductive approach to establishing worker requirements. After the major job tasks and duties are clarified, judgments must be made as to what traits (predictor constructs) are thought to be relevant to performance, which usually calls for inferences (inductions) on the part of incumbents, supervisors, or other subject matter experts. Alternatively, such experts can be given a trait (construct) framework (or theory) first and then asked to rate the job in terms of the attributes involved. In this case the investigator would be using a more deductive approach. Thus, jobs (tasks) could be rated in light of Fleishman's taxonomy of physical abilities (for example, Fleishman & Hogan, 1978), the scales of the General Aptitude Test Battery (GATB), or the dimensions of the sixteen personality factors (PF).

We are unaware of any research comparing these two approaches to predictor construct development, but it is quite likely that differing sets of traits or trait definitions would result. What seems certain, however, is that the latter would lead to higher resulting validity (irrespective of the particular traits identified), owing to the superior measurement systems available.

Often the particular way of choosing or operationalizing constructs is driven by pragmatic forces. For instance, an academic researcher is interested in the dynamics of a particular theory. Thus, she or he will investigate only certain constructs. The practitioner who favors a particular approach to job analysis, like the position analysis questionnaire (PAQ), will usually end up with a particular and restricted set of constructs. Finally, because selection research is often driven by problems of turnover or poor productivity (Boehm, 1980), the search for predictor constructs frequently is guided by the belief of managers that something is not quite right with the current pool of employees. As a result, managers not only raise the alarm but also offer their "solutions" in terms of the traits involved.

A case in point is American industry's current fascination with "integrity tests." For better or worse, many organizational decision makers have recognized a symptom (theft, "shrinkage"), presumed its cause (employees who lack certain qualities, like integrity), and proposed a solution (the use of integrity tests as screening devices). In this case, even though the symptoms may be real, changing the selection system may not be the best response. But more important, a lack of conceptual and theoretical clarity of the notion of "integrity" has severely hampered the formulation of the most appropriate scientific and policy response (Sackett & Harris, 1989). The applied researcher knows only too clearly how easy it is to spend resources chasing elusive constructs (for example, a "good personality"). Establishing a set of predictor constructs that are both necessary and sufficient for effective personnel selection is a complex task. At this time, this goal seems very elusive. However, in addressing developments in this area, there are some distinctions that seem important to maintain when describing current predictor construct work or making recommendations for future practice.

  • *Constructs in use.* It seems clear that most, if not all, human social discourse is built around the use of personal constructs. Thus, to the extent selection systems involve real-time inferences and human judgments, we can expect to see the effects of these constructs in our data and in personnel decisions. It is just very difficult to overcome these human tendencies. On the other hand, the good news is that we are at a point where we know how to recognize, measure, and make use of these constructs in personnel systems.

  • *Constructs as conceptualized.* Research and practice associated with developing and using predictor constructs are quite varied in the quality of conceptualization involved. Put differently, the proliferation of potential predictor constructs and disagreement over their relative importance can often be traced to problems of construct definition. The good news here is that we have approaches to critical thinking, theory building, and construct definition that are well suited to remedying this situation.

  • *Constructs as inferred.* Although many professional investigators start with a set of constructs in mind, most psychologists work differently. As noted, they usually operate to infer the qualities of interest from job analysis data or from original observations. The nature and number of constructs, then, will be strongly affected by the procedures followed for job analysis and for obtaining expert judgments. To the extent that well-developed and well-documented systems (like the PAQ or Behaviorally Anchored Rating Scales (BARS) procedures, or the Fleishman taxonomy for physical abilities) are used, we would expect to see this process facilitated. Using ad hoc or idiosyncratic approaches or lists tends to produce problematic inference-to-construct processes, yielding potentially irreproducible construct lists.

•   *Constructs as measured.* With few exceptions, we do not have standardized or agreed-upon ways to measure or index predictor constructs, even where we enjoy conceptual clarity or a strong inferential base. Moreover, the construct validity of measures is often asserted rather than empirically established by investigators. In addition, the most popular approaches to assessing predictor constructs—the selection interview and assessment centers—do not involve a standard format. If there is anything positive about this situation, it is that more applied researchers seem willing to spend the time required "up front" to establish the nature of constructs (Mitchell & Klimoski, 1982).

Common Constructs in Personnel Assessments

It has been implied throughout this chapter that the number and nature of traits to be considered in a selection program should depend on the needs and purpose of the investigator. True, the constructs of greatest interest will be those that contribute to both prediction and understanding of behavior or performance in a given context. But we must address the question, What are *the* best predictor constructs? We cannot really say, a priori, what constitutes the most defensible list.

What is offered in this section, then, is a description and analysis of the constructs nominally associated with a selected set of common predictor techniques. The term *nominal* is used to acknowledge that, correctly or not, certain constructs are often associated with a given method. To the extent possible, however, we separate claims from what can be supported by research.

Standardized Personality Measures

It seems reasonable to assert that a major contribution of psychologists over the last century has been the creation and development of standardized tests as a way to measure and understand individual differences. The number of available tests is enormous (compare Ghiselli, 1973; Hogan, 1991). Their nature, complexity, and format vary considerably. And it is probably true that a test can be found for just about any personal attribute of interest. Fortunately, test theory and technology allow for valid measurement of most of these constructs (Ackerman & Humphreys, 1991).

When standardized tests are considered as the measurement approach, there is a tendency to think of them in terms of the construct being measured. For example, we speak not of a test of "interpersonal dominance" so much as "an interpersonal dominance test." Although this is not bad per se, it often has the effect of causing us to presume a test measures what its name implies. This is an assumption that must be verified.

Personality tests are thought to get at constructs that imply "typical behavior" (Cronbach, 1970). Personality constructs have the flavor of dispositions, and thus are relevant to consistencies in behavior over time. Although there is controversy over just how best to define personality (for example, Gough, 1976; Funder, 1991), most writers do conceptualize it as a dynamic psychological structure determining adjustment to the environment but manifest in the regularities and consistencies in the behavior of the individual over time (Snyder & Ickes, 1985).

In their review of a dispositional approach to behavior, Snyder and Ickes (1985) point to Blass (1977), London and Exner (1978), and Robinson and Shaver (1973) for fairly comprehensive lists. They themselves choose to stress three constructs: authoritarianism, need for social approval, and Machiavellianism. These three constructs are stressed not because they are the most well developed or for the quality of the measures available, but because investigators have found them to be particularly interesting in light of their implications for human social relations.

In contrast, Gough (1976) was more pragmatic in his approach. He selected for review six personality domains (constructs) for which he felt there was relatively good measurement and which were likely to have relevance to I/O psychology. Either these constructs had already demonstrated this relevance or, in his judgment, the available research could easily be extrapolated to the world of work. His nominations were authoritarianism, conformity (versus independence), need for achievement, socialization/moral judgment, social sensitivity, and field independence. About the same time, Browne and Howarth (1977) thought that up to twenty personality domains could be empirically derived from a large pool of items.

As implied, there is a large number of personality attributes that can be imagined. In fact, at one time Allport (1937) reported finding 17,953 trait terms in an unabridged dictionary. More recently, however, there seems to be a convergence among writers that the number of distinct personality dimensions or concepts is much smaller. Digman (1990), among others, has argued that a strong case can be made for as few as five overarching concepts that could be used to summarize the personality trait domain: extroversion or surgency (perhaps a mixture of ambition and sociability), emotional stability (or its opposite, neuroticism), agreeableness, conscientiousness, and openness to experience. Barrick and Mount (1991) provide empirical support for not only the existence of these five dimensions but also their potential value to personnel selection. Their meta-analysis revealed that all five could predict one or more aspects of job performance for five occupational groupings. Even more impressive, scores on the conscientiousness dimension, although operationalized in very different ways across the 117 studies reviewed, were found to predict criterion variables (such as job proficiency and training proficiency) with an average estimated true correlation in the range of .20 to .23.

Finally, it is useful to examine what personality domains are stressed by psychologists doing individual assessment in organizations. Ryan and Sackett (1987) report a list that was developed from surveys completed by over three hundred respondents. How it was determined that these dimensions were important for the individual assessment task varied by respondent. But rarely was a formal job analysis involved. Informal conversation and personal preferences were most often the bases for the choice of constructs.

Even if there were a consensus on just *what* personality constructs are relevant and potentially useful for personnel selection, deciding *how* to measure them would be a major obstacle. With few exceptions, there is no commonly accepted way to measure most of these constructs — Gough's (1976) position notwithstanding. It is not that we have too few measures; quite the contrary, there are often many approaches to measuring a given attribute.

Quite often, however, an investigator will make use of a standard multiattribute personality inventory to solve the measurement problem. As the term implies, such measures have been developed (through item or factor analysis) to produce scores on a number of relatively independent personality traits. Some common personality inventories include the Minnesota Multiphasic Personality Inventory, Edwards Personal Preference Schedule, California Psychological Inventory, Guilford-Zimmerman Temperament Survey, Gorden Personal Profile, Thurstone Temperament Survey, and Jackson Personality Research Form.

The research evidence on the relevance of personality attributes to criteria of interest to I/O psychologists (for example, attendance, performance, accidents) is voluminous. Fortunately, much of it has been summarized (for example, Guion & Gottier, 1965; Ghiselli, 1966; Schmitt, Gooding, Noe, & Kirsch, 1984). Unfortunately, the tone of these reviews is rather critical, with careful analysis of published studies finding little support for such constructs.

Now it is quite possible that there is no basis in fact for the argument that personality influences job-relevant behaviors. However, recent research seems to lay the blame for this inconclusiveness on poor thinking and inappropriate choice of measures. To put it more positively, when investigators carefully conceptualize the role of personality vis-à-vis the criterion domain(s) of interest, when they select appropriate, construct-valid measures based on a job analysis, or when they systematically develop new measures built around a construct model of effectiveness, personality attributes are found to be relevant and potent predictors (Guion, 1987; Schneider & Schmitt, 1986; Miner, 1978; Inwald, 1988).

Perhaps one of the better examples of a fruitful approach to incorporating personality constructs into a selection paradigm is found in the work of Borman, Rosse, and Abrahams (1980). These investigators used a construct model to link criterion dimensions and personality predictor domains. For a sample of navy recruiters, they found item composites (derived from carefully written and validated new items and old items on the Jackson Personality Research and the Strong-Campbell Interest forms) could successfully and differentially predict criterion (performance) dimensions. What was particularly significant was that new items could be successfully written for the predictor construct domains. The authors apparently understood the constructs involved. Unlike the case in many studies, the resultant personality measures also showed good discriminant validity. Some other "success stories" include those presented by Barrick and Mount (1991), Day and Silverman (1989), Inwald (1988), and Hogan, Hogan, and Busch (1984).

In 1965, Guion and Gottier concluded their gloomy review of the evidence for the usefulness of personality constructs and measures in personnel selection at that time by acknowledging (but only grudgingly) that there *may* be some places and some situations where they can offer helpful predictions (p. 159). Recent research reveals that we have the technology to establish just where and under what conditions this can occur. It remains to be seen whether this knowledge gets put into practice.

To summarize the nature of the constructs prevalent in the use of personality measures in the selection context, we highlight a recent paper describing a major research effort aimed at predicting and understanding performance in the U.S. military (Peterson et al., 1990). One of the results of this effort was the specification of the predictor domain for a sample of nineteen military jobs. To give a sense of the scope and organization of the predictor domain, the authors prepared a "hierarchical map," which is reproduced in Table 4.1.

Table 4.1. Map of Predictor Construct Domain for Project A.

Constructs	Clusters	Factors
1. Verbal comprehension		
5. Reading comprehension		
16. Ideational fluency	A. Verbal ability/general intelligence	
18. Analogical reasoning		
21. Omnibus intelligence/ aptitude		
22. Word fluency		
4. Word problems		
8. Inductive reasoning: concept formation	B. Reasoning	
10. Deductive logic		
2. Numerical computation	C. Number ability	**Cognitive abilities**
3. Use of formula/number problems		
12. Perceptual speed and accuracy	N. Perceptual speed and accuracy	
49. Investigative interests	U. Investigative interests	
14. Rote memory	J. Memory	
17. Follow directions		
19. Figural reasoning	F. Closure	
23. Verbal and figural		

* *

6. Two-dimensional mental rotation		
7. Three-dimensional mental rotation		
9. Spatial visualization	E. Visualization/ spatial	**Visualization/ spatial**
11. Field dependence (negative)		
15. Place memory (visual memory)		
20. Spatial scanning		

* *

24. Processing efficiency		
25. Selective attention	G. Mental information processing	**Information processing**
26. Time sharing		

* *

13. Mechanical comprehension	L. Mechanical comprehension	**Mechanical**
48. Realistic interests	M. Realistic versus artistic interests	
51. Artistic interests (negative)		

* *

Table 4.1. Map of Predictor Construct Domain for Project A, Cont'd.

Constructs	Clusters	Factors
28. Control precision		
29. Rate control	I. Steadiness/precision	
32. Arm-hand steadiness		
34. Aiming		
27. Multilimb coordination	D. Coordination	**Psychomotor**
35. Speed of arm movement		
30. Manual dexterity		
31. Finger dexterity	K. Dexterity	
33. Wrist-finger speed		
****
39. Sociability	Q. Sociability	
52. Social interests		**Social Skills**
50. Enterprising interests	R. Enterprising interests	
****
36. Involvement in athletics	T. Athletic abilities/energy	
37. Energy level		**Vigor**
41. Dominance	S. Dominance/self-esteem	
42. Self-esteem		
****
40. Traditional values		
43. Conscientiousness	H. Traditional values/ conventionality/ nondelinquency	
46. Nondelinquency		
53. Conventional interests		
44. Locus of control	O. Work orientation/locus of control	**Motivation/ stability**
47. Work orientation		
38. Cooperativeness	P. Cooperation/emotional stability	
45. Emotional stability		

Source: Peterson et al., 1990, pp. 252–253.

Note the structure of the predictor battery itself. As represented in the table, constructs are clustered, and clusters are organized around factors. This makes explicit the notion of "level of generality" of constructs raised earlier. It can be clearly seen how constructs can be extended in this manner. In discussing the predictor domain, investigators could use any or all of the three levels. Similarly, measures could be selected or developed for the various levels according to the logic developed in other chapters of this book (for example, Chapters Two, Three, and Nine).

Biodata

The use of biographical information in the context of personnel selection goes back to the earliest days of the practice of I/O psychology (Owens, 1976; Schmitt & Klimoski, 1991), and its value in this context has been repeatedly demonstrated (Hunter & Hunter, 1984; Reilly & Chao, 1982; Schmitt, Gooding, Noe, & Kirsch, 1984). Criterion validities in the range of .25 to .50 have often been reported (Schneider & Schmitt, 1986).

The traditional approach to the use of biodata has been an empirical one in which information from objectively scored items of a demographic, life-style, experience, and preference nature is statistically related to criterion information (Mitchell & Klimoski, 1982). Thus, even though biodata could often predict job-relevant behavior, exactly why this occurred was problematic. The usual rationale offered for the validity of biodata was one of behavioral consistency. To the extent that the measure could capture the essential pattern of past behavior, it was thought, it should be able to predict future behavior (Owens, 1976). Unlike tests, which could be thought of as "signs" (surrogates for causes), biodata served as a "sample" of the behavior domain of interest. The validity of this assertion notwithstanding, it is interesting to note that even having a rationale did not serve to drive the selection of items of biodata instruments in early prediction and selection research.

In much of this early work on biodata, the techniques of choice were factor analysis and, later, subgroup analysis. The factor analysis approach revealed that reliable, meaningful, and useful dimensions (constructs) of life history information could indeed be created. But the particular constructs uncovered varied (for example, drive, financial responsibility, favorable self-perception), influenced by such things as the particular set of items chosen for inclusion in the inventory, the response format used, and the sample studied. Clearly, if the goal was to identify *general* life history constructs, a broader approach had to be taken.

In a program of research, Owens and his colleagues (for example, Schoenfeldt, 1974; Owens, 1971, 1976; Neiner & Owens, 1985; Shaffer, Sanders, & Owens, 1986; Mumford, Stokes, & Owens, in press) took such an approach. Starting with conceptual models of human development and vocational choice, and informed by life history interviews, known life history correlates of job requirements, or empirical findings regarding the factor loadings of biodata items, Owens developed a general instrument. This was then administered to large samples of undergraduates. Analysis of this measure revealed two reliable and interpretable factor structures, one each for males and females. Table 4.2 illustrates his findings.

Owens found that these dimensions are robust across samples, are consistent with past research (for example, Baehr & Williams, 1967), and relate well to measured variables in a manner consistent with theory. Moreover, they appear to provide the basis for a conceptualization of human development, adjustment, and achievement called the Ecology model (Mumford, Stokes, & Owens, in press).

In a sense, the factors in Table 4.2 are "criterion free" constructs of life history. They come out of an instrument primarily driven by human development theory. However, an alternative approach to construct definition is to have items and resulting dimensions derive from a knowledge of a phenomenon of interest. This has been done for such things as supervisory effectiveness (Rothstein, Schmidt, Erwin, Owens, & Sparks, 1990), success in training (Alker & Owen, 1977), career success (Mitchell & Klimoski, 1982), and antisocial behaviors on the job (Haymaker, 1986). These two represent a rational approach to instrument and ultimately, construct development. The investigators used judgment (and theory) to select or develop items that have relevance (often content relevance) to the criterion. Thus, items were selected to reflect either the developmental life history antecedents of the constructs thought to be important for predicting or understanding criterion behavior or the contemporary defining elements of these constructs, or both. In one study, however, which involved a contrast of the rational with the traditional empirical approaches to prediction

Table 4.2. Biodata Factors—Male and Female College Students.

		Rank	Percentage Variance
	Factor name—males (n = 1,037)		
I	Warmth of parental relationship	1	3.5
II[a]	Emotional maturity or adjustment	17	1.2
III	Intellectualism	4.5	2.3
IV	Academic achievement (self-perceived)	2.5	3.1
V	Social introversion	2.5	3.1
VI	Scientific interest	10	1.8
VII	Socioeconomic status	7	2.1
VIII	Independence/dominance	6	2.2
IX	Parental control versus freedom (bipolar)	8	2.0
X[a]	Literary-historical interest	11	1.6
XI	Positive academic attitude	12.5	1.5
XII	Sibling friction	18	1.1
XIII	Religious activity	15.5	1.3
XIV	Athletic interest	4.5	2.3
XV	Social desirability	9	1.9
XVI[a]	Family size	19	0.9
XVII[a]	Math achievement (or math-English discrepancy)	12.5	1.5
XVIII[a]	Interest in vocational courses	15.5	1.3
XIX[a]	English achievement	14	1.4
			36
	Factor name—females (n = 897)		
I	Warmth of maternal relationship	1	4.3
II	Leadership (social)	2	3.2
III	Academic achievement (self-perceived)	3	3.1
IV	Parental control versus freedom (bipolar)	5	2.4
V	Cultural-literary interests (reading)	6	2.0
VI	Scientific-artistic interest	9	1.8
VII	Socioeconomic status	4	2.6
VIII	Expression of negative emotions (anger)	11	1.7
IX[a]	TV (daytime)	16	1.4
X	Athletic participation	7	1.9
XI	Conformity to female role	9	1.8
XII	Maladjustment	9	1.8
XIII	Popularity with opposite sex	12.5	1.6
XIV[a]	Math versus English	14.5	1.5
XV	Positive academic attitude	14.5	1.5
XVI[a]	Only child	18	1.1
XVII[a]	Language achievement	19	1.0
XVIII	Daddy's girl	17	1.3
XIX	Social maturity	12.5	1.6
			38

[a]Not used for subsequent subgrouping.
Source: Owens, 1976, p. 622.

(Mitchell & Klimoski, 1982), the latter did somewhat better at predicting ($r = .46$) the licensure of real estate sales people.

The problems facing biodata users interested in underlying traits or attributes relate to conceptualizing, inferring, and measuring constructs. Currently, it is not uncommon to rely on post hoc dimensional analysis to identify these and ad hoc approaches to label them. Thus, the comparability of the constructs reported across studies is questionable. The evidence for the constructs themselves is frequently weak.

However, the technology and theory of biodata do allow for a construct approach to prediction. In this regard, investigators may wish to follow either of the themes described in this section. Given the developmental work of Owens and his colleagues, it would be advantageous to make use of his instrument and the constructs that it measures. Of course, anyone doing this would have to make a case that these particular predictor constructs are potentially linked to explaining the criterion of interest. It remains to be seen just how easy this would be to do for dependent variables relevant to personnel selection specialists. Alternatively, current research evidence goes a long way to guide the construction of construct-based biodata instruments that could be used in particular settings. Such tools, because they measure only those factors of importance to the job in question, may be more efficient than Owens's questionnaire and thus the better direction to go. In any event, if there is a desire for a construct-based selection device, there is no reason the biodata form should be overlooked.

The Selection Interview

The employment interview is thought to be the most prevalent method for assessing individuals prior to an offer to hire (Schneider & Schmitt, 1986). Because of its importance to personnel selection, it is the topic of a specific chapter in this book (Chapter Five). Thus, it is not surprising that a great deal of practical, theoretical, and scientific material on the interview exists. This section does not attempt to repeat what is found in Chapter Five, but focuses instead on the constructs implicitly and explicitly measured by the interview.

A clue to what predictor constructs are measured by the interview can be found in the research studies on interviews themselves. Such insight might be gained by looking at the types of judgments and dependent variables involved. Several studies have, in fact, looked at more or less job-specific constructs. One example is reported by Hakel (1971), who examined postinterview ratings on the traits of conscientiousness, knowledge and judgment, and expected level of job performance.

Many investigators have favored assessing the impact of one or more interviewer variables on more global criteria, including hirability (Dipboye, Stramler, & Fontenelle, 1984), suitability (Rothstein & Jackson, 1980), and applicant qualifications (Parsons & Liden, 1984).

When the interview is designed and structured around a particular job, the predictor constructs usually take on the flavor of worker requirements. For instance, Landy (1976) evaluated ratings of candidates for a police officer's job on nine dimensions based on a job analysis (for example, appearance, communications skills). However, as is often the case with a priori dimensions, the factor analysis of these ratings yielded only three factors: manifest motivation, personal stability (for example, responsibility), and communications skills. He did find evidence that the first two of these was predictive of police officer job performance as rated by supervisors.

A final set of clues regarding the predictor constructs measured by the interview comes from reviews of the literature. Arvey and Campion (1982) thought that six constructs were stated or implied by the literature (including intelligence, general impression, and sociability). More recently, Campion, Pursell, and Brown (1988) suggest that the interview may allow the measurement of two domains: cognitive attributes (thinking, job knowledge) and motivation. The Harris (1990) summary argues for practical/social intelligence, achievement, interpersonal skills, and behavioral intentions as likely constructs. Finally, Buckley and Weitzel (1989) emphasize cognitive ability, interpersonal skills, job knowledge/skill/ability, and motivation. Not surprisingly, these overlap considerably with the lists derived from the individual studies mentioned earlier.

Could it be that the interview measures all these attributes? Could it potentially be "all things to all people"? The answer seems to be a qualified yes. The interview seems to be a very versatile measurement approach (which may account, in part, for its durability over the years).

It may be clear by now that the particular constructs assessed (intentionally or unintentionally) by the interview are affected by its design and structure. However, it appears that even loosely structured or haphazardly designed experiences allow for the assessment of intellective and interpersonal qualities. They also allow for the measurement of at least a generalized impression. Thus, it is quite reasonable for interviewers to validly observe and rate an applicant in terms of attractiveness, sociability, liking, verbal facility, and so on. Two points follow from this observation. First, it is reasonable to ask interviewers for assessments of these attributes based on almost any interview experience. Second, it may be almost impossible to prevent such assessments from taking place in any interview.

More structured interviews, especially those based on a job analysis, allow for and encourage the valid assessment of particular job-relevant attributes. This is true especially where interviewers are well trained and where the constructs involved are well defined, distinct, and can indeed be inferred from the interview exchange (with or without the support of application materials).

In the most tightly designed interviews, such as the situation interview (Latham, Saari, Pursell, & Campion, 1980) or the oral trade tests (Tiffin & McCormick, 1965), it seems that the construct assessed is performance. In this case, the applicant is literally "scored" on how well he or she deals with questions relevant to job content or with make-believe situations. Moreover, it is easy to see how the interviewer could easily go on to infer an applicant's hirability from such evidence. Performance in the interview designed in this manner could easily be expected to predict later job performance.

In terms of the themes developed in this chapter, it seems that all four issues (constructs in use, constructs as conceptualized, constructs as inferred, and constructs as measured) are problematic for the interview. In particular, the interview is one

domain where the investigator or practitioner needs to be aware
of the implications of "constructs in use." The available evidence
is that constructs such as the potential good employee and good
job incumbent *can* be distinguished by judges. But the tendency
to use these may also overwhelm attempts to assess specific job-
relevant attributes. Also of particular concern should be the way
we go about measuring job-relevant traits. Although there is
no shortage of examples or programs, at the present time there
is also no standard way of getting at them. There is no such
thing as *the* employment interview (Wiesner & Cronshaw, 1988).

Assessment Centers

Unlike the selection interview, assessment centers are usually designed around a set of constructs (Klimoski & Brickner,
1987; Zedeck, 1986). A job analysis is used to identify assessment dimensions. These become the basis for exercises that in
turn are used to obtain evidence of individual capabilities. Assessment centers are most frequently used to aid in decisions
relating to promotions to management positions. Recent reviews
of the assessment center literature have established both their
validity and utility (Cascio & Silbey, 1979; Gaugler, Rosenthal,
Thornton, & Bentson, 1987; Hunter & Hunter, 1984; Klimoski
& Strickland, 1977; Schmitt, Gooding, Noe, & Kirsch, 1984).

Zedeck (1986) points out that in the assessment center literature, the term *dimension* can be used to denote a set of tasks
or behaviors that are similar in features *or* performances that
require the same ability (p. 280). A particular center can be
built around a smaller or greater number of dimensions, ostensibly reflecting the job requirements involved or the need or
desire to get at attributes that are more or less specific, or both.
For instance, investigators reporting recently on two operational
centers describe them as using from eight (Bycio, Alvares, &
Hahn, 1987) to seventeen (Dugan, 1988) dimensions.

Despite favorable results, Klimoski and Brickner (1987) argue that the assessment center paradigm has several weaknesses.
Most notably, it fails to fulfill its claims as an approach to the
measurement of individual difference constructs. To put it an-

other way, although assessment centers are built around a well-developed set of procedures to ensure trait measurement, the evidence is that most staff at most centers are not able to produce a differentiated set of construct-valid assessments (Huck, 1973; Sackett & Hakel, 1979; Schmitt, 1977). For instance, Bycio, Alvares, and Hahn (1987) examined the pattern of data from ratings on eight abilities across five center exercises. This (and previous research) caused the authors to pronounce: "The preponderance of evidence suggests that the method does not measure large sets of job related abilities" (p. 470). Indeed, several writers have argued against the use of dimensional ratings entirely and in favor of giving some overall center performance "score" to participants (Klimoski & Brickner, 1987; Sackett, 1987).

Actually, for purposes of assisting in selection and promotion decisions, there is no reason why global assessments derived from assessment center observations cannot be used. The evidence is consistent in this regard. Overall assessment judgments do predict a variety of important criteria. Yet, this may not be the best way to go. For example, the assessments do not "inform" such decisions. By themselves they do not contribute to an understanding of why such predictions "work" (Klimoski & Brickner, 1987).

In their analysis, Klimoski and Brickner (1987) argue that improvements *could* be made in the quality of construct ratings if more attention were given to the dimensions themselves. Picking up on Zedeck's (1986) observation regarding the way dimensions are used in assessment centers, they recommend using fewer dimensions, dimensions at a higher level of abstraction, and/or more "natural" dimensions. The latter would reflect the personal constructs used by those in the organization and the assessment center staff in their spontaneous cognitions of (in this case) managerial effectiveness.

Fortunately, there is some recent evidence on the consequences of doing some of these things. For example, Gaugler and Thornton (1989) found that the number of dimensions to be assessed (three, six, or nine) affected rating variability, rating level, and accuracy. Shore, Thornton, and Shore (1990) showed that the nature of dimensions (their definition, level of abstraction, and naturalness), as well as the number involved, affected construct validity. Ratings on the more global (and natural) dimensions of interpersonal style and performance were distinct and could be systematically related to personality and cognitive abilities marker variables. What was especially nice to see was that ratings on the performance dimension (but not the style dimension) were strongly related to measured cognitive abilities. This implies that the staff could separate style from performance.

As stressed in this chapter, an important aspect of construct measurement is its operational definition. Reilly, Henry, and Smither (1990) demonstrate that the benefits of a behavioral checklist approach to assessment center ratings stem, in part, from the way it clarifies just what behaviors define a dimension. The checklist serves to guide observation during the exercises and reduces some of the information-processing burden facing the rater by making explicit just what to look for while observing.

Reilly, Henry, and Smither (1990) also report as an outcome of their checklist development work that some of the dimensions actually have few (four) behavioral referents across the exercises whereas others have many (thirty-two). They speculate that some of the difficulty with construct measurement in assessment centers may be because the opportunity to observe (infer) behavior relevant to various dimensions is quite variable in typical centers. A rater would thus have many chances to form a valid impression for some dimensions, little chance for others. This too may contribute to the reliability of inferences and enhance construct validity.

In addition to dealing with issues of constructs as conceptualized and measured, as in the case of the interview, investigators also have to be diligent regarding the operation of constructs-in-use. At present, despite the vast resources devoted to developing and implementing assessment centers, there is little research on the tendencies to use generalized evaluative categories (interpersonal constructs) in this context. Indeed, as pointed out elsewhere (Klimoski & Strickland, 1977), such tendencies may actually account for the obtained validities of the method.

Maintaining the Integrity of Predictor Constructs

It is not enough that we can establish that a given selection device *can* measure particular constructs. It is still necessary to ensure that prediction devices, in use, *continue* to index the construct qualities of interest. Here are some issues that affect predictor construct integrity.

• *Construct stretching.* The point has already been made that, although a construct name is attached to a test or the output of a procedure, there is no guarantee that this construct is actually measured. Osigweh (1989) warns of another possibility — the unwarranted application of construct terms to concepts that seem or sound similar. He suggests that construct extension should be done carefully and only after there are strong theoretical or empirical arguments in favor of doing so. Are "dominance" and "the need for power" the same thing? Do "oral communication skills" refer to both formal presentations and the spontaneous use of language for clarity and impact? If so, arguments must be carefully crafted to assert that they are. This caveat is related to the call for better construct definition, but it is also a warning about the pitfalls of unwarranted generalizations.

• *Modifying measures.* Schmitt and Klimoski (1991) highlight the tendency of some investigators to modify or adapt tests to meet their needs. Most often this involves changing the wording or language to be more appropriate for a particular subject or applicant population. It is also common to shorten measures to meet time constraints placed on test administration. These and other changes will have an effect on both the psychometric and construct properties of a measure.

• *Respondent characteristics.* In the context of this section, *respondent characteristics* refers to the attributes of the individuals to be assessed relative to the attributes of the individuals who were used in the development of the predictor device or method (Mitchell, 1985). The case of tests is most clear. If, for example, the level of language skills is lower for the applicant population than for the scale development sample, the construct or dimensional integrity of a test may be compromised. The medium or modality used may also make a difference. If a test is to be taken in written form, to administer it orally may produce an undesired impact. This issue takes on increased importance at this time as organizations in the United States move forward to comply with the Americans with Disabilities Act, which was signed into law by President Bush in 1991. The impact of various accommodations offered to applicants with disabilities must be evaluated relative to the impact they will have on the valid measurement of predictor constructs.

   • *Adequate behavior sampling.* This concept is well integrated into test construction practices. We readily acknowledge the benefits of a longer test for increased reliability. But an analogous notion is only now being integrated into interview and assessment center design. Investigators must allow for multiple opportunities to observe the manifestation of individual qualities of interest (Banks & Roberson, 1985; Kamouri & Balzer, 1990). This is particularly true when we are trying to assess "typical" behaviors. Thus, what we are arguing for goes beyond simply obtaining multiple observations at a given time.

   • *Consistency in administering measures.* Consistency in implementing measures is observed to varying degrees in the methods reviewed above. Still, it is unsettling to discover how little information is typically given regarding the actual administration or implementation of predictor measures in articles or technical reports. We clearly understand the consequence for construct measurement of variability in administration of tests (Brown, 1979). We also now realize the consequences of conducting interviews or assessment centers in different ways. We do not pay enough attention, however, to what happens *after* design and development, after selection programs are implemented (Brown, 1979; Latham & Saari, 1984; Schmitt, Schneider, & Cohen, 1990).

Conclusion

   Valid construct measurement in selection programs requires theory to inform practice. We must have a good (theory-driven) conceptualization of the performance domain of interest. Ideally, we should also have a model of the role of individual differences in affecting levels of performance in that domain.

Similarly, we must have practice informing theory, which in this case implies an understanding of the realities of predictor construct measurement. This includes what operationalizations are feasible, as well as the place where subjectivity will almost inevitably occur and the likely consequences of that subjectivity. The sections on personal constructs and on the nature and impact of impression formation in the interview are most explicit in this regard.

Finally, valid predictor construct measurement will only occur if we exert constant diligence. The complex nature of psychological constructs, the difficulty of good measurement, and the tendency for selection systems to take on a life of their own mean that to demonstrate good measurement under ideal (for example, experimental) conditions is not enough. We must continue to ensure that good predictor construct measurement exists in practice.

References

Ackerman, P. L., & Humphreys, L. G. (1991). Individual differences theory in industrial organizational psychology. In M. D. Dunnette & L. M. Hough (Eds.), *Handbook of industrial and organizational psychology* (2nd ed.). Palo Alto, CA: Consulting Psychologists Press.

Alker, H. A., & Owen, D. W. (1977). Biographical, trait and behavioral sampling predictors of performance in a stressful life situation. *Journal of Personality and Social Psychology, 35,* 717–723.

Allport, G. W. (1937). *Personality: A psychological interpretation.* Troy, MO: Holt, Rinehart & Winston.

Arvey, R. D., & Campion, J. E. (1982). The employment interview: A summary and review of recent research. *Personnel Psychology, 35,* 281–321.

Baehr, M., & Williams, W. (1967). Underlying dimensions of personnel background data and the relationship to occupational classification. *Journal of Applied Psychology, 65*(6), 662–671.

Banks, C. O., & Roberson, L. (1985). Performance appraisers as test developers. *Academy of Management Review, 10,* 128–142.

Barrick, M. R., & Mount, M. K. (1991). The big five personality dimensions and job performance: A meta-analysis. *Personnel Psychology, 44,* 1–26.

Blalock, H. M. (1969). *Theory construction: From verbal to mathematical formulations.* Englewood Cliffs, NJ: Prentice-Hall.

Blass, T. (Ed.). (1977). *Personality variables in social behavior.* Hillsdale, NJ: Erlbaum.

Boehm, V. R. (1980). Research in the real world: A conceptual model. *Personnel Psychology, 33,* 495–504.

Borman, W. C. (1987). Personal constructs performance, schemata and "folk theories" of subordinate effectiveness: Explorations in an army officer sample. *Organizational Behavior and Human Decision Processes, 40,* 307–322.

Borman, W. C., Rosse, R. L., & Abrahams, N. M. (1980). An empirical construct validity approach to strategy predictor-job performance limits. *Journal of Applied Psychology, 65,* 662–671.

Brown, S. H. (1979). Validity distortions with a test in use. *Journal of Applied Psychology, 64*(4), 460–462.

Browne, J. A., & Howarth, E. (1977). A comprehensive factor analysis of personality questionnaire items: A test of twenty putative factor hypotheses. *Multivariate Behavioral Research, 12,* 399–427.

Buckley, M. R., & Weitzel, H. (1989). Review of research on the selection interview. In R. W. Eder & G. R. Ferris (Eds.), *The employment interview: Theory, research, and practice.* Newbury Park, CA: Sage.

Bycio, P., Alvares, K. M., & Hahn, J. (1987). Situational specificity in assessment center ratings: A confirmatory factor analysis. *Journal of Applied Psychology, 72,* 463–474.

Campion, M. A., Pursell, E. D., & Brown, B. K. (1988). Structured interviewing: Raising the psychometric properties of the employment interview. *Personnel Psychology, 41,* 25–42.

Cantor, N., & Mischel, W. (1979). Prototypes in person perception. In L. Berkowitz (Ed.), *Advances in experimental social psychology.* San Diego, CA: Academic Press.

Cascio, W. F., & Silbey, V. (1979). Utility of the assessment center as a selection device. *Journal of Applied Psychology, 64,* 107–118.

Cooper, W. H. (1981). Ubiquitous halo. *Psychology Bulletin, 90,* 218–244.

Cronbach, L. J. (1970). *Essentials of psychological testing.* New York: HarperCollins.

Day, D. V., & Silverman, S. B. (1989). Personality and job performance: Evidence of incremental validity. *Personnel Psychology, 42,* 25–36.

Digman, J. M. (1990). Personality structure: Emergence of the five factor model. In M. R. Rosenzweig & L. W. Porter (Eds.), *Annual Review of Psychology.* Palo Alto, CA: Annual Reviews.

Dipboye, R. L., Stramler, C. S., & Fontenelle, G. A. (1984). The effects of the application of recall of information from the interview. *Academy of Management Journal, 27,* 561–575.

Dugan, B. (1988). Effects of assessor training on information use. *Journal of Applied Psychology, 73,* 743–748.

Fleishman, E. A., & Hogan, J. E. (1978). *A taxonomic method for assessing the physical requirements of jobs: The physical abilities analysis approach.* Washington, DC: Advanced Resources Research Organization.

Funder, D. C. (1991). Global traits: A neo-Allportian approach to personality. *Psychological Science, 2,* 91–102.

Gaugler, B. B., Rosenthal, D. B., Thornton, G. C., & Bentson, C. (1987). Meta-analysis of assessment center validity. *Journal of Applied Psychology, 72,* 493–511.

Gaugler, B. B., & Thornton, G. C. (1989). Number of assessment center dimensions of a determinant of rating accuracy. *Journal of Applied Psychology, 74,* 611–618.

Ghiselli, E. E. (1966). *The validity of occupational aptitude tests.* New York: Wiley.

Ghiselli, E. E. (1973). The validity of aptitude tests in personnel selection. *Personnel Psychology, 26,* 461–477.

Gough, H. (1976). Personality and personality assessment. In M. D. Dunnette (Ed.), *Handbook of industrial and organizational psychology,* Skokie, IL: Rand McNally.

Guion, R. M. (1987). Changing views for personnel selection research. *Personnel Psychology, 4,* 199–213.

Guion, R. M., & Gottier, R. F. (1965). Validity of personality measures in personnel selection. *Personnel Psychology, 18,* 135–164.

Hakel, M. D. (1971). Similarity of post-interview trait rating intercorrelations as a contributor to interaction agreement in a structured employment interview. *Journal of Applied Psychology, 55,* 443–448.

Harris, M. M. (1990). Reconsidering the employment interview: A review of recent literature and suggestions for future research. *Personnel Psychology, 42,* 691–726.

Haymaker, J. C. (1986, August). *Biodata as a predictor of employee integrity and turnover.* Paper presented at the meeting of the American Psychological Association, Washington, DC.

Hogan, J., Hogan, R., & Busch, C. M. (1984). How to measure service orientation. *Journal of Applied Psychology, 69,* 167–175.

Hogan, R. T. (1991). Personality and personality management. In M. D. Dunnette & L. M. Hough (Eds.), *Handbook of Industrial and Organizational Psychology* (Vol. 2). Palo Alto, CA: Consulting Psychologists Press.

Huck, J. R. (1973). Assessment centers: A review of the external and internal validities. *Personnel Psychology, 26,* 191–212.

Hunter, J. E. (1986). Cognitive ability, cognitive aptitudes, job knowledge and job performance. *Journal of Vocational Behavior, 29,* 340–362.

Hunter, J. E., & Hunter, R. F. (1984). Validity and utility of alternative predictors of job performance. *Psychology Bulletin, 96,* 72–98.

Inwald, R. R. (1988). Five-year follow-up of department terminations as predicted by 16 pre-employment psychological indicators. *Journal of Applied Psychology, 73,* 703–710.

Jackson, D. N., Peacock, A. C., & Holden, R. R. (1982). Professional interviewer's trait inferential structures for diverse occupational groups. *Organizational Behavior and Human Decision Processes, 29,* 1–20.

Jackson, D. N., Peacock, A. C., & Smith, J. P. (1980). Impressions of personality in the employment interview. *Journal of Personality and Social Psychology, 39,* 294–298.

Kamouri, A. L., & Balzer, W. K. (1990). The effects of performance sampling methods on frequency estimation, probability estimation and evaluation of performance information.

Organizational Behavior and Human Decision Processes, 45, 285–316.

Kelly, G. A. (1955). *The psychology of personnel constraints.* New York: Norton.

Kenny, D. A., & Albright, L. (1987). Accuracy in interpersonal perception: A social relations analysis. *Psychology Bulletin, 102,* 390–402.

Klimoski, R. J., & Brickner, M. (1987). Why do assessment centers work? Puzzle of assessment center validity. *Personnel Psychology, 40,* 243–260.

Klimoski, R. J., & Strickland, W. J. (1977). Assessment centers — valid or merely prescient? *Personnel Psychology, 30,* 353–361.

Landy, F. (1976). The validity of the interview in police officer selection. *Journal of Applied Psychology, 61,* 193–198.

Latham, G. P., & Saari, L. M. (1984). Do people do what they say? Further studies on the structured interview. *Journal of Applied Psychology, 69,* 569–573.

Latham, G. P., Saari, L. M., Pursell, E. D., & Campion, M. A. (1980). The situational interview. *Journal of Applied Psychology, 65,* 422–427.

Lewin, K. (1945). The research center for group dynamics at Massachusetts Institute of Technology. *Sociometry, 8,* 126–135.

London, H., & Exner, J. (Eds.). (1978). *Dimensions of personality.* New York: Wiley.

Lord, R. L. (1985). Accuracy in behavioral measurement: An alternative definition based on raters' cognitive schema and signal detection theory. *Journal of Applied Psychology, 70,* 66–71.

Mancuso, J. C., & Adams-Webber, J. (1982). *The construing person.* New York: Praeger.

Miner, J. B. (1978). Twenty years of research on role motivation theory of managerial effectiveness. *Personnel Psychology, 31,* 739–760.

Mitchell, T. R. (1985). An evaluation of the validity of correlational research conducted in organizations. *Academy of Management Review, 10,* 192–205.

Mitchell, T. R., & Klimoski, R. J. (1982). Is it rational to be empirical: A test of methods for scoring biodata. *Journal of Applied Psychology, 67,* 411–418.

Mumford, M. D., Stokes, G. S., & Owens, W. A. (in press). *Patterns of life adaptation: The ecology of human individuality.* Hillsdale, NJ: Erlbaum.

Neiner, A. G., & Owens, W. A. (1985). Using biodata to predict job choice among college students. *Journal of Applied Psychology, 70*(1), 127–136.

Osigweh, C.A.B. (1989). Concept fallibility in organizational science. *Academy of Management Review, 14,* 579–594.

Owens, W. A. (1971). A quasi-actuarial basis for individual assessment. *American Psychologist, 26,* 974–991.

Owens, W. A. (1976). Background data. In M. D. Dunnette (Ed.), *Handbook of industrial and organizational psychology.* Skokie, IL: Rand McNally.

Parsons, C. K., & Liden, R. C. (1984). Interviewer perceptions of applicant qualifications: A multivariate field study of demographic characteristics and non-verbal cues. *Journal of Applied Psychology, 69,* 557–568.

Pervin, L. A. (1989). Persons, situations, interactions: The history of a controversy and a discussion of a theoretical model. *Academy of Management Review, 4,* 350–360.

Peterson, N. G., Hough, L. M., Dunnette, M. D., Rosse, R. L., Houston, J. S., Toquam, J. L., & Wing, H. (1990). Project A: Specification of the predictor domain and development of new selection and classification tests. *Personnel Psychology, 43,* 247–276.

Pulakos, E., Borman, W. C., & Hough, L. M. (1988). Test validation for scientific understanding: Two demonstrations of an approach to strategy predictor-category linkages. *Personnel Psychology, 41,* 703–716.

Raza, S. M., & Carpenter, B. N. (1987). A model of hiring decisions in real employment interviews. *Journal of Applied Psychology, 72,* 596–603.

Reilly, R. R., & Chao, G. T. (1982). Validity and fairness of some alternative employee selection procedures. *Personnel Psychology, 35,* 1–62.

Reilly, R. R., Henry, S., & Smither, J. W. (1990). An examination of the effects of using behavior checklists on the construct validity of assessment center dimensions. *Personnel Psychology, 43,* 71–84.

Robinson, J. P., & Shaver, P. R. (Eds.). (1973). *Measures of social psychological attitudes.* Ann Arbor, MI: Institute for Social Research.

Rothstein, H. R., Schmidt, F. L., Erwin, F. W., Owens, W. A., & Sparks, C. P. (1990). Biographical data in employment selection: Can validities be made generalizable? *Journal of Applied Psychology, 75,* 175–184.

Rothstein, M., & Jackson, D. N. (1980). Decision making in the interview: An experimental approach. *Journal of Applied Psychology, 65,* 271–283.

Runkle, P. J., & McGrath, J. E. (1972). *Research on human behavior: A systematic guide to methods.* Troy, MO: Holt, Rinehart & Winston.

Ryan, A. M., & Sackett, P. R. (1987). A survey of individual assessment practices by I/O psychologists. *Personnel Psychology, 40,* 455–588.

Sackett, P. R. (1987). Assessment centers and content validity: Some neglected issues. *Personnel Psychology, 40,* 13–25.

Sackett, P. R., & Hakel, M. D. (1979). Temporal stability and individual differences in using assessment information to form overall ratings. *Organizational Behavior and Human Decision Process, 23,* 120–137.

Sackett, P. R., & Harris, M. M. (1989). Honesty testing for personnel selection: A review and critique. *Personnel Psychology, 37,* 221–245.

Schmitt, N. (1977). Interrater agreement on dimensionality and combination of assessment center judgments. *Journal of Applied Psychology, 62,* 171–176.

Schmitt, N., Gooding, R. Z., Noe, R. A., & Kirsch, M. (1984). Meta-analysis of validity studies published between 1964–1982 and an investigation of study characteristics. *Personnel Psychology, 37,* 407–422.

Schmitt, N., & Klimoski, R. J. (1991). *Research methods in human resources management.* Cincinnati, OH: South-Western.

Schmitt, N., Schneider, J. R., & Cohen, S. A. (1990). Factors affecting the validity of a regionally administered assessment center. *Personnel Psychology, 43,* 1–12.

Schneider, B., & Schmitt, N. (1986). *Staffing organizations* (2nd ed.). Glenview, IL: Scott, Foresman.

Schoenfeldt, L. F. (1974). Utilization of manpower: Development and evaluation of an assessment classification model with jobs. *Journal of Applied Psychology, 59,* 583–595.

Seiss, T. F., & Jackson, D. N. (1970). Vocational interests and personality: An empirical integration. *Journal of Counseling Psychology, 17,* 27–35.

Shaffer, G. S., Sanders, V., & Owens, W. A. (1986). Additional evidence for the accuracy of biographical data: Long term retest and observer ratings. *Personnel Psychology, 39,* 791–809.

Shore, T. H., Thornton, G. C., III, & Shore, L. M. (1990). Construct validity of two categories of assessment center ratings. *Personnel Psychology, 43,* 101–116.

Snyder, M., & Ickes, W. (1985). Personality and social behavior. In G. Lindzey & E. Aronson (Eds.), *Handbook of social psychology* (3rd ed.). New York: Random House.

Tiffin, J., & McCormick, E. J. (1965). *Industrial psychology* (5th ed.). Englewood Cliffs, NJ: Prentice-Hall.

Webster, E. C. (1962). *Decision making in the employment interview.* Montreal: Industrial Relations Center, McGill University.

Weick, K. E. (1989). Theory construction as disciplined imagination. *Academy of Management Review, 14,* 516–531.

Wiesner, W. H., & Cronshaw, S. (1988). A meta-analytic investigation of the impact of interview format and degree of structure on the validity of the employment interview. *Journal of Occupational Psychology, 61,* 275–290.

Zedeck, S. (1986). A process analysis of the assessment center method. In B. M. Staw & L. L. Cummings (Eds.), *Research in organizational behavior* (Vol. 12). Greenwich, CT: JAI Press.

5

Cognitive and Behavioral Processes in the Selection Interview

Robert L. Dipboye, Barbara B. Gaugler

Given the choice between an unscored, highly subjective selection interview and the best psychometric instruments that psychological research and theory have to offer, most employers would choose the interview. Like a favorite old pair of shoes, the interview is familiar and comfortable. Interviews were used to select employees long before psychologists introduced ability tests, assessment centers, personality inventories, biographical data, and other objective methods and are likely to remain the dominant method of selection. Not only do interviews fulfill important functions (for example, recruiting) that more quantitative methods cannot, but their ubiquitous use suggests that no other area of research has as much potential for improving selection in organizations. Rather than lamenting their existence, a better approach is to seek to understand and improve them. This chapter starts by reviewing the evidence that structured interviews are superior in their predictive validity to less structured procedures. To account for these differences, we examine surface features that distinguish structured interviews from unstructured ones and the cognitive and behavioral processes that possibly underlie these surface features. Finally, we discuss the alternative effects that prior impressions can have on mediating processes and the implications of these effects for the validity of the interviewer's judgments.

135

Do Selection Interviews Predict Job Performance?

Selection interviews usually are intended to predict the future job success of applicants. Consequently, criterion-related validation is a crucial strategy for evaluating interviewer judgments and decisions. The reviews of this literature conducted between 1949 and 1982 tended to be pessimistic (Reilly & Chao, 1982; Schmitt, 1976; Ulrich & Trumbo, 1965; Wagner, 1949). For instance, Reilly and Chao (1982) found that the average validity of the interview ($r = .19$) was much lower than the average validity of mental ability tests ($r = .45$), biographical data ($r = .35$), and peer evaluations ($r = .37$). However, these reviews were limited in at least two respects: they failed to comprehensively cover the unpublished as well as published validation research, and by relying on observed correlations without correcting for statistical artifacts, they likely overestimated the true variation in validities and underestimated the true mean validity of the interview.

Two recent meta-analyses provide a more comprehensive, quantitative review of interview validation research to overcome the limitations in previous qualitative reviews (McDaniel et al., 1987; Wiesner & Cronshaw, 1988). Wiesner and Cronshaw (1988) report an average corrected validity coefficient in predicting job performance criteria of .47, with structured interviews having significantly higher validity (corrected mean $r = .62$) than unstructured ones (corrected mean $r = .31$). McDaniel et al. (1987) reported similar findings, although the differences in validity between structured and unstructured interviews were smaller than those reported by Wiesner and Cronshaw. The conclusions reached in these meta-analyses are much more optimistic than those of previous reviews. Indeed, the level of criterion-related validity attained by structured interviews was comparable to that shown for mental ability tests, and even unstructured interviews appeared sufficiently valid to be useful in employee selection.

The results of these meta-analyses are encouraging, but they pose a dilemma similar to that facing the assessment center (Klimoski & Brickner, 1987). Interviews appear to work better than previously believed, but there is little understanding of why. Schuler (1989) aptly described the current state of ignorance when he asserted that "the employment interview does not exist" but instead is a "kind of cover that can be filled with different constructs, methods, and modes" (p. 344). For both practical and scientific reasons, research is needed that goes beyond criterion-related validity and examines processes in the form of the interviewer's information gathering, judgment, and decision making. The practical benefits of process research would come from addressing questions that continue to nag the application of interview procedures: what is interview "structure," and what essential features need to be incorporated when structuring an interview? What psychological constructs (such as social skills, motivation, or cognitive ability) should be the focus of interviews, and what behaviors and statements (such as statements about past performance or future intentions) need to be sampled in the interview session to assess these constructs? How can structured interviews achieve high levels of predictive validity without becoming simple oral tests that duplicate what could be accomplished with less costly paper-and-pencil instruments (Dipboye, 1989; Harris, 1989)? Once a procedure is designed that is shown to be valid, what should be done to maintain its validity? Progress will be made in answering these and other practical questions only if attention is given to what goes on in the interview as well as to the predictive validity of interviewer judgments. There is also value in studying interview processes solely for the sake of understanding, apart from any practical payoffs that may result from this research. The widespread use of the interview is evidence of its unique position among selection procedures. The interview is not just another selection procedure; it is an organizational phenomenon, and as such deserves the same attention from researchers that would be given to any interesting behavioral event. Moreover, inquisitiveness should lead to research on all types of interviews, including those that are unstructured and unscored.

At the same time that we advocate more attention to process, we do not mean to imply that validity and other practical outcomes should be ignored. To the contrary, future research should avoid the tendency to focus rather narrowly on individual aspects of the interview to the neglect of the entire process. At one time interview studies consisted mostly of macroanalytic evaluations of interviews with little attention given to the underlying sources of the reliability and validity of interviewer judgments. The microanalytic investigations initiated by Webster (1982) and his colleagues brought attention to social and cognitive processes but tended to ignore outcomes in the form of the validity of interviewer judgments. Both macroanalytic and microanalytic research has provided important insights, but future work should give more attention to the *interrelationships* of social processes involved in the interaction of interviewer and applicant, cognitive processes involved in the interviewer's judgment of the applicant, and the validity of the interviewer's final judgments.

In examining the interrelationships of process and outcomes, in the remainder of this chapter we build on a unitarian view of validity as opposed to the traditional separation of criterion, construct, and content validity (Binning & Barrett, 1989; Schneider & Schmitt, 1986). Evidence that higher prediction is obtained with interviews that are more structured provides a starting point for our analysis. Criterion-related evidence is only one type of data that can be used in evaluating interviews, however, and should be supplemented with process research. From this broader perspective, all validation is essentially construct validation and should be guided by an a priori explication of why interviews may succeed or fail in selecting applicants. Thus, we present in this chapter a model to help organize past research and to provide an agenda for future research.

What Are the Surface Features That Account for the Success of Structured Interviews?

A first step in examining the construct validity of interviews is to delineate the surface features that distinguish highly structured interviews from those less structured. This distinction is more complex than previous discussions of the interview would lead us to believe. For convenience we refer to structured and unstructured interviews in this chapter, but closer examination reveals that, contrary to the categorical definition used in the literature, "structure" is multidimensional and continuous in nature. Several features of structured interviews serve as potential sources of predictive validity. Next we describe how some interviews may succeed because of these characteristics, whereas others fail because they lack the same features.

- *Standardized questioning of the applicant.* This is the most salient feature of structured interviews, but wide variations still exist in how rigidly the various structured interview procedures require interviewers to adhere to the same line of questioning. The Highly Structured Interview (Campion, Pursell, & Brown, 1988) and the Situational Interview (Latham, 1989) are perhaps the most standardized and require all interviewers to ask the same questions without follow-ups and probes. The Patterned Behavior Description Interview (Janz, 1982) and the Selection Interview Blueprint of the Life Insurance and Research Association (Brown, 1979) allow follow-ups, whereas the Multimodal Employment Interview (Schuler, 1989) provides for a period of free questioning in addition to a list of standardized queries. In support of standardization, there is some evidence that interrater agreement is much higher when follow-up questions are not permitted than when interviewers are allowed to follow their own line of questioning (Schwab & Heneman, 1969). Yet, much of the practical advice on how to interview is based on the assumption that skill in asking follow-up questions is crucial to assessing applicant qualifications, and some theory in the area of social perception supports this contention (Argyle, 1969). How much and what type of follow-up questioning should be allowed have yet to be investigated.

- *Job analysis.* Although a standardized interview can be developed without a job analysis, most structured interviews base questions and evaluative procedures on systematic and thorough job analyses. For example, the Situational Interview, the Patterned Behavior Description Interview, the Highly Structured Interview, and the Multimodal Employment Interview all contain questions developed from job analysis and are tailored to the particular job. The results of Wiesner and Cronshaw's (1988) meta-analysis suggest that interviews based on a systematic job analysis are more valid than those that are not.

• *Information about job requirements.* Some structured interview procedures provide interviewers with common information about the knowledge, skills, and abilities required in the job. Job information can instill a common framework and thus improve the reliability and content validity of interview procedures. Providing interviewers with a complete set of job specifications can do much to eliminate bias and improve the reliability of their judgments (Langdale & Weitz, 1973; Wiener & Schneiderman, 1974).

• *Ancillary data.* Interviews differ to the extent that interviewers are allowed to use ancillary data. The typical unstructured interview provides interviewers with information on the applicant (for example, biographical data, test scores, reference letters) both before and after the interview. However, structured interviews frequently either prohibit interviewers from viewing paper credentials prior to the interview (Campion, Pursell, & Brown, 1988) or provide for a formal preview of application materials (Brown, 1979). There is some evidence that agreement among interviewers is higher when they do not preview the paper credentials of applicants (Dipboye, Fontenelle, & Garner, 1984). An implication of these findings is that previewing credentials also adversely affects the criterion-related validity of interviewer judgments, but so far there is no research directly testing this possibility.

• *Note-taking.* Structured interview procedures such as the Selection Interview Blueprint and the Patterned Behavior Description Interview recommend or require that interviewers take extensive notes during the interview session. Note-taking can lead to more accurate recall (Macan & Dipboye, 1986; Schuh, 1980) and serves as another potential source of higher predictive validities. Yet, a continuing concern that has received little attention in interview research is that note-taking can reduce rapport and interfere with information gathering.

• *Delayed evaluation of applicants.* Another difference between some structured interviews and unstructured procedures is the phase in the interview process at which applicants are evaluated. In some structured interviews, such as the Situational Interview and the Patterned Behavior Description Interview, interviewers are required to record applicants' responses during the session but do not evaluate their performance until the interview is finished. The failure to separate these two phases may introduce systematic biases in the interviewer's judgments and adversely influence information gathering (see Thornton & Byham, 1982, for a discussion related to assessment centers).

• *Well-defined rating scales.* Structured interviews often anchor the rating scales used by interviewers with behaviorally specific examples of what constitutes good, average, or poor answers on a dimension. At least two studies have shown that Behaviorally Anchored Rating Scales (BARS) can improve the reliability (Maas, 1965) and accuracy (Vance, Kuhnert, & Farr, 1978) of interviewer judgments relative to the traditional graphic rating scales so often found in less structured interviews.

• *Decomposed rating procedures.* Unstructured interviews usually require interviewers to make holistic judgments of applicant qualifications (for example, a single rating of hirability), whereas structured interviews often decompose the overall judgment of qualifications into component dimensions (for example, separate ratings of education, work experience, and social skill). There is some evidence that a decomposition strategy can yield higher-quality judgments than a holistic strategy (Einhorn, 1972), thus providing another explanation for the higher validities achieved in some structured procedures.

• *Mechanical combination of ratings.* After decomposing ratings into separate dimensions, structured interviews frequently combine these separate ratings using simple averaging. In contrast, some unstructured procedures require interviewers to arrive at an overall, global evaluation (for example, an evaluation of overall job qualifications) based on idiosyncratic, clinical combinations of the information gathered about the applicant. Mechanical combination of ratings has been found to yield higher-quality judgments than differential weighting (Einhorn & Hogarth, 1975) and may be a source of the higher validities of structured procedures (Campion, Pursell, & Brown, 1988; Harris, 1989; Maurer & Fay, 1988).

• *Multiple interviewers.* In cases where the structured interview is conducted by a panel (for an example see Campion, Pursell, & Brown, 1988), the participation of multiple interviewers offers another possible explanation for the high level of validity. Note, however, that Wiesner and Cronshaw (1988) found no difference in validity between structured panel interviews and structured individual interviews. Unfortunately, they compared only a few studies, and the results may well have been confounded by other factors, such as whether the interviews were based on job analysis, were conducted for purposes of research, or contained structured rating scales.

• *Trained interviewers.* Comprehensive interviewer training programs frequently accompany the introduction of structured interviews and offer another source of their superior reliability and validity (Latham, Saari, Pursell, & Campion, 1980). The research evaluating the effects of interviewer training has yielded generally positive results (Dougherty, Ebert, & Callender, 1986; Maurer & Fay, 1988; Vance, Kuhnert, & Farr, 1978). There is no empirical evidence, however, regarding the relative efficacy of training interviewers in how to gather information versus how to rate and evaluate applicants.

• *Needed research.* In summary, the prototypical aspect of structured interviews is the standardized questioning and evaluation procedures, whereas the hallmark of unstructured interviews is the freedom of interviewers to pursue their own line of questioning and to base their evaluations on whatever they deem reasonable. It is impossible to conclude, however, that only standardization is responsible for the success of structured interviews, given the other factors that invariably confound comparisons of different types of structured interviews. As has been shown above, structured interview systems contain a surprising variety of other features (see also Campion, Pursell, & Brown, 1988; Harris, 1989; Mauer & Fay, 1988). Differences in these surface features may account for the large variation in predictive validities that have been found for structured interviews (Wiesner & Cronshaw, 1988).

To understand why structured interviews succeed where others fail, research is needed in which two or more of these surface features are varied independently and the consequences for reliability and validity are observed. This research could show that standardized questioning and evaluation alone are insufficient and that achieving a high level of validity requires the inclusion of a variety of features (for example, job analysis, training, effective use of ancillary data, multiple interviewers). It is also possible that this research could show that including only a few of these features is sufficient to achieve substantial validity, and that developing effective interview procedures requires less effort and cost than existing structured procedures.

Cognitive and Behavioral Processes in the Interview

An examination of the effects of the various surface features of interviews helps show why interviewers succeed or fail in predicting criteria, but a comprehensive understanding of interview validity and reliability requires a deeper examination of the cognitive and behavioral processes underlying interviewer judgments. The contribution of previous interview research has been limited by the fragmented nature of the investigations on this topic. Several reviewers have called for a more integrated approach (Arvey & Campion, 1982; Dipboye & Macan, 1988; Schmitt, 1976) incorporating social process, information processing, and outcomes of the interview into one framework. The framework presented in Figure 5.1 builds on these suggestions in explaining how behavioral and cognitive events unfold in the interview.

At the beginning of the process, information is available about the applicant (for example, test scores, the application, references) and the job (such as formal specifications of the knowledge, skills, abilities, and personal characteristics required for successful performance). Interviewers attempt to simplify their task by relying on knowledge structures to form cognitive representations of the applicant and the job. As more information about the applicant is obtained, interviewers either stick to their initial categorizations or shift their attention to specific individuating information about the applicant (Fiske & Neuberg, 1990). Interviewers judge the applicant throughout the

Figure 5.1. Interviewer Information Processing and Decision Making.

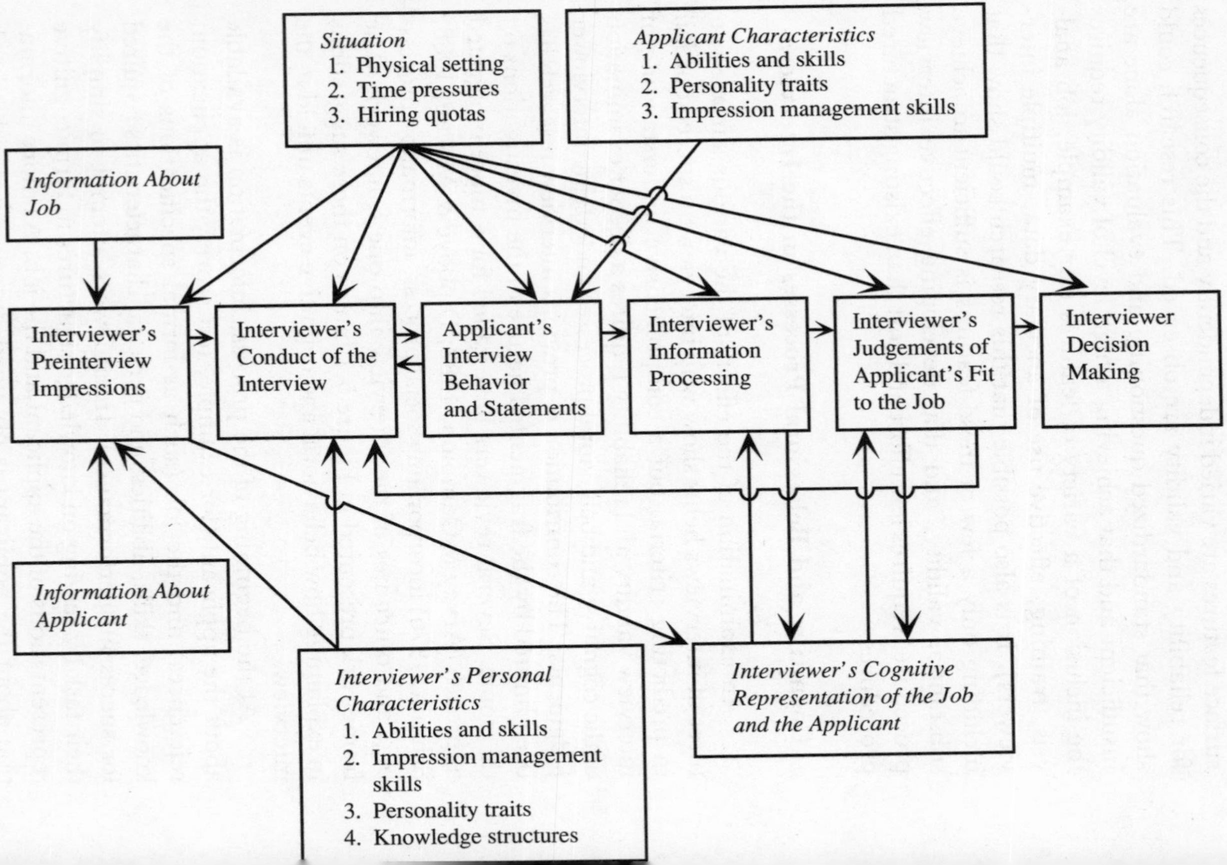

interview, but their first impressions are often formed prior to the actual interview from the information available. Even in the absence of information about a specific applicant, interviewers may have a predisposition to evaluate positively or negatively as the result of such factors as information about the applicant pool (Macan & Dipboye, 1990) or the affectivity of the interviewer (Brief, Burke, George, Robinson, & Webster, 1988). The preinterview impressions, along with situational factors and personal characteristics of the interviewer, influence how the interviewer conducts the session.

How the applicant presents his or her qualifications during the interview session is subject to three primary factors: how the interviewer conducts the interview, the situation, and the applicant's characteristics. Information made available during the interview is subsequently encoded, retrieved, and integrated by the interviewer to judge the applicant's fit to the job. This sequence—interview conduct, applicant performance, information processing, and judgment of fit—is repeated throughout the interview session and terminates with a final postinterview judgment of the applicant's fit to the job. Eventually the interviewer decides to hire, reject, or gather more information about the applicant. As indicated in the model, the interviewer's final judgment of the applicant's fit to the job is usually important in this decision, but situational factors such as the physical setting, time pressures, and hiring quotas also play a role. For example, where there are many positions to be filled and few applicants, the interviewer's final judgment is less likely to affect the employment decision than in a labor market where many applicants are competing for relatively few positions.

A logical hypothesis that can be derived from this framework is that structured interviews have higher criterion-related validity because interviewer judgments are better measures of applicant characteristics that are predictive of job performance (for example, personality traits or mental ability). The multitrait-multimethod (MTMM) approach (Campbell & Fiske, 1959) offers a strategy that could be used to evaluate this possibility, which would require that the same constructs (for example, personality traits, abilities) be measured with multiple selection procedures (for example, structured interview, unstructured interview, paper-and-pencil tests, situational exercises). Comprehensive MTMM assessments of interviewer judgments have not appeared in the literature, but several studies have examined the convergence between interviewer judgments of applicant qualifications and mental ability tests, objectively scored application materials, or personality test scores (James, Campbell, & Lovegrove, 1984; Kinicki & Lockwood, 1985; McDaniel et al., 1987). The correlations are typically quite low, usually in the vicinity of $r = .20$ or lower. These unimpressive results may reflect the fact that most of this research has involved unstructured interviews. Evidence that structured procedures show stronger convergent validity was provided in two recent studies. Schuler (1989) used a structured procedure that emphasized personality attributes and found that interviewer evaluations of the applicants were strongly related to applicants' scores on extroversion ($r = .49$), inhibition ($r = -.42$), social competence ($r = .56$), dominance ($r = .52$), and self-acceptance ($r = .40$). Consistent with the emphasis on personality, a lower correlation was found with applicant scores on mental ability ($r = .23$). Using a structured procedure that focused on knowledge, skills, and abilities, Campion, Pursell, and Brown (1988) found high correlations between interviewer judgments and scores on tests of mathematical aptitude ($r = .40$), mechanical aptitude ($r = .70$), following oral instructions ($r = .52$), and reading standard scales ($r = .66$).

Why may structured interviews measure job-relevant characteristics of the applicant better than unstructured ones? We propose six outcomes of the interview process, derived from the model in Figure 5.1, as potential explanations. Four of these outcomes follow from the conduct of the session and raise the possibility that structured interviews are predictive because they obtain job-related samples of applicant behavior. A fifth outcome pertains to how the interviewer processes information and leads to the hypothesis that interviewers using structured procedures are more accurate and less biased. A sixth outcome is that individual interviewers differ in their conduct of the interview and in processing information, and consequently differ in the validity of their judgments. Structured procedures may improve validity through reducing these differences and thereby improving reliability of interviewer judgments.

Can Sampling of Applicant Behavior Account for the Effects of Structure on Prediction?

The linkage in Figure 5.1 between the interviewer's conduct of the interview and the applicant's statements and behavior can be described as a process of information sampling on the part of the interviewer (Motowidlo, 1986). From this perspective, the superior predictive validity of the structured interview is the consequence of the interviewer's obtaining samples of information that are representative of all the job-related information that might have been learned about the applicant during the interview. What the applicant does and says supposedly provides the information that determines the interviewer's success or failure in predicting future performance. An examination of the interview process in Figure 5.1 suggests four possible outcomes of this sampling process.

Outcome 1: What they say is what you get. Interviews contain samples of applicants' statements of what they intend to do in the future or have done in the past. In structured interviews, statements are sampled that are good indicators of what the applicants will do in the future. For example, the Situational Interview (Latham, 1989) is based on the theory that intentions and goals are the best predictors of future job performance. Questions are intended to present crucial situations, and the statements made by applicants are taken at face value — the assumption is that what the applicant intends to do is indeed what the applicant will do. Similarly, the Patterned Behavior Description Interview (Janz, 1982) samples past behavior on the theory that it is the best predictor of future behavior. Again, applicant statements of past behavior are taken at face value on the assumption that they are honest and relatively free of social desirability biases. In contrast, unstructured interviews fail because they do not sample the statements that are valid indicators of future behavior.

The Situational Interview and the Patterned Behavior Description Interview both achieve respectable levels of prediction, but there is no direct evidence to support the theories underlying these procedures (Latham, 1989). To provide this evidence, applicants' statements of past behavior or future intentions should be validated against specific observations of behavior on the job. If applicants say they would cooperate with other employees in attempting to accomplish job objectives, then this intention could be validated by determining if in fact there was specific evidence of cooperative behavior on the job. Likewise, if applicants in the Patterned Behavior Description Interview are asked how they have dealt with specific situations in the past, then research could be conducted to assess whether these accounts are actually predictive of similar behaviors on the job.

Outcome 2: What they do is what you get. Apart from what they say they have done or will do, applicants also exhibit a variety of verbal and nonverbal behaviors in the interview session that can reflect important job-related constructs. Thus, poor eye contact and a halting tone of voice on the part of a sales applicant could indicate a lack of the social skills needed for the job. From this perspective, structured interviews are more predictive than unstructured ones because they elicit interview behaviors from the applicant that reveal personal characteristics (see Figure 5.1) related to future job performance.

Structured interviews such as the Situational Interview treat interview behaviors as extraneous and rely instead on the content of what is said (outcome 1). Examples of structured interviews that do provide evaluation of interview behavior are those in which the applicant must perform a work sample in the session (such as being asked by the interviewer to "sell me this pencil"). Another exception is the Multimodal Employment Interview (Schuler, 1989), which provides for periods of free conversation in which the applicant can be observed and evaluated. Even where no provision is made for evaluating interview behavior, however, the verbal and nonverbal behaviors accompanying applicants' answers to questions seem likely to influence interviewers' judgments (Forbes & Jackson, 1980). Again, the research needed to assess whether structured interviews succeed because they sample applicant behavior in the interview session has not yet been conducted. To fully evaluate this hypothesis would require that applicant behaviors in the session be recorded and then coded by observers other than the interviewer. The relationships of these coded verbal and nonverbal behaviors to job criteria could then be examined to determine the extent to which the interview samples behaviors that contribute to prediction. For example, a determination could be made of whether eye contact, posture, and facility in the use of language are actually related to social skills exhibited in the job.

Outcome 3: What you get is what they want you to see. Another possibility is that applicants' behavior in an interview consists largely of impression management and reflects more the ability of applicants to project positive impressions than the ability to perform the job (Baron, 1989). Structured interviews may discourage impression management to a greater degree than unstructured ones and thereby provide a more valid basis for prediction. In highly structured interviews, the opportunities for applicants to manipulate and shape the interviewer's impressions in a favorable direction are limited by the standardization of questioning. Discussion is focused on those topics deemed important from the job analysis, and digression is discouraged so that all designated topics can be adequately covered during the time allowed.

The assumption underlying this hypothesis is that impression management is most often a source of error in interviewer judgments. However, it is important to acknowledge that there are jobs for which an applicant's skill in managing impressions is criterion-related. For instance, determining what will positively impress other persons in a situation and then successfully projecting that image are skills that would seem crucial to success in many jobs requiring intense interpersonal interaction (for example, sales and management). One reason that some interview procedures succeed may be that they are able to capture the impression management skills important for successful performance on the job. Research is needed that assesses the extent to which structured and unstructured interviews are vulnerable to faking and that identifies the circumstances in which impression management contributes to and detracts from criterion-related validity.

Outcome 4: What you get is the product of what you have done. Ideally, interviewers attempt to create a communication climate in which applicants disclose information about themselves without being biased by the interviewer's conduct of the session. Contrary to this ideal, the way interviewers conduct interviews can be biased by their impressions of the applicant, and the interviewer's conduct can subsequently influence the applicant's behavior (Dipboye, 1982; Dipboye & Macan, 1988; Dougherty, Turban, & Callender, 1992). For example, interviewer impressions of an applicant can be self-fulfilling in that subsequent conduct of the interview evokes applicant behavior consistent with the interviewer's impressions. In these cases, what the applicant says or does reflects the interviewer's conduct of the interview rather than the applicant's intentions or personal characteristics. A source of the higher validity in structured versus unstructured interviews is their greater success in removing interviewer behavior as a cause of variance in applicant behavior.

Although self-fulfilling prophecies are another possible cause of the lower validities of unstructured interviews, it is important to recognize that the occurrence of a self-fulfilling prophecy does not necessarily mean that the interviewer's judgment is totally erroneous. Indeed, if preinterview impressions are based on information that is a valid source of prediction (for example, mental ability test scores), then these impressions can lead to valid predictions even though they bias applicant behavior. In these cases self-fulfilling prophecies may not be as much a threat to validity as to incremental validity, that is, the usefulness of the interview in increasing prediction beyond the level achieved with ability tests and other sources of preinterview impressions (Dipboye, 1989). Again, research is needed to understand how self-fulfilling prophecies may lessen the ability of the interview to contribute unique information to the prediction of job criteria.

Can Information Processing Account for Effects of Interview Structure on Prediction?

To successfully predict an applicant's performance in the job, interviewers must obtain adequate samples of behavior and statements that are related to job criteria. That is not enough, however. As shown in Figure 5.1, interviewers also must process information made available in the session, judge the applicant's fit to the job, and then render some final decision. This brings us to a fifth potential outcome of the process.

Outcome 5: What you see is not what you get. Interviewers using less structured interview formats may be more likely to rely on broad categories representing what it takes to be successful in the job or what the applicant is like, to the neglect of specific information about the job and the applicant. A possible reason for the success of more highly structured interviews, on the other hand, is that interviewers attend to diagnostic information about the applicant and are more accurate in mapping judgments onto underlying attributes. There is evidence for a variety of biases in information processing and judgment that may account for the poorer prediction of unstructured interviews. This includes biases in causal attributions, inaccurate retrieval of information, rating effects (for example, halo, leniency, negativity), and the influence of irrelevant characteristics of the applicant (for example, sex and race).

In asking applicants about activities, events, and performances in their past and observing their behavior in the interview itself, interviewers assess the causes of applicants' behavior and achievements. They must determine whether the applicant's behavior in the interview (for instance, nervousness) was caused by situational factors, such as the interviewer's own behavior, or originated from personal characteristics. If attributable to the applicant, the interviewer further determines whether the behavior reflects a temporary state that is unlikely to be repeated or a stable trait likely to influence future performance on the job. Similarly, interviewers must assess whether events reported by the applicant in the interview (such as problems in a previous job) were the outcomes of situational factors or stable attributes of the applicant. A possible reason for the greater validity of structured interviews is that they allow for more accurate attributional analyses by removing the influence of the interviewer on the applicant and by focusing the interviewer's attention on job-related characteristics of the applicant.

Interviewers are vulnerable to a variety of attributional biases in their attempts to explain applicants' behavior (Herriot,

1989). As indicated earlier, an applicant's behavior in the interview is influenced by the interviewer's conduct of the session; but research on attributional biases suggests that interviewers fail to take into account the influence of their own actions and instead see the traits of the applicant as the primary cause of the applicant's behavior. Interviewers also have been shown to attribute applicant behavior that violates their expectancies to external or unstable factors and behavior that confirms their expectancies to stable traits (Phillips & Dipboye, 1989; Tucker & Rowe, 1979).

In addition to being vulnerable to biases in causal attributions, interviews may also suffer from biases in the recall of information gathered from the interviewee. Given the large amount of information interviewers typically must retrieve, it is not surprising that they are subject to considerable error in recalling information from an interview (Carlson, Thayer, Mayfield, & Peterson, 1971). The basic research and theory in social cognition suggest that much of the error in interviewer memory stems from the cognitive representations that interviewers form of the applicant and the influence of these representations on their encoding and retrieval of information (Wyer & Srull, 1989). According to schematic processing models, once interviewers form a representation of the applicant, they tend to forget information inconsistent with the representation while recalling information consistent with it (Wyer & Srull, 1989). A representation of the applicant can form around an explicit early judgment and subsequently bias recall of information from the interview (Dipboye, Stramler, & Fontenelle, 1984). Structured procedures may increase the accuracy of recall by providing for more accurate and differentiated cognitive representations of the applicant and the job. Also, procedures such as note-taking, guided questioning, and the use of multiple interviewers may improve recall by reducing reliance on global cognitive representations and focusing the interviewer's attention on individual items of information.

The research on interviewer judgment has demonstrated a variety of rating biases (Arvey & Campion, 1982; Schmitt, 1976), including negativity effects, in which greater weight is given to negative than to positive information, and context effects, in which the qualification level of other applicants influences evaluations of the target applicant. The most common context effect is contrast, in which the ratings of the target applicant are displaced away from the ratings of the other applicants. Thus, an applicant would receive more positive ratings than deserved when the other applicants were unqualified, but the same applicant would receive less positive ratings than deserved when the other applicants were highly qualified. Other rating effects are primacy, in which the first information presented affects subsequent judgments more than information presented later, and halo, in which interviewers fail to differentiate among various dimensions of the applicant's performance in the interview. Halo is perhaps the most pervasive of these biases and poses the greatest threat to the construct validity of interviewer judgments. Possibly indicating halo bias, a general performance factor is frequently found in factor analyses of interviewer evaluations of applicants (Dipboye, Gaugler, & Hayes, 1990; Hakel, 1971; Kinicki & Lockwood, 1985; Kinicki, Lockwood, Hom, & Griffeth, 1990; Liden & Parsons, 1986; Rynes & Gerhart, 1990). Similarly, research on assessment center ratings has failed to show strong support for their construct validity and has consistently found that dimension ratings are dominated by a single general factor (Klimoski & Brickner, 1987).

Another way in which structured interviews can improve information processing and consequently yield more valid predictions is by reducing the influence of irrelevant applicant characteristics. A variety of irrelevant factors have been shown to influence interviewer judgments, including applicant gender (Hitt & Barr, 1989), race (Parsons & Liden, 1984), physical disability (Johnson & Heal, 1976), and age (Avolio & Barrett, 1987). The findings from research conducted on these demographic biases appear mixed and generally inconclusive, however. The evidence regarding the effects on interviewer judgments of applicant attractiveness and similarity to the interviewer is somewhat clearer. Interviewers appear to evaluate a physically attractive applicant more positively (Hayes, Macan, & Speroff, 1992; Stone, Stone, & Dipboye, 1992). There is evidence that an interviewer evaluates an applicant's qualifications more positively the more similar the opinions and other characteristics of applicant and interviewer (Graves & Powell, 1988; Orpen, 1984) and the more the interviewer personally likes the applicant (Graves & Powell, 1988; Keenan, 1977; Raza & Carpenter, 1987).

Reviewing the various biases that occur in evaluating applicants shows that the judgments of interviewers in less structured interviews are subject to a variety of factors other than the attributes presumed to underlie applicant behaviors and statements. All these biases can be interpreted as evidence of categorical information processing, in which interviewers rely on broad cognitive categories (such as stereotypes of the ideal employee) in attempting to process information and form judgments. There are at least two reasons why interviewers may rely on categories in rendering judgments of applicants in unstructured interviews: in the attempt to distinguish signal from noise and make sense of the large amount of information about applicants, interviewers rely more on ill-defined and diffuse cognitive structures, such as prototypes of the ideal applicant. Also, postinterview judgments from an unstructured procedure are accompanied by stronger affect, which in turn leads to broader and less complex categorizations (Baron, 1989). Whether categorization is less likely to occur in structured interviews is speculation on our part, because most of the research in which the above biases have been demonstrated has used unstructured interview procedures. Another direction for research, then, is to compare structured and unstructured interview formats on the degree of bias that occurs in interviewers' information processing and judgment.

Can Interviewer Differences Account for the Effects of Interview Structure on Prediction?

An implication of the model depicted in Figure 5.1 is that interviewers take different approaches to interviews and these differences influence how they conduct the interview and process information. Structuring the interview achieves better prediction as a consequence of reducing these individual differences, whereas unstructured interviews suffer from unreliability of judgments by allowing these differences to influence information gathering and processing. This leads us to a sixth possible outcome of the interview process.

Outcome 6: What you see is not what I see. The few studies that have examined the issue show large differences among interviewers in the predictive validity of their judgments (Dipboye, Gaugler, & Hayes, 1990; Dougherty, Ebert, & Callender, 1986; Kinicki, Lockwood, Hom, & Griffeth, 1990). Moreover, aggregating the judgments of different interviewers and ignoring these differences can lead to an underestimation of the true validity of an interview procedure (Dreher, Ash, & Hancock, 1988). For example, Dipboye, Gaugler, and Hayes (1990) examined differences in the validity of judgments made by five interviewers who used unstructured procedures to evaluate 446 applicants for corrections officer positions. With aggregated interviewer judgments, predictive validity ranged from .07 (n.s.) to .12 ($p < .05$) in the prediction of job success and two dimensions of training success. Examination of the predictive validity of judgments made by individual interviewers, however, showed wide variation. Two interviewers had mean-corrected validities of .44 ($p < .05$) and .29 ($p < .05$), respectively, in predicting job performance. In comparison, the obtained and corrected validities for the other three interviewers ranged from .02 to .09.

The model of interviewer judgments presented in Figure 5.1 suggests that individual differences in interviewer validity may originate from differences in how information is gathered and processed. These variations in process, in turn, may result from differences among interviewers in their ability, experience, and other personal characteristics. Research has shown that interviewers differ considerably in the weight they place on various factors when evaluating applicants (Dipboye, Gaugler, & Hayes, 1990; Dougherty, Ebert, & Callender, 1986; Kinicki, Lockwood, Hom, & Griffeth, 1990; Valenzi & Andrews, 1973). We are aware of no research, however, that has examined whether interviewers with high validity conduct interviews or process information differently from those with lower validity or whether differences in the complexity of the knowledge structures of interviewers underlie differences in information processing and gathering.

A logical prediction is that differences among interviewers in validity and in interview processes are reduced to the extent that the interview is structured. Again, an MTMM framework is a possible strategy for exploring this aspect of construct validity.

One possible MTMM approach is to use the individual interviewer and the type of interview (for example, structured versus unstructured) as the bases for classifying methods. The dimensions on which applicants are evaluated could be the "traits" cutting across individual interviewer and interview method. Such a design would allow comparison of the variations among interviewers as a function of both interview type and evaluative dimension.

Although standardization should improve validity by reducing differences among interviewers, one wonders whether the standardization is maintained over time. Structured interviews may be a welcome relief for interviewers who dislike interviewing and for whom interviewing is an unwanted burden. The same procedures could be seen as a significant source of boredom or loss of power by interviewers who like to interview, who are firmly convinced of their ability to judge others, and who consider interviewing an important part of their position. Indeed, highly structured interviewing programs have been observed to degrade into less structured programs (Latham & Saari, 1984), and a possible reason for this degradation is that interviewers attempt to enrich their activities through adding a "personal touch." We suspect that there is less variation among interviewers in validity and in the interview process shortly after implementation of a structured procedure but that variation increases over time. Such findings would suggest that it is not enough to structure the interview and that efforts must be made to ensure interviewers' continued acceptance and of commitment to the interviewing procedures.

Alternative Effects of Prior
Impressions on the Interview Process

So far we have explored several aspects of the model presented in Figure 5.1: how gathering information, processing that
information, and individual differences among interviewers may
account for the successes and failures of selection interviews.
Another important feature of the model is that gathering and
processing information follow from prior impressions that the
interviewer forms about the applicant. As noted by Motowidlo
(1986), "People do not observe information about a job applicant all at once. Instead, they pick up bits of information se-
quentially over the course of the interview. The way information bits are distributed in this temporal stream, especially in
the early portions of the stream, can have important effects on
the interviewer's judgments and decisions" (pp. 7–8). This brings
us to a process issue that seems crucial to understanding the
interview—the nature of the linkage between the impressions
interviewers form in the early period of the interview and how
they subsequently conduct the interview, process information,
and make judgments.

A productive approach to understanding this linkage is to
adopt a strong-inference strategy (Platt, 1964), in which alternative, competing hypotheses are set forth and research is then
conducted to identify the boundaries of each. We focus here on
three alternative linkages. Interviews can be guided by a confirmatory process in which the interviewer attempts to maintain consistency with an initial categorization of the applicant.
Another possibility is a diagnostic process in which the interviewer seeks information that will help test prior impressions.
A third possibility is a disconfirmatory process in which the interviewer forms an initial impression and then focuses on information that is inconsistent with that impression.

A confirmatory process may emerge because interviewers
cannot attend to all the detail potentially made available in the
interview and, as implied in Figure 5.1, resort to cognitive
representations of the applicant to some degree. Interviewers

guided by confirmatory processes begin with a preconception of the applicant, and the subsequent gathering and processing of information are driven by the attempt to support this preconception (Dipboye, 1982). Thus, if the interviewer had a prior impression of the applicant as highly extroverted, then the applicant might be asked, "What do you like most about working with large groups of people?" The applicant's answer is taken as evidence in support of the applicant's extroversion despite the fact that most applicants could not help but provide extroverted answers to such a leading question. The interviewer's causal attributions for the applicant's behavior further sustain initial impressions. If a behavior of the applicant violates initial impressions, it is attributed to factors external to the applicant, but a behavior consistent with initial impressions is seen as further proof that the initial impression was correct (Phillips & Dipboye, 1989; Tucker & Rowe, 1979). When the interviewer forms final judgments of the applicant's qualifications, recalling and interpreting information are biased in the direction of initial impressions. Thus, if initial impressions of the applicant are unfavorable, interviewers may be more likely to retrieve negative than positive information from the interview (Dipboye, Stramler, & Fontenelle, 1984). In the final judgment of the applicant, the interviewer evaluates the fit of the applicant to a prototype or exemplar. Items of information are weighted according to their consistency with the prior impression; those that are consistent with it influence the final judgment of fit more than those seen as inconsistent with it. When the similarity of the applicant to the prototype or exemplar reaches a certain threshold, then the applicant is categorized as qualified or unqualified. At this point, the interviewer uses schemata to infer other attributes that are consistent with the category.

In contrast, interviewers guided by diagnostic processes test their prior impressions rather than seek to confirm them. (Here we rely on Trope and Bassok's (1982) definition of a "diagnosing strategy" as one in which "to test the hypothesis that a target person belongs to one trait-category rather than to another, the information gatherer asks about features that maximally discriminate between the two categories" (p. 31). We

broaden their definition, however, to include not only information gathering but also information processing and judgment.)
Similar to the confirmatory process described above, interviewers
are likely to categorize applicants in their initial encounter; but
in contrast to confirmatory processes, interviewers attempt to
"scientifically" evaluate these categorizations. In gathering information, interviewers keep in mind alternative possibilities
and ask those questions that best differentiate between applicants who conform to initial impressions and those who do not.
Thus, these interviewers prefer open-ended and double-edged
questions and avoid closed-end questions that lead the applicant in a biased direction (Macan & Dipboye, 1988). Ideally,
the interview is conducted in such an evenhanded fashion that
all applicants have an equal opportunity to convey their qualifications and the interviewer has a minimal influence on their
responses. Interviewers' causal attributions of applicants comply
with a covariation model such as that of Kelley (1967): interviewers attribute behavior to particular factors only to the extent
that the factors are consistently and distinctively related to the
behavior. In recalling information about the applicant, interviewers remember items that clearly differentiate between levels of
qualifications. In judging the applicant's fit to the job, the interviewer examines information on an item-by-item basis, asssess-
ing the extent to which each item fits the interviewer's representation of the job requirements. Those items that are diagnostic
in differentiating between levels of qualifications are given greater
weight regardless of consistency with prior impressions.

Under other circumstances, disconfirmatory processes
dominate in the interview (Miller & Turnbull, 1986). In these
cases the interviewer again is guided by the degree of consistency
of information with prior impressions rather than by the diagnosticity of the information. Unlike in the confirmatory process,
however, the interviewer seeks and emphasizes information that
is inconsistent with prior impressions. As an example, imagine
an interviewer who has an initial impression of the applicant
as a highly extroverted person but then asks for information that
would disconfirm the initial impression (for example, "Have you
ever felt shy?"). Because most people would probably respond

in the same way ("yes"), the item is both inconsistent with the initial impression of extroversion and nondiagnostic in assessing this impression. Disconfirmatory processes are most likely to emerge when interviewers fear that they will be judged by others as biased against or in favor of particular applicants (Neuberg, 1989; Binning, Goldstein, Garcia, & Scattaregia, 1988). For example, an interviewer who is prejudiced against women applicants may attempt to compensate by being particularly lenient in questioning and evaluating them.

To further illustrate the three contrasting processes, consider an interviewer whose initial impression of an applicant for a sales position is that the applicant possesses the high degree of extroversion required for successful performance. Interviewers who are guided mainly by diagnostic processes would focus on information that distinguishes the highly extroverted applicant from those who are less extroverted. Interviewers who are primarily concerned with consistency would gather, process, and utilize information that is consistent with high extroversion (in the case of a confirmatory process) or inconsistent with high extroversion (in the case of a disconfirmatory process), regardless of the diagnosticity of the information in assessing the validity of the initial impression. We hypothesize that interviews achieving higher levels of criterion-related validity are characterized to a greater degree by diagnostic processes and to a lesser degree by confirmatory and disconfirmatory processes. Rather than consisting of only one of the three processes, however, the typical interview is likely to consist of a mixture, with the relative dominance of the processes determined by characteristics of the situation, the interviewer, and the applicant.

Few attempts have been made in research on selection interviews to determine the conditions under which each of the alternative processes is dominant, but previous research on social cognition suggests potentially important moderators (Dipboye, 1992). There is evidence that confirmatory processes are more likely where the hypotheses tested are one-sided (for example, "Is this applicant introverted?"), whereas diagnostic processes seem more likely where alternative hypotheses are tested ("Is this applicant introverted or extroverted?") (Kruglanski &

Mayseless, 1988). Other research shows that persons are more likely to use confirmatory processes when they do not think that their decisions will be reviewed for accuracy, whereas they may be more likely to use diagnostic processes when they are concerned about the accuracy of their judgments (Kruglanski & Mayseless, 1988; Neuberg, 1989). Confirmatory processes occur when there are situational pressures that commit interviewers to their prior impressions, whereas diagnostic processes occur when subjects feel free to revise their initial impressions (Schoorman, 1988). Finally, confirmatory processes seem more likely when individuals experience cognitive overload as the result of a large amount of complex information (Payne, 1976) or time pressures (Wright, 1974).

Several of the factors shown to support diagnostic processes seem more characteristic of highly structured interviews than less structured procedures. Structured interviews provide interviewers with a large amount of high-quality information about the job and the applicant while avoiding cognitive overload by restricting the questions that can be asked and using decomposed rating procedures (see Harris, 1989, p. 713, for a similar observation). Recognize, however, that highly structured interviews in which the questioning of applicants is completely standardized and probing is not allowed can take information gathering, information processing, and judgment out of the hands of the interviewer. Consequently, the alternative strategies may only explain differences in criterion-related validity where the interviews are unstructured or semistructured, not where the interviewer serves as a mere recorder of events.

In attempting to assess the boundary conditions of each process, interviewers' self-reports are of dubious validity given that most interviewers probably believe they follow a diagnosing strategy. To fully explore the conditions under which each of the above processes emerges requires objective measures of diagnosticity. One approach to measuring diagnosticity is to have judges rate the extent to which items or questions are diagnostic in differentiating among various levels of an attribute (Kruglanski & Mayseless, 1988). An even more objective approach is to examine the actual ability of items or questions to distinguish between criterion groups (Martin, 1987). Questions that are most diagnostic in assessing an attribute would be those that differentiate between applicants known to be low and high on the attribute. Although it seems possible to use these or other procedures in the field, a rigorous examination of the processes outlined here would require the control afforded by laboratory settings.

Conclusion

This chapter begins with a discussion of how recent meta-analyses have made a valuable contribution by providing quantitative evidence of the superior prediction of highly structured interviews compared to less structured interviews. A primary theme of the chapter is that research is needed to explore the process factors that underlie this difference in prediction.

While our call for more research on the behavioral and cognitive processes of different types of selection interviews may seem uncontroversial, it directly contradicts one of Wiesner and Cronshaw's (1988) major conclusions. On the basis of their meta-analysis finding that unstructured interviews have no situational specificity, that is, no meaningful variance in unstructured interviews remains after correcting for statistical artifacts, they call for a moratorium on research on the unstructured interview and on the interview process in general. We obviously disagree with this conclusion.

Meta-analytic procedures are both an art and a science, and judgments are required at many junctures that may influence the results and their implications (Gaugler, Rosenthal, Thornton, & Bentson, 1987). Several of the choices made by Wiesner and Cronshaw raise concerns as to the validity of their conclusion that unstructured interviews have no situational specificity. One concern is that their corrections for range restriction and criterion unreliability may have been based on unrepresentative samples of reliabilities and selection ratios. In making these corrections, researchers often rely on artificial distributions based on other research conducted on similar criteria.

Wiesner and Cronshaw chose an alternative strategy of correcting for the influence of statistical artifacts on validity distributions by constructing their own distributions of artifacts from reliability and range restriction data provided by the studies used in the meta-analysis. Unfortunately, only a few studies provided the data needed to perform the corrections, thus casting doubt on the accuracy of their corrections. Also, only those interviews that used some kind of rating instrument were selected for inclusion in the meta-analyses for the obvious reason that validity coefficients could only be computed when there were ratings. Consequently, the unstructured interviews on which their meta-analysis was based are probably more structured and more valid than those conducted in the workplace (see McDaniel et al., 1987 for a similar observation). Finally, even if one accepts the conclusion that no meaningful variance in the predictive validity of unstructured interviews remains after corrections for statistical artifacts are applied, research on unstructured interviews and potential moderators is still needed. As Sackett, Harris, and Orr (1986) argue, falsely concluding that variance remains after correcting for statistical artifacts and continuing to search for potential moderators of validity is a less serious error than falsely concluding the reverse and closing the door to research that may uncover moderators.

Research is needed on the behavioral and cognitive processes that are responsible for the differences observed in interviewer validities. The logical place to begin is by examining the surface features that are crucial to distinguishing between effective and ineffective interviews, followed by research probing the behavioral and cognitive processes underlying interviewer validity. To fully investigate these matters requires a variety of methods and settings. Moreover, understanding the interview process will require an investigation of both highly structured and less structured procedures. Knowing what does work requires some understanding of what does not work. If research shows that unstructured interviews cannot be significantly improved, scientific curiosity still should lead us to explore why they fail while more structured programs succeed.

164   **Personnel Selection in Organizations**

References

Argyle, M. (1969). *Social interaction.* Hawthorne, NY: Aldine.

Arvey, R. D., & Campion, J. E. (1982). The employment interview: A summary and review of recent research. *Personnel Psychology, 35,* 281–322.

Avolio, B. J., & Barrett, G. V. (1987). Effects of age stereotyping in a simulated interview. *Psychology and Aging, 2,* 56–63.

Baron, R. A. (1989). Impression management by applicants during employment interviews: The "too much of a good thing" effect. In R. W. Eder & G. R. Ferris (Eds.), *The employment interview: Theory, research and practice.* Newbury Park, CA: Sage.

Binning, J. F., & Barrett, G. V. (1989). Validity of personnel decisions: A conceptual analysis of the inferential and evidential bases. *Journal of Applied Psychology, 74,* 478–494.

Binning, J. F., Goldstein, M. A., Garcia, M. F., & Scattaregia, J. H. (1988). Effects of preinterview impressions on questioning strategies in same- and opposite-sex employment interviews. *Journal of Applied Psychology, 73,* 30–37.

Brief, A. P., Burke, M. J., George, J. M., Robinson, B., & Webster, J. (1988). Should negative affectivity remain an unmeasured variable in the study of job stress? *Journal of Applied Psychology, 73,* 193–198.

Brown, S. H. (1979, April). *The results of a fifteen year research program investigating the selection interview.* Paper presented at the meeting of the Eastern Psychological Association, Philadelphia.

Campbell, D. T., & Fiske, D. W. (1959). Convergent and discriminant validation by the multitrait-multimethod matrix. *Psychological Bulletin, 56,* 81–105.

Campion, M. A., Pursell, E. D., & Brown, B. K. (1988). Structured interviewing: Raising the psychometric properties of the employment interview. *Personnel Psychology, 41,* 25–42.

Carlson, R. E., Thayer, P. W., Mayfield, E. C., & Peterson, D. A. (1971). Improvements in the selection interview. *Personnel Journal, 50,* 268–275.

Dipboye, R. L. (1982). Self-fulfilling prophecies in the selection recruitment interview. *Academy of Management Review, 7,* 579–587.

Dipboye, R. L. (1989). Threats to the incremental validity of interviewer judgments. In R. W. Eder & G. R. Ferris (Eds.), *The employment interview: Theory, research, and practice.* Newbury Park, CA: Sage.

Dipboye, R. L. (1992). *Selection interviews: Process perspectives.* Cincinnati, OH: South-Western.

Dipboye, R. L., Fontenelle, G. A., & Garner, K. (1984). Effects of previewing the application on interview process and outcomes. *Journal of Applied Psychology, 69,* 118–128.

Dipboye, R. L., Gaugler, B., & Hayes, T. (1990, April). *Individual differences among interviewers in the incremental validity of their judgments.* Paper presented at the meeting of the Society for Industrial and Organizational Psychology, Miami, FL.

Dipboye, R. L., & Macan, T. (1988). A process view of the selection/recruitment interviews. In R. S. Schuler, S. A. Youngblood, & V. L. Huber (Eds.), *Readings in personnel and human resource management.* St. Paul, MN: West.

Dipboye, R. L., Stramler, C., & Fontenelle, G. A. (1984). The effects of the application on recall of information from the interview. *Academy of Management Journal, 27,* 561–575.

Dougherty, T. W., Ebert, R. J., & Callender, J. C. (1986). Policy capturing in the employment interview. *Journal of Applied Psychology, 71,* 9–15.

Dougherty, T. W., Turban, D. B., & Callender, J. C. (1992, May). *Expectancy confirmation behavior of employment interviewers.* Paper presented at the meeting of the Society for Industrial and Organizational Psychology, Montreal, Quebec.

Dreher, G. F., Ash, R. A., & Hancock, P. (1988). The role of traditional research design in underestimating the validity of the employment interview. *Personnel Psychology, 41,* 315–327.

Einhorn, H. J. (1972). Expert measurement and mechanical combination. *Organizational Behavior and Human Performance, 7,* 86–106.

Einhorn, H. J., & Hogarth, R. M. (1975). Unit weighting schemes for decision making. *Organizational Behavior and Human Performance, 13,* 171–192.

Fiske, S. T., & Neuberg, S. L. (1990). A continuum of impression formation from category-based to individuating processes: Influences of information and motivation on attention and interpretation. In M. P. Zanna (Ed.), *Advances in Experimental Social Psychology* (Vol. 23). San Diego, CA: Academic Press.

Forbes, R. J., & Jackson, P. R. (1980). Nonverbal behaviour and the outcome of selection interviews. *Journal of Occupational Psychology, 53,* 65–72.

Gaugler, B. B., Rosenthal, D. B., Thornton, G. C., III, & Bentson, C. (1987). Meta-analysis of assessment center validity. [Monograph]. *Journal of Applied Psychology, 72,* 493–511.

Graves, L. M., & Powell, G. N. (1988). An investigation of sex discrimination in recruiters' evaluations of actual applicants. *Journal of Applied Psychology, 73,* 20–29.

Hakel, M. D. (1971). Similarity of post-interview trait rating intercorrelations as a contributor to interrater agreement in a structured employment interview. *Journal of Applied Psychology, 55,* 443–448.

Harris, M. J. (1989). Reconsidering the employment interview. *Personnel Psychology, 42,* 691–727.

Hayes, T. L., Macan, T. M., & Speroff, L. (1992, May). *An empirical cross-validation of two interview process models.* Paper presented at the meeting of the Society for Industrial and Organizational Psychology, Montreal, Quebec.

Herriot, P. (1989). Attribution theory and interview decisions. In R. W. Eder & G. R. Ferris (Eds.), *The employment interview: Theory, research and practice.* Newbury Park, CA: Sage.

Hitt, E. R., & Barr, S. H. (1989). Managerial selection decision models: Examination of configural cue processing. *Journal of Applied Psychology, 74,* 53–61.

James, S. P., Campbell, I. M., & Lovegrove, S. A. (1984). Personality differentiation in a police-selection interview. *Journal of Applied Psychology, 69,* 129–134.

Janz, T. (1982). Initial comparisons of patterned behavior description interviews versus unstructured interviews. *Journal of Applied Psychology, 67,* 577–580.

Johnson, R., & Heal, L. W. (1976). Private employment agency responses to the physically handicapped applicant in a wheelchair. *Journal of Applied Rehabilitation Counseling, 7,* 12–21.

Keenan, A. (1977). Some relationships between interviewers' personal feelings about candidates and their general evaluation of them. *Journal of Occupational Psychology, 50,* 275–283.

Kelley, H. H. (1967). Attribution theory in social psychology. In D. Levine (Ed.), *Nebraska Symposium on Motivation* (Vol. 15). Lincoln: University of Nebraska Press.

Kinicki, A. J., & Lockwood, C. A. (1985). The interview process: An examination of factors recruiters use in evaluating job applicants. *Journal of Vocational Behavior, 26,* 117–125.

Kinicki, A. J., Lockwood, C. A., Hom, P. W., & Griffeth, R. W. (1990). Interviewer predictions of applicant qualifications and interviewer validity: Aggregate and individual analyses. *Journal of Applied Psychology, 75,* 477–486.

Klimoski, R., & Brickner, M. (1987). Why do assessment centers work? The puzzle of assessment center validity. *Personnel Psychology, 40,* 243–260.

Kruglanski, A. W., & Mayseless, O. (1988). Contextual effects in hypothesis testing: The role of competing alternatives and epistemic motivations. *Social Cognition, 6,* 1–21.

Langdale, J. A., & Weitz, J. (1973). Estimating the influence of job information on interviewer agreement. *Journal of Applied Psychology, 57,* 23–27.

Latham, G. P. (1989). The reliability, validity, and practicality of the situational interview. In R. W. Eder & G. R. Ferris (Eds.), *The employment interview: Theory, research and practice.* Newbury Park, CA: Sage.

Latham, G. P., & Saari, L. M. (1984). Do people do what they say? Further studies on the situational interview. *Journal of Applied Psychology, 69,* 569–574.

Latham, G. P., Saari, L. M., Pursell, E. D., & Campion, M. A. (1980). The situational interview. *Journal of Applied Psychology, 65,* 422–427.

Liden, R. C., & Parsons, C. K. (1986). A field study of job applicant interview perceptions, alternative opportunities and demographic characteristics. *Personnel Psychology, 39,* 109–122.

Maas, J. B. (1965). Patterned scaled expectation interview: Reliability studies on a new technique. *Journal of Applied Psychology, 49,* 431–433.

Macan, T. M., & Dipboye, R. L. (1986, April). *Biases in interviewers' processing of information in the employment interview.* Paper presented at the meeting of the Southwestern Psychological Association, Fort Worth, TX.

Macan, T. M., & Dipboye, R. L. (1988). The effects of interviewers' initial impressions on information gathering. *Organizational Behavior and Human Decision Processes, 42,* 364–387.

Macan, T. M., & Dipboye, R. L. (1990). The relationship of the interviewers' preinterview impressions to selection and recruitment outcomes. *Personnel Psychology, 43,* 745–769.

Martin, C. L. (1987). A ratio measure of sex stereotyping. *Journal of Personality and Social Psychology, 52,* 489–499.

Maurer, S. D., & Fay, C. (1988). Effect of situational interviews, conventional structured interviews, and training on interview rating agreement: An experimental analysis. *Personnel Psychology, 41,* 329–345.

McDaniel, M. A., Whetzel, D. L., Schmidt, F. L., Hunter, J. E., Maurer, S., & Russell, J. (1987). *The validity of employment interviews: A review and meta-analysis.* Unpublished manuscript.

Miller, D. T., & Turnbull, W. (1986). Expectancies and interpersonal processes. In M. R. Rosenzweig & L. W. Porter (Eds.), *Annual review of psychology.* Palo Alto, CA: Annual Reviews.

Motowidlo, S. J. (1986). Information processing in personnel decisions. In K. M. Rowland & G. R. Ferris (Eds.), *Research in personnel and human resources management* (Vol. 4). Greenwich, Conn.: JAI Press.

Neuberg, S. L. (1989). The goal of forming accurate impressions during social interactions: Attenuating the impact of negative expectancies. *Journal of Personality and Social Psychology, 56,* 374–386.

Orpen, C. (1984). Attitude similarity, attraction, and decision making in the employment interview. *Journal of Psychology, 117,* 111–120.

Parsons, C. K., & Liden, R. C. (1984). Interviewer perceptions of applicant qualifications: A multivariate field study of demographic characteristics and nonverbal cues. *Journal of Applied Psychology, 69,* 557–568.

Payne, J. W. (1976). Task complexity and contingent processing decision making: An information search and protocol analysis. *Organizational Behavior and Human Performance, 16,* 366–387.

Phillips, A., & Dipboye, R. L. (1989). Correlational tests of predictions from a process model of the interview. *Journal of Applied Psychology, 74,* 41–52.

Platt, J. R. (1964). Strong inference. *Science, 146,* 347–353.

Raza, S. M., & Carpenter, B. N. (1987). A model of hiring decisions in real employment interviews. *Journal of Applied Psychology, 72,* 596–603.

Reilly, R. R., & Chao, G. T. (1982). Validity and fairness of some alternative employee selection procedures. *Personnel Psychology, 35,* 1–61.

Rynes, S., & Gerhart, B. (1990). Interviewer assessments of applicant "fit": An exploratory investigation. *Personnel Psychology, 43,* 13–35.

Sackett, P. R., Harris, M. M., & Orr, J. M. (1986). On seeking moderator variables in the meta-analysis of correlational data: A Monte Carlo investigation of statistical power and resistance to type I error. *Journal of Applied Psychology, 71,* 302–310.

Schmitt, N. (1976). Social and situational determinants of interview decisions: Implications for the employment interview. *Personnel Psychology, 29,* 79–101.

Schneider, B., & Schmitt, N. (1986). *Staffing organizations.* Glenview, IL: Scott, Foresman.

Schoorman, F. D. (1988). Escalation bias in performance appraisals: An unintended consequence of supervisor participation in hiring decisions. *Journal of Applied Psychology, 73,* 58–62.

Schuh, A. J. (1980). Effects of early interruption and note taking on listening accuracy and decision making in the interview. *Bulletin of the Psychonomic Society, 13,* 263–264.

Schuler, H. (1989). Construct validity of a multimodal employment interview. In B. J. Fallon, H. P. Pfister, & J. Brebner (Eds.), *Advances in industrial organizational psychology.* Amsterdam: North-Holland.

Schwab, D. P., & Heneman, H. G. III (1969). Relationship between interview structure and interviewer reliability in an employment situation. *Journal of Applied Psychology, 53,* 214–217.

Stone, E. F., Stone, D. L., & Dipboye, R. L. (1992). Stigmas in organizations: Race, handicaps, and physical unattractiveness. In K. Kelley (Ed.), *Issues, theory, and research in industrial and organizational psychology.* Amsterdam: Elsevier Science.

Thornton, G. C., III, & Byham, W. C. (1982). *Assessment centers and managerial performance.* San Diego, CA: Academic Press.

Trope, Y., & Bassok, M. (1982). Confirmatory and diagnosing strategies in social information gathering. *Journal of Personality and Social Psychology, 43,* 22–34.

Tucker, D. H., & Rowe, P. M. (1979). Relationships between expectancy causal attributions and final hiring decisions in the employment interview. *Journal of Applied Psychology, 64,* 27–34.

Ulrich, L., & Trumbo, D. (1965). The selection interview since 1949. *Psychological Bulletin, 63,* 100–116.

Valenzi, E., & Andrews, I. R. (1973). Individual differences in the decision process of employment interviewers. *Journal of Applied Psychology, 58,* 49–53.

Vance, R. J., Kuhnert, K. W., & Farr, J. L. (1978). Interview judgments: Using external criteria to compare behavioral and graphic scale ratings. *Organizational Behavior and Human Performance, 22,* 279–294.

Wagner, R. (1949). The employment interview: A critical summary. *Personnel Psychology, 2,* 17–46.

Webster, E. C. (1982). *The employment interview: A social judgment process.* Schonberg, Ontario, Canada: S.I.P. Publications.

Wiener, Y., & Schneiderman, M. L. (1974). Use of job information as a criterion in employment decisions of interviewers. *Journal of Applied Psychology, 59,* 699–704.

Wiesner, W. H., & Cronshaw, S. (1988). The moderating impact of interview format and degree of structure on interview validity. *Journal of Occupational Psychology, 61,* 275–290.

Wright, P. (1974). The harassed decision maker: Time pressures, distractions, and the use of evidence. *Journal of Applied Psychology, 59,* 555–561.

Wyer, R. S., Jr., & Srull, T. K. (1989). *Memory and cognition in its social context.* Hillsdale, NJ: Erlbaum.

6

Fairness in Selection: Current Developments and Perspectives

Richard D. Arvey, Paul R. Sackett

One of the great issues of modern times, at least within the United States, has had to do with achieving equality and fairness for all members of our society. Within the field of industrial and organizational (I/O) psychology, this issue has often been hotly debated, researched, and litigated from the perspective of selection fairness. Indeed, when one of us pulled together the few strands of psychological research and legal precedents over ten years ago (Arvey, 1979) to summarize what we knew then about selection fairness, the field was just beginning to develop. Since then, much has happened. While the basic contours and shape of the field have remained the same, we believe that there has been considerable expansion and pushing of the "frontiers" associated with the domain of selection fairness. In this chapter we summarize our views of these trends and comment on what we consider to be the frontier components.

We note at the outset that we do not mean to be comprehensive. Instead, we wish to summarize the salient literature and themes of selection fairness. Similarly, we do not intend to be particularly statistical, technical, or legalistic in our presentation, but, again, to summarize the developments in the field.

We believe that (1) the basic definition and conceptualization of selection fairness have undergone a transformation, (2) there has been expansion in the legal domain vis-à-vis selection fairness, (3) selection fairness has been expanded to be more inclusive and comprehensive, and (4) there have been several technical and value-orientation developments in the field.

Expansion of the Definition of Fairness

It is worthwhile to examine the definition of fairness. Dictionary definitions of *fair* offer a variety of synonyms, such as *just, equitable, unbiased,* and *honest.* This suggests that the concept of fairness in selection would be a broad-based construct, incorporating selection system content and process issues as well as the perspectives of all stakeholders in the selection process. However, in selection, initial conceptualizations of fairness were associated solely with minority group issues. Arvey (1979), for instance, stated that his treatment of fairness would focus on blacks, women, the elderly, and the handicapped.

Within psychology, fairness was also treated for some time as a psychometric characteristic of a selection device. Various models of fairness emerged in the late 1960s and early 1970s and were the subject of considerable debate. For example, Peterson and Novick (1976) systematically compared the various models. Shortly thereafter Hunter and Schmidt (1976) clarified the point that fairness is a philosophical concept, not a technical characteristic of a test. The Cleary regression model is now referred to not as a model of fairness, but of predictive bias. Predictive bias is a technical quality of a test that can and should be examined; fairness is in the eye of the beholder.

This view, that fairness is more subjective in nature, is now reflected in current professional standards. The Society for Industrial and Organizational Psychology's (SIOP) *Principles for the Validation and Use of Personnel Selection Procedures* (1987) state that "fairness is a social rather than a psychometric concept. Its definition depends on what one considers to be fair. Fairness has no single meaning, and, therefore, no single statistical or psychometric definition. Fairness, or lack of fairness, is not a property of the selection procedure, but rather a joint function of the procedure, the job, the population, and how the scores derived from it are used" (p. 18). Similarly, the American Educational Research Association, American Psychological Association, and National Council of Measurement in Education's *Standards for Educational and Psychological Testing* (1985) acknowledge the regression model as the appropriate approach to predictive bias, but note that "unlike selection bias, however, fairness is not a technical psychometric term; it is subject to different definitions in different social and political circumstances" (p. 13).

We too wish to move beyond the view of fairness as a psychometric characteristic of a test and instead consider it as a psychological "construct." As such, perceptions of fairness will constitute the important "observables" or measurements of the construct along which individuals may differ. Moreover, we view the selection system content, context, process, and outcome factors as potential contributors to fairness. Here, we explore potential determinants of these fairness perceptions. We also explore how these perceptions may vary across different stakeholders in the selection process. Stakeholders include individual applicants, both minority and majority, advocacy groups for various minority groups, I/O psychologists and other human resource professionals, the hiring organization, and society at large.

It should be clear that we see the notion of fairness as not just pertaining to minority group issues. While these issues are clearly important, questions about what is right, just, and equitable go beyond minority issues.

Also, our view is consistent with other developing literatures. The idea that fairness is a subset or part of other definitions of justice has not gone unnoticed. Greenberg (1986), Folger (1987), Folger and Greenberg (1985), Tyler and Bies (1990), Sashkin and Williams (1990), and others have called attention to the notion that organizational justice may be viewed from two perspectives: *distributive justice,* wherein the relative outcomes of various parties are examined for equity, and *procedural justice,* in which the processes and procedures by which decisions are made and outcomes (for example, rewards, punishments) allocated are examined for fairness. Several articles and research pieces have highlighted the importance of both procedural and distributive justice concepts in performance appraisal processes, compensation systems, dispute resolution, and other organizational phenomena. Only recently, however, has any specific attention been given to the notion that selection procedures and outcomes can be examined within a similar framework. Schmitt (1991) presents his view that employee perceptions of various selection procedures relate to their perceptions of distributive and procedural justice. Our view is consistent with these developments. Although we do not explicitly identify each variable in our proposed model within this framework, many of them fit nicely within this taxonomic system.

In Table 6.1 we offer a set of potential determinants of perceived selection system fairness. This view is derived from a very Western (particularly U.S.) perspective. Other cultures and nationalities may not adopt or apply these particular concepts and considerations in their specific selection practices. We hypothesize that perceptions of fairness can be influenced by variables in each of the five categories listed: selection system content, selection system development process, selection system administration process, selection system context, and selection system outcomes. We also hypothesize that different stakeholders will be sensitive to different variables in forming their perceptions of the fairness of a selection system.

In the following sections we offer comments about each of the potential determinants in Table 6.1. We acknowledge that much of what follows is speculative and without the benefit of much, if any, empirical work; we view this as a starting point for discussion and research.

Selection System Content

We have somewhat loosely placed several issues and variables within the selection system content category. We hypothesize that the following elements are related to perceptions of selection fairness.

**Table 6.1. Potential Determinants of
Perceived Selection System Fairness.**

Selection system content
  Merit-based variables
  Job-relatedness
  Objectivity versus subjectivity
  Use of illegal variables
  Thoroughness of coverage of knowledge, skills, and abilities
  Invasiveness
  Fakability

Selection system development process
  Adequacy of job analysis
  Adequacy of validity evidence
  Search for alternatives
  Involvement of professionals
  Representation in process

Selection system administration process
  Consistency across candidates
  Opportunity to review score and scoring
  Prior information about content and purpose
  Confidentiality
  Opportunity for reconsideration

Selection system context
  Company history
  Selection ratio
  Organizational resources (for example, time, money)

Selection system outcomes
  Maximize performance and utility
  Maximize representativeness

Merit-based Variables. "Merit-based" variables are perceived as fairer than those not based on merit. Merit-based hiring practices have been a central facet of government and have received great social acceptance over the years. The major premise underlying meritocracy is described in a recent National Research Council report (Hartigan & Wigdor, 1989): "The qualification that merits rewards in the allocation of jobs is talent (ability, experience), not family connections, social class, political loyalty, virtue, need, or other criteria that are irrelevant to performance" (p. 32).

Job-Relatedness. "Job-related" variables are perceived as fairer than unrelated ones. That is, variables that seem prima facie related to the job (face validity), directly reflect the job (content-oriented validity), demonstrate empirical relationships to important aspects of the job (criterion-related validity), or reflect central psychological constructs important to the job (construct validity) are perceived as fairer than variables with no direct or empirical or theoretical relationship to the job. As we know, the job-relatedness standard is the major bulwark on which organizations must rely if their selection procedures are challenged in a Title VII case. Here we suggest that the important thing is for organizations to document some linkage between the variable and the job, rather than simply assume validity.

In addition, there are some variables explicitly considered and weighted in selection processes that are considered fair and legal but have no established job-relatedness. A good example is the use of veterans preference often used by civil service departments, in which point scores are automatically added to test scores for applicants who served in the U.S. military. The philosophy behind this particular practice is that this variable serves as a reward for prior national service.

Objectivity Versus Subjectivity. Objectivity versus subjectivity in scoring can be viewed quite differently by different stakeholders. Within psychology, objectivity is clearly viewed as a virtue. The SIOP *Principles* (1987) are explicit in their preference for more objective predictors (p. 12). However, groups critical of traditional approaches to testing argue against objective tests. They tend to equate "objective" with "multiple choice" and argue that such tests are unfair. Although the primary target of these critics is educational testing, they apply similar arguments to employment testing. One hears calls for "authentic assessment," which refers to evaluation of performance samples rather than paper-and-pencil tests.

Use of Illegal Variables. We expect little controversy here: variables that are explicitly illegal are perceived as unfair to almost all constituencies. Thus, the Civil Rights Act of 1964 as amended, as well as other legislation treated later in this chapter, makes it illegal for organizations to use such information as race, sex, national origin, age, religion, and disability status in making selection decisions. Congress has made it explicit that the use of such variables is illegal except in very limited cases (for instance, bona fide occupational qualifications, affirmative action staffing), and their use in making selection decisions may also violate U.S. norms of fairness.

Thoroughness of Coverage of Knowledge, Skills, and Abilities (KSAs). The central idea here is that a selection system that focuses on only a single KSA or subset of KSAs may be viewed as unfair. There may be no quarrel with what is included in the selection system, but with what is not. We see this as more likely to affect the perceptions of job applicants and the public at large than to affect the perceptions of I/O psychologists. Within the psychological community, in fact, it is well accepted that there is no obligation to measure all important KSAs. The issue is whether there is support for the inference of a relationship between predictor scores and important aspects of job performance. However, the failure to measure what applicants believe to be important KSAs is a commonly heard lay criticism of selection systems. This concern is exacerbated when the selection device chosen has adverse impact on members of protected groups and unmeasured KSAs are hypothesized to have less adverse impact.

Invasiveness. Information that constitutes an invasion of privacy will be considered less fair than information that does not. Although we recognize that just what is considered to be an invasion of privacy in the selection domain is not entirely clear, the use of tests or interviews that probe candidates' personal lives, explore sexual habits, or somehow invade these emotional components or thoughts believed to be private may be perceived to be unfair. There are situations, however, where such personal information may be considered private but nonetheless relevant to the job (for example, a person may be suicidal yet be applying for a safety-sensitive position). We could modify our proposition to state that gathering information of a private nature will be considered relatively more fair if the information is job-related and has important ramifications in terms of losses and gains (or utility) to the organization and the public. Perhaps a good example of this is the current use of drug tests to detect substance abuse among employees working in safety-sensitive positions.

Fakability. Information that is easily faked and distorted may be perceived by applicants as unfair. Thus, selection systems wherein applicants can easily "fake good" and otherwise manage their impressions will be considered less fair than those where fakability is not an issue. Applicants may feel torn between a perception that they can be successful in their job search if they "tell the company what they want to hear" in an interview or on a personality inventory and a personal moral code that dictates responding honestly.

Selection specialists, on the other hand, are likely to be less concerned about fakability in and of itself and more concerned about the effects of fakability on validity. If evidence shows that most applicants respond honestly, even though they can fake well if instructed to do so, and thus validity is minimally influenced by faking, selection specialists are not likely to view this as a serious fairness issue.

Selection System Development Process

We hypothesize that the selection system concept variables above are more important to the fairness perceptions of applicants than to the fairness perceptions of selection specialists. Conversely, the first three variables in the selection system development process are hypothesized as more important to selection specialists. We suspect that many may concur with a statement made by Guion (1965) in the earliest days of concern about fairness and discrimination in employment: "[Unfairness and discrimination] is an emotionally charged topic, but if agreement is reached first on the nature of the criterion to be predicted, and second on maximum accuracy of prediction as the proper goal of the test specialist, then the issues and questions reduce to technical ones" (p. 491).

Adequacy of Job Analysis. Other chapters in this book treat the role of job analysis in criterion development and in predictor selection and development. We simply note here that proper grounding in an appropriate job analysis is generally acknowledged within the psychological community as a prerequisite to an acceptable and fair selection system.

Adequacy of Validity Evidence. Validity is also treated in detail elsewhere in this book. We do not discuss technical aspects of validity here, but simply note that use of appropriate validation strategies to support inferences made from selection devices is mandated by the SIOP *Principles* (1987).

We suggest that validity evidence is likely to be viewed differently by selection specialists and the general public. Conceptually, selection specialists ask, Does the success rate achieved using the selection system produce an improvement over the success rate achieved without it? The general public tends to ask, Does the selection system make mistakes? Selection specialists view the base rate as the standard of comparison; the general public may view perfect accuracy of prediction as the standard. This is exemplified by Senator Edward Kennedy's comments made in the course of debate about the passage of the 1989 Employee Polygraph Protection Act to the effect that even if the 95 percent accuracy claims of polygraph proponents are accurate, if one million preemployment polygraph exams are given annually, a 5 percent error rate means that fifty thousand innocent people are misclassified, and any device that misclassifies fifty thousand people per year should be prohibited. In short, different constituencies may view the same validity evidence quite differently.

Search for Alternatives. The concept of a search for alternatives relates to the "minority issues" interpretation of fairness. Conceptually, it is hard to argue with the idea that if an alternative is available that serves the employer's interests equally well but has less adverse impact, it should be used. From this it follows that any party who believes that such an alternative is available will view the existing selection system as unfair. In practice, it is difficult to find predictors that are equally valid but with less adverse impact. More often, a reduction in adverse impact is accompanied by a loss in validity (or reliability). However, Maxwell and Arvey (in press) show that among psychometrically unbiased tests (as defined by Cleary, 1968), alternative tests with less adverse impact will also be accompanied by an increase in validity.

The typical discussion of selection alternatives focuses on *replacing* one predictor with another. Another possibility is to consider *supplementing* the valid predictor with adverse impact with additional predictors with less or no adverse impact. If the focus is on one particular criterion, then a regression approach is available to determine the optimal way to combine predictors. The resulting composite will have less adverse impact if the additional predictor contributes to the regression equation. Another interesting approach is to incorporate multivariate procedures wherein multiple predictors predict multiple-criterion variables.

Here we presume a criterion-related validity framework; if the basis for the selection system is judgmental rather than empirical, the mechanisms for evaluating alternatives are even less clear. Thus, the apparently straightforward notion of using alternative predictors if appropriate is perhaps more open to dispute than is recognized in the I/O literature.

Involvement of Professionals. The issue here is whether perceptions of fairness may be affected by the belief that the selection system in question was developed by experts, independent of the actual technical quality of the system. It is, of course, hoped that involvement by selection specialists does in fact affect selection system quality.

Representation in the Process. We hypothesize that representative involvement in the selection system development process and the evaluation of applicants can contribute to perceptions of the system's fairness. Selection specialists increasingly attempt to involve minority group subject matter experts (SMEs) in job analysis activities, in selection system content development and review, and in assessor, interviewer, and rater roles if appropriate given the type of selection system. To the extent that this involvement is visible, it may influence the fairness perceptions of applicants and minority advocacy groups. Representation by an even wider stakeholder group (union representatives, attorneys, community advisory groups, and so on) is sometimes now made a part of selection system development, operations, and evaluation.

Selection System Administration Process

The variables in the administration process deal with issues of procedural justice and due process; we suspect that such variables have a substantial impact on fairness perceptions shared by a number of different constituents.

Consistency Across Candidates. Three separate issues exist here: consistency in selection system content, consistency in scoring, and consistency in score interpretation. We do not see the first issue as controversial; standardization of selection system content and administration conditions are generally acknowledged as essential features of a selection system. Violations of this aspect of consistency (for instance, asking particular interview questions only of women) commonly evoke strong reactions.

Consistency in scoring deals with reliability and lack of bias in the scoring process, and is a focal issue when the selection system involves judgmental scoring, as in an interview or assessment center. That the scoring process should be reliable and unbiased is also not controversial. Selection specialists may look for technical evidence on this issue; applicants may look for signals of fairness and consistency, such as multiple raters and minority involvement in the scoring process.

The issue of consistency in actions taken once initial scores are available deals with adjusting the scores of a subset of applicants on some basis. In some settings this is done without much apparent controversy. The practice of adding points to the scores of veterans in some public-sector settings is a well-known example of this. The issue of score adjustment on the basis of race or gender is an incendiary issue. Debate tends to deal with two settings: physical ability tests, which have substantial adverse impact on women, and cognitive ability tests, which have substantial adverse impact on some racial and ethnic minority groups, particularly blacks and Hispanics.

Score adjustment takes several forms, including converting scores to percentiles within race or gender groups, adding a fixed number of points to the scores of particular subgroups, and more elaborate approaches, such as that described in the

National Research Council report on the General Aptitude Test Battery (see Hartigan & Wigdor, 1989), in which the proposed adjustment was a function of the degree of validity of the selection system.

Disputes about score adjustment can be argued on legal, technical, and social grounds. Legally, various commentators differ strongly as to the permissibility of the practice (for example, Hartigan & Wigdor, 1989). Moving beyond legal issues, the argument tends to be cast in terms of individual merit versus social good. Opponents of score adjustment tend to argue for the sanctity of individual merit and the inappropriateness of minority group membership as a factor in selection decisions. Arguments about attaching social stigma to members of the aided minority group are also common. Proponents can take multiple positions. One is that proportional representation in employment is appropriate in a pluralistic society, even at the expense of individual merit. Merit is valued; it simply is not the only thing valued. A second is to express general skepticism about the validity of selection systems and to assert that such systems do not truly assess merit.

We believe that there is value in considering different scenarios in which score adjustment may be considered legitimate.

• Scenario 1: Multiple KSAs are believed to contribute in a compensatory manner to job performance. A selection system with adverse impact on one group is used as an initial screen to identify a smaller subset of applicants who will move on for additional screening. Adjusted scores are the basis for referral for additional screening. Final hiring is based on an appropriately weighted composite of unadjusted scores across the complete set of screening devices.

• Scenario 2: Multiple KSAs are believed to contribute in a compensatory manner to job performance. A selection system that is based on the measurement of one KSA and shows validity but has adverse impact on one group is developed and used as the *sole* basis for the selection decision. Hiring decisions are based on adjusted scores.

• Scenario 3: Multiple KSAs are believed to contribute in

a compensatory manner to job performance. A thorough state-of-the-art selection system is developed to measure all relevant KSAs; the resulting system is found to have adverse impact on one group. Scores are adjusted and selection decisions are based on adjusted scores.

In the first scenario, the adoption of a score adjustment could be motivated by an attempt to obtain as accurate an assessment of merit as possible by increasing the pool of minority candidates who move on for additional screening. This concern for merit, though, is specific to the minority group, as majority group members with below-threshold scores do not have the same opportunities.

In scenario 2, an argument for score adjustment might be based on the incompleteness of the selection system: if other measures that have less adverse impact and contribute to validity had been developed, a system incorporating these other measures would have had less adverse impact. Thus, the decision to adopt a score adjustment procedure is based on the premise that the present system is incomplete and that, if other measures were included, less adverse impact might be achieved. In essence, this option is based on the assumption that less adverse impact in selection would occur if all possible predictors were available; but because they are not, adjustments are appropriate and even necessary. In this case, though, the remedy of score adjustment benefits both those whose standing would rise as a result of a more thorough selection system and those whose standing would fall.

In the third scenario, absent bias in the selection procedure, any argument for score adjustment would be based solely on the belief that increased minority employment is an important social goal and that deviation from merit hiring is a viable method of achieving that goal.

The three scenarios offered here are not a comprehensive list. They are intended to illustrate that different rationales may underlie support for score adjustment in different situations. We suggest the possibility that beliefs about the appropriateness of score adjustment may vary across situations.

Opportunity to Review Score and Scoring. Opportunities for an applicant to see a scoring key for a written exam, to verify the accuracy of exam scores, and to file challenges to the appropriateness of the keyed response to particular items are not uncommon, and are sometimes legally mandated, in public-sector settings. Such a procedure may contribute to applicant perceptions that the selection system is open and above-board. We have no data, but it is our sense that such procedures are extremely rare in private-sector settings. We wonder about the trade-off between increased perceptions of fairness and the costs to organizations of such practices (for example, loss of test security).

Prior Information About Content and Purpose. We suggest that informing candidates in advance of the content and purpose of components of the selection system can contribute to perceptions of fairness. One issue is uncertainty reduction. Particularly when the selection device in question is unfamiliar to a candidate (for instance, an assessment center or individual assessment by a psychologist), the result can be a feeling of "I didn't do well because I didn't know what to expect." Another issue is candidate concerns about opportunities to prepare. These can range from something as simple as informing candidates of procedures beforehand ("If I'd known they were going to give me a test, I'd have brought my reading glasses") to announcing test dates well in advance (for instance, for public safety jobs, such as fire fighter, where the content of a physical ability test may be announced months in advance of the test date to ensure that all candidates have equal opportunity to prepare and practice).

Confidentiality. There should be little controversy about the notion that data obtained in the selection process should be made available only on a need-to-know basis. The SIOP *Principles* (1987) endorse this notion; failure to follow this policy may contribute to candidate perceptions of unfairness.

Opportunity for Reconsideration. Receiving a second chance if performance on a selection device falls below the organization's standards may contribute to perceptions of fairness on the part of applicants. This is also consistent with professional standards: the SIOP *Principles* (1987) call for providing such opportunities wherever technically feasible.

Selection System Context

We believe selection systems include several contextual variables that affect perceptions of fairness.

Company History. The notion here is that various parties view organizational activities in the selection arena in the context of a company's history. The activities of an organization with a stellar track record in terms of minority employment, for example, may be perceived differently from the same activities by a company with a record of intentional discrimination. Suspicion about potential unfairness based on past experiences may lead to heightened awareness of variables that may be overlooked in other settings.

Selection Ratio. This variable reflects an extremely common lay perception of selection systems, namely, a belief that if a candidate is above some threshold in terms of qualifications, he or she deserves to be hired. That many such candidates are turned away when applicants exceed openings is a fact of life perhaps not obvious to the candidate who says, "It's not fair: I met all the stated qualifications, yet wasn't hired." When extremely high applicant-to-opening ratios are paired with top-down selection, large numbers of very well qualified candidates can be turned away.

Organizational Resources (for Example, Time, Money). Factors such as emergency hiring needs or financial constraints may result in selection systems developed with less care and resource allocations than a company would prefer. We wonder whether various stakeholders differentially factor in such variables when assessing the fairness of a selection system.

Selection System Outcomes

It is possible that for some individuals or groups, all of the above selection system variables are irrelevant to their perceptions of fairness: all that matters is the outcome of the selection process. Two key outcomes are described below.

Maximization of Performance. For some selection specialists, this may be viewed as a moral imperative: a fair selection system is one that maximizes utility given the constraints of the situation.

For job applicants, value to the organization may be of little importance. For society at large, this is likely to be one valued outcome, though perhaps not the only one.

Maximization of Representation. For some stakeholders, this may be *the* fundamental determinant of fairness precepts. For others it may be a valued outcome, but only if its achievement does not require any compromising of the preceding variable, namely, maximizing performance and utility. To the extent that representativeness and performance are not compatible (for instance, because of differential preparation for a given occupation by subgroup), this reflects the converse of concern for maximizing performance.

Consequences of Perceptions of Fairness

A system perceived as unfair can have a variety of consequences, which are likely to differ for various constituencies. For job applicants, the consequences are likely to be different for successful and unsuccessful applicants. Applicants who were successful in obtaining a job through a system they believe is unfair may be troubled by feelings of inequity; a link to higher rates of eventual turnover might be hypothesized. Applicants who were rejected by a system perceived as unfair may feel a sense of moral outrage, with various behavioral manifestations. Filing a discrimination complaint may be the prototypical example. Closer to home, a scathing diatribe calling for a reduction in funding to our employer, the School of Management at the University of Minnesota, recently appeared in a local paper, written by an individual rejected for a faculty position in the school. Lounsbury, Bobrow, and Jensen (1989) show that individuals rejected for a job because of their test performance hold a more negative view of tests than those unaffected or selected via tests.

Our sense is that word gets around about how firms treat applicants and that perceptions of selection system fairness can have considerable effect on subsequent applicant pools. Rynes, Bretz, and Gerhart (1991) offer an interesting example of this in a case study of college students using a university placement center. Interviews with students made it very clear that word of mouth travels quickly about recruiters and recruiting practices.

Expansion of the Legal Frontiers

There have been three important legal developments regarding selection fairness, which we summarize here. We think these cases have five major implications.

1. *Watson* v. *Fort Worth Bank* (1988) suggests that there will be expanded review and scrutiny of previously rarely touched and litigated selection tools. Selection methods regarded as relatively subjective in nature (for example, the interview) are clearly fair game to plaintiffs.

2. The *Price Waterhouse* v. *Hopkins* (1989) decision indicates that greater probative weight will be given to psychological constructs by the courts, such as sex-role stereotyping, managerial leadership qualities, and the like.

3. As a result of *Wards Cove Packing Company* v. *Antonio* (1989), more precise statistical evidence will probably be required to trigger an adverse impact finding. Thus, just showing an "imbalance" by comparing the proportions of minorities to an external market may not be sufficient to determine whether adverse impact has occurred.

4. There clearly seems to be some lightening of the burden necessary for employers to meet the business necessity rule. By indicating that organizations have the burden of providing evidence of a business justification for their employment practices (versus the more difficult burden of persuasion), recent legal findings declare that organizations need only show a manifest relationship between the selection device and the legitimate goals of the employer. In the *Wards Cove* case, the

Court said, "The touchstone of the inquiry is a reasoned review of the employer's justification for the use of the challenged practice" (p. 4507). Similarly, the Court said that there is no requirement that the challenged practice be "essential" or "indispensable" to the employer's business for it to pass muster. Thus, rigid adherence to the validity provisions in the *Uniform Guidelines* (1978) may not be necessary under this standard. In *Watson,* the Court also appears to relax the evidentiary standards needed to demonstrate business necessity. In this case the Court said there need only be a "manifest" relationship between the selection practice and job performance. This linkage could be required by a variety of methods, including the results of studies, expert testimony, and prior successful experience.

5.   The *Wards Cove* case indicates that plaintiffs must show that a particular specific selection procedure is responsible for the claimed discrimination. That is, organizations cannot be required to show that each and every one of their selection procedures is job-related if a bottom-line figure shows adverse impact.

These rulings and others apparently convinced civil rights advocates that the Supreme Court had substantially reduced the protection afforded by the Civil Rights Act of 1964 and the more than twenty-five years of litigation and legal precedents that followed (Rasky, 1989). Thus, a new version of the Civil Rights Act is being fashioned.

Expansion of Coverage

Another area of expansion in selection fairness has to do with the number and kinds of people affected. In our previous discussion we make clear that fairness and perceptions of fairness pertain to all individuals. That is, no one group or membership is singled out as having an especially privileged view or corner on the market in terms of being treated fairly in an organization's selection process. However, we can point to several recent events and activities that clearly suggest that particular populations are receiving targeted attention.

Americans with Disabilities Act (ADA)

The ADA was signed into law in July 1990. It prohibits discrimination against "qualified individuals with disabilities," defined as individuals who, with or without reasonable accommodation, can perform the essential functions of the position. A disability is defined as "a) a physical or mental impairment that substantially limits one or more of the major life activities, b) a record of such an impairment, or c) being regarded as having such an impairment." Major life activities include performing manual tasks, walking, seeing, hearing, speaking, learning, and working. The Equal Employment Opportunity Commission is required by law to issue interpretive guidelines. A draft was made available for public comment in March 1991; the ADA went into effect in July 1992.

The ADA requires reasonable accommodation of an individual with a disability, both on the job and in preemployment screening. We outline here a number of unanswered questions about the impact of the ADA on selection system development and use. Answers to these questions will emerge over time; our intent here is to sensitize readers to the fact that this is an area in flux.

The proposed regulations indicate that an organization cannot accommodate a disabled individual unless the organization knows of the disability, and also indicate that the organization cannot inquire into the presence of a disability. There is the explicit statement that "this provision only requires that an employer provide, upon request, alternative accessible tests to individuals with disabilities." We wonder whether applicants will be required to make this request prior to administration of the test in question, or whether they will be allowed to do so after going through the process and being rejected.

A serious concern arises regarding the administration of selection devices in alternative formats. For example, for any test of speed, even minor format changes can produce dramatic changes in test outcomes. And given the ADA's treatment of each individual as distinct, rather than categorizing disabilities, the development of norms for various groups of disabled individuals does not seem possible. Also, for some tests, a change in format changes the nature of the test. Consider, for example, the fairly commonly used measurement of reasoning ability via number series problems. For a blind applicant, it appears that an oral administration would produce a confounding of memorization skills and reasoning skills. If a different type of reasoning test is used for the blind applicant, how is the score on the alternative test compared to scores on the original test? Even in what appear to be the least controversial situations, we see some difficulties. For example, a commonly used example of reasonable accommodation is the oral administration of a multiple-choice job knowledge test to a blind applicant. The construct of interest is job knowledge; we can assume that the job requires reading, but if the blind applicant has sufficient knowledge to merit being hired, he or she can be accommodated via a reader. We wonder, however, whether the test scores are truly comparable. The sighted applicant can easily and quickly scan and rescan the alternatives as often as he or she desires, whereas the blind applicant must ask to have the alternatives reread, a much slower and more laborious process. It is not clear how much this format change would affect scores. Even if the effect was not large, in a setting where there are large numbers of applicants who are being rank-ordered on the basis of the test, a change in score of a few points could have a large effect on one's position on a hiring list.

Related to some of the above issues is the distinction between making a pass-fail decision about an individual applicant and rank-ordering a group of applicants. The model that seems to run through the regulations is the first: use of the phrase "qualified individual with a disability" in the act implies a dichotomy. A change in test format may have limited impact if the question is one of making a determination of whether an applicant exceeds some threshold level of the attribute being measured (that is, only applicants very close to the cutoff would be affected). A change in format may be much more problematic if there is a need to slot the disabled applicant's score into a score distribution.

In short, the ADA will bring to the fore a variety of issues regarding the selection of individuals with disabilities. We predict that the attention of I/O psychologists will increasingly be devoted to this area.

Reverse Discrimination Cases

Several "reverse discrimination" cases have been filed claiming that the rights of whites or males have been violated because of preferential treatment of minorities or affirmative action efforts on the part of an organization. For example, in Minneapolis a case was filed recently by forty-four males who claimed that their rights had been violated when applying for a fire fighter position because of preferential treatment given to females and minorities (*United Firefighter Candidates* v. *City of Minneapolis*, 1991). This case and others exemplify the notion that whites and males, as well as minority group members, have perceptions of what is fair in selection settings.

Discrimination Against Asians

Some recent literature suggests that Asians may also be targets of discrimination. A *Wall Street Journal* article ("Asian-Americans Charge," 1985) indicates that Asians feel prejudice when attempting to move into managerial ranks. Occupational stereotypes may also operate with regard to Asians. For example, Leong and Hayes (1990) published the results of a study showing that Asians are rated as less likely to succeed as insurance salespersons but more likely to succeed as engineers, computer scientists, and mathematicians. These stereotypes may operate as barriers to Asians applying for nonstereotypical jobs.

Recent Technical Developments and Issues

In addition to the trends already discussed, there are several recent technical developments. They involve the following themes.

Test Bias

Over the years, much research has been conducted regarding test bias. It is probably safe for us to make the following statements regarding the outcomes of such research efforts as they pertain to cognitive tests.

• Research has clearly shown that racial differences exist on many, if not most, cognitively oriented tests used for selection purposes. Although the reasons for such differences are complex, they are indeed real. That is, the differences are not artifactually produced, not a function of test unreliability, not based on some inherent natural or cultural bias in the test, but reflect true score differences (compare Arvey, 1972; Jensen, 1980). Such tests, if used for selection purposes in combination with a top-down selection procedure where candidates are rank-ordered by scores and the individuals with the highest scores are offered the job, will almost always produce adverse impact.
• Research has clearly shown that cognitive-oriented tests are *not* differentially valid. That is, if a test is valid for one group, it is highly probable that it will be valid for other groups.
• Research has demonstrated that cognitively oriented tests tend to be valid across a wide variety of jobs, locations, and other situations. That is, the validities tend to generalize across multiple settings—the theory of validity generalization has a solid research foundation. This is not to say that there are not substantial criticisms of the theory. However, these criticisms tend to aggregate around questions concerning the validity of the corrections made for artifacts. The findings that psychological tests used in employment settings show nonzero correlations across multiple settings and jobs are widely accepted.
• Convincing research evidence has established that the regression lines for minority and nonminority groups or for different gender groups tend to be the same. If differences are found, the regression line for the minority groups typically shows a lower intercept value. Thus, if a common regression line were used to make selection decisions, the predicted criterion values for the minority groups would be overpredicted, thus providing them with greater advantage than if the regression line cal-

culated for the members of that group alone had been used to make predictions.

- Criterion performance differences between minority and nonminority groups continue to be found. However, in many instances, the differences on performance measures tend *not* to be as great as the differences observed on the employment tests. Thus, minorities tend to show greater differences on tests than on job performance measures the tests are designed to predict. This finding is consistent with finding intercept differences in regression lines.

Given this background, there have been several recent developments in examining test bias.

Perspectives on the Correct Model of Test Bias

The different models and approaches to determine whether a test or predictor is fair have been well described previously (compare Arvey & Faley, 1988; Peterson & Novick, 1976; Crocker & Algina, 1986). Three of the best known are (1) the "Cleary model," where test fairness is achieved if the prediction of job performance is the same for minority and nonminority candidates given the same level of test score (Cleary, 1968); (2) the constant ratio model, where a test is fair if the proportion qualified by the test in relationship to the proportion that can actually perform the job satisfactorily is the same across groups; and (3) the conditional probability model, where the probability of being selected given a particular criterion score should be the same for all groups.

These models have been around for almost two decades, and the debate has been intense. Perhaps the most outspoken and recognized proponent of the Cleary model has been Gottfredson (1990), who suggests that any deviation from this model violates the principle of meritocracy. There are several points we can make about these models.

- One's choice of the "correct" model is essentially based on one's value orientation. In essence, it reflects a political or social value concerning the kinds of results one would like to see as a result of selection procedures. Similarly, the manner in which tests can be used for selection purposes also reflects value orientations. For example, adopting an approach where applicants who score the highest are first selected, then the next highest scorers are selected, and so forth (the top-down approach), will almost certainly greatly advantage nonminority members because of the clear test differentials on cognitive tests, even though the regression lines are the same. There is no question that this approach maximizes productivity within an organization. Yet there may be very little representation of minority group members in jobs filled by testing.

- The choice of a model is not "scientific." That is, there is no scientific evidence or standard that can be applied to say that one should adopt a strictly merit-driven model or approach. In our opinion, the debate has been muddled by claims that the adoption of something other than the Cleary model is not scientific. Again, the choice of any of these models and perspectives is value-driven and not based on any scientific theory or set of evidence.

- Different constituents may have different opinions and values concerning which model is correct or should be applied. For example, government agencies may have the objective of ensuring that minority group members are simply employed, regardless of the relative outcomes to the organization, because of greater society benefits and public policy decision making. Fire fighters may value hiring the absolutely most physically qualified in order to ensure their own personal safety when working with colleagues. It seems to us that most I/O psychologists have essentially allied with organizations in terms of maximizing productivity and utility in this debate.

- The presumption that selection should be based on the principle of meritocracy is not shared by everyone, and it is violated in many instances. I/O psychologists seem to be the standard-bearers of this flag, even when there is clear evidence that other criteria are accepted and used (such as veterans preference, seniority rules) by a variety of constituents.

Perhaps the conflict is best illustrated by the debate over a recent report issued by the National Research Council, which was charged by the National Academy of Sciences to evaluate the General Aptitude Test Battery (GATB) by the U.S. Employment Service (USES). The USES had been using the GATB to test and *refer* applicants to businesses unwilling or not capable of engaging in testing practices. The USES had adopted a procedure whereby a within-group top-down scoring procedure was used. Each candidate received a score based on his or her percentile ranking within a particular minority or majority group. The objective of this procedure was to balance the need to refer the most qualified individuals yet ensure that minority group members would also be referred in proportion to their representation in the applicant group, an outcome that would almost surely not be achieved if strict top-down procedures were used. This practice was challenged by the U.S. Department of Justice, and a study was commissioned to review the GATB as well as to forge a set of recommendations regarding the use of the GATB in the context of race-conscious procedures. The National Research Council recommended that, indeed, race-conscious procedures should be used and explicitly adopted the conditional probability model previously mentioned (Hartigan & Wigdor, 1989). The report articulated the notion that minority applicants who are at the same level of performance as nonminority members should have similar probabilities of being referred to employers. They summarize the research on the GATB as indicating that minorities have proportionally lower test scores than nonminorities compared to their job performance scores. Thus, given a particular cutoff score, greater false negatives occur for minorities than nonminorities, and more false acceptances occur for nonminorities than minorities. Indeed, the number of false negatives increases as test validity decreases. They recommend that this procedure be accomplished by using "score-adjustments" based on candidates' predicted level of job performance. In a separate report, the chair and a member of the council (Wigdor & Sackett, in press) refer to this system as a "performance fair" referral system.

These reports prompted several criticisms and attacks, including the following:

- Gottfredson (1990) objects to the race-conscious selection procedure because it violates the principle that employers should hire the most qualified (meritocracy), and it creates a double standard.

- From a technical perspective, Gottfredson (1990) also eschews the score-adjustment procedure because it affords the lowest-scoring (or least talented) minority members greater score adjustments, thus further diminishing the principle that employers hire the best qualified even within racial subgroups.

- Gottfredson (1990) also argues that score adjustments are recommended only for minority members who are subject to false-negative outcomes, but that similar adjustments should be made for all individuals similarly situated, including nonminorities.

- Schmidt (1990) argues that the National Academy of Sciences panel violated scientific and scholarly values by using "complex statistical sleight of hand techniques to obfuscate and disguise this problem . . . to provide a bogus statistical, psychometric, and scientific justification for score adjustments" (p. 5).

Whereas there has been no formal counter to these criticisms, we suspect that counterarguments could be made owing to the referral nature of the system (see the above discussion of the National Research Council report), the different perspectives and values concerning meritocracy versus representativeness, the designation of the conditional probability model as the preferred model, and other technical considerations. We expect a considerable amount of future discussion and debate on this subject.

Search for Item Differences

Several recent developments concern examining tests on an item-by-item basis to discover which items are the culprits in forging overall test differences. One method of examining tests for bias at the item level is simply to examine the relative difficulty level of items across racial subgroups. One interesting case using this methodology involved the Educational Testing

Service (ETS), which had been sued by an insurance company, Golden Rule, claiming that the examination produced by ETS for licensing insurance agents was racially discriminatory. Although the case was settled out of court, ETS agreed to construct future examinations by including items where the difficulty index level of items was greater than 40 percent and there was not more than a 15 percent difficulty index difference between whites and blacks.

Other quite sophisticated models using item response theory models may be employed to examine test items for bias. An excellent reference is a book edited by Berk (1982) that presents a variety of methods to examine test bias at the item level. One of the interesting premises associated with many of these models and procedures is the notion that a test is biased if it yields different item parameter values for individuals with equal ability levels. For example, Ironson (1982) offers this definition of item bias: "An item is considered unbiased if individuals with equal ability, but from different groups, have the same probability of answering the item correctly" (pp. 117–118). That is, the conditional probability model is invoked, but at the item response level. Tenopyr (1990) found that many of the methods of studying possible differential item functioning are problematic because of the large sample sizes required and the problem of using an internal criterion (usually total test score) versus some external standard.

Another problem or issue with these methods is, What happens to the psychometric properties of the test if such items are deleted? One hypothesis is that the external validity of the test (as well as its reliability) will diminish. If so, then this line of technical exploration may have limited benefit. This proposition was provided support through a study conducted by Roznowski (1987) showing that items manifesting group differences are not necessarily biased and do not lead to relatively poor composite scores on a test of intelligence.

Fairness Issues with Physical Ability Testing

Fleishman (1988) identifies physical ability testing as one of the new frontiers in personnel selection research. Physical ability tests typically demonstrate an adverse effect on females and trigger lawsuits (Arvey & Faley, 1988; Hogan & Quigley, 1986). The physical testing practices used to select candidates for fire fighter and police officer jobs are facing increased legal scrutiny. In meeting the burden of demonstrating job-relatedness, jurisdictions have often used content-oriented validation strategies. However, under the withering scrutiny of litigation, problems have surfaced when organizations have attempted to show the content validity of these physical ability tests, including the following:

- Challenges are made that the job analysis failed to adequately tap relevant physical duties and performance requirements. This argument typically falls under the criticism either that the agency failed to include relevant physical duties or that there was a failure to determine the relative importance or frequency of such duties.
- The adequacy of the job analysis is challenged via assertions that the sample was not sufficiently large, that inappropriate raters were used, or that the sampling plan was inadequate.
- An issue has surfaced involving whether the physical ability test events over- or underemphasize relevant aspects of the job. A variation on this theme is that the test events do not have the "proper mix" of aerobic and anaerobic capacities.
- A challenge is made that there is not sufficient fidelity between the test events and the job. One variation on this claim is that the response properties of the test event are unlike the response properties in the job.

Our informal examination of the responses of professional I/O psychologists to these kinds of potential and real challenges when developing physical ability tests suggests that there appears to be an incredible obsession with job analysis activities, even to the point where resources devoted to test development suffer. For example, comprehensive sampling of the population, instead of random sampling, appears to be the norm in gathering job analysis information. The largest sample size possible is used. Molecular job analysis procedures are used, where jobs are broken down into minute components. A variety of systems are employed to obtain judgments and proportional weighting of both tasks and KSAs, as well as test components. Selection methods using physical ability testing seem to be driven by legal precedents in contrast to theory and informed judgment.

At some point, we expect a shift back toward theory and research-oriented practices in this particular selection arena. For example, one of us (Arvey) is finishing a research piece detailing a construct validation approach to developing physical ability test events for selecting police officers. This research uses a variety of data and evidence (both logical and empirical) to confirm inferences that a set of physical ability tests are related to two important constructs — strength and endurance — and that these two constructs are important facets of job performance.

Conclusion

This chapter has two major components. The first is a presentation of an expanded view of potential determinants of selection system fairness. We note that the perspectives of different stakeholders — applicants, organizations, I/O psychologists, society at large — may differ. Everyone supports fairness, but striving for fairness may mean different things to different groups. We think there would be considerable value in determining what affects each group's perceptions of fairness. Once this is known, there is the possibility of more productive dialogue about the fairness issue.

The second component is an overview of key themes that have emerged over the last two decades in the area of litigation over selection systems and in the area of psychometric treatments of selection system fairness. The issues remain thorny. Most organizations value productivity; a great many also value cultural diversity. When selection systems known to contribute to the first detract from the second, as in the case of valid selection systems with adverse impact on protected groups, conflict arises. No clear solution has emerged, although what is surfacing is a clear sense that fairness is a social issue rather than a scientific one. As psychologists, we can bring scientific evidence to bear to describe the consequences of using different selection systems and using them in different ways, but we do not have any special knowledge as to the "right" approach to defining and measuring fairness. We do seem to be making progress, however. Out of the conflict and divergency in thinking and values, we are learning more about what we mean by "fairness" and how to achieve it.

References

American Educational Research Association, American Psychological Association, and National Council of Measurement in Education. (1985). *Standards for educational and psychological testing.* Washington, DC: American Psychological Association.

Arvey, R. D. (1972). Some comments on culture-fair tests. *Personnel Psychology, 25,* 443–448.

Arvey, R. D. (1979). *Fairness in selecting employees.* Reading, MA: Addison-Wesley.

Arvey, R. D., & Faley, R. H. (1988). *Fairness in selecting employees* (2nd ed.). Reading, MA: Addison-Wesley.

Asian-Americans charge prejudice slows climb to management ranks. (1985, September 11). *Wall Street Journal.*

Berk, R. A. (Ed.). (1982). *Handbook of methods for detecting test bias.* Baltimore, MD: Johns Hopkins University Press.

Cleary, T. A. (1968). Test bias: Prediction of grades of Negro and white students in integrated colleges. *Journal of Educational Measurement, 5,* 115–124.

Crocker, L., & Algina, J. (1986). *Introduction to classical and modern test theory.* Troy, MO: Holt, Rinehart & Winston.

Fleishman, E. A. (1988). Some new frontiers in personnel selection research. *Personnel Psychology, 41,* 679–702.

Folger, R. (1987). Distributive and procedural justice in the workplace. *Social Justice Research, 1,* 143–159.

Folger, R., & Greenberg, J. (1985). Procedural justice: An interpretive analysis of personnel systems. In K. M. Rowland & G. R. Ferris (Eds.), *Research in Personnel and Human Resource Management, 3,* 141–183.

Gottfredson, L. S. (1990, April). *Affirmative action and the merit principle.* Paper presented at the meeting of the Society for Industrial and Organizational Psychology, Miami, FL.

Greenberg, J. (1986). Determinants of perceived fairness of performance evaluations. *Journal of Applied Psychology, 71,* 340–342.

Guion, R. M. (1965). *Personnel testing.* New York: McGraw-Hill.

Hartigan, J. A., & Wigdor, A. K. (1989). *Fairness in employment testing: Validity generalization, minority issues, and the General Aptitude Test Battery.* Washington, DC: National Academy Press.

Hogan, J., & Quigley, A. (1986). Physical standards for employment and the courts. *American Psychologist, 41,* 1193–1217.

Hunter, J. E., & Schmidt, F. L. (1976). Critical analysis of the statistical and ethical implications of various definitions of test bias. *Psychological Bulletin, 83,* 1053–1071.

Ironson, G. (1982). Use of chi-square and latent trait approaches for detecting item bias. In R. Berk (Ed.), *Handbook of methods for detecting test bias.* Baltimore, MD: Johns Hopkins University Press.

Jensen, A. R. (1980). *Bias in mental testing.* New York: Free Press.

Leong, F. T., & Hayes, T. J. (1990). Occupational stereotyping of Asian Americans. *Career Development Quarterly, 39,* 1443–1454.

Lounsbury, J. W., Bobrow, W., & Jensen, J. B. (1989). Attitudes toward employment testing: Scale development, correlates, and "known group" validation. *Professional Psychology, 20,* 340–349.

Maxwell, S. E., & Arvey, R. D. (in press). The search for predictors with high validity and low adverse impact: Compatible or incompatible goals? *Journal of Applied Psychology.*

Peterson, N. S., & Novick, M. R. (1976). An evaluation of some models for culture-fair selection. *Journal of Educational Measurement, 14,* 3–29.

Price-Waterhouse v. *Hopkins.* 109 S. Ct. 1775 (1989).

Rasky, S. (1989, December 30). Rights groups work on measure to reverse court's bias rulings. *New York Times,* p. A-11.

Roznowski, M. (1987). Use of tests manifesting sex differences as measures of intelligence: Implications for measurement bias. *Journal of Applied Psychology, 72,* 480–483.

Rynes, S., Bretz, B., & Gerhart, B. (1991). The importance of recruitment in job choice: A different way of looking. *Personnel Psychology, 44,* 487–522.

Sashkin, M., & Williams, R. L. (1990). Does fairness make a difference? *Organizational Dynamics, 19,* 56–71.

Schmidt, F. L. (1990, April). *Affirmative action in the 1990's.* Paper presented at the meeting of the Society for Industrial and Organizational Psychology, Miami, FL.

Schmitt, N. (1991). *Beyond differential prediction: Fairness in selection.* Paper presented at the Conference on Human Rights and Employment: Interdisciplinary Perspectives, McGill University, Montreal, Canada.

Society for Industrial and Organizational Psychology (1987). *Principles for the validation and use of personnel selection procedures.* College Park, MD: Author.

Tenopyr, M. L. (1990). *Employment research in multi-ethnic societies.* Paper presented at the meeting of the International Association of Applied Psychology, Kyoto, Japan.

Tyler, T. R., & Bies, R. J. (1990). Beyond formal procedures: The interpersonal context of procedural justice. In J. S. Carroll (Ed.), *Applied social psychology and organizational settings.* Hillsdale, NJ: Erlbaum.

Uniform guidelines on employee selection procedures, Section 3,D. (1978). *Federal Register, 43,* (166), 38297.

United Firefighter Candidates v. *City of Minneapolis.* District Court, Fourth Judicial District, September 3, 1991.

Wards Cove Packing Company v. *Antonio.* 57 *LW* 4583 (1989).

Watson v. *Fort Worth Bank.* 108 S. Ct. 2777 (1988).

Wigdor, A. K., & Sackett, P. R. (in press). Employment testing and public policy: The case of the General Aptitude Test Battery. In H. Schuler, J. Farr, & M. Smith (Eds.), *Personnel selection and assessment: Organizational and individual perspectives.* Hillsdale, NJ: Erlbaum.

7

Computerized Psychological Testing: Impacts on Measuring Predictor Constructs and Future Job Behavior

Michael J. Burke

The focus of this chapter is on how the current and future use of computers in presenting test stimuli is likely to affect the inferences we make about the measurement of our predictor constructs and future on-the-job behavior. Advances in two areas of computerized psychological testing have the potential to affect the measurement of our predictor constructs in personnel selection and the inferences we make about future job behavior as a result of scores on these selection procedures. These are developments in (1) computer-based testing (CBT) technology related to administering and scoring conventional (paper-and-pencil) tests and providing interpretive reports for such tests and (2) computer-adaptive testing (CAT), in which a computer program adjusts the test difficulty to the ability of the individual being tested.

This chapter comprises four sections. The first section presents a brief history of CBT and CAT. The second establishes a general framework for studying current and future uses of CBT and CAT in estimating attribute–job performance relationships. The third section focuses on issues in CBT such as the equivalence of computer-administered and paper-and-pencil versions of conventional tests, the criterion-related validity evidence for computer-based tests, and the potential scientific and practical benefits and disadvantages of CBT. The fourth section provides an overview of CAT with emphasis on discussing measurement precision in CAT and conventional tests, criterion-related validity evidence for CAT in military settings, and unique threats to construct validity in CAT. Although issues related to measuring predictor constructs and estimating criterion-related validity coefficients for computer-based and computer-adaptive tests are not always mutually exclusive, this general distinction between CBT and CAT will assist in discussing several different research and practice issues that arise with each type of testing.

This chapter is not intended to provide a comprehensive review of developments in CBT and CAT. Rather, the intent is to focus on key research and practice developments that appear to have the most relevance for improving measurement of our predictor constructs and understanding human attribute–job performance relationships.

Brief History of Computer-Based and Computer-Adaptive Testing

Use of computers in psychological testing has steadily increased over the last three decades. During this time, computers have primarily assisted in administering and scoring tests and in providing interpretive reports for personality and interest measures. Several critical reviews of use of computers in psychological testing over the first twenty-five years (compare Bartram & Bayliss, 1984; Burke & Normand, 1987; Skinner & Pakula, 1986) have generally concluded that although computerized psychological testing systems (CBT or CAT) have the potential for being practical, cost-effective, and psychometrically sound means of assessing individuals, this potential has yet to be fully realized and a number of important science and practice issues remain to be addressed. To best understand the recent progress and hope for CBT and CAT, we first take a look at their past.

Based on the optical scanning device invented by Reynold B. Johnson (see Downey, 1965) and other developments in scanning technolology as of 1970, high-capacity optical scanners were originally used in testing mainly to read, score, and store test information in a computer-compatible medium for future data analysis and reporting. Baker (1971) provides an in-depth discussion of these early high-capacity test scoring systems. Sampson (1983) chronicles how later developments in mark sensing optical scanning led to the use of large time-sharing computers for scanning (while allowing clerical personnel to edit answer sheets simultaneously), scoring, and profiling standardized tests.

Quick to follow the use of these mainframe computers for scoring and analyzing test data were the uses of mainframe computers and other automated devices for a variety of assessment purposes, such as direct computer interviewing and administration of personality inventories (for example, see Gedye, 1968; Slack, Hicks, Reed, & Van Cura, 1966; Stillman, Roth, Colby, & Rosenbaum, 1969). Although these as well as many other early uses of computer technology in testing represented advances in the practice of psychological testing, the reliance on mainframes and special automated devices posed numerous technological problems, as these testing systems were relatively inflexible and costly.

Primarily within the area of personality assessment, computer-based test interpretations closely followed the use of computers in scoring and analyzing test data. The first such computer-based interpretive system was developed at the Mayo Clinic (Pearson, Swenson, Rome, Mataya, & Brannick, 1965; Rome et al., 1962). Other early interpretive systems were developed for the Sixteen Personality Factor Test Questionnaire (16PF) (Eber, 1964), Rorschach (Piotrowski, 1964), Holtzman inkblot technique (Gorham, 1967), and Thematic Apperception Test (TAT) (Smith, 1968). Most of these systems were not refined. This was probably in part due to the open-ended nature of the possible responses and the inherent difficulty in scoring and developing interpretive systems for such response data.

The next major development in computerized psychological testing was the on-line administration of tests. The first such system, by Elwood and Griffin (1972), administered the Wechsler Adult Intelligence Scale (WAIS). This was followed by an early on-line system for administering the Minnesota Multiphasic Personality Inventory (MMPI) by Lushene, O'Neil, and Dunn (1974). The proliferation of computer software for administering, scoring, and interpreting personality inventories in the late 1970s and early 1980s, coupled with the advent of the minicomputer, led to increased use of minicomputer testing technology in the practice of clinical psychological testing. Subsequent developments during the mid-1980s in microcomputer technology and the increased availability of computer testing software that was not bundled with a particular type of hardware for most conventional psychological tests spelled the demise of minitesting technology.

A more recent innovation in microcomputer technology is the possibility of linking a microcomputer with a tabletop scanner. The microcomputer works with the scanner to pick up marks on scannable forms, processes this information, and usually communicates its results via a computer printer. Other developments in microcomputer technology have not only improved the traditional test administration, scoring, analysis, and reporting phases, but have also led to the use of computers in item writing, item banking, and test construction (see Baker, 1989). That is, microcomputers are now used with graphics software capabilities to create and store test items. Often accompanying the storage of each item is descriptive information specifying the item's content as well as its psychometric properties. The resulting set of items is generally called an item pool or item bank, and the process of storing the items via the computer is known as item banking (see Millman & Arter, 1984; Roid, 1989). A result of these important additional uses of microcomputers is the possibility of integrating the total testing process within the framework of a single hardware and computer software system. With a few exceptions, however, several computer programs are currently necessary to perform the major steps in the total testing process. As emphasized by Baker (1989), even in these situations the computer programs are not necessarily compatible with one another.

One state-of-the-art system that integrates hardware and software into a total testing system and has applicability to personnel testing is the MicroCAT system (Assessment Systems

Corporation, 1989). MicroCAT, although oriented toward CAT, supports all aspects of the testing process and most combinations of item response theory and classical test theory with adaptive and conventional testing. Informative reviews of MicroCAT with respect to its advantages and disadvantages in the total testing process are presented by Baker (1989) and Stone (1989). In particular, Stone stresses that although some individuals may consider the item analysis procedures based on item response theory to be MicroCAT's strength, its primary strength lies in the development and banking of items composed of both text and graphics, and in the administration of such items on the computer.

The work of Loevinger (1947) can be considered the origin of CAT procedures in testing systems such as MicroCAT's. Loevinger posited that a test should be thought of as a collection of items that were all chosen to measure the same underlying trait or ability. This notion was to become the fundamental tenet of item response theory (IRT).

Later developments in IRT, beginning with the work of Fred Lord (1952) and continuing through the 1960s and 1970s, emphasized the test item as the unit of measurement. IRT assumed an underlying trait on which a set of prespecified items were linearly arrayed from the easiest to the most difficult. In essence, each item was considered to provide information about ability within a certain range of the continuum. Once items were considered as individual tools for use in estimating a person's ability (standing on the underlying trait), the goal of testing was to present only enough items to obtain an accurate estimate of where the person was on the underlying trait continuum. The strategy of tailoring a test to present, via computer, only enough items to obtain an accurate estimate of an examinee's ability became known as computerized adaptive testing. And as noted by Wainer (1990), many believe that adaptive testing is the raison d'être of IRT.

CAT, the dynamic selection of items to match the performance of an examinee during the computer administration of a test, is now an accessible methodology for use in standardized testing (Reckase, 1989). Most current computer-adaptive tests based on IRT select precalibrated items (that is, items with known item characteristics and, thus, information) to maximize test information. Several large-scale testing programs now use adaptive testing (Kingsbury, 1990; Ward, Kline, & Flaugher, 1986); several major investigations of adaptive testing have been conducted (Moreno, 1987; Olsen, Maynes, Slawson, & Ho, 1986; Stevenson & Salehi, 1986); and, as noted above, a system that incorporates adaptive testing is commercially available. In addition, a set of technical guidelines has been developed for assessing computerized adaptive testing (Green, Bock, Humphreys, Linn, & Reckase, 1984).

The current and possible future uses of CAT and CBT for more appropriately estimating attribute–job performance relationships are discussed later in this chapter. Initially, a discussion of important issues in estimating attribute–job performance relationships with CBT and CAT predictor measures is presented. This discussion provides a general framework for studying current and future uses of CBT and CAT in estimating attribute–job performance relationships.

Estimating Attribute–Job Performance Relationships with Computer-Based and Computer-Adaptive Test Scores

Fundamental to the development and application of useful selection methods such as CBT or CAT procedures is the need for appropriate taxonomic systems that classify and interrelate characteristics of people and jobs over time. An example of such a system is presented in Table 7.1, which shows a hypothetical matrix representing the relationships between human attributes and various jobs or job performance dimensions. The values in the matrix can be viewed as quantitative measures of association (for example, validity coefficients, covariances, expert ratings of relevance) indicating the degree of relationship between the two domains.

There are at least three important issues encountered in developing and quantifying a matrix such as that in Table 7.1 (Burke & Pearlman, 1988; Peterson & Bownas, 1982). These

Table 7.1. Hypothetical Attribute–Job Performance Matrix.

	AT 1	AT 2	AT 3	AT 4
J/JPD 1	34	37	11	20
J/JPD 2	19	18	28	46
J/JPD 3	78	70	39	55
J/JPD 4	30	32	49	16

Note: AT = attribute; J/JPD = job or job performance dimension.

issues are central to our understanding of, and ability to accurately quantify, the inferences from computer-based and computer-adaptive personnel selection test scores and the productivity implications of such inferences.

The first issue concerns which human attribute and job performance categories should be included in the system. As discussed by Burke and Pearlman (1988), determining the human attribute and job performance categories is fundamentally a theoretical sampling issue concerning the representativeness and comprehensiveness of the system, which in turn depends on how the domain of relevant jobs or job performance dimensions is defined and what categories of human attributes are hypothesized to explain or predict most of the predictable variance in individual performance within this domain. For example, if the job domain were defined as "managerial," would categories representing cognitive ability attributes be sufficient to account for most of the criterion variance, or would the inclusion of attribute categories such as temperament, interest, and psychomotor abilities enhance prediction? Within the context of the present chapter, would the development of new tests such as those for time sharing, divided attention, ability to concentrate, and ability to function under time pressures as noted in Fleishman (1988) lead to the development of new attribute categories or a modification of existing ones?

A third set of categories that might be added to the matrix in Table 7.1 to form a cube would be time-related categories. At the present, time does not play a central role in the estimation of attribute–job performance relationships. Even for most selection test validation studies that involve job incumbents, the measurement of attributes is static, at one point in time, with very little or no attribute measurement over time. This practice is understandable considering the purposes of selection test validation studies, the potential costs versus benefits involved in the measurement of currently defined attributes over time, and the limitations of current testing technology and information management systems. It is plausible that developments in computer testing technology and information systems management will provide opportunities for more efficient continuous or dynamic (over time) measurement of attributes and linkage to job performance. This would seem to be particularly relevant in the future with respect to the measurement of attributes based on new dynamic (changing) test stimuli and their relation over time to job performance that may also change.

The second issue in constructing an attribute–job performance matrix (Table 7.1) is how specific or general these categories should be. This can be viewed as an issue of differential prediction or the degree to which attribute–job performance relationships are moderated by the level of specificity with which they are defined and measured. Continuing the above example for the managerial job domain, would the relationships between two information processing attribute categories, such as processing efficiency and selective attention, and job performance be relatively constant across attributes (for example, like that shown across attribute categories 1 and 2 for job or job performance dimensions in Table 7.1)? If these relationships are relatively constant, it implies that the taxonomy of attributes is likely too specific and less than optimal; that is, it means that the specific attributes (for example, the information processing attributes) could be aggregated to a more general level with little loss of information (at least with respect to their relationship with performance in the set of jobs).

A current issue in CBT and CAT is whether or not the predictor constructs measured by such computerized tests differentially predict job performance in relation to their paper-and-pencil counterparts. A related issue is whether or not computerized and conventional versions of the same tests provide equivalent measurement. In our opinion, a more important future issue is whether the generality or specificity of measurement of attributes (such as memory, visual spatial ability, complex reasoning, and so on) via new types of computerized tests *enhances* the job inferences we can make from our present selection test scores for analogous conventional tests.

The issue of the optimal level of generality or specificity of attribute categories, which CBT and CAT have the possibility of informing, is crucial to the utility of the framework in personnel selection and classification. Fortunately, within the areas of computer-based and computer-adaptive testing of human attributes, researchers can now begin with some provisional assumptions or hypotheses concerning the appropriate level of generality. The work of Hunter (1983a, 1983b, 1983c, 1985), recent validity generalization/meta-analytic findings in applied settings, and the results of a large-scale military validation study (see Campbell et al., 1990; Campbell, McHenry, & Wise, 1990; Peterson et al., 1990; Young, Houston, Harris, Hoffman, & Wise, 1990; Wise, McHenry, & Campbell, 1990) provide information for specifying a priori the level of generality of various attribute categories.

The final issue in developing an attribute–job characteristic matrix is how the values of the matrix will be determined. (See Burke and Pearlman, 1988; Peterson and Bownas, 1982; and Peterson et al., 1990, for a discussion of methodological issues in quantifying such a matrix.)

Discussion of more specific science and practice issues concerning the measurement of attributes with CBT and CAT and the criterion-related validity evidence for attribute–job performance relationships based on CBT and CAT is offered next. Minimal reference is made to criterion measurement, because the focus of this chapter is on CBT and CAT in the measurement of human attributes.

Computer-Based Testing

There are a number of construct validity issues concerning the computer administration of conventional tests. In this section, we discuss research on the equivalence of conventional

and computer-administered versions of the same test as well as
criterion-related validity evidence for computer-administered
tests. Furthermore, we discuss the possibilities of CBT relative
to the development of new item types and dynamic test stimuli.

Test Equivalence Issues

Central to the computer administration of conventional tests
are issues concerning the equivalence of conventional and computer-administered versions. Several studies have compared conventional and computer versions of the same test for personality
inventories (for example, see Honaker, Harrell, & Buffaloe, 1989),
aptitude tests (for example, see Harrell, Honaker, Hetu, & Oberwager, 1987; Hunter & Burke, 1987; Lee, Moreno, & Sympson,
1986), and a variety of other measures (see Greaud & Green,
1986; Kiely, Zara, & Weiss, 1986; Silver & Bennett, 1987). Two
recent reviews (Bunderson, Inouye, & Olsen, 1989; Mazzeo &
Harvey, 1988) of these studies have concluded that the research
in this area is still quite shallow. Although such conclusions were
reached in these reviews primarily on the basis of a comparison
of differences in mean test scores between the two versions, the
magnitude of these mean differences is often quite small.

The concern over mean differences between different modes
of administration is not highly important for most ability tests used
by personnel psychologists as long as the two versions measure the
same construct. Within a selection validation context, resolving
more important issues, such as whether approximately identical
frequency distributions of test scores in which no change is observed in examinee ranks between the two versions, provides
greater evidence for assessing equivalence. Although the study
used a small sample size of thirty-four, Silver and Bennett (1987)
imply that the examinee ranks (that is, norms) changed from
paper-and-pencil to computer versions of a clerical aptitude test.

Notable exceptions are the differences found in scores on
speed tests (Greaud & Green, 1986; Henly, Klebe, McBride,
& Cudeck, 1989; Silver & Bennett, 1987) and some personality
tests (Mazzeo & Harvey, 1988). It appears, as is even the case
with nonspeeded tests in educational testing (see Olsen, Maynes,

Slawson, & Ho, 1986), that the speed of responding on a computer keyboard tends to favor the computer-administered group. However, in Silver and Bennett's (1987) study, and in a study by Martin and Wilcox (1989), the computer-administered test groups performed lower on a clerical perceptual speed and accuracy test and a block-design task, respectively. Another exception is the computer administration of personality tests, where omit rates seem to be higher (see Mazzeo & Harvey, 1988). Clearly, one should be cautious in using normative data from conventional administration of personality or speed measures for interpreting computer-administered scores for such measures.

Test equivalence appears to be more straightforward for nonspeeded ability tests used in personnel selection. A high degree of equivalence would generally be expected between different modes for power tests that are fixed in length, have little if any change in format, and require some form of multiple-choice response (Burke & Normand, 1987). Several concerns, however, related to the equivalence of computer and conventional versions of the same test may arise even for power tests from human factor design considerations.

Some human factor considerations that may facilitate or inhibit examinee-computer interaction include the clarity of instructions for taking the test, amount of practice before starting the test, difficulties related to reading and understanding items on a computer screen, availability of a backup key for error checking and correction, flexibility to skip items in highly speeded tests, and amount of time between an individual's answer to an item and the computer's response. For instance, Allred and Green (1984) note that human factor design considerations may affect test-taking strategies. Green (1988) also discusses the possible need to modify computer versions of some conventional tests, such as the need to use multiple screens for comprehension test items. Such human factor considerations that alter test-taking strategies and modify the type of item presented can affect the construct being measured.

Although some improvements have been made over the past five years with respect to computer software and hardware design features, several human factor design issues remain, and several more important issues related to providing item feedback and considering what is presented on computer screens have emerged. A more detailed discussion of developing issues related to the presentation of stimuli on computer screens is presented in a special issue of *Computers in Human Behavior* (Morrison, 1989). Also, Wise and Plake (1989) discuss why it is recommended that test developers consider not providing item feedback on computer-based tests until its effects on examinee test performance are better understood.

The preceding discussion on test equivalence issues between computer-administered and conventional versions of the same test leads to the conclusion that, where feasible, it would be helpful to conduct studies to compare computer-administered and conventional versions of tests. Hofer and Green (1985) and the *Guidelines for Computer-Based Tests and Interpretations* (American Psychological Association, 1986) provide valuable insights concerning the effect of different kinds of information on the equivalence of tests and the legitimacy of generalizing inferences from test scores when the tests have different modes of administration. Peterson, Kolen, and Hoover (1989) also present a number of equating research designs and conceptual issues to attend to when conducting equating studies. Furthermore, Turban, Sanders, Francis, and Osburn (1989) present an approach for evaluating predictor construct equivalence between an experimental test and a currently used test, where the latter test has been shown to correlate with job performance and it is assumed that the factor structure of job performance has remained essentially the same. Their approach provides a general framework, in a personnel selection context, for determining whether computer-administered tests of constructs and conventionally administered tests of the same constructs can be substituted for one another without the necessity of conducting new criterion-related validity studies.

Other Construct-Related Differences

Another interesting construct validity issue is whether examinees differentially respond to questions probing highly sensitive personal topics and admit more to engaging in socially undesirable behavior when examined via computer than when interviewed in person. Several authors indicate that individuals may respond more honestly on a computer to questions probing sensitive personal issues (see Evan & Miller, 1969; Koson, Kitchen, Kochen, & Stodolosky, 1970; O'Brien & Dugdale, 1978) and possibly admit to engaging in more socially undesirable behaviors (Carr, Ghosh, & Ancil, 1983; Greist & Klein, 1980; Lucas, Mullins, Luna, & McIroy, 1977; Slack & Van Cura, 1968). Such findings may in part be due to the use of inappropriate equating designs and inadequate statistical analyses (see Schuldberg, 1988).

A more recent study by Martin and Nagao (1989) found that within the context of laboratory simulation in which undergraduates were interviewed for low- or high-status positions, subjects in computer-administered interviews reported their grade point averages and scholastic aptitude scores more accurately than did those given paper-and-pencil forms. However, the magnitude of the differences between computer-administered interviews and paper-and-pencil forms in terms of Scholastic Aptitude Test (SAT) score and grade point average (GPA) bias (that is, reported minus actual) and overreporting was very small. Likewise, Lautenschlager and Flaherty (1990) found little difference between social desirability responses for individuals taking computer-administered versus paper-and-pencil tests.

An unanswered question, arising from the above studies in clinical and undergraduate student populations, is whether or not in applied settings individual responses to sensitive items on integrity tests or background information forms are influenced by the mode of test administration. As with concerns over many human factor design considerations and issues of equating, this question will likely become moot as computerized testing becomes more common in our society.

Criterion-Related Validity of Computer-Based Tests

Although issues of measurement equivalence of computer-based and conventional versions of the same test have been examined in several studies, criterion-related validity studies for computer-based tests in applied settings are sparse. An early industrial criterion-related CBT study (Burke, 1984) estimated the predictive effectiveness, for a sample of 217 clerical employees, of a battery of ten clerical ability tests (described in Normand & Burke, 1984), a word processing test, and a personality scale for forecasting job proficiency criteria in three clerical job families: general clerk, transcriber/word processor, and quantitative clerk. Two tests explicitly developed to take advantage of the computer medium, a reasoning ability test and a test for following directions, had a corrected (for criterion unreliability) multiple correlation of .63 with an overall job performance rating criterion for the general clerk job family. The reasoning ability test was also a significant predictor of job performance for the other two job families. In addition, the disattenuated (for criterion unreliability) bivariate validity coefficient of .54 for the reasoning ability test contrasts with the value of .38 for the mean of Pearlman, Schmidt, and Hunter's (1980) distribution of operational true validity coefficients for reasoning ability in stenography, typing, filing, and related occupations. Also, Silver and Bennett (1987) report, for a sample of thirty-four secretaries, that a computer version of a clerical aptitude test correlated .62 with an interactive criterion task, in contrast with a .55 validity coefficient for the paper-and-pencil version of the test.

Another study (Marshall-Meis, Eisner, Schemmer, & Yarkin-Levin, 1983), described in Fleishman (1988), estimates the criterion-related validity of tests of decision making, information processing, attention to detail, sensory alertness, problem sensitivity, problem solving, and time sharing for predicting job performance for positions in energy control centers. It was noted that the validity coefficients of computer-administered tests were no better than the predictions obtained from combinations of printed tests.

More recently, McHenry, Hough, Toquam, Hanson, and Ashworth (1990) report, for a sample of 4,039 incumbents in nine military jobs, criterion-related validity results for a combination of computer-administered perceptual/psychomotor tests;

conventional cognitive ability, temperament/personality, interest, and job outcome preference predictor measures; and criterion measures of job-specific and general task proficiency. The newly developed cognitive ability composites (including the new computer-administered perceptual/psychomotor tests) were found to add small increments to the prediction of job-specific (.02) and general soldiering (.04) task proficiency over and above conventional cognitive ability composites. Noteworthy were the findings that the new composites predicted general soldiering proficiency equally as well (.65) as the conventional cognitive ability composites. Another important finding relative to the development of a matrix such as that in Table 7.1 was that temperament/personality scales considerably improved the prediction of several job performance dimensions over and above cognitive ability composites (which included the newly developed computer-administered perceptual/psychomotor tests).

Development of New Item Types and Dynamic Test Stimuli

Although the magnitude of possible increases in criterion-related validity coefficients may not be large relative to the validity of conventional cognitive ability test composites, CBT, as noted, affords the opportunity for developing new types of tests that may increase validity coefficient estimates for some jobs (for example, the measurement of dynamic spatial and reasoning abilities: Hunt & Pellegrino, 1985; Pellegrino, Hunt, Abate, & Farr, 1987; Snow, Bethel-Fox, & Seibert, 1985). Research on the development and application of new item and test types has been somewhat slow in the field of personnel selection. This in part is likely due to the relatively high development costs and necessary technical expertise required for such applications. The primary exceptions in personnel selection are the new types of tests for spatial and reasoning abilities discussed above, developed as part of Project A, and the computer-interactive performance tests noted in Fleishman (1988) and Bartram and Bayliss (1984). In addition, some examples of new item types developed for educational testing that involve dynamic test stimuli are presented in WICAT Systems' (1988) Learner Profile (a battery of forty-five computer-based and computer-adaptive tests covering a variety of learning-oriented aptitude and preference dimensions).

We are rapidly moving away from static computer screens to dynamic visual and auditory stimuli on computer screens. These are exciting developments that signal the potential for developing new forms of dynamic test stimuli (for example, see Hunter & Burke, 1987) and computer simulations of real-life situations (for instance, see Greitzer, Hershman, & Kelly, 1981; Jacoby, Kuss, Mazursky, & Troutman, 1985; Wolfe, 1990) and for presenting actual situations through computer-videotape linkages. For example, Kennedy, Bittner, Harbeson, and Jones (1982) and Jones, Kennedy, and Bittner (1981) present early examples of the use of video games for selection and training. Bartram and Bayliss (1984) describe the development of novel computerized tests for selection studies in the U.S. Air Force and the MicroPAT battery developed for pilot selection in the U.K. Army Air Corps (also see Bartram, 1987). In addition, there are a variety of video-related computer applications in business school training (see Wolfe, 1990) and in industries such as manufacturing, merchandising, and air traffic control (Hall, Cunningham, Roache, & Cox, 1988). These latter computer systems are largely used for training purposes or to support employee tasks.

The measurement of responses to dynamic stimuli such as computer-based simulations or video displays in personnel selection contexts and the developing capabilities for dynamic (continuous) and portable measurement in remote sites (for example, see Bittner, Smith, Kennedy, Staley, & Harbeson, 1985; Popper, Dragsbaek, Siegel, & Hirsch, 1988) will likely present new challenges and raise new questions for industrial and organizational psychologists and allied professionals in the fields of business, psychometrics, and cognitive psychology. In particular, new questions are likely to arise as a result of not only the dynamic test stimuli but also the new types of temporal controls on presenting and responding to test stimuli. Models derived from the cognitive sciences may assist in understanding the constructs involved in tests with dynamic stimuli (Bunderson, Inouye, & Olsen, 1989; Snow & Lohman, 1989). However, as discussed by Dunlap, Kennedy, Harbeson, and Fowlkes (1989), cognitive constructs may assist us in describing and understanding our predictor measures but may be less useful for prediction purposes in selection contexts. Nevertheless, an understanding of the constructs measured by foreseeable new types of tests with dynamic stimuli in industrial settings may fundamentally advance personnel selection by providing a better understanding of the job behaviors such dynamic measures will be designed to predict.

The ability of computers to not only present dynamic stimuli but also synthesize dynamic responses (for example, auditory responses) may also assist in testing individuals with disabilities. Microcomputers in conjunction with specialized data input and output devices provide individuals with visual, auditory, or physical limitations opportunities to complete various tests with minimal assistance (see Low & Beukelman, 1988; Wilson, Thompson, & Wylie, 1982). In a personnel selection context, the future use of computer technology for assessing individuals with disabilities may assist in more appropriate job matching by obviating the need for a clinical (in lieu of statistical) prediction of their job performance. Such use of computers and related technology for personnel selection testing may become more prominent as the implications of the Americans with Disabilities Act are better understood.

Other benefits of computer-based tests are that they appear to be well accepted by examinees (for example, see Burke, Normand, & Raju, 1987), have acceptable to high levels of reliability (for example, see Barrett, Alexander, Doverspike, Cellar, & Thomas, 1982), provide economy and speed in test scoring, and can produce relatively accurate interpretations (for example, see Space, 1981; Vale, Keller, & Bentz, 1986). Particularly in the area of personality assessment, use of computer-based interpretive reports, although controversial, is common (see Farrell, 1989).

Even though ensuring the quality of computer-based test interpretations is relatively straightforward in ability testing, it is a difficult process in other assessment areas (see Conoley, Plake, & Kemmerer, 1990). Nevertheless, the Buros Institute of Mental Measurements is beginning a review dedicated to evaluation of computer-based test interpretation systems (Plake, Conoley, Kramer, & Murphy, 1989).

In sum, CBT offers several practical and possible scientific advantages. A few shortcomings in classical test theory, upon which most computer-based tests are constructed and interpreted, have been pointed out, however (see Hambleton, 1989). As discussed below, the concept of CAT based on item response theory is an attractive alternative that may overcome many of the shortcomings of classical test theory, which forms the basis for CBT.

Computer-Adaptive Testing

CAT, as noted previously, is a testing procedure in which a computer program adjusts or tailors the difficulty of a test to the examinee's ability. Item response theory provides the psychometric basis for most CAT procedures. These computer-adaptive procedures use item pools containing items that supposedly all measure a unidimensional trait and that have been precalibrated using an IRT model (see Hambleton, 1989; Harris, 1989) rather than group test statistics. Hsu and Yu (1989) review studies comparing selected IRT item calibration programs.

Items are selected for administration in CAT according to the amount of information they provide about the trait (for instance, ability) level of the examinee. The CAT item administration strategy is to select from the item pool those items that are most useful in estimating the trait level of an examinee at the most recent estimate of ability. Implementing this strategy is accomplished by primarily administering easy items to examinees with estimated low ability and difficult items to examinees with estimated high ability. The test stops when a given level of precision has been reached or when a fixed number of items have been administered. When the test stops, the examinee's final trait estimate can be taken as the test score. A critical feature of CAT is that this final trait estimate is independent of the particular set of items given to the examinee. A result is that examinee scores can be compared even though the examinees might have been administered different sets of items of varying difficulty.

Reliability Issues

Similar to concerns about the equivalence of computer-based and conventional versions of paper-and-pencil tests are questions about the relationship between scores on conventionally administered (or even CBT versions) and computer-adaptive tests. One question concerns whether the precision of measurement obtained with CAT differs from that obtained with paper-and-pencil testing. In CAT, reliability is generally considered in terms of precision of examinee ability estimates. The test practitioner has some control over the reliability or precision of CAT scores, because a prespecified level of precision, as noted above, is often used as a stopping rule for a testing session.

For comparisons between CAT and conventionally administered tests, it is likely that the computer-administered test will be scored on a scale using an IRT model (see Hambleton, 1989) and that the conventional test will use summed test scores and indices of precision developed from classical test theory (Thissen, 1990). For such cases, only an incomplete comparison between the two modes of administration can be made. The primary indices of measurement precision available for the conventional test are internal consistency estimates of reliability and test-retest and alternate form reliabilities. The primary indices for CAT are marginal reliability (see Thissen, 1990) and alternate form reliability.

The existence of alternate forms in CAT, referring to alternate item pools, allows one to assess to what extent two item pools are equally related to the same psychological construct. If CAT is to progress in industrial settings in the future, then assessment of alternate form reliability will become more important. In contrast to internal consistency reliability estimates in conventional testing, CAT alternate form reliability assessments using different item pools will more directly show variation due to item sampling.

Several studies (for example, see Divgi, 1989; Henly, Klebe, McBride, & Cudeck, 1989; McBride & Martin, 1983; McKinley & Reckase, 1980; Moreno, Wetzel, McBride, & Weiss, 1984; Sympson, Weiss, & Ree, 1982) have compared the measurement precision of CAT subtests with paper-and-pencil versions of the same subtests. Although not a straightforward assessment of alternate form reliability, a study by Moreno, Wetzel, McBride, and Weiss (1984) found, for a sample of 270 marines, that the Armed Services Vocational Aptitude Battery (ASVAB) subtests for arithmetic reasoning, word knowledge, and paragraph comprehension correlated .80, .80, and .51 with the respective paper-and-pencil ASVAB subtests administered prior to enlistment. These relationships with CAT-ASVAB subtests were virtually identical when compared to scores on an alternate form paper-and-pencil ASVAB administered two weeks after entering for active duty. The CAT and conventionally administered ASVAB subtest correlations were comparable to the alternate form reliabilities for the two conventional versions of the ASVAB subtests, even though the CAT subtests contained only half the number of items. Sympson, Weiss, and Ree (1982) also found that computer-adaptive ASVAB tests could provide levels of measurement precision obtainable only with much longer ASVAB tests. Similar findings were also obtained in the studies by McBride and Martin (1983) and McKinley and Reckase (1980). In sum, these studies provide evidence that roughly equivalent ability estimates can be obtained between conventional and CAT versions of ability tests with reduced testing time.

Content-Related Validity Issues

Closely related to issues of measurement precision in CAT are content-related validity concerns. Steinberg, Thissen, and Wainer (1990) discuss why there are problems for the maintenance of content-related validity evidence in CAT unlike those found in conventional tests. The argument is that in the administration of computer-adaptive tests there may be an interaction between item content and the item selection procedures. The possibility comes about in CAT because items are selected for presentation on the basis of high discrimination at a particular level of ability. Evidence that the representation of content does not differ across levels of ability is required to ensure that a computer-adaptive test produces the equivalent of parallel forms (Steinberg, Thissen, & Wainer, 1990). Although Green (1988) has pointed out that balancing content may not always be possible, it is generally considered that item selection procedures are adequate (Reckase, 1989) or can be modified to ensure content representativeness (Kingsbury, 1990).

The issue of ensuring content representativeness (or balance) across levels of ability in CAT is somewhat different from notions of content sampling in content-oriented validation strategies (see Society for Industrial and Organizational Psychology, 1987). A content-oriented personnel selection test validation strategy is an attempt to establish that test performance is a representative sample of job performance or job-required knowledge. A primary concern in personnel selection test validation is whether or not the entire measure contains a representative sample of the content domain, whereas in CAT there is the additional concern of whether or not there is content representativeness (or what is sometimes referred to as content balance) of items at each level of ability.

Criterion-Related Validity Issues

When the criterion-related validity evidence for CAT versus conventional testing in applied settings is considered, the few studies involving military samples indicate that the two versions yield similar results (for example, see McBride & Martin, 1983; Moreno, Wetzel, McBride, & Weiss, 1984; Sands & Gade, 1983; Sympson, Weiss, & Ree, 1982). For instance, Sands and Gade (1983) found, for a sample of 312 individuals, that the fifteen-item Computerized Adaptive Screening Test (used for predicting army recruits' performance) predicted Armed Forces Qualification Test (AFQT) scores as accurately as the much longer Enlistment Screening Test. Moreno, Wetzel, McBride, & Weiss (1984) also found that AFQT scores could be predicted as accurately by three CAT-ASVAB subtests as by four conventionally administered ASVAB subtests. These results lead to a tentative conclusion that computer-adaptive ability tests are likely to yield comparable validity coefficient estimates in organizational settings relative to similar types of conventional tests.

Criterion-related validity coefficients for CAT, based on item pools for conventional tests, will not necessarily be expected to enhance our understanding of attribute–job performance relationships in a matrix such as that shown in Table 7.1. From a pragmatic perspective, several key questions then arise. One, is CAT cost-effective relative to conventional testing? Second, does CAT offer potential solutions to other practical testing problems? At present, it is very unlikely that CAT will be found very cost-effective relative to conventional testing when considered in an economic utility analysis. As computers come to play a more central role in personnel selection testing and test publishers or consortia make available calibrated item pools for CAT applications, it is possible that CAT will become more cost-effective and viable as a personnel selection method for more organizations.

CAT, however, does offer several scientific and practical advantages that are not considered in our typical selection test utility analyses. These include all the benefits of CBT, such as the development of new item types, plus improved test security (see Bunderson, Inouye, & Olsen, 1989), the flexibility for the test practitioner to construct tests and create items by computer (see Baker, 1989), the use of IRT models and programs in the score-equating process, and possibly, greater measurement precision throughout the ability range in comparison to conventional tests.

Unique Threats to Construct Validity of Computer-Adaptive Tests

Unfortunately, CAT has all the human factor concerns noted previously for CBT. Moreover, there are unique threats to the construct validity of computer-adaptive tests. These include departures from unidimensionality in an item pool, context effects that influence the interpretation of an item purely as a result of the item's relationship (for instance, location) to other items in the test (Kingston & Dorans, 1984; Yen, 1980), the disproportionately negative impact of a flawed item on test results in CAT versus conventional testing, the potential demotivating and anxiety-producing effects of CAT item-difficulty ordering (see Wainer & Kiely, 1987; Rocklin & O'Donnell, 1987), and, as noted above, the possibility of unbalanced content.

This list of potential threats to the construct validity of CAT may appear to embody the "kiss of death" for CAT. Such is likely not the case. Many of these concerns, although clearly varied in degree of threat to the viability of IRT-based CAT, may be overcome by suggested modifications to CAT (see Wainer & Kiely, 1987; Rocklin & O'Donnell, 1987) or monitored through empirical research. For instance, Wainer and Kiely (1987) propose the use of "testlets" to retain the advantages of CAT while requiring that items be selected for presentation in prearranged clusters to reduce problems with context effects, item ordering, and content balancing. The notion of testlets is expanded on in Wainer et al. (1990).

What general lessons can applied psychologists involved in personnel selection learn from the concerns raised about CAT in military and educational testing? One, IRT models that form the basis for CAT are not panaceas. The models, with the primary exception of the Rasch model, were developed to fit data. As heuristic techniques, they serve valuable purposes in offering tentative solutions to many practical testing problems (see Hambleton, 1989; Lord, 1980). Perhaps in the long term we will have new theoretical models of test performance that yield tests constructed on the basis of such theory. For instance, Wainer et al. (1990) note that an ultimate goal for research in the measurement of individual differences in cognition (see Embretson, 1985) may be the development of tests in which a well-understood theory of cognitive processing may be used to determine the properties (parameters) of the test items. In the short term, even given the additional research needs and limited applicability of CAT for many organizational testing situations (see Vale, 1991), we do have IRT heuristics and commercially available and viable procedures for potential CAT applications.

A second lesson from CAT use in military and educational testing is that, even with the increased technical sophistication of the IRT literature and algorithms for implementation of CAT, the test practitioner and developer need not be removed from the test development process. Developing systems such as those in the MicroCAT Testing System offer flexibility to the practitioner in the development and inclusion of new items in CAT item pools. As aptly stated by Wainer and Kiely (1987, p. 200) in discussing CAT, "our advocacy of not allowing an algorithm to build the test unaided until the algorithm contains as much wisdom as the expert test developer is not radical — it is merely sensible." In sum, although there are serious issues with the application of the most common IRT models to many tests used in industry today, developments in IRT-based CAT procedures are likely to enhance the organizational applicability of alternative forms of CAT such as testlets.

Conclusion

Computer-based and computer-adaptive testing offers the potential for progressively developing knowledge of human attribute–job performance relations. Continued developments in computerized psychological testing may assist in addressing important issues in this area by helping to develop and quantify matrices such as that shown in Table 7.1.

With respect to issues concerning which human attribute and job performance categories should be included in such a system and how specific or general these categories should be, the findings from Project A (see McHenry, Hough, Toquam, Hanson, & Ashworth, 1990) and the work of Hunter (1983a) indicate that general cognitive ability, perceptual abilities, and psychomotor abilities predict a large portion of the predictable variance in general job proficiency. Furthermore, as discussed, it was found in Project A that temperament/personality scales considerably improved the prediction of several job performance dimensions (that is, effort and leadership, personal discipline) over and above cognitive ability composites that included the newly developed computer-administered perceptual/psychomotor tests.

The findings from these studies as well as meta-analytic studies (Hunter & Schmidt, 1990) indicate that a relatively small number of general human attribute and job performance categories are necessary for the broader purpose of maximizing the gain in predictive efficiency for many jobs. The Project A results also suggest that new computer-administered item types for tests of cognitive and perceptual/psychomotor abilities may modify the measurement of such attributes and add small increments to the prediction of general job proficiency over and above general cognitive ability composites. Although the magnitudes of validity increments for computer-administered cognitive ability and perceptual/psychomotor tests that include new item types may not be large relative to conventional tests, these small validity coefficient increments may represent important gains in selection utility.

More important, the development of dynamic test stimuli may lead to an extension of existing attribute categories for some human resource allocation systems. Because computers are capable of both presenting dynamic auditory and visual stimuli and synthesizing human motor and auditory responses, it is possible that computerized ability assessment related to behavioral content — for instance, in terms of Guilford's (1959, 1967; Guilford & Hoepfner, 1971) notions of the structure of intellect — may assist in evaluating interpersonal abilities (for example, with respect to productively analyzing, evaluating, and responding to the verbal and nonverbal behavior of another individual or group of individuals). The most interesting possibilities for computer-based assessment of interpersonal or behavioral content abilities with dynamic test stimuli are jobs that have a major performance dimension concerning dealing with other people. In addition, as discussed, dynamic test stimuli, including computer simulations and presentations of real-life situations based on computer-videotape linkages, may very well lead to the development of other new attribute categories and refinements in the measurement of existing cognitive, perceptual, and psychomotor attribute categories (for instance, through use of matrices such as that shown in Table 7.1).

To date, attention to the refinement of personality test interpretive systems in CBT and to the application of IRT models in CAT have dominated the development of new types of items and tests necessary for the expansion of our attribute–job performance knowledge base. This is understandable given the historical context in which the two forms of computerized assessment developed.

It is time to move on to aggressively pursue the possibilities of computers for assisting in the development of new item types. Theoretical and applied developments may, alone or in various combinations, drive the development or modification of human attribute categories. These advances may include theoretical developments within substantive areas of psychology, such as cognitive psychology; appropriate recognition of the deficiencies in conventional testing of many constructs; increased understanding and progress in computer technology in presenting dynamic test stimuli and synthesizing human auditory, psychomotor, and physiological response data; and the development of tests for attributes that were not conceived of in the conventional test mode of administration. In sum, the present and future uses of computers in assessing individual differences clearly present challenges and opportunities for expanding both the science and practice of personnel selection.

References

Allred, L. J., & Green, B. F. (1984). *Analysis of experimental CAT ASVAB test data.* Unpublished manuscript, Johns Hopkins University, Department of Psychology, Baltimore, MD.

American Psychological Association. (1986). *Guidelines for computer-based tests and interpretations.* Washington, DC: Author.

Assessment Systems Corporation. (1989). *Users manual for the MicroCAT testing system* (3rd ed.). St. Paul, MN: Author.

Baker, F. B. (1971). Automation of test scoring, reporting, and analysis. In R. L. Thorndike (Ed.), *Educational measurement.* Washington, DC: American Council on Education.

Baker, F. B. (1989). Computer technology in test construction and processing. In R. L. Linn (Ed.), *Educational measurement* (3rd ed.). New York: American Council on Education and Macmillan.

Barrett, G. V., Alexander, R. A., Doverspike, D., Cellar, D., & Thomas, J. C. (1982). The development and application of a computerized information processing test battery. *Applied Psychological Measurement, 6,* 13–29.

Bartram, D. (1987). The development of an automated testing system for pilot selection: The MicroPAT project. *Applied Psychology: An International Review, 36,* 279–298.

Bartram, D., & Bayliss, R. (1984). Automated testing: Past, present, and future. *Journal of Occupational Psychology, 57,* 221–237.

Bittner, A. C., Smith, M. G., Kennedy, R. S., Staley, C. F., & Harbeson, M. M. (1985). Automated portable test (APT) system: Overview and prospects. *Behavior Research Methods, Instruments, & Computers, 17,* 217–221.

Bunderson, C. V., Inouye, D. K., & Olsen, J. B. (1989). The four generations of computerized educational measurement. In R. L. Linn (Ed.), *Educational measurement* (3rd ed.). New York: American Council on Education and Macmillan.

Burke, M. J. (1984). *Eastman Kodak computerized clerical test validation report.* Psych Systems Technical Report. Baltimore, MD: Psych Systems.

Burke, M. J., & Normand, J. (1987). Computerized psychological testing: Overview and critique. *Professional Psychology, 18,* 42–51.

Burke, M. J., Normand, J., & Raju, N. S. (1987). Examinee attitudes toward computer-administered ability testing. *Computers in Human Behavior, 3,* 95–107.

Burke, M. J., & Pearlman, K. (1988). Recruiting, selecting, and matching people with jobs. In J. P. Campbell and R. J. Campbell (Eds.), *Productivity in organizations.* San Francisco: Jossey-Bass.

Campbell, C. H., Ford, P., Rumsey, M. G., Pulakos, E. D., Borman, W. C., Felker, D. B., de Vera, M. V., & Riegelhaupt, B. J. (1990). Development of multiple job performance measures in a representative sample of jobs. *Personnel Psychology, 43,* 277–300.

Campbell, J. P., McHenry, J. J., & Wise, L. L. (1990). Modeling job performance in a population of jobs. *Personnel Psychology, 43,* 313–333.

Carr, A. C., Ghosh, A., & Ancil, R. J. (1983). Can a computer take a psychiatric history? *Psychological Medicine, 13,* 151–158.

Conoley, C. W., Plake, B. S., & Kemmerer, B. E. (1990). Developing and applying evaluative criteria to computer-based tests. *The Score, 12,* 5.

Divgi, D. R. (1989). Estimating reliabilities of computerized adaptive testing. *Applied Psychological Measurement, 13,* 145–149.

Downey, M. T. (1965). *Ben T. Wood, educational reformer.* Princeton, NJ: Educational Testing Service.

Dunlap, W. P., Kennedy, R. S., Harbeson, M. M., & Fowlkes, J. E. (1989). Problems with individual difference measures based on some componential cognitive paradigms. *Applied Psychological Measurement, 13,* 9–17.

Eber, H. (1964, August). *Computer reporting of 16PF data.* Paper presented at the meeting of the American Psychological Association, Washington, DC.

Elwood, D. L., & Griffin, H. R. (1972). Individual intelligence testing without the examiner: Reliability of an automated method. *Journal of Consulting and Clinical Psychology, 38,* 9–14.

Embretson, S. (1985). *Test design: Developments in psychology and psychometrics.* San Diego, CA: Academic Press.

Evan, W. M., & Miller, J. R. (1969). Differential effects on response bias of computer versus conventional administration of a social science questionnaire. *Behavioral Science, 14,* 216–227.

Farrell, A. D. (1989). Impact of computers on professional practice: A survey of current practices and attitudes. *Professional Psychology, 20,* 172–178.

Fleishman, E. A. (1988). Some new frontiers in personnel selection research. *Personnel Psychology, 41,* 679–701.

Gedye, J. L. (1968). The development of a general purpose psychological testing system. *Bulletin of the British Psychological Society, 21,* 101–102.

Gorham, D. R. (1967). Validity and reliability of a computer-based scoring system for inkblot responses. *Journal of Consulting Psychology, 31,* 65–70.

Greaud, V. A., & Green, B. F. (1986). Equivalence of conventional and computer presentation of speed tests. *Applied Psychological Measurement, 10,* 23–34.

Green, B. F. (1988). Construct validity of computer-based tests. In H. Wainer & H. Braun (Eds.), *Test validity.* Hillsdale, NJ: Erlbaum.

Green, B. F., Bock, R. D., Humphreys, L. G., Linn, R. L., & Reckase, M. D. (1984). Technical guidelines for assessing computerized adaptive tests. *Journal of Educational Measurement, 21,* 347–360.

Greist, J. H., & Klein, M. H. (1980). Computer programs for patients, clinicians, and researchers, in psychiatry. In H. B. Sidowski, J. H. Johnson, & T. A. Williams (Eds.), *Technology in mental health care delivery systems.* Norwood, NJ: Ablex.

Greitzer, F. L., Hershman, R. L., & Kelly, R. T. (1981). The air defense game: A microcomputer program for research on human performance. *Behavior Research Methods and Instrumentation, 13,* 57–59.

Guilford, J. P. (1959). Three faces of intellect. *American Psychologist, 14,* 469–479.

Guilford, J. P. (1967). *The nature of human intelligence.* New York: McGraw-Hill.

Guilford, J. P., & Hoepfner, R. (1971). *The analysis of intelligence.* New York: McGraw-Hill.

Hall, A. D., Cunningham, B., Roache, R. P., & Cox, J. W. (1988). Factors affecting performance using touch-entry systems: Tactual recognition fields and system accuracy. *Journal of Applied Psychology, 73,* 711–720.

Hambleton, R. K. (1989). Principles and selected applications of item response theory. In R. L. Linn (Ed.), *Educational measurement* (3rd ed.). New York: American Council on Education and Macmillan.

Harrell, T. H., Honaker, L. M., Hetu, M., & Oberwager, J. (1987). Computerized versus traditional administration of the Multidimensional Aptitude Battery–Verbal Scale: An examination of reliability and validity. *Computers in Human Behavior, 3,* 129–137.

Harris, D. (1989). Comparison of 1-, 2-, and 3-parameter IRT models. *Educational Measurement, 8,* 35–41.

Henly, S. J., Klebe, K. J., McBride, J. R., & Cudeck, R. (1989). Adaptive and conventional versions of the DAT: The first complete test battery comparison. *Applied Psychological Measurement, 13,* 363–371.

Hofer, P. J., & Green, B. F. (1985). The challenge of competence and creativity in computerized psychological testing. *Journal of Consulting and Clinical Psychology, 53,* 826–838.

Honaker, L. M., Harrell, T. H., & Buffaloe, J. D. (1989). Equivalency of microtest computer MMPI administration for standard and special scales. *Computers in Human Behavior, 4,* 323–337.

Hsu, T., & Yu, L. (1989). Using computers to analyze item response data. *Educational Measurement, 8,* 21–28.

Hunt, E., & Pellegrino, J. (1985). Using interactive computers to expand intelligence testing: A critique and prospectus. *Intelligence, 9,* 207–236.

Hunter, D. R., & Burke, E. F. (1987). Computer-based selection testing in the Royal Air Force. *Behavior Research Methods, Instruments, & Computers, 19,* 243–245.

Hunter, J. E. (1983a). *Test validation for 12,000 jobs: An application of job classification and validity generalization analysis to the General Aptitude Test Battery* (USES Test Research Report No. 45). Washington, DC: U.S. Department of Labor.

Hunter, J. E. (1983b). *Validity generalization of the ASVAB: Preliminary report.* Rockville, MD: Research Applications.

Hunter, J. E. (1983c). *Validity generalization of the ASVAB: Second report.* Rockville, MD: Research Applications.

Hunter, J. E. (1985). *Differential validity across jobs in the military.* Unpublished manuscript, Michigan State University, East Lansing.

Hunter, J. E., & Schmidt, F. L. (1990). *Methods of meta-analysis.* Newbury Park, CA: Sage.

Jacoby, J., Kuss, A., Mazursky, D., & Troutman, T. (1985). Effectiveness of security analyst information accessing strategies: A computer interactive assessment. *Computers in Human Behavior, 1,* 95–113.

Jones, M. B., Kennedy, R. S., & Bittner, A. C. (1981). A video game for performance testing. *American Journal of Psychology, 94,* 143–152.

Kennedy, R. S., Bittner, A. C., Harbeson, M., & Jones, M. B. (1982). Television computer games: A "new look" in performance testing. *Aviation, Space, and Environmental Medicine, 53,* 49–53.

Kiely, G. L., Zara, A. R., & Weiss, D. J. (1986). *Equivalence of computer and paper-and-pencil Armed Services Vocational Aptitude Battery tests* (Research Report No. AFHRL-TP-86-13). Brooks Air Force Base, TX: Air Force Human Resources Laboratory.

Kingsbury, G. G. (1990). Adapting adaptive testing with the MicroCAT testing system. *Educational Measurement, 9,* 3–6, 29.

Kingston, N. M., & Dorans, N. J. (1984). Item location effects and their implications for IRT equating and adaptive testing. *Applied Psychological Measurement, 8,* 146–154.

Koson, D., Kitchen, C., Kochen, M., & Stodolosky, D. (1970). Psychological testing by computer: Effect on response bias. *Educational and Psychological Measurement, 30,* 803–810.

Lautenschlager, G. J., & Flaherty, V. L. (1990). Computer administration of questions: More desirable or more social desirability. *Journal of Applied Psychology, 75,* 310–314.

Lee, J., Moreno, K. E., & Sympson, J. B. (1986). The effects of mode of test administration on test performance. *Educational and Psychological Measurement, 46,* 467–474.

Loevinger, J. (1947). A systematic approach to the construction and evaluation of tests of ability. *Psychological Monographs, 61,* 4.

Lord, F. M. (1952). A theory of test scores. *Psychometric Monographs, 7,* 1–84.

Lord, F. M. (1980). *Applications of item response theory to practical testing problems.* Hillsdale, NJ: Erlbaum.

Low, D., & Beukelman, D. R. (1988). The use of microcomputer technology with persons unable to speak: An overview. *Computers in Human Behavior, 4,* 355–366.

Lucas, R. W., Mullins, R. J., Luna, C. B., & McIroy, D. C. (1977). Psychiatrists and a computer as an interrogator of patients with alcohol-related illnesses: A comparison. *British Journal of Psychiatry, 131,* 160–167.

Lushene, R. E., O'Neil, H. F., & Dunn, T. (1974). Equivalent validity of a completely computerized MMPI. *Journal of Personality Assessment, 38,* 353–361.

Marshall-Meis, J. C., Eisner, E. J., Schemmer, F. M., & Yarkin-Levin, K. (1983). *Development of selection and evaluation methods in energy control centers* (ARRO Technical Report No. 3072/R83-14). Bethesda, MD: Advanced Research Resources Organization.

Martin, C. L., & Nagao, D. H. (1989). Some effects of computerized interviewing on job applicant responses. *Journal of Applied Psychology, 74,* 72–80.

Martin, T. A., & Wilcox, K. L. (1989). HyperCard administration of a block-design task. *Behavior Research Methods, Instruments, & Computers, 21,* 312–315.

Mazzeo, J., & Harvey, A. L. (1988). *The equivalence of scores from automated and conventional versions of educational and psychological tests: A review of the literature* (Research Report No. CBR 87-8, ETS RR 88-21). Princeton, NJ: Educational Testing Service.

McBride, J. R., & Martin, J. T. (1983). Reliability and validity of adaptive ability tests in a military setting. In D. J. Weiss (Ed.), *New horizons in testing: Latent trait theory and computerized adaptive testing.* San Diego, CA: Academic Press.

McHenry, J. J., Hough, L. M., Toquam, J. L., Hanson, M., & Ashworth, S. (1990). Project A validity results: The relationship between predictor and criterion domains. *Personnel Psychology, 43,* 335–354.

McKinley, R. L., & Reckase, M. D. (1980). Computer applications to ability testing. *Association for Educational Data Systems Journal, 13,* 193–203.

Millman, J., & Arter, J. A. (1984). Issues in item banking. *Journal of Educational Measurement, 21,* 315–330.

Moreno, K. E. (1987, August). *Military applicant testing: Replacing paper-and-pencil with computerized adaptive tests.* Paper presented at the meeting of the American Psychological Association, New York.

Moreno, K. E., Wetzel, C. D., McBride, J. R., & Weiss, D. J. (1984). Relationship between corresponding Armed Services Vocational Aptitude Battery (ASVAB) and computerized adaptive testing (CAT) subtests. *Applied Psychological Measurement, 8,* 155–164.

Morrison, G. R. (1989). Reconsidering CBI screen design: Alternatives to text-based designs. *Computers in Human Behavior,* 5, 153.

Normand, J., & Burke, M. J. (1984). *Clerical assessment battery: Test manual.* Baltimore, MD: Psych Systems.

O'Brien, T., & Dugdale, V. (1978). Questionnaire administration by computer. *Journal of the Market Research Society, 20,* 228–237.

Olsen, J. B., Maynes, D. M., Slawson, D. A., & Ho, K. (1986, April). *Comparison and equating of paper-administered, computer-administered and computerized adaptive tests of achievement.* Paper presented at the meeting of the American Educational Research Association, San Francisco.

Pearlman, K., Schmidt, F. L., & Hunter, J. E. (1980). Validity generalization results for tests used to predict job proficiency and training success in clerical occupations. *Journal of Applied Psychology, 65,* 373–406.

Pearson, J. S., Swenson, W. M., Rome, H. P., Mataya, P., & Brannick, T. C. (1965). Development of a computer system for scoring and interpretation of the Minnesota Multiphasic Personality Inventory in a medical setting. *Annals of the New York Academy of Science, 126,* 682–692.

Pellegrino, J. W., Hunt, E. B., Abate, R., & Farr, S. (1987). A computer-based test battery for the assessment of static and dynamic spatial reasoning abilities. *Behavior Research Methods, Instruments, & Computers, 19,* 231–236.

Peterson, N. G., & Bownas, D. A. (1982). Skill, task structure, and performance acquisition. In M. D. Dunnette & E. A. Fleishman (Eds.), *Human performance and productivity. Vol. 1: Human capacity assessment.* Hillsdale, NJ: Erlbaum.

Peterson, N. G., Hough, L. M., Dunnette, M. D., Rosse, R. L., Houston, J. S., Toquam, J. L., & Wing, H. (1990). Project A: Specification of the predictor domain and development of new selection/classification tests. *Personnel Psychology, 43,* 247–276.

Peterson, N. S., Kolen, M. J., & Hoover, H. D. (1989). Scaling, norming, and equating. In R. L. Linn (Ed.), *Educational measurement* (3rd ed.). New York: American Council on Education and Macmillan.

Piotrowski, Z. A. (1964). A digital computer interpretation of inkblot test data. *Psychiatric Quarterly, 38,* 1–26.

Plake, B. S., Conoley, J. C., Kramer, J. J., & Murphy, L. U. (1989). Buros bulletin. *Educational Measurement, 8,* 20–21.

Popper, R., Dragsbaek, H., Siegel, S., & Hirsch, E. (1988). Use of pocket computers for self-administration of cognitive tests in the field. *Behavior Research Methods, Instruments, & Computers, 20,* 481–484.

Reckase, M. D. (1989). Adaptive testing: The evolution of a good idea. *Educational Measurement, 8,* 11–15.

Rocklin, T., & O'Donnell, A. M. (1987). Self-adapted testing: A performance-improving variant of computerized adaptive testing. *Journal of Educational Psychology, 79,* 315–319.

Roid, G. H. (1989). Item writing and item banking by microcomputer: An update. *Educational Measurement, 8,* 17–20.

Rome, H. P., Swenson, W. M., Mataya, P., McCarthy, C. E., Pearson, J. S., Keating, F. B., & Hathaway, S. R. (1962). Symposium on automation techniques in personality assessment. *Proceedings of the Staff Meetings of the Mayo Clinic, 37,* 61–82.

Sampson, J. P. (1983). Computer-assisted testing and assessment: Current status and implications for the future. *Measurement and Evaluation in Guidance, 5,* 293–299.

Sands, W. A., & Gade, P. A. (1983). An application of computerized adaptive testing in U.S. Army recruiting. *Journal of Computer-Based Instruction,* 87–89.

Schuldberg, D. (1988). The MMPI is less sensitive to the automated testing format than it is to repeated testing: Item and scale effects. *Computers in Human Behavior, 4,* 285–298.

Silver, E. M., & Bennett, C. (1987). Modification of the Minnesota Clerical Test to predict performance on video display terminals. *Journal of Applied Psychology, 72,* 153–155.

Skinner, H. A., & Pakula, A. (1986). Challenge of computers in psychological assessment. *Professional Psychology, 1986, 17,* 44–50.

Slack, W. V., Hicks, G. P., Reed, C. Z., & Van Cura, L. J. (1966). A computer-based medical history system. *New England Journal of Medicine, 274,* 194–198.

Slack, W. V., & Van Cura, L. J. (1968). Patient reaction to computer-based medical interviewing. *Computers and Biomedical Research, 1,* 527–531.

Smith, M. S. (1968). The computer and the TAT. *Journal of School Psychology, 6,* 206–214.

Snow, R. E., Bethel-Fox, C. E., & Seibert, W. F. (1985). *Studies in cine-psychometry* (Technical Report, Aptitude Research Project). Stanford, CA: Stanford University, School of Education.

Snow, R. E., & Lohman, D. F. (1989). Implications of cognitive psychology for educational measurement. In R. L. Linn (Ed.), *Educational measurement.* New York: American Council on Education and MacMillan.

Society for Industrial and Organizational Psychology (1987). *Principles for the validation and use of personnel selection procedures* (3rd ed., pp. 18–24). College Park, MD: Author.

Space, L. G. (1981). The computer as psychometrician. *Behavior Research Methods and Instrumentation, 13,* 595–606.

Steinberg, L., Thissen, D., & Wainer, H. (1990). Validity. In H. Wainer (Ed.), *Computerized adaptive testing: A primer.* Hillsdale, NJ: Erlbaum.

Stevenson, J. W., & Salehi, S. (1986, April). *Project Adapt: An investigation of testing procedures for functional testing.* Paper presented at the meeting of the American Educational Research Association, San Francisco.

Stillman, R., Roth, W. T., Colby, K. M., & Rosenbaum, C. P. (1969). An on-line computer system for initial psychiatric inventory. *American Journal of Psychiatry, 125,* 8–11.

Stone, C. A. (1989). Testing software review: MicroCAT version 3.0. *Educational Measurement, 8,* 33–38.

Sympson, J. B., Weiss, D. J., & Ree, M. J. (1982). *Predictive validity of conventional and adaptive tests in an air force training environment* (Research Report No. AFHRL TR 81-40). Brooks Air Force Base, TX: Manpower and Personnel Division, Air Force Human Relations Laboratory.

Thissen, D. (1990). Reliability and measurement precision. In H. Wainer (Ed.), *Computerized adaptive testing: A primer.* Hillsdale, NJ: Erlbaum.

Turban, D. B., Sanders, P. A., Francis, D. J., & Osburn, H. G. (1989). Construct equivalence as an approach to replacing validated cognitive ability selection tests. *Journal of Applied Psychology, 74,* 62–71.

Vale, C. D. (1991). Computerized adaptive testing. In J. W. Jones, B. D. Steffy, & D. W. Bray (Eds.), *Applying psychology in business.* Lexington, MA: Lexington Books.

Vale, C. D., Keller, L. S., & Bentz, V. J. (1986). Development and validation of a computerized interpretation system for personnel tests. *Personnel Psychology, 39,* 525–542.

Wainer, H. (1990). Introduction and history. In H. Wainer (Ed.), *Computerized adaptive testing.* Hillsdale, NJ: Erlbaum.

Wainer, H., Dorans, N. J., Green, B. F., Mislevy, R. J., Steinberg, L., & Thissen, D. (1990). Future challenges. In H. Wainer (Ed.), *Computerized adaptive testing: A primer.* Hillsdale, NJ: Erlbaum.

Wainer, H., & Kiely, G. (1987). Item clusters and computerized adaptive testing: A case for testlets. *Journal of Educational Measurement, 24,* 185–201.

Ward, W. C., Kline, R. G., & Flaugher, J. (1986). *College board computerized placement tests: Validation of an adaptive test of basic skills* (Research Report No. RR-86-29). Princeton, NJ: Educational Testing Service.

WICAT Systems (1988). *Learner profile and WICAT test of basic skills.* Orem, UT: WICAT Systems.

Wilson, S. L., Thompson, J. A., & Wylie, G. (1982). Automated psychological testing for the severely physically handicapped. *International Journal of Man-Machine Studies, 17,* 291–296.

Wise, L. L., McHenry, J., & Campbell, J. P. (1990). Identifying optimal predictor composites and testing for generalizability across jobs and performance factors. *Personnel Psychology, 43,* 355–366.

Wise, S. L., & Plake, B. S. (1989). Research on the effects of administering tests via computers. *Educational Measurement, 8,* 5–10.

Wolfe, J. (1990). The evaluation of computer-based business

games: Methodology, findings, and future needs. In J. W. Gentry (Ed.), *ABSEL guide to experiential learning and simulation gaming.* New York: Nichols.

Yen, W. M. (1980). The extent, causes, and importance of context effects on item parameters for two latent trait models. *Journal of Educational Measurement, 17,* 297–311.

Young, W. Y., Houston, J. S., Harris, J. H., Hoffman, G., & Wise, L. (1990). Large-scale predictor validation in Project A: Data collection procedures and data base preparation. *Personnel Psychology, 43,* 301–311.

8

Who's Selecting Whom?
Effects of Selection Practices
on Applicant Attitudes and Behavior

Sara L. Rynes

In evaluating test use in selection and classification, one should not focus on one value basis to the exclusion of all others. To do so engenders too narrow a validation inquiry and reduces our sensitivity to side effects that are likely to be seen as adverse by other value positions (Messick, 1989, p. 87).

Nearly all the chapters in this book are dedicated in one way or another to speculating about how employers can make "better" selection decisions. Whole chapters are devoted to expanding criterion spaces, to implementing new selection technologies, and, more generally, to examining various ways of increasing productivity and reducing "counterproductive" behaviors through selection.

This chapter adopts a rather different and less well researched perspective: the applicant's. The dramatic expansion of selection techniques in recent years makes it increasingly important that we develop a better understanding of applicant reactions, particularly because many of the "high growth" areas in selection (drug testing, personality assessment, handwriting

Note: The author wishes to thank Michael K. Mount for thought-provoking discussions and comments on an earlier version of this manuscript.

analysis, integrity testing, background checking) are potentially invasive, lack obvious relatedness to job content, and have generated considerable public controversy (see, for example, Bible, 1990; Goldberg, Grenier, Guion, Sechrest, & Wing, 1991; Inwald, 1990; O'Bannon, Goldinger, & Appleby, 1989; Rothfeder, 1989; U.S. Congress, 1990).

Although the perspective taken here is unabashedly the applicant's, it should not be assumed that applicant and employer interests are necessarily inconsistent in selection. For example, recent movements toward greater interview structure have not only increased interview validities (Harris, 1989), but also probably reduced the number of irrelevant, offensive, and discriminatory questions at the same time. Similarly, adopting work samples or simulations generally increases applicant acceptability while simultaneously providing high predictive validity (see, for example, Cascio & Phillips, 1979).

More generally, to the extent that unimpressive or offensive selection procedures reduce applicant pools or job acceptance rates, the overall utility of a selection system is reduced as well (Boudreau & Rynes, 1985; Murphy, 1986). Additionally, legal challenges to devices regarded as overly invasive, face-invalid, or potentially discriminatory also reduce the overall payoff from those devices (Bible, 1990; "This Is," 1989; McKenna, 1982). Also, despite the fact that many selection procedures (including some controversial ones) appear to have generalizable validities, there is little reason to believe that most procedures are currently as valid as they could be (Colberg, 1985; Drasgow & Hulin, 1991). Nor is there any reason to believe that most devices could not simultaneously be made more valid *and* more acceptable to applicants.

While experts debate the pros and cons of alternative procedures in cool, scientific terminology (construct validity, empirical validity, item response theory, hit rates, validity scales, dollar-valued utility, impression management, predictor and criterion spaces), applicant reactions to them are often vividly personal and highly emotional. Consider the following examples, volunteered by the author's M.A. and M.B.A. students during the 1990–91 recruiting season.

- A married graduate student with a 3.9 + grade point average reported that the first three questions in one company's psychological assessment procedure involved inquiries about her personal relationships with her husband and children. Although the company asked her what she thought of the procedure before she left, she lied because she was afraid that telling the truth would eliminate her from further consideration. Because of dual-career constraints, she continued to pursue an offer, but noted that if she got one, her first on-the-job priority would be to try to get the assessor fired.

- A male M.B.A. told how he had originally planned to refuse to submit to psychological testing, but was persuaded by his girlfriend that it would be a more effective form of protest to pursue the offer and then pointedly turn it down.

- The first interview question asked of a female M.A. student was, "We're a pretty macho organization. . . . Does that bother you?" Unfortunately, it did, and she simply wrote the company out of her future interviewing plans. (When I later relayed this incident to an audience of corporate recruiters, a male recruiting director raised his hand and asked, "What's wrong with that?")

- Another M.A. student told the class that she "felt more like a criminal than a job applicant" after being escorted by a uniformed guard to a doorless toilet stall for drug testing.

The preceding examples illustrate that job applicants are not merely passive "receptors" of selection procedures. Rather, applicants react—sometimes very strongly—to what they are asked to do or say to get a job. Sometimes a negative experience results in withdrawal from the application process. Other times the applicant does not quit, but goes forward with a very different agenda than before the incident.

Over and above affective responses, applicants can also be quite proactive in attempting to influence selection outcomes. For example, beyond the generally accepted tendency to "put one's best foot forward," applicants sometimes mount elaborate countermoves designed to confound selection procedures. For example, a recent National Public Radio broadcast reported how stepped-up drug surveillance in professional sports led first to an active trade in "clean" urine and more recently to a brisk trade in alleged chemical "blocking devices." Seligman (1991) described a recent incident where half the police officers taking a promotional exam "prepared" for the test by obtaining questions from prior test-takers and sharing them with other applicants. Kleinmuntz (1985) outlined how really "dedicated" liars can learn to reduce polygraph effectiveness through such activities as biofeedback, powdering fingertips with talc, or contracting anuses and pressing toes to the floor during testing. More generally, the literature on coaching, practice, impression management, and other applicant influence tactics has mushroomed in recent years (for example, Leary & Kowalski, 1990; Sackett, Burris, & Ryan, 1989).

The remainder of this chapter addresses two questions: (1) How are applicants' attitudes toward organizations affected by selection procedures, and to what extent may those attitudes affect application behaviors, job choice decisions, and early work expectations? and (2) How do applicants attempt to influence the outcome of selection procedures, and what are the effects of those attempts? Because research is not well developed in either of these areas, the chapter raises as many questions as it answers. Nevertheless, it is hoped that the reader will come away with a better understanding of what is known (and not known) with respect to each of these topics, as well as an increased appreciation of the complexities of obtaining valid answers to these questions.

Affective Reactions Toward Selection Devices

Consider for a moment the case of an M.B.A. student who has spent her last two years preparing to qualify for a position at an elite consulting firm. Her first direct contact with the firm is a panel stress interview, from which she emerges with a very pessimistic impression of how well she did. As she leaves the reception room, she is stopped by a Ph.D. candidate who asks her to fill out his dissertation questionnaire. On the questionnaire, the applicant rates the recruiters as "rude, hostile, and threatening," says she is not interested in pursuing a second interview, and gives the firm the second-lowest rating on an overall attractiveness scale, filling in the open-ended portion with the explanation "too intense and very arrogant."

Drawing on this and other similar questionnaires, the author publishes a study concluding that applicants dislike threatening recruiters and that recruiters' actions are very important to job choices. A few months later, the researcher bumps into the applicant and asks how her job search is going. Imagine his surprise when she says that she has just accepted a job with this very same firm, explaining that it is "very selective, very challenging, and the premier employer in its field."

What are we to make of this example? Here, the most widely used method of assessing applicant reactions to employment interviews (for example, Powell, 1984; Rynes & Miller, 1983; Schmitt & Coyle, 1976) has failed to capture any of the important dynamics of this woman's job search and choice: her early strong preference for the firm; the spillover from her self-perceived performance onto questionnaire evaluations of the firm; the possibility that her preferences did not actually shift at all, but only her assessment of *who* would be doing the choosing (she or they), or the possibility that the stress interview might in fact have made the firm even more attractive through its blatant elitism (for example, Goodman, 1982).

To date, very few studies of applicant reactions would be likely to capture any of the preceding complexities, because the vast majority of such research has consisted of one-shot paper-and-pencil questionnaires. This method is incapable of detecting changes in preferences over time; of understanding how personal insecurities, time pressures, and social comparisons in placement offices influence applicants' public statements and actual decisions; of determining how often applicants do something other than what they say they will do; and so on. Indeed, the most improbable event in the preceding scenario may well be the researcher's (inadvertent) acquisition of subsequent information that caused him to rethink both his methods and his findings. These caveats should be kept in mind when evaluating the research conducted to date.

Descriptive Findings: Best- and Least-Liked Procedures

The most unequivocal finding from previous research of this type is that applicants favor procedures with a strong relationship to job content, particularly when administered in non-paper-and-pencil formats, such as work samples or simulations (Cascio & Phillips, 1979; Rynes & Connerley, 1991; Schmidt, Greenthal, Hunter, Berner, & Seaton, 1977; Smither & Pearlman, 1991; Stoffey, Millsap, Smither, & Reilly, 1991). From the applicant's perspective, such procedures appear to have several advantages: they are likely to be seen as both necessary and fair, are delivered in face-valid formats, and bypass many applicants' fears of paper-and-pencil evaluation of ability or achievement.

In addition, recent research also suggests that some "controversial" procedures (for example, drug and integrity tests, personality inventories) are nonetheless generally accepted by most applicants, at least in the abstract (for instance, Murphy, Thornton, & Reynolds, 1990; Ryan & Sackett, 1987a; Rynes & Connerley, 1991). In part, this is because most applicants, like employers, have come to view drugs and dishonesty as serious problems for business and society. However, at least in the case of drug testing, it also partially reflects the belief that so many employers are adopting the practice that there is little point in objecting to it (Rynes & Connerley, 1991).

Still, studies have found that there are wide individual differences in reactions to these procedures, with some applicants being strongly opposed to them and others actually liking them (Murphy, Thornton, & Reynolds, 1990; Rynes & Connerley, 1991; Sackett, Burris, & Callahan, 1989). To date, research has been largely unsuccessful in pinpointing personal characteristics that account for these differences, other than Murphy, Thornton, and Reynolds's (1990) finding that those who actually use drugs are more negatively disposed to drug testing.

Although applicant reaction research is relatively scarce (particularly outside the drug testing domain), research to date has uncovered only a few selection devices that receive markedly negative reviews, at least in the abstract. However, Rynes and

Connerley (1991) did obtain very negative reactions to psychological assessment and to handwriting analysis. Supplementary analyses suggested that applicants were very skeptical about employers' need to acquire such information, as well as their ability to correctly evaluate it.

There also appear to be some acceptability problems with interviews — not in the abstract, but in the way some interviews actually play out in real selection situations. For example, despite more than twenty-five years of federal Equal Employment Opportunity legislation, it is apparently still quite common for women and minorities to be asked offensive or discriminatory questions ("Black Applicants," 1991; "True Colors," 1991; Rynes, Bretz, & Gerhart, 1991). Indeed, the apparently widespread existence of discriminatory treatment has led the Equal Employment Opportunity Commission to announce that it will begin accepting charges of discrimination from "testers" — individuals who make applications for the sole purpose of uncovering discrimination (Scovel, 1991).

There appear to be other common problems with interviews as well. For example, many interviewers still ask superficial or shoot-from-the-hip questions. These interviews tend to receive very negative evaluations from applicants (Rynes & Connerley, 1991), perhaps in part because they signal low preparation or apparent interest in the applicant (Rynes & Miller, 1983).

During their pretest, Rynes and Connerley (1991) also found very mixed reactions to behavior description interviews, or BDIs (for example, "Tell me about a time when you had to . . . "). Although some applicants thought that these interviews were a good, in-depth way to assess candidates, others had encountered the same questions so many times that they regarded the interviews as both boring and fakable. BDIs also tended to be somewhat disliked by students with little work experience who felt, correctly or not, that descriptions of their classroom experiences would never count for as much with interviewers as "real" work-based incidents.

Despite these occasionally negative reactions, research suggests, on balance, that the typical applicant (more accurately, the typical college student responding to a hypothetical questionnaire) gives employers a fair amount of leeway in conducting selection procedures. As one applicant put it, "If they're going to pay me $45,000 a year, I guess they can ask me pretty much anything they want."

Nevertheless, although most practices appear to be at least minimally acceptable, they are not equally well regarded. Furthermore, the potential spillover from impressions of selection procedures to more general perceptions of organizations may be considerable (Robertson, Iles, Gratton, & Sharpley, 1991; Stoffey, Millsap, Smither, & Reilly, 1991), although the limited research on this question suffers from substantial methodological limitations.

Factors Underlying Likes and Dislikes

Although rank orderings of relative acceptability are interesting and somewhat useful, they tell us little about the underlying factors that make procedures liked, disliked, or neutral. Recently, several researchers have attempted to discover some of these underlying characteristics.

Stoffey, Millsap, Smither, and Reilly (1991) examined whether differences in acceptability for three selection devices (biodata inventory, cognitive ability test, in-basket simulation) could be explained by using a justice theoretic framework (for example, Greenberg & Tyler, 1987). Using this framework, they predicted that perceived job-relatedness would influence perceptions of selection fairness, which in turn would influence perceived fairness of human resource practices more generally, which in turn would influence overall organizational attractiveness and job pursuit intentions. Although the methodology (a cross-sectional questionnaire with items that basically "walk through" the hypothesized model) appears to have strong demand characteristics, results were supportive.

A similar study by Reilly, Millsap, and Stoffey (1991) using two thousand real job applicants also supported a "justice" interpretation of applicant reactions. However, in addition to investigating procedural justice (roughly, perceived fairness of a procedure), this study also investigated the effects of "distributive" justice (that is, actual test scores or selection outcomes).

Specifically, the authors gave applicants honest feedback about their test results and subsequently asked whether they would encourage others to apply to the company. Results suggested that perceived fairness of the procedure greatly dominated self-performance as a predictor of recommendations to peers.

Rynes and Connerley (1991) based their underlying factors on open-ended pretest interviews designed to determine why applicants did, or did not, like particular selection devices. Transcripts revealed that three considerations were mentioned far more frequently than others: perceived likelihood of accurate evaluation, perceived employer need to acquire the information revealed by the procedure, and perceived ability of applicants to do well on the procedure (a distributive justice concept). Interestingly, although the first two concerns are probably related to perceived "fairness," that word was mentioned only three times in 121 queries about particular selection procedures (forty-one subjects responding to three procedures each).

Pretest findings were then incorporated into a larger study ($n = 390$) where thirteen selection scenarios were rated in terms of each of the three factors (faith in scoring, need to know, likely self-performance) as well as overall attitudes toward the organization. All three factors were significant predictors of overall attitudes; however, effect sizes for expected self-performance were generally dwarfed by beliefs about evaluative accuracy and perceived need to acquire the information.

In combination, these last two studies suggest that applicants evaluate selection devices more on the basis of perceived legitimacy than on personal self-interest. Although there are potential problems with socially desirable responding in both studies, the fact that Reilly, Millsap, & Stoffey (1991) obtained their results from real applicants following actual test feedback reduces this concern. A more serious concern seems to be whether justice theory, by itself, adequately captures the entire set of factors that influence applicant impressions.

Needed Research

In terms of purely descriptive research (that is, identifying applicant likes and dislikes rather than underlying processes), the most pressing need is to move toward greater task fidelity: more precision in the specification of procedures, and greater hands-on involvement of subjects with those procedures. To date, most studies have asked subjects either to respond to fairly generic descriptions of procedures (for example, Rynes & Connerley, 1991; Smither & Pearlman, 1991; Stoffey, Millsap, Smither, & Reilly, 1991) or to complete only one of many alternative instruments from a whole class of procedures (Ryan & Sackett, 1987a). In addition, respondents have rarely been actual job applicants.

These are important limitations, because the effects of selection procedures on applicant impressions are almost certain to vary with specific differences in format and administration. For example, virtually no one objects to being interviewed in the abstract, although many object to the interviews they actually encounter during job search. Similarly, applicants may tell researchers that they do not mind personality inventories but become outraged when asked to respond to such items as "When a man is with a woman, he is usually thinking about things related to her sex," or "I have no difficulty in starting or holding my bowel movements" (examples from a current lawsuit: "This Is," 1989). Generally speaking, then, the superficial way in which most studies of applicant reactions have been conducted would be expected to suggest minimal "problems" relative to those that are actually occurring in real life.

Several important concerns might be addressed by using more intensive methodologies (such as having subjects actually complete a test or inventory, scoring it, and providing feedback; or having subjects "talk through" a procedure as they complete it). For example, such methods should prove helpful in (1) assessing the incremental acceptability of using more contextually relevant items for personality, biodata, or ability tests; (2) determining what specific kinds of items are most likely to be regarded as offensive, discriminatory, redundant, invalid, or misleading; (3) assessing when an instrument, as a whole, is perceived as too difficult, too long, too simplistic, or too repetitive; or (4) determining reactions to alternative administrative formats (written versus oral, essay versus multiple choice, computerized versus face-to-face).

In short, the kinds of test development procedures currently used to enhance item reliability and validity can, and should, be applied with equal vigor to assessing applicant acceptability. Although test developers are continually urged to consider acceptability issues (Anastasi, 1988; Drasgow & Hulin, 1991) and although some surely do, even the most cursory examination of some of the most commonly used instruments (Ryan & Sackett, 1987b; Sackett & Harris, 1984; Sackett, Burris, & Callahan, 1989) reveals a striking number of highly personal, seemingly irrelevant, and potentially sexist or racially divisive items.

Although it is possible that making questions more acceptable to applicants may also make them less valid, it is equally possible that it may make them *more* valid. For example, the author recently read a list of common integrity test items to her students as part of an informal class discussion. Students had widespread objections to certain kinds of questions, in particular those that asked whether they had *ever* done something bad (stolen, cheated, lied, taken drugs, or whatever) and those that asked about very minor transgressions (such as making a personal phone call on company time).

Their "problem" with these items was their belief that virtually *everyone* had done these things, at some level, at some point in their lives (probably an accurate assumption; see Patterson & Kim, 1991). Furthermore, they also suspected that anyone who *had not* done any of these things would probably make a pretty "low-level" employee (again, a suspicion with at least some empirical grounding; see Hogan & Hogan, 1989).

For these reasons, these kinds of items placed subjects in a game of "psychological warfare" with the test developers and users: Should they tell the truth, or should they give the "right" answer? What would other applicants do? Would there be a subsequent opportunity to explain that the negative incidents occurred long ago? Could they "trust" test developers and employers to know the *real* base rates for these behaviors in the population, or to be able to distinguish those who take the test in good faith from those who lie through their teeth?

These are legitimate applicant concerns, even if such tests on average show midrange, generalizable validities. Even granting the premise that empirical validity should be the dominant criterion for assessing integrity tests, there has been no published work demonstrating that these kinds of items yield any higher validities than items requiring less "gamesmanship." The only distinction that has been analyzed to date is the one between narrow-purpose (overt) and broader-purpose (personality-based) measures, and then only with respect to whole tests rather than specific items (Ones, Viswesvaran, & Schmidt, 1991). Given that the *specifics* of acceptability and item-type validities have barely been touched in this area, it may well be possible to make modifications that simultaneously increase both acceptability and validity.

Similarly, in the cognitive ability area, concerns regarding applicant acceptability might be minimized in several ways: by framing test items in more employment-related contexts (Anastasi, 1988; Rynes & Connerley, 1991), by demonstrating that there is a logical basis for all items, and by ensuring that there is only one logically correct answer per item (Colberg, 1985). At least in theory, all three steps might be expected to enhance validity at the same time that they improve acceptability (Arvey, Strickland, Drauden, & Martin, 1990; Colberg, 1985; Rynes & Connerley, 1991; Smither & Pearlman, 1991).

Similar steps should be taken to evaluate alternative structured interview formats (for example, past-oriented BDIs versus future-oriented simulation questions). Special attention to interviews is merited because they are such ubiquitous selection devices, because many common questions are now widely publicized and rehearsed before interviews (Sackett, Burris, & Ryan, 1989; Shook, 1988; Solomon, 1989), and because attempts to make interviews more valid by increasing their structure run the risk of becoming too impersonal and unattractive to applicants (see, for example, the procedure described by Pursell, Campion, & Gaylord, 1980).

Finally, although it has become almost trite to call for subjects other than college students in applicant attraction research, changing work force characteristics make this plea a serious one. Particular attention should be focused on the most rapidly growing segments of the labor force, including racial and ethnic minorities, midlife career changers, and people returning to the labor force after their children are grown. Focus on these groups is merited because of not only their numbers but also their potentially different outlook on selection procedures. For example, Arvey, Strickland, Drauden, and Martin (1990) observed racial differences in test-taking motivation and age and sex differences in test anxiety and perceived test difficulty. Highly skilled technical applicants are another important group because of their high demand and short supply. Little explicit attention has been paid to what kinds of selection procedures are attractive or impressive to these groups. And finally, because high-tech occupations are increasingly populated by individuals born in other countries, international and multicultural differences in expectations and impression formation must also be taken into account.

To identify the factors and processes that underlie applicant likes and dislikes, intensive qualitative research should be pursued *before* conducting additional large-sample surveys based on researchers' prior conceptualizations (Patton, 1990). One potentially useful method would be to let applicants "talk through" their reactions to a wide variety of selection devices—whether they like them and why or why not, what they assume about organizations that use various procedures, and so on. Responses could then be content-coded and sorted into a parsimonious number of relatively independent categories. By pursuing such basic research, we may avoid the opposing dangers of either prematurely settling on one (potentially deficient) model, such as justice or expectancy theory, or contribution to underlying process obfuscation via proliferation of seemingly different but actually similar constructs (as has happened in other areas, such as personality assessment and expatriate selection; Digman, 1989; Ones & Schmidt, 1991).

Another important need is to get a better idea of the practical importance of applicant reactions to selection procedures. Although we now know a fair amount about applicant likes and dislikes in this area, we have little idea how often these preferences actually translate into withdrawals from the application process, negative "PR" to friends and other applicants, offer turndowns, or filed complaints.

It is the author's strong belief that these phenomena are best studied through intensive investigation of applicants throughout the search process. Although negative selection procedures, by themselves, may rarely lead to automatic disqualification of an employer, they may well exert indirect or interactive pressures that, over time, cause a job to be rejected. For example, Rynes, Bretz, and Gerhart (1991) found that poor first interviews and recruiting delays often acted as "early warning devices," creating more wary applicants and closer scrutiny of subsequent interactions. These kinds of signaling, attentional, and attributional processes are likely to be quite common in nonroutine decisions (such as job choice) characterized by high importance, sequential search, and imperfect information (see Schwab, Rynes, & Aldag, 1987; Soelberg, 1967; Rynes, Bretz, & Gerhart, 1991, for elaboration of these points). Despite their commonness, however, they are *not* likely to be detected via simplistic importance rating or ranking surveys.

Finally, as the use of "nontraditional" selection procedures becomes more widespread, it will be increasingly important to monitor the effects of rejections and how rejections are communicated. At present, most organizations send impersonal, uninformative rejection letters (for example, the company was not able to hire all well-qualified candidates; the candidate does not meet the company's specific needs at this time). Although applicants may regard these kinds of explanations as sufficient when interviews and application blanks are the only selection procedures, it is less clear that they will suffice when procedures with less face validity are employed.

Offhand, it seems reasonable to expect that the further selection devices stray toward personality, values, or life-style inquiries, the more employers should be prepared to address questions from rejected applicants or their lawyers. However, given the large number of personality, handwriting, and integrity tests that are proprietarily scored by vendors (Goldberg, Grenier, Guion, Sechrest, & Wing, 1991; O'Bannon, Goldinger, & Appleby, 1989), it is unclear how many managers would presently be well equipped to provide satisfactory explanations to aggrieved applicants.

Applicant Self-Presentation Strategies and
Attempts to Manipulate Selection Outcomes

At the same time that applicants form affective reactions to selection procedures, they also adopt proactive strategies to try to influence selection outcomes. However, as in the case of affective reactions, determining all possible linkages between selection devices and the reactive behaviors they inspire is exceedingly difficult. Consider the following excerpt from Michael Lewis's *Liar's Poker* (1989, pp. 29–30):

> *Square Young Male Recruiter:*   Why do you want to be an investment banker?
>
> *Lewis:*   (Mumble, mumble . . .) Well, really, when you get right down to it, I want to make money.
>
> *Square Recruiter:*   That's not a good reason. . . . Frankly, we try to discourage people from our business who are too interested in money. That's all. [Lewis is prematurely dismissed.]

> A friend who eventually landed a job with the firm explained: "It's taboo (to talk about money). . . . You're supposed to talk about the challenges, and the thrill of doing deals, and the excitement of working with such high-caliber people, but never, ever mention money."
>
> Learning a new lie was easy. Believing it was another matter. . . . That money wasn't the binding force was, of course, complete and utter bullshit. But inside the Princeton University Career Services Office in 1982, you didn't let the truth get in the way of a job. . . . Set questions were posed, to which set answers were expected. A successful undergraduate investment banking interview sounded like a monastic chant. . . . I flattered the bankers. At the same time, I seethed at their hypocrisy.

On its face, the "monastic chant" of the successful investment banking interview would appear to be a psychometric disaster: after a minimal amount of social learning, applicants'
responses display systematic self-enhancement biases and no variance. Still, one may argue that the required deception had high
overall utility in that it selected (and self-selected) individuals
who could lie successfully without batting an eyelash — an apparently useful trait in investment banking. An additional advantage of the interview was that it accurately communicated
to new recruits that open discussions about money and earnings were "taboo" outside the firm. This prohibition was useful
because such discussions might have raised questions about how
so much money was actually being made — questions that, if pursued, would clearly have revealed unabashed ripping off of un-
suspecting clients ("the fools in the market"). And finally, the
overall selection process undeniably yielded trainees who generated billions of dollars in revenues for their firms, although partitioning those billions into subsets attributable to individual initiative versus other causes is hardly straightforward (Bianco,
1987).

Nevertheless, although Lewis and his colleagues did (eventually) come to enjoy the "thrill of doing deals and the excite-
ment of working with . . . high-caliber people," it is also true
that they demanded salaries and bonuses of unprecedented magnitude, and abandoned their employers in droves as soon as their
allegedly "unimportant" salaries fell behind those of competitors. Moreover, it is also true that the prevailing ethic of deception eventually caught up with many investment firms, including Lewis's own employer.

Did the investment banking selection system contribute to
these negative outcomes? Did all investment bankers, like Lewis,
lie to get hired? Or did some lie only to themselves? Does the
distinction make any difference in terms of predicting sales? Ethical violations? Successful evasion of detection for ethical violations? More to the point, to what extent can we, as outsiders,
ever know?

The current tendency seems to be to provide either very
optimistic (for example, Hogan, 1991) or guardedly optimistic

(for example, Goldberg, Grenier, Guion, Sechrest, & Wing, 1991; Hough, Eaton, Dunnette, Kamp, & McCloy, 1990) answers to these questions. Indeed, some experts seem largely willing to close the book on these questions (for instance, Hogan, 1991). The truth is, however, that existing research has just begun to scratch the surface in terms of understanding the full range of applicant strategies in response to the wide variety of selection devices now in use. Moreover, the evidence that does exist is often weaker and more contradictory than is generally recognized.

The remainder of this chapter briefly describes evidence concerning the extent of deception in actual selection situations, reviews evidence concerning the effects of such behaviors on validity, and identifies some of the most important areas for future research.

Extent of Deception

Although many studies have examined the extent to which applicants can or do "fake good" in experimental situations, evidence concerning actual distortion in real selection situations is considerably more scarce, particularly for certain devices. For example, almost nothing is known about how many applicants withhold or misrepresent important information in employment interviews, or what percentage suspend drug use just long enough to "beat" a drug test.

On the other hand, there is a bit more evidence concerning distortion on paper-and-pencil devices, particularly application blanks and skills inventories. Although results are mixed, a preponderance of the evidence suggests that distortion on these devices is relatively common and sometimes serious (Sloane, 1991). For example, Goldstein (1971) reported that 15 percent of nursing applicants claimed previous employment that they did not appear to have. Another 25 percent provided reasons for leaving that were clearly discrepant with prior employers' accounts, and 42 percent overreported the length of previous employment (by sixteen months, on average). Similarly, both Anderson, Warner, and Spencer (1984) and the New York Port

Authority (cited in Sloane, 1991) found that more than a third of actual applicants claimed to have nonexistent skills that were "planted" on application blanks to detect deception. Finally, both Gatewood and Feild (1990) and Sloane (1991) cite surveys showing that practitioners believe fraudulent representation to be on the increase.

On the more optimistic side, Cascio (1975) reported a median correlation of .94 between police applicants' responses to seventeen application blank items and posthire self-reports of those same items. Similarly high correlations were reported by Keating, Paterson, and Stone (1950) between self-reports of work history to employment counselors (not actual employers) and prior employers' records.

At least three factors emerge as possible explanations of differences across studies. One is the extent to which applicant self-reports and verification responses are obtained in maximally different ways. Generally speaking, the greater the independence of the two sources, the greater the amount of detected deception. (The Keating research is a possible exception, although self-revelations in that study were made to a relatively nonthreatening source.)

A second possible moderator concerns the kinds of items included in the comparisons. Because lying appears to be more common on items with the strongest social norms against deviant responses (McDaniel & Timm, 1991), observed or inferred deception would be expected to correlate directly with normative item "sensitivity." Although this issue has received attention across items *within* studies of deception (particularly those based on response latencies), it has been completely ignored in comparisons *across* studies. Cascio's (1975) study, for example, included a number of seemingly innocuous items (such as "number of siblings" or "number of schools attended before age 18"), a fact which may have reduced applicants' perceived *need* to lie on the application blank.

A third possible explanation of differences across studies concerns the way in which data are analyzed and reported. Generally speaking, correlational formats have produced more comforting conclusions than have tallies of raw discrepancies.

One possible explanation for these results is that some distortions may be relatively "unimportant" — at least in the sense of leaving applicant rank orderings roughly consistent with true-score orderings.

Several studies have also attempted to discover the extent of deception on psychological instruments such as personality inventories or integrity tests. On first blush, one would expect applicants to practice more deception on these devices than on application blanks or skills inventories because of the greater difficulty (for employers) of externally verifying responses.

Nevertheless, recent reviews of this literature have been considerably more upbeat than most studies of application blanks. For example, Hogan (1991) recently concluded that "all empirical data converge on the finding that the incidence of faking on personality inventories in real applicant populations is low" (p. 904).

Still, several factors argue against prematurely dismissing the faking question as "answered." One is that the optimism expressed in recent literature reviews has been based on a small number of studies with small sample sizes. For example, the "converging data" cited by Hogan (1991) consisted of only four studies with sample sizes of 30, 56, 92, and 245. Furthermore, two of the four compared interest (not personality) inventory responses of high school students who were and were not applying for college scholarships — a scenario with questionable generalizability to most employment situations.

In addition, virtually all optimistic assessments have depended on comparing responses from a group with presumed incentive to fake (such as real applicants) against responses obtained under "pure research" conditions (for example, Hough, Eaton, Dunnette, Kamp, & McCloy, 1990). The assumption, of course, is that responses obtained purely for research purposes are in fact "accurate." However, this assumption would seem to be open to question, as explained below.

The study that has contributed the most to recent optimism regarding applicant distortion is the large-sample, multifaceted research project by Hough et al. (1990). In a small substudy of that project (the largest study cited by Hogan, 1991), the researchers found little difference between the responses of just-sworn-in soldiers (who were told the results would be used for career purposes) and those of longer-service soldiers under pure research instructions.

The main portion of this study ($n = 9,188$) was designed to examine not the extent of deception, but rather whether deception moderates validity. Nevertheless, this part of the investigation also yielded indirect evidence regarding the extent of deception, because it depended on being able to sort subjects into groups that were likely to have responded in an "accurate" versus an "overly desirable" (p. 588) fashion. To accomplish this, the authors first obtained personality scores from 245 active soldiers under either "fake good," "fake bad," or "be honest" instructions in a pure research setting. Then, a much larger sample was asked to respond honestly, also under pure research conditions. Soldiers from this second group who scored at or above the mean in the earlier "fake good" condition were then categorized as having given "overly desirable" (that is, probably faked) responses.

Using this method, approximately 2,450 respondents appeared to be fakers (as compared with 5,950 "accurates"; Hough, Eaton, Dunnette, Kamp, & McCloy,1990). Thus, probable "fakers" represented approximately 29 percent of all respondents, even under pure research conditions!

This is a potentially important finding, in that it appears to raise serious problems for assessing applicant deception via comparisons with pure research responses. Although "fake good" instructions have long been recognized as too inflated for use as accuracy base rates (see, for example, Ruch & Ruch, 1967; McDaniel & Timm, 1991), "honest" instructions under pure research conditions have generally been assumed to produce accurate scores. Hough, Eaton, Dunnette, Kamp, & McCloy's (1990) results appear to challenge that assumption.

A third reason for caution is that much of the recent optimism regarding applicant honesty derives from findings that at least some applicants *do* admit to surprisingly negative thoughts and behaviors (for example, Cunningham, 1989; Goldberg, Grenier, Guion, Sechrest, & Wing, 1991, p. 13). Although this is indeed comforting evidence, it says very little about the proportion of applicants who do *not* admit to such activities and are subsequently hired. Nor does it ensure against the possibility that applicants who successfully distort predictor data may also be more successful at manipulating criterion scores to their advantage. For example, supervisory performance evaluations appear to be positively influenced by employee flattery, a form of self-serving manipulation (Wayne & Ferris, 1990), just as sales of investment instruments are correlated with willingness and ability to deceive customers (Lewis, 1989). In short, there is little reason to believe that fakers who "slip through the net" are disproportionately likely to be detected posthire.

Fourth (and perhaps relatedly), one has to wonder whether the narrow range of occupations typically examined in this research (entry-level military, police, and retailing positions) might not have produced an overoptimistic feeling about our ability to detect deception. For example, limited evidence suggests that two of the reasons applicants "fail" these devices are that they do not recognize the need to take them seriously, and even when they do, they are not very good at "psyching them out" (see Cunningham, 1989). At least on the basis of armchair hypothesizing, one would expect to see fewer such errors of judgment in higher-level occupations, particularly ones that depend on interpersonal influence and manipulation for on-the-job success (for example, consulting, sales, law, or even purveying integrity tests; see Goldberg, Grenier, Guion, Sechrest, & Wing, 1991; Inwald, 1990; Sackett, Burris, & Callahan, 1989).

Although it seems to be part of a developing conventional wisdom that scores on personality and integrity tests (and hence, presumably, the extent of manipulation) are largely uncorrelated with intelligence (for instance, Sackett, Burris, & Callahan, 1989; Schmidt, Ones, & Hunter, in press), the evidence to date is actually rather weak. Sackett, Burris, and Callahan (1989) cite only three studies with modest sample sizes — one with 104 convenience store applicants, one with 97 unspecified applicants, and one with 193 students. Second, intelligence has been operationalized in questionable ways (for example, as educational level or via vocabulary tests). Third, questions have been raised as to whether even conventional cognitive ability measures adequately capture "street smarts" or success in dealing with the external environment (Sackett, Burris, & Callahan, 1989; Sternberg, 1985). And finally, at least one study ($n = 72$) has found that more intelligent salespeople are less likely to admit to counterproductive behaviors (Barrick, Mount, & Strauss, 1991).

Finally, one has to wonder why *applicants* would be so honest in responding to selection devices, given the extent to which *employees* are widely assumed to be *dis*honest by test purveyors and the employers who engage them. Put another way, if people are so devious as employees, what underlying mechanism would make them more honest as applicants? That deception appears to be quite common on devices where verification is most straightforward ("bogus" skills inventories or application blanks) suggests that recent optimism about the honesty of applicants on psychological inventories may say more about our limited ability to detect such deception than about applicants' true honesty levels.

Effects of Lying, Faking, and Impression Management on Validity

Given that deception can, and unquestionably sometimes does, result in hiring individuals who would otherwise not be hired, it is important to learn the extent to which deception may be affecting our ability to accurately predict performance.

Again, multiple studies have examined this question, and once again results have been mixed. Some studies have suggested that distortion does not affect predictive ability (for example, Haymaker, 1986; Hough, Eaton, Dunnette, Kamp, & McCloy, 1990; Paajanen, 1987), but others have concluded that it does—some in a negative direction (for example, Anderson, Warner, & Spencer, 1984; Dunnette, McCartney, Carlson, & Kirchner, 1962) and others in a positive one (Ruch & Ruch, 1967).

Again, it is difficult to say exactly what accounts for these differences. Although the three studies showing small or no differences are based on larger samples than the others, the various studies differ in other ways as well, including predictor type (biodata, skills inventories, personality measures), sample (armed services, retail clerks, clericals, sales), and method of analysis (for instance, subgroup analysis, comparisons of partial versus nonpartial correlations, use of corrected versus uncorrected scores, and moderated regression).

A different kind of evidence concerning this issue was recently reported by Mount, Holt, and Barrick (1991). There, a large sample of managers ($n = 13,445$) completed a conscientiousness inventory that was also filled out (with respect to those same managers) by at least two peers, two subordinates, and two superiors. Using overall performance evaluations as the criterion (ratings were made by a supervisor not included in the conscientiousness rating study), the authors obtained uncorrected validity coefficients of .12 for self-reports, .25 for peer assessments, .28 for subordinate ratings, and .35 for supervisor assessments. (Analogous validities corrected for unreliability were .19, .39, .43, and .54.) Thus, self-reports were substantially less useful predictors than all forms of assessment by others.

In sum, one can find empirical evidence (along with accompanying theoretical explanations) to support virtually any position: that distortion reduces validity, that it makes little or no difference, or that it actually enhances it (on this last point, see Ruch & Ruch, 1967). As such, continued attention to the effects of deception or socially desirable responding appears warranted, with emphasis on identifying the factors (both real and artifactual) responsible for observed differences across studies. Variables that merit investigation include differences in occupational samples, task instructions, type of selection device, basis for estimating extent of deception, presence or absence of warnings regarding deception, method of analysis, and type of criterion measure. Special emphasis should be placed on securing large samples, examining the effects of alternative analyses on the same data set (similar to earlier efforts regarding test fairness; see Arvey & Faley, 1988), and describing each of the preceding variables in sufficient detail for accurate coding in future meta-analyses.

Observations and Future Research Suggestions

According to Hogan (1991), "further advances in personality assessment will be based on a better understanding of the processes that mediate the manner in which people respond to personality test stimuli" (p. 901). This author concurs with that sentiment, and indeed would extend it to include *all* selection stimuli. At present, there is no overarching theory of how applicants respond to selection devices and, as a result, no clear picture of all possible effects of those responses.

At least two characteristics of previous research have impeded broader understanding of applicants' responses to selection demands. One is the extremely indirect nature of most attempts to infer applicant intentions and motivations. The other is the fragmented way in which these issues have been studied, with each type of selection device being examined in relative isolation from other types.

Regarding the first point, nearly all the research designed to investigate whether or how applicants lie, fake, or manage impressions has been notably indirect. Rather than observing applicants "in action" or even asking them how or why they respond as they do, researchers have tended almost exclusively to try to *infer* motivations from observed scores or correlations among sets of scores (for exceptions see Arvey, Strickland, Drauden, & Martin, 1990; Cunningham, 1989). Although comparing one set of researcher-generated scales with other researcher-generated scales is undoubtedly a useful way of learning, it is probably less efficient (and complete?) than if a wider range of strategies and tactics were used. For example, traditional item analyses and correlations among obtained scores might be supplemented with more direct process-oriented methods such as role-playing or protocol analysis. Because many of these studies would have to be performed in experimental settings, they may be inappropriate for addressing certain types of issues (for example, determining the extent to which faking actually occurs in real applicant settings).

On the other hand, these more intimate forms of investigation may prove very helpful in illuminating a variety of important process questions, such as, What factors increase or decrease motivation to do or say whatever it takes to get a job? What kinds of assumptions and judgments underlie decisions about whether (or how much) to distort? How do people "draw the line" between what they are willing, and not willing, to distort? What kinds of questions or procedures are most likely to elicit flippant or even spitefully deceptive responses?

More generally, a clearer picture is needed of how applicants frame the task of responding to a selection situation. Hogan (1991, p. 902) speculates that applicants' responses (to personality devices) represent "automatic and often nonconscious efforts on the part of test-takers to negotiate an identity with an anonymous interviewer [the test author]." Ruch and Ruch (1967) hypothesize (with respect to sales applicants) that "responses become to a large degree a measure of their image of the job's demands." In addition, they speculate that the willingness of good salespeople to commit so-called sensible deception *enhances* validity, because the good salesperson "is better *able* than the poor salesman to put his best foot forward, regardless of what his 'true' personality dynamics really are" (p. 201, emphasis added).

Therefore, Hogan (1991) envisions personality test-taking as much like a "confessional" to an unseen priest, whereas Ruch and Ruch (1967) see it as a kind of "intelligence test" that virtually requires some deception to be successful. These distinctions are potentially important, because they may well have implications for the *incremental* validities of personality and integrity devices when added to other selection procedures.

In addition, Ruch and Ruch's (1967) definition seems to contain a larger role for the environment ("image of the *job's* demands") in applicants' responses than does Hogan's (1991), with its emphasis on "automatic" and "nonconscious" responses to "anonymous" testers and employers. These distinctions bring to mind the self-monitoring literature (Snyder, 1979), which proposes that individuals vary in the extent to which their actions are typically driven by external, versus internal, states. Ruch and Ruch's (1967) definition almost perfectly describes the mental processing of "high self-monitors," who Snyder claims often succeed in such occupations as politics, acting, sales, or management precisely because of their willingness (and ability) to adopt whatever posture is required at the moment. In contrast, low self-monitors are believed to have a more rigid concept of "who they really are" and hence are more likely to view adaptations to situational demands as somehow unprincipled or untrue to themselves.

At least two observations flow from the preceding views of the selection task. One is that successful hurdling of a selection barrier requires both the *ability* to figure out the "right answer" and the *willingness* to give it. The indirect nature of most prior research has impeded a clear vision of either construct (except perhaps in the area of cognitive ability testing), as well as possible interactions between the two.

Of the two constructs, ability to fake has probably been the less well examined. For example, investigations of faking ability with respect to personality devices have extended only to demonstrating that *groups* given "fake good" instructions score higher than groups given "honest" instructions. Questions about the factors that underlie *individual* differences in "fake good" abilities have gone largely unexamined.

The absence of studies examining faking ability applies equally to impression management (IM) interview research, where the typical study has treated IM as an independent, rather than dependent variable. That is, in the typical study, actors employ one IM strategy versus another, with the objective of determining which strategy is "most effective" (see Gerstein, Ginter, & Graziano, 1985; Stevens, Mitchell, & Tripp, 1990). The failure to examine IM skills as dependent variables in interview research represents a substantial missed opportunity, given that the exhibited range of self-presentational skills is likely to be far greater in interpersonal settings than in paper-and-pencil ones.

Another observation about the faking *motivation* research is that even in work that focuses on the interplay between individuals and environments (for example, Snyder's), interest in differences due to the environment per se has taken a back seat

to interest in individual predispositions. Thus, studies of applicant reactions have tended to ignore the effects of such factors
as labor market conditions (tight or loose), the vacancy (highly
desired or not), and the selection device itself (challenging versus
simple-minded, straightforward versus manipulative, informal
versus formal, cognitive- versus values-based).

To completely ignore these variables is to (implicitly) assume
that applicant motivations and behaviors in selection do not depend on such factors as financial desperation, number of perceived
options, interest in the company, and so on. Such an assumption seems highly untenable. For example, a student recently explained that he ended up accepting a job at a "surprising" company in the following way: "I wasn't really interested initially,
so I answered the interviewer's questions exactly the way I really
felt, and they seemed to be really impressed by that. They called
me back the very next day, and *I* was really impressed with that."
Thus, future models of applicant reactions should focus on not
only individual characteristics but also potentially relevant characteristics of labor markets, vacancies, and selection devices.

Beyond the indirect nature of inquiry into these areas, the
other main impediment to broader understanding of applicants'
responses to selection demands has been the tendency to study
applicant reactions piecemeal, device by device. For example,
cognitive ability test developers have been preoccupied with such
issues as test security, cheating, guessing, and "faking bad" (in
military draft situations) and have devised parallel forms, item
analysis, and item response theory to try to deter and detect
such transgressions. With personality tests, the issues have been
lying, "faking good," self-deception, and self-monitoring, with
solutions offered in the form of "lie scales" or correction formulas. With interviews, the problem is described as one of impression management and addressed (to the extent it has been addressed at all) via tightly structured questioning and interview
procedures. In drug testing, the concern is "tampering" and is
dealt with through both preventative (escorted lavatory trips)
and detective (for example, temperature testing) strategies.

This fragmentation by devices has inhibited various forms
of conceptual integration. For example, we have at present only

a murky picture of the relationships between the wide range of phenomena that might be classified as "distortive" or "manipulative" (see Sackett, Burris, & Ryan, 1989, for an interesting review). A potential list of such activities ranges from clearly illicit behaviors such as lying, cheating, stealing answer keys, switching urine samples, or having surrogates take tests under false identities, to deceptive but probably less reprehensible activities such as embellishing behavioral description incidents, selectively withholding information, feigning greater enthusiasm than is actually felt, temporarily suspending recreational drug use, or consistently giving oneself the benefit of the doubt on ambiguous questions, to "preparational" activities such as asking preceding applicants to describe interview questions or assessment center exercises, purchasing professional interview training or résumé construction services, or taking tests over and over again to capitalize on measurement error.

At present, we do not know whether all these various behaviors merely represent differing degrees of the same underlying phenomenon or a variety of relatively independent dimensions. After all, each tactic is designed to produce observed scores that are "overpositive" relative to true scores. Still, the author (perhaps like most readers) suspects that multiple dimensions are involved. But if so, what distinguishes their use (and longer-term implications)—legality? prevalence in the population? applicant intent? degree of "motivation" implied by their use?

A related impediment to integration has been the marked tendency to study paper-and-pencil devices rather than other formats. Paper-and-pencil techniques are more constrained than other formats in that applicants are typically restricted to a predetermined set of items and response options and are prevented from using strategies that employ interpersonal or body language tactics. Although these features make data from paper-and-pencil instruments more tractable, a price is paid in terms of probable failure to observe the full range of applicant tactics that occur in real-world selection.

The lack of research regarding applicant responses to interview stimuli is particularly striking. For example, despite growing evidence that structured interviews are superior to unstructured ones (Harris, 1989), there has been virtually no interest in determining the role that applicants' cognitive processes may have in producing improved validities. Conventional explanations have emphasized the job-analytic foundations of structured interviews, the standardization of information-gathering procedures, and the emphasis on past behaviors (at least in BDI formats). However, alternative (partial) explanations include reduced ability to fake responses (and hence greater potential variability across applicants) or increased motivation to perform well on more challenging or job-related questions.

To date, however, we have barely tried to find out whether applicants *like* these new interviews, let alone how they have changed the task of responding. Nor do we know the implications, over time, of standardized questions becoming more and more widely disseminated and practiced (Sackett, Burris, & Ryan, 1989). In summary, at the risk of making a too obvious point, we know more about applicants' reactions to relatively little used selection procedures than we do about the one that is virtually universal.

Conclusion

Two additional points are important. First, although this chapter segments applicants' affective reactions from their self-presentational strategies, in reality the two may be interrelated. For example, it seems reasonable to expect that applicants would be more motivated to do well on procedures that are regarded as legitimate and challenging, and less motivated on ones regarded as irrelevant, silly, or none of the employer's business.

Second, applicant reactions to selection devices are probably deeply embedded in the broader social, economic, and political environment. For example, it is difficult to imagine Vietnam-era college seniors marching to the urinal saying, "I don't particularly like drug testing, but I can see that marijuana creates a serious problem for society," or "Everyone is doing it, so I may as well just go along with it." Yet these are quite common sentiments today, given dwindling economic competitiveness, the "War on Drugs," a weak market for college graduates

(Deutschmann, 1991), increasing political conservatism, and diminished concern about civil liberties (Caminiti, 1990). Therefore, because reactions to selection devices are embedded in a broader context, research conducted at one time and place should not automatically be assumed to generalize to others.

References

Anastasi, A. (1988). *Psychological testing* (6th ed.). New York: Macmillan.

Anderson, C. D., Warner, J. L., & Spencer, C. C. (1984). Inflation bias in self-assessment examinations: Implications for valid employee selection. *Journal of Applied Psychology, 69,* 574–580.

Arvey, R. D., and Faley, R. H. (1988). *Fairness in selecting employees* (2nd ed.). Reading, MA: Addison-Wesley.

Arvey, R. D., Strickland, W., Drauden, G., & Martin, C. (1990). Motivational components of test-taking. *Personnel Psychology, 43,* 695–716.

Barrick, M. R., Mount, M. K., & Strauss, J. P. (1991). *Big five and ability predictors of citizenship, delinquency and sales performance.* Working paper, University of Iowa, Iowa City.

Bianco, A. (1987, August 17). The decline of the superstar. *Business Week,* pp. 90–98.

Bible, J. D. (1990). When employers look for things other than drugs: The legality of AIDS, genetic, intelligence, and honesty testing in the workplace. *Labor Law Journal, 41,* 195–213.

Black applicants are victims of bias in study of hiring. (1991, May 15). *Kansas City Star,* pp. A-1, A-7.

Boudreau, J. W., & Rynes, S. L. (1985). Role of recruitment in staffing utility analysis. *Journal of Applied Psychology, 70,* 453–366.

Caminiti, S. (1990, July 2). A bright future for conservatism. *Fortune,* pp. 89–90.

Cascio, W. F. (1975). Accuracy of verifiable biographical information blank responses. *Journal of Applied Psychology, 60,* 767–769.

Cascio, W. F., & Phillips, N. (1979). Performance testing: A rose among thorns? *Personnel Psychology, 32,* 751–766.

Colberg, M. (1985). Logic-based measurement of verbal reasoning: A key to increased validity and economy. *Personnel Psychology, 38,* 347–360.

Cunningham, M. R. (1989). Test-taking motivations and outcomes on a standardized measure of on-the-job integrity. *Journal of Business and Psychology, 4,* 119–127.

Deutschmann, A. (1991, July 29). The trouble with MBAs. *Fortune,* pp. 67–79.

Digman, J. M. (1989). Five robust trait dimensions: Development, stability, and utility. *Journal of Personality, 57,* 195–214.

Drasgow, F., & Hulin, C. L. (1991). Item response theory. In M. D. Dunnette & L. M. Hough (Eds.), *Handbook of industrial and organizational psychology* (2nd ed., Vol. 1.) Palo Alto, CA: Consulting Psychologists Press.

Dunnette, M. D., McCartney, J., Carlson, H. C., & Kirchner, W. K. (1962). A study of faking behavior on a forced-choice self-description checklist. *Personnel Psychology, 15,* 13–24.

Gatewood, R. D., & Feild, H. S. (1990). *Human resource selection.* New York: Dryden.

Gerstein, L. H., Ginter, E. J., & Graziano, W. G. (1985). Self-monitoring, impression management, and interpersonal evaluations. *Journal of Social Psychology, 125,* 179–389.

Goldberg, L. R., Grenier, J. R., Guion, R. M., Sechrest, L. B., & Wing, H. (1991). *Questionnaires used in the prediction of trustworthiness in pre-employment selection decisions.* Washington, DC: American Psychological Association.

Goldstein, I. L. (1971). The application blank: How honest are the responses? *Journal of Applied Psychology, 53,* 491–492.

Goodman, E. K. (1982, September). Only the best and the brightest need apply. *Savvy,* pp. 34–38.

Greenberg, J., & Tyler, T. R. (1987). Why procedural justice in organizations? *Social Justice Research, 2,* 127–141.

Harris, M. M. (1989). Reconsidering the employment interview: A review of recent literature and suggestions for future research. *Personnel Psychology, 42,* 691–726.

Haymaker, J. C. (1986). *Biodata as a predictor of employee integrity and turnover.* Paper presented at the meeting of the American Psychological Association, Washington, DC.

Hogan, J., & Hogan, R. (1989). How to measure employee reliability. *Journal of Applied Psychology, 74,* 273–279.

Hogan, R. (1991). Personality and personality measurement. In M. D. Dunnette & L. M. Hough (Eds.), *Handbook of industrial and organizational psychology* (2nd edition, Vol. 2). Palo Alto, CA: Consulting Psychologists Press.

Hough, L. M., Eaton, N. K., Dunnette, M. D., Kamp, J. D., & McCloy, R. A. (1990). Criterion-related validities of personality constructs and the effect of response distortion on those validities. *Journal of Applied Psychology, 75,* 581–595.

Inwald, R. (1990, June). Those little "white lies" of honest test vendors. *Personnel,* pp. 52–58.

Keating, E., Paterson, D. C., & Stone, H. C. (1950). Validity of work histories obtained by interview. *Journal of Applied Psychology, 34,* 6–11.

Kleinmuntz, B. (1985, July–August). Lie detectors fail the truth test. *Harvard Business Review,* pp. 36–42.

Leary, M. R., & Kowalski, R. M. (1990). Impression management: A literature review and two-component model. *Psychological Bulletin, 107,* 34–47.

Lewis, M. (1989). *Liar's poker: Rising through the wreckage on Wall Street.* New York: W. W. Norton.

McDaniel, M. A., & Timm, H. W. (1991, April). *Lying takes time: Predicting deception in biodata using response latency.* Working paper, Booz-Allen & Hamilton.

McKenna, C. (1982, January 23). Grievance filed against Vikings. *Minneapolis Tribune,* p. B-1.

Messick, S. (1989). Validity. In R. Linn (Ed.), *Educational measurement* (3rd ed.). New York: Macmillan.

Mount, M. K., Holt, K., & Barrick, M. R. (1991, September). *Concurrent validity of peer, subordinate, supervisor and self ratings of conscientiousness.* Working paper, University of Iowa, Iowa City.

Murphy, K. M. (1986). When your top choice turns you down. *Psychological Bulletin, 99,* 133–138.

Murphy, K. M., Thornton, G. C., & Reynolds, D. H. (1990). College students' attitudes toward employee drug testing programs. *Personnel Psychology, 43,* 615–631.

O'Bannon, R. M., Goldinger, L. A., & Appleby, G. S. (1989). *Honesty and integrity testing: A practical guide.* Atlanta, GA: Applied Information Resources.

Ones, D. S., & Schmidt, F. (1991). *Expatriate selection.* Unpublished manuscript, University of Iowa, Iowa City.

Ones, D. S., Viswesvaran, C., & Schmidt, F. L. (1991). *Integrity testing: Empirical confirmations and refutations using meta-analysis.* Unpublished manuscript, University of Iowa, Iowa City.

Paajanen, G. E. (1987). *The prediction of counterproductive behavior by individual and organizational variables.* Unpublished doctoral dissertation, University of Minnesota, Minneapolis.

Patterson, J., & Kim, P. (1991). *The day America told the truth.* Englewood Cliffs, NJ: Prentice-Hall.

Patton, M.Q. (1990). *Qualitative evaluation and research methods* (2nd ed.). Newbury Park, CA: Sage.

Powell, G. N. (1984). Effects of job attributes and recruiting practices on applicant decisions: A comparison. *Personnel Psychology, 37,* 721–732.

Pursell, E., Campion, M. A., & Gaylord, S. (1980, November). Structured interviewing: Avoiding selection problems. *Personnel Journal, 59,* 907–912.

Reilly, R. R., Millsap, R. E., & Stoffey, R. (1991, April). *The influence of selection procedures on attitudes about the organization and job pursuit intentions.* Paper presented at the meeting of the Society for Industrial and Organizational Psychology, St. Louis, MO.

Robertson, I. T., Iles, P. A., Gratton, L., & Sharpley, D. (1991). The impact of personnel selection and assessment methods on candidates. *Human Relations, 44,* 963–982.

Rothfeder, J. (1989, September 4). Is nothing private? *Business Week,* pp. 74–82.

Ruch, F. L., & Ruch, W. W. (1967). The K-factor as a validity suppressor variable in predicting success in selling. *Journal of Applied Psychology, 51,* 201–204.

Ryan, A. M., & Sackett, P. R. (1987a). Pre-employment honesty testing: Fakability, reactions of test-takers, and company image. *Journal of Business and Psychology, 3,* 248–256.

Ryan, A. M., & Sackett, P. R. (1987b). A survey of individual assessment practices by I/O psychologists. *Personnel Psychology, 40,* 455–489.

Rynes, S. L., Bretz, R., & Gerhart, B. (1991). *The importance of recruitment in job choice: A different way of looking.* Working paper, University of Iowa, Iowa City.

Rynes, S. L., & Connerley, M. L. (1991, August). *Selecting with an eye to attraction: Applicant reactions to alternative selection procedures.* Working paper, University of Iowa, Iowa City.

Rynes, S. L., & Miller, H. E. (1983). Recruiter and job influences on candidates for employment. *Journal of Applied Psychology, 68,* 147–154.

Sackett, P. R., Burris, L. R., & Callahan, C. (1989). Integrity testing for personnel selection. *Personnel Psychology, 42,* 491–529.

Sackett, P. R., Burris, L. R., & Ryan, A. M. (1989). Coaching and practice effects in personnel selection. In C. L. Cooper & I. Robertson (Eds.), *International review of industrial and organizational psychology.* New York: Wiley.

Sackett, P. R., & Harris, M. M. (1984). Honesty testing for personnel selection: A review and critique. *Personnel Psychology, 37,* 221–246.

Schmidt, F. L., Greenthal, A., Hunter, J. E., Berner, J., & Seaton, F. (1977). Job sample vs. paper-and-pencil trades and technical tests: Adverse impact and examinee attitudes. *Personnel Psychology, 30,* 187–197.

Schmidt, F. L., Ones, D. S., & Hunter, J. E. (in press). Personnel selection. In *Annual Review of Psychology* (Vol. 43). Palo Alto, CA: Annual Reviews.

Schmitt, N. W., & Coyle, B. (1976). Applicant decisions in the employment interview. *Journal of Applied Psychology, 61,* 184–192.

Schwab, D. P., Rynes, S. L., & Aldag, R. J. (1987). Theories and research on job search and choice. In K. Rowland & G. Ferris (Eds.), *Research in personnel and human resource management* (Vol. 5). Greenwich, CT: JAI Press.

Scovel, K. (1991). Testers to expose illegal hiring practices. *Human Resource Executive, 5*(3), 10.

Seligman, D. (1991, January 14). Great moments in law enforcement. *Fortune,* p. 112.

Shook, R. L. (1988). *Honda: An American success story.* Englewood Cliffs, NJ: Prentice-Hall.

Sloane, A. A. (1991). Countering resume fraud within and beyond banking: No excuse for not doing more. *Labor Law Journal,* 303–311.

Smither, J. W., & Pearlman, K. (1991, April). *Perceptions of the job-relatedness of selection procedures among college recruits and recruiting/employment managers.* Paper presented at the meeting of the Society for Industrial and Organizational Psychology, St. Louis, MO.

Snyder, M. (1979). Self-monitoring processes. In L. Berkowitz (Ed.), *Advances in experimental social psychology* (Vol. 12). San Diego, CA: Academic Press.

Soelberg, P. O. (1967). Unprogrammed decision making. *Industrial Management Review, 8,* 19–29.

Solomon, J. (1989, December 4). The new job interview: Show thyself. *The Wall Street Journal,* pp. B-1, B-7.

Sternberg, R. J. (1985). Human intelligence: The model is the message. *Science, 230,* 1111–1118.

Stevens, C. K., Mitchell, T. R., & Tripp, T. M. (1990). Order of presentation and verbal recruitment strategy effectiveness. *Journal of Applied Social Psychology, 20,* 1076–1092.

Stoffey, R., Millsap, R. E., Smither, J. W., & Reilly, R. R. (1991, April). *Relationships between perceived fairness of selection and perceptions of the organization.* Paper presented at the meeting of the Society for Industrial and Organizational Psychology, St. Louis, MO.

This is your life. (1989, December). *Harper's,* pp. 19–21.

True colors. "Prime Time." (1991, September 25). New York: American Broadcasting Corporation.

U.S. Congress. Office of Technology Assessment. (1990, September) *The use of integrity tests for pre-employment screening.* Washington, DC: U.S. Government Printing Office.

Wayne, S. J., & Ferris, G. R. (1990). Influence tactics, affect, and exchange quality in supervisor-subordinate interactions: A laboratory experiment and field study. *Journal of Applied Psychology, 75,* 487–499.

9

The Concept of Validity

Neal Schmitt, Frank J. Landy

In this chapter we trace the development of ideas about appropriate ways of testing hypotheses regarding predictor-criterion relationships. Various approaches to the validation of tests were evident in the work of early industrial and organizational (I/O) psychologists such as Munsterberg. Impatience with theory and emphasis on the practical led to almost sole reliance on criterion-related studies in which the theoretical meaning of the criterion, the predictor, or both were given little attention. Much current research reflects a desirable emphasis on theory, including the realization that all test validation research involves inferences about psychological constructs.

Historical Foundation of the Strategies and Concept of Validation

Among the leading early twentieth-century applied psychologists in the United States and Europe who were combining an interest in the measurement of individual differences with a desire to predict behavior (for example, Lippman and Stern in Germany and Walter Dill Scott in the United States), Hugo Munsterberg was one of the most prominent (or at least one of the most vocal) advocates of industrial testing (Landy, 1991b).

275

His major contributions came during the period 1910–1916, and his continuing development of the industrial testing paradigm was cut short by his untimely death. Nevertheless, in his published works in 1913 and 1915, he articulated a logic and a superstructure for industrial testing. In addition, he anticipated the most commonly used validation strategies, which are the central issue of this chapter.

Munsterberg was trained as a brass-instrument experimental psychologist in the tradition of his mentor, Wilhelm Wundt. Although he rebelled against the rigid search for general laws of behavior that defined turn-of-the-century structuralism, he did not abandon the structuralist methods of measurement. He was interested in such basic processes as memory, reaction time, letter and number identification, and visual and auditory perception, and he developed elaborate schemes for measuring these attributes. His departure from the structuralists was in the goal of such measurement (Landy, 1991b). The structuralists wanted to map out the nature of mental life (or consciousness) and, as a result, develop general laws of behavior. The more Munsterberg measured these traditional attributes, the more he was struck with the substantial differences that appeared among those tested. He was an ardent Darwinist and, as a result, believed that these individual differences were not just the random variation of the Darwinist mechanism, but also the raw material for the natural selection that might favor some of these differences. He was convinced that differences in these attributes would likely lead to differences in all sorts of behavior, including industrial behavior. Thus, Munsterberg was interested in looking for individual attributes that might predict job success. To be sure, Cattell, Jastrow, and others had a broad appreciation for the potential value of the differential psychology paradigm, but it was Munsterberg who most forcefully articulated the industrial testing model.

Munsterberg had another reason for pursuing testing. After the turn of the century, a tendency had developed to classify individuals in terms of national characteristics. This was known as "group" psychology. Stereotypes of Swedes, Germans, Italians, Slavs, and other European immigrants had developed. Munsterberg (1915) was opposed to this ersatz psychology and thought that tests should be used to replace nationality as a personnel decision tool.

Munsterberg took two very different approaches to the development of tests. These approaches are exemplified in his description of tests used for hiring telephone operators versus those he developed for hiring trolley drivers (Munsterberg, 1913). In examining the job of telephone operator, Munsterberg concluded that there were many different and discrete pieces to that job and that those pieces were supported by discrete abilities. As a result, he developed a very elaborate test battery to measure clerical skills, perceptual and motor skills, memory, and reaction time. The measurement of these abilities was based on the laboratory paradigm, and no attempt was made to make them look like any of the work conducted by telephone operators. Viteles (1932) would later dub these "analytic" tests, because they decomposed complex behavior in terms of the multiple-constituent attributes that supported this behavior. He developed the tests to tap underlying cognitive, motor, and perceptual-motor abilities that he thought (based on his observations and discussions) were necessary for success on the job. To put it slightly differently, he developed the working hypothesis that the same abilities necessary to do well on the test were necessary to do well on the job. This is a fairly basic statement of the construct validation strategy. He was confident that most basic abilities had been identified in earlier laboratory work by the structuralists and that these abilities (that is, constructs) defined the attribute skeleton required to develop the necessary tests.

In contrast to this method of test development, consider his approach to predicting the success of trolley operators. His analysis of that job convinced him that there was really only one criterion of interest — frequency of accidents. His review of company records for the Boston Railway Company as well as critical incident interviews of incumbent trolley operators and their supervisors suggested that driver safety was a paramount issue and that a good test would reduce accidents and, more important, save the companies enormous amounts of money that was currently devoted to repairing damage and settling claims.

Munsterberg's job analysis convinced him that the actions of the trolley operator were so integrated and "holistic" that it made no sense to break them down in order to find discrete attributes (constructs) that might predict operator success. Instead, he decided to develop a simulation of the work to be performed. He was concerned with, among other things, identifying current trolley operators who were poor risks for safe performance and trolley operators who would quit after short periods of time. Turnover among trolley operators was a serious problem, and Munsterberg believed that those most likely to quit were those who lacked the requisite abilities. As a result, he developed a laboratory simulation of the trolley operator's task demands. He constructed a wooden apparatus with a series of windows in it that showed the subject a moving "street" scene. In this scene, the "trolley" was stationary and the scene moved past the trolley. The subject was required to anticipate which objects (people, animals, other vehicles) might cross the trolley tracks at a point that would bring them into contact with the trolley. The subject could control the speed of the "trolley" by cranking the moving scene at a faster or slower rate. The subject's score was a combination of speed and accuracy in predicting probable contacts (potential accidents). In contrast to the telephone operator test battery, this was clearly a work sample and was intended to simulate, to the greatest extent possible, the exact tasks that were to be carried out by the operator. Thus, we have an early illustration of the content-oriented test development model.

In the application of both test development strategies, Munsterberg suggested that the test development be followed by a criterion-related study comparing success rates before testing was introduced to similar measures after testing. In addition to this primitive form of empirical validation, he also suggested (when possible) including both concurrent and predictive designs similar to those with which current I/O psychologists are familiar. In fact, in the telephone operator study described above, Munsterberg was more the victim than the designer of a concurrent validation study. Company management was skeptical of the new "tests" and decided to determine for itself the effectiveness of this method of hiring. Without Munsterberg's knowledge, the company placed some of its most effective operators into the subject pool to see how well they did on the tests. Much to their surprise (and Munsterberg's belated relief), the top-performing operators generally received the highest test scores.

There was one validation "strategy" that separated Munsterberg from his contemporaries. He placed great faith in the reactions of incumbents to his tests. This was something more than what we might label "face validity," perhaps closer to our current use of subject matter experts for pilot testing. Munsterberg frequently asked incumbent test subjects if their "experience" in taking the test was similar to their "experience" when doing the job. If they reported similar experiences, then he was convinced that he was tapping the right abilities and attributes. This could be dubbed a "soft" version of known-group validation.

Munsterberg's logic for validation was very straightforward. He pursued validation for two reasons: First, he knew that business managers would be persuaded by results, not theories or promises. Thus, he needed to demonstrate to them that he could actually give them better workers. This was the reason that many early industrial psychologists (including Munsterberg) were so enthusiastic about criterion-related models. It also led to a continuing debate between Munsterberg, who claimed that "psychotechnics" (as testing was called then) was value-free, and those who doubted that science supported by the desires of management could be without values (Goldman, 1918; Roback, 1917). It is interesting to note that shades of the same debate can be seen in Messick's (1980b) argument that the *effects* of testing must be considered in evaluating validity.

The second reason for Munsterberg's interest in criterion-related models was his desire to "test" the theories of job performance he had developed—theories that he carefully concealed from the business owners lest he lose their interest. In many respects, the validation study was the scientific icing on the cake. It was here that Munsterberg saw some value to correlation coefficients. He had little enthusiasm for the practical value of statistical analysis (beyond simple grouping methods). In a book entitled *Business Psychology* (1915), he writes that "the study of correlations is very interesting because it allows theoretical insight into the far-reaching mental connections. It shows how far apparently different acts have common causes or some common elements. *But their practical importance seems as yet negligible"* (p. 247; italics added).

Munsterberg was as interested in the reactions of managers and incumbents to his tests as he was in the tests' actual predictive power. There might have been several reasons for his lack of enthusiasm for empirical validation. The most parsimonious explanation is that he was not a very good statistician. Harold Burtt, one of his graduate students and later a renowned industrial psychologist, reports that few depended on Munsterberg for help in analysis. "He was an idea man," Burtt recalls (Landy, 1991a), and not much help when it came time for statistical analysis. In addition, Munsterberg came from a tradition in which theories were developed deductively, not inductively. Thus, statistical analysis was, if anything, broadly confirmatory rather than exploratory. Munsterberg believed that for any serious theoretical work, it was necessary to go into the laboratory and experimentally control the independent variable and measurement method. With respect to theory building, he frequently described the whole testing enterprise as a "short-cut" method (1913).

At that time (circa 1910), correlation coefficients were still considered rather novel as devices for demonstrating relationships. It was only after Munsterberg's death that the validity coefficient began to emerge as the statistical test "of choice." Burtt (1917) completed some analyses of Munsterberg's test data after his death and reported correlation coefficients with some hesitancy. (Munsterberg had never used correlation coefficients in any of his reports, but Burtt had been a math major at Dartmouth and felt more at home with statistical analysis.) Munsterberg was criticized by later I/O psychologists (for instance, Viteles and Kornhauser) for his lack of sophisticated statistical analysis, but this criticism was not actually warranted given the tenor of the times in which he worked.

Munsterberg used an additional method of "validation" in his early test development for the position of ship captain. He pointed out that one could not do a proper criterion-related study since (fortunately!) so few ship collisions occurred for any given captain that one might need to wait for twenty years to gather any criterion data. Munsterberg had already decided (from his job analysis) that decision speed and accuracy were the critical attributes for the successful ship captain. On that assumption, he asked the friends and acquaintances of incumbent ship captains if they were capable of making quick and accurate decisions. He then compared the judgments of those observers with the results of his tests of the captains. The actual test consisted of determining the frequency of appearance of a particular letter embedded in other letters printed on a card; the task was to identify the letter that appeared most frequently on the card. The subject's score was a combination of accuracy and time. Munsterberg reported that the judgment of friends corresponded to the test scores such that those subjects reported to be most capable of making quick and accurate decisions were also the ones with the best test scores. He replicated the results with Harvard students, having them take the test and obtaining peer judgments of their decision-making skills. Munsterberg considered this to be confirmatory evidence for his technique (and his "theory"). Today, we would be inclined to accept such evidence as part of a larger nomothetic network describing a test instrument, that is, a contribution to construct validity examinations.

The Role of the Criterion

With the exception of his recognition that some criteria were more important than others (for example, frequency of accidents for trolley operators), Munsterberg was not particularly interested in the criterion construct. If the managers felt that performance increased and the incumbents reported that the same abilities were called into play in the test as were used on the job, Munsterberg was happy. The next generation of I/O psychologists was less casual about the choice of criterion, however. As an example, in one of the early modern books on personnel psychology, Burtt (1929) cautions the practitioner about the choice of the criterion by stating, "The need, however, is not merely for a criterion as such, but for as reliable and accurate a one as possible. The value of the entire project depends upon it because it is the standard used in evaluating tests" (p. 141).

In fact, Burtt devotes an entire chapter to the criterion in his book, and it might well have been written today insofar as it articulates problems that face us currently in criterion development and measurement. This concern for the criterion problem was echoed by contemporaries such as Viteles (1932), who goes so far as to endorse a construct validity study of supervisory ratings that were to be used as criteria in a validation analysis. Walter Van Dyke Bingham expressed similar concerns for criterion development (for example, Bingham & Freyd, 1926).

The Modern Era

The watershed for the "modern" era of validity studies was the publication of Viteles's book on industrial psychology in 1932. Among other things, this book anticipates the whole movement toward utility analysis as the justification for testing. According to Viteles, the justification of a test development project "requires an estimate of the cost of operation of the new method in relation to possible savings in cost of turnover, spoiled work, accidents, cost of production, etc., in relation to the gain in the way of improved adjustment of the individual worker" (p. 202).

The major distinction between the approach articulated by Viteles and the work of those who had preceded him was his emphasis on the nature of abilities. He refined a technique known as the job psychograph, which had been developed by a German colleague (Lippman, 1916). The psychograph was an elaborate listing of the various knowledge, skills, and abilities that might be used as resources for completion of job tasks. Viteles considered task analysis a preliminary step in the more important procedure of identifying critical human attributes in successful performance.

With respect to validation strategies, Viteles was straightforward. He was a strong advocate of criterion-related testing, suggesting a concurrent study followed by a predictive study. He accepted the distinction that Munsterberg had made between more laboratory-type tests and work samples but added a refinement: he classified tests into three types, analytic, analogous, and work sample. Analytic tests were discrete laboratory-based tests of basic abilities. They had little phenotypic similarity to industrial tasks. In contrast, analogous tests were intended to duplicate essential characteristics of a job but were administered in miniature or in a simulated environment. Work sample tests were exact work tasks carried out in a natural work location. Viteles (1932) presents a rather elaborate discussion of when each type of test is appropriate. The discussion is based on a notion of common and specific factors underlying performance. In this respect, he anticipated the later work of Thurstone (1938) and Harman (1960) in factor analysis. He presents quite a lucid discussion of constructs, their meaning, and their measurement.

With respect to the presentation of validity evidence, Viteles (1932) suggests a combination of expectancy charts and correlation coefficients. His standards for acceptable validity (shared by his contemporaries) are instructive. He endorses the following value judgments for various levels of validity presented first by Hull (1928): below .45 or .50 was considered practically useless; from .50 to .60, of some value; from .60 to .70, of considerable value; from .70 to .80, of decided value, but rarely found; and above .80, not found by present methods (Viteles, 1932, p. 38). It seems our forefathers were more exacting in challenging themselves and their colleagues.

Link (1919) reports correlation coefficients from .55 to .72 between performance on basic mental tasks and productivity for munitions workers. He reports even better correlations with the Stenquist Mechanical Abilities Test to select machinists. Here his validity coefficients between the test and supervisory ratings for three groups were .50, .65, and .90! To be fair, the sample size in each case was twelve. Nevertheless, the standards were high.

It is clear that early I/O psychologists were firmly wedded to the criterion-related model. Nevertheless, they recognized the value of multiple test development techniques, including construct- and content-oriented strategies. It is not difficult to understand the devotion to criterion-related strategies if one considers the zeitgeist. Behaviorism was on the ascendancy. Munsterberg was closely allied to this approach (Landy, 1991b), as were most other applied psychologists of the time. This was part and parcel of the American development called functionalism, which was to replace European structuralism. In recalling this period, Viteles (personal communication, 1988) expresses great impatience with "theorists." He and his colleagues (for example, Kornhauser) had little tolerance for those who were not driven by statistical analysis. The concern was more for rigorous analysis than for rigorous design or thought. It was this style of thought that led to the dust bowl empiricism of the 1940s and the dearth of theory in the 1960s. In many respects, we are still trying to shake this legacy. That we have been able to shed this earlier pragmatism is testimony to the insight of people like Cronbach, Meehl, and others who saw the importance of going beyond the simple models of the behaviorists. We have come to realize that virtually all behavior of interest to the psychologist is rooted in various constructs.

Rethinking the Tripartite Approach to Validity

A historical review illustrates that, although various facets of the validation question arose early in the history of personnel selection research, the overarching model was a criterion-related analysis. In fact, even the foundation for the tripartite approach was serendipitous. With the burgeoning post–World War II testing boom, there were many questionable tests appearing. As a service to consumers of testing, the American Psychological Association formed a committee to develop standards by which users could judge the adequacy of tests. It was this committee (with key members Lee Cronbach and Paul Meehl) that suggested alternative ways for evaluating test adequacy. Instead of concentrating solely on correlations with criteria, they suggested that content and construct questions were of equal, or possibly greater, importance. In fact, the work of this committee resulted in the first set of standards for educational and psychological tests (American Psychological Association, 1954).

The introduction of alternative methods for evaluating validity was a small revolution but one which never progressed beyond the simple point that there *were* alternative designs. Instead, the three methods suggested entered a state of suspended

animation and were eventually calcified in professional literature and the *Uniform Guidelines* (1978).

Perhaps the beginning of our recognition that we should
view all validation as construct validation was the reminder that
validation is concerned with supporting the inferences we make
from test scores, and is not some attribute of the tests or test items
themselves (for example, Cronbach, 1971; Guion, 1980). We
have continued to speak of different analytic strategies (for example, Lawshe, 1985; Society for Industrial and Organizational
Psychology, 1987) even though we recognize that all approaches
are really addressing some question about construct validity. Content, criterion-related, and construct strategies (Society for Industrial and Organizational Psychology, 1987) are the most frequently used forms of presenting evidence for the validity of our
inferences about selection procedures, but we are becoming increasingly aware that validation need not (and should not) be
limited to these few strategies (Binning & Barrett, 1989; Landy,
1986; Messick, 1980a, 1980b, 1988).

Marshaling evidence of validity is now seen as a process
of theory development and testing (Binning & Barrett, 1989;
Landy, 1986). We must develop and articulate theories of job
performance and define logically the constructs that are central
to these theories. We must establish a "nomological network"
that relates constructs important in the job performance domain
to the constructs we choose to identify qualified job applicants.
This requires evidence that the measures we use to operationalize constructs in the predictor and performance domains possess a logical relationship to these constructs and empirically
consistent relationships to other measures of the construct. There
must be a continual process of hypothesis generation, testing,
and challenging. A criterion-related validity coefficient may or
may not constitute good evidence of the validity of inferences
from test scores. The appropriateness of this evidence would
depend on the degree to which the criterion in the study was
linked to the constructs underlying the performance domain and
whether the test or test items measured constructs about which
we had reasonable hypotheses concerning their relevance to the
performance domain. As we saw earlier, even the earliest personnel researchers (Burtt, 1929; Viteles, 1932) recognized the

importance of understanding the criterion construct. For example, an empirical criterion-related study of the validity of *available* biographical data in predicting *available* measures of absenteeism probably would not constitute very good evidence in support of the inferences drawn from those biodata.

These ideas about evidencing validity have been articulated by various authors (Anastasi, 1986; Guion, 1980, 1987; Landy, 1986; Messick, 1988; Tenopyr, 1977). Perhaps the most detailed analysis of the inferences underlying construction validation is presented by Binning and Barrett (1989). We first present a brief description of their model of the inferential linkages involved in building theories of job performance. In the next section of this chapter we examine the degree to which recent research and validation efforts constitute evidence for one or more of the linkages they identified.

Like Nunnally (1978), Binning and Barrett point out that the first four inferences depicted in Figure 9.1 are all involved in construct validation. Specifically, construct validation involves demonstrating evidence for four inferences or linkages: (1) X and Y are related, (2) X is a measure of construct 1, (3) Y is a measure of construct 2, and (4) construct 1 is related to construct 2. Inference 1 is the only one that can be empirically tested directly, and evidence concerning at least three of the inferences (1, 2, 3, 4) is necessary to justify the fourth linkage. Typical practice is to gather empirical evidence that X and Y are related (traditional criterion-related validity) and to assume that two of the other three inferences are correct. Use of the term *construct validity* to describe evidence supporting any of these inferences is using that term in its most general sense. Psychometricians and researchers have most often been interested in construct-measure linkages (linkages 2 and 4) (Campbell & Fiske, 1959; Cronbach & Meehl, 1955). In developing a new test, one may be primarily interested in inference 2 or 4. However, in theory building, one is interested in the validity of the construct; hence, all four linkages are equally important. Binning and Barrett (1989) point out that in personnel selection research, we are interested in linkage 5 in Figure 9.1; that is, the linkage between a specific measure (X) and the performance domain (construct 2).

Figure 9.1. Inferential Linkages in
Construct Validation and Theory Building.

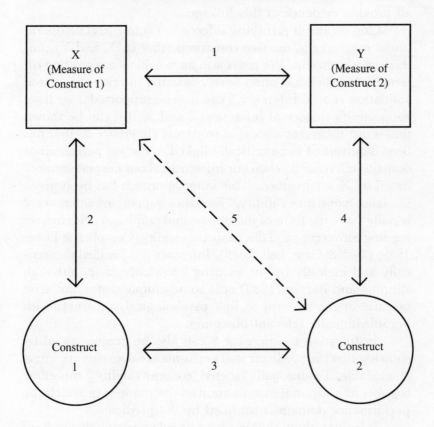

In the traditional personnel selection model outlined in the preface of this book (Figure P.1), we begin with a job analysis, which serves to define the performance domain. We also develop specific operational criteria that we believe define this performance domain (linkage 4) and select or develop procedures or operationalizations (linkage 2) of the constructs we hypothesize are related to the performance domain (linkage 3). In a criterion-related study, we gather empirical evidence of the relationship between the operationalizations of the two constructs (linkage 1). Ultimately, in the selection context, the central interest is in inference 5, the linkage between the available information on job applicants and aspects of future performance. Content, construct, and criterion-related validation strategies all provide evidence of this linkage.

One means of justifying inference 5 is to correlate operational measures of the two constructs (that is, X and Y), but this is not sufficient. We must also have evidence regarding inference 4, which has often been neglected in criterion-related validation efforts. Inference 5 can also be supported if we have supporting evidence of inferences 2 and 3. If it can be shown that a test measures a specific construct (inference 2) that has been determined to be critically linked to the job performance domain (inference 3), then our inferences about job performance based on X are justified. This latter approach has been given the label "construct validity." Evidence supporting inference 2 usually takes the form of judgments and empirical evidence regarding convergent and discriminant validity (Campbell & Fiske, 1959; Cook & Campbell, 1979). Inference 3 is justified theoretically and logically by the existing knowledge base, although Binning and Barrett (1989) note some unique issues that arise because of the attempt to link psychological constructs with organizationally relevant outcomes.

Justification of inference 5 can also be demonstrated by showing that the predictor and performance domains are interchangeable. Traditionally labeled "content validity," this effort consists of a rational examination of the manner in which the performance domain is sampled by the predictor.

It is clear, then, that our traditional operationalizations of content, construct, and criterion-related validity all involve support for one or more of the inferences essential to construct validation and theory development. Theory and hypotheses are necessary at all stages in a traditional validation design. Defensibility of linkage 5 in Figure 9.1 depends on the degree to which our inferences about the meaning of job analyses data are valid and the degree to which we are correct about the relevant predictor and criterion constructs and their interrelationships.

Having examined the types of inferences for which we seek support in validation research, we now examine how some recent research in personnel selection provides evidence regarding the various inferences discussed above. Indirectly, we are asking how these approaches contribute to theory development and construct validation in selection research.

Construct-Relevant Research in Selection

The appropriateness of inferences in selection depends on all aspects of our activity as personnel selection researchers, but the foundation of our theories regarding work performance rests on job analyses. The information we obtain from job experts can be influenced by several organizational and social factors that may affect the degree to which job analyses truly reflect critical performance constructs.

Research on Job Analysis

Theory-relevant research on job analysis takes two different approaches. Recently, researchers have explored the extent to which ratings of job dimensions depend on subject matter experts' ethnic status or gender (Schmitt & Cohen, 1989), their rated similarity to each other (Mullins & Kimbrough, 1988), their knowledge of the job (DeNisi, Cornelius, & Blencoe, 1987), and their performance level (Conley & Sackett, 1987). In all these studies, there was little evidence that substantially different job analysis data were generated by different subgroups of people. Recent research has also been directed to gaining an understanding of subject matter experts' decision making in evaluating tasks (Cornelius & Lyness, 1980; Sanchez & Levine, 1989) and ascertaining the psychometric quality of task ratings (Wilson, Harvey, & Macy, 1990). This research is useful in that it helps us understand the quality and determinants of job analysis information, but the knowledge base in this area has developed only recently and in piecemeal fashion.

Several job analysis procedures represent theories of work performance. The development of the Position Analysis Questionnaire (PAQ) by McCormick and his colleagues (McCormick, Jeanneret, & Meecham, 1972) was an effort to develop an instrument that would be applicable across all jobs. These researchers built their instrument around the notion that work could be described on the basis of activities involving information input, worker processing activities, and worker output. That this information processing model of worker activity was not adequate is evident in that McCormick, Jeanneret, and Meecham (1972) found it necessary to include three other sections: interpersonal activities; physical, psychological, and social aspects of jobs; and miscellaneous items regarding work schedules, job demands, and level of responsibility. Nevertheless, the PAQ has proved to be applicable to a wide variety of different jobs, and the availability of the PAQ data base has proved to be a rich source of data about the world of work (for example, Gael, 1988; McCormick, 1979).

From a historical perspective, however, we still seem to have missed some of the lessons that might have been learned from our predecessors. As described previously, the job psychograph (Lippman, 1916; Viteles, 1932) was, above all, a search for relevant knowledge, skills, and abilities (KSAs), not a search for generic tasks or task groups. It is in this area that many of the more modern approaches to job analysis have fallen short. Support for this concern arises from the dearth of KSA taxonomies available to the I/O psychologist. To be sure, some work has been done. For example, the Fleishman taxonomy is a complete and well-developed "full service" description of cognitive, perceptual-motor, and motor abilities (Fleishman and Quaintance, 1984). Similarly, the French kit of cognitive abilities (French, Ekstrom, & Price, 1963) and even Guilford's (1967) structure of the intellect model (though incomplete) represent attempts to map out ability domains. Nevertheless, the I/O practitioner often knows more about tasks than about abilities. (We return to Fleishman's taxonomy shortly.)

Another theory of work grew out of the job analyses conducted during the development of various editions of the *Dictionary of Occupational Titles (DOT)*. Functional job analysis (Fine & Wiley, 1974) is a conceptual system used to define the level and orientation of worker activity. Fine maintained that the tasks people do can be organized along three dimensions that reveal the *level* of their involvement with data, people, and things.

Actions on each of these three dimensions are classified on scales ranging from simple to complex. In addition, the *orientation* of a worker with respect to data, people, or things is described by the percentage of time workers spend on each dimension. This theory of work has been used as part of the basis for coding jobs in the *DOT*, but its potential use as a means to ascertain worker requirements does not appear to have been exploited.

As indicated above, Fleishman and his colleagues (Fleishman & Quaintance, 1984) engaged in several decades of work devoted to development of a performance taxonomy. To generalize about conditions that affect human performance (including individual differences), they maintained that it is necessary to consider the properties of tasks as important constructs in psychological research and theory. A useful taxonomic system in personnel selection would include "concepts for linking the characteristics of job tasks, their performance requirements and the capacities measured by selection tests" (Fleishman & Quaintance, 1984, p. 8). These taxonomic requirements sound very much like the inferential linkages discussed in the previous section of this chapter. Fleishman and Quaintance (1984) describe several taxonomies, but the most developed and applicable to personnel selection is their ability requirements approach. This approach was developed from factor analytical and experimental studies of human performance in various areas. One recent list of the abilities they found useful in describing requirements of different jobs contained fifty-two abilities (Fleishman & Quaintance, 1984, appendix B). The ultimate aim for personnel selection applications, however, should be to define the common ability requirements of different tasks. We still lack a system linking task characteristics and ability requirements in spite of repeated calls for such a system (for instance, Dunnette, 1976; Burke & Pearlman, 1988; Peterson & Bownas, 1982; Goldstein, Zedeck, & Schneider, 1992).

Job Performance Constructs

Criteria in selection research have often received little attention, as researchers have seemed interested only in establishing an empirical relationship between a predictor and some available criterion. Without serious consideration of the construct validity of the performance measure (linkage 4 in Figure 9.1), however, such criterion-related evidence is of dubious value. Although it is clear that the early I/O psychologists understood the importance of selecting the right criterion measures, it is not clear why this lesson was forgotten. It may simply be that the blush of success in the development of predictors that occurred in the context of World War II turned the heads of the I/O psychologists toward tests. One could market tests, but not criteria. For a period of several decades, until the appearance of social criticism (for example, Martin Gross's book *The Brain Watchers,* 1962), the predictor was king. It was common to throw out a test and start over again when a predictor-criterion correlation was nonsignificant. Seldom did the researcher consider the possibility that the problem might be with the criterion.

Recently, however, there has been burgeoning research directed toward a further understanding of job performance criteria. Research has been conducted to examine the meaning and accuracy of performance appraisals (for example, Sulsky & Balzer, 1988), the degree of convergence across rating sources (Harris & Schaubroeck, 1988), and the ability, knowledge, experience, and motivational precursors of supervisory ratings (Borman, White, Pulakos, & Oppler, 1992; Schmidt, Hunter, & Outerbridge, 1986; Schmidt, Hunter, Outerbridge, & Goff, 1988). Sackett, Zedeck, and Fogli (1988) extend the distinction between maximum and typical measures of ability to measures of grocery store clerks' performance. There is continuing debate about the existence and meaning of performance changes across time (Ackerman, 1987, 1989; Henry & Hulin, 1987, 1989; Barrett, Caldwell, & Alexander, 1989; Schmidt, Hunter, Outerbridge, & Goff, 1988). Extension of the performance domain to a discussion of organizational citizenship behaviors (for instance, Organ, 1990) and customer service behavior (for example, Rafaeli & Sutton, 1990) has taken place.

There have also been methodological and theoretical advances in the study of criteria as well. Fichman (1988, 1989), Harrison and Hulin (1989), and Morita, Lee, and Mowday

(1989) provide alternative methods of analyzing turnover and absence measures that should enhance our understanding of these criteria. Pritchard, Jones, Roth, Steubing, and Ekeberg (1988) provide a new method of measuring productivity at the unit or group level that incorporates both quality and quantity indices. Vance, Coovert, MacCallum, and Hedge (1989) use confirmatory factor analyses of ratings and job sample measures to examine the construct validity of the performance domain of air force jet engine mechanics.

One aim of the Project A research was to develop a model of the domain of job performance among army enlistees (Campbell, Henry, & Wise, 1990). Using exploratory and confirmatory factor analyses of a battery of job performance measures, including job knowledge tests, job sample tests, rating scales, training achievement tests, and archival data, Campbell et al. (1990) propose a model of performance containing five performance and two method dimensions. The model described in Chapter Three of this book provides further clarification of the performance construct.

Clearly, the research identified in this section goes well beyond a simple search for an available criterion against which to "validate" some predictor. The increased attention being given to performance constructs is well overdue and should be extremely important in enhancing our understanding of ability-performance linkages.

Predictor Constructs

Much more research has been directed to gaining an understanding of individual differences in ability and potential and the structure of those differences (Thurstone, 1938; Guilford, 1967). As well as taxonomies of human cognitive ability, we have information on the structure of psychomotor abilities, personality, and vocational preferences. Research in these various areas has usually been isolated to a single domain, however. Few studies have examined on a systematic basis the interrelationships between aptitude tests, personality measures, and psychomotor ability measures, much less attempted to link these various ability domains to aspects of the performance domain.

A grand design for linking ability and job performance constructs is presented by Peterson & Bownas (1982). Aspects of this "grand design" have been implemented in the army's Project A. Hypotheses were derived from models of the underlying dimensionality of predictor scores regarding the likelihood of differential relationships between predictors and criteria (Wise, McHenry, & Campbell, 1990) that resulted from a similar attempt to model the job performance construct (see the description of Campbell, McHenry, & Wise, 1990, above). Test batteries designed to be maximally predictive of different jobs were constructed and evaluated. These batteries included measures from different aspects of the predictor domain that used different methods of measurement.

On a smaller scale, Arnold, Rauschenberger, Soubel, and Guion (1982) investigated the performance-related constructs underlying physical ability tests, and Pulakos, Borman, and Hough (1988) examined personality and cognitive ability constructs. Further, I/O psychologists have pursued research directed at understanding the constructs measured in assessment centers (Klimoski & Brickner, 1987; Sackett, 1987), biodata (Mumford & Owens, 1987), personality (Borman, Rosse, & Abrahams, 1980), and interviews (Eder & Ferris, 1989). Such studies are relatively new to our field. They are not directed solely at documenting linkage 1 in Figure 9.1, but most often linkage 2. These studies, we believe, will have the greatest impact on the long-term development of our field.

Alternate Methods of Validation

In describing the validation process earlier in this chapter, we discussed the traditional validation strategies as they relate to various inferences we make in validation research. In this section of the chapter, we highlight three other efforts at providing support for inferences about predictor-performance domain linkages: rational validity, validity generalization, and synthetic validity. In the last section we describe in some detail other research programs or studies that may serve as models for research that would more thoroughly assess the inferences made by selection researchers and practitioners.

Validity Generalization

Perhaps one of the most important developments in social science research in the last decade is the use of meta-analyses (Hunter & Schmidt, 1990) to integrate the findings of research studies. In personnel selection, validity generalization research has provided support for inferences that tests measure underlying attributes that are not confounded with the sample on which the validation study is based. Concern about construct validity always involves questions about whether inferences about a test–job performance relationship can be generalized to a new sample (Landy, 1986). Cumulation across replications of test–job component relationships is a valuable method of supporting such inferences. It is important, however, to keep in mind the challenges to generalization. (Figure 9.2 presents those challenges graphically.) The goal is to achieve the widest generalizability possible. The validity generalization models and meta-analytic techniques support such generalizability determinations.

Validity generalization research has indicated that inferences derived from several different selection procedures (cognitive ability, assessment centers, interviews, for example) generalize across a wide variety of samples and situations. We should remember, however, that the data base used in validity generalization research comprises studies in which the focus of attention was the first linkage in Figure 9.1. If linkage 4 (the linkage between the measure of performance and the performance construct) was neglected in this body of research, we have a knowledge base that is deficient with respect to construct validity. Research such as that of Schmidt, Hunter, Outerbridge, and Goff (1988), which is directed to understanding the supervisory rating criterion used in these studies, is particularly important in providing insight into the data base underlying validity generalization studies. Further, since most of the studies used in validity generalization analyses have employed a rating criterion,

Figure 9.2. Generalizability Domains.

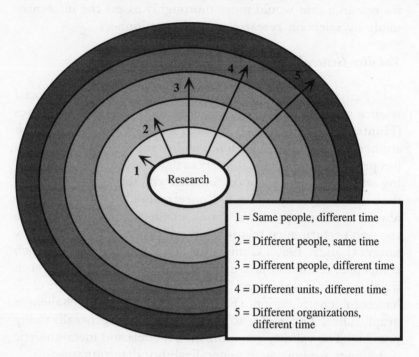

1 = Same people, different time

2 = Different people, same time

3 = Different people, different time

4 = Different units, different time

5 = Different organizations,
    different time

it is important that we continue to conduct studies regarding the performance construct (such as those described earlier) and the appropriateness of inferences one can make from various predictors about this widened performance domain.

We also believe much could be learned by examining situations in which a variety of selection procedures are used in the same studies. Estimates of mean-corrected validity coefficients on a single predictor are often in the high .40s and .50s. Since scores from some of these selection procedures (interviews, cognitive ability tests, biodata) are often uncorrelated, the results of independent meta-analyses suggest that researchers could achieve near perfect validity if a combination of procedures was used. Meta-analyses of the interrelationships of predictor constructs are important to understanding the predictor domains as well as the real limits of our ability to draw inferences about job applicants' future work performance.

Rational Validity

In another demonstration that empirical estimates of test-criterion relationships may not be the best basis on which to support inferences about test scores, Schmidt, Hunter, Croll, & McKenzie (1983) show that psychologists with experience and expertise in personnel selection can estimate relationships between subtests of the Navy Basic Test Battery (NBTB) and overall training success in a navy training school. These judges were given descriptions of the tests used and the job duties of people performing nine different navy jobs. They were asked to estimate the criterion-related validity of the six NBTB tests for predicting training school success. Their results indicate that these experts slightly underestimated (.02) empirical validity, but that expected values of their estimates, even estimates of a single judge, were less variable than criterion-related estimates based on sample sizes typically available to personnel researchers. In a follow-up study, Hirsh, Schmidt, and Hunter (1986) found that less experienced judges (recent Ph.D.'s in I/O psychology) produced judgments with greater systematic and random error.

The set of predictor instruments and the training criterion used in these two studies may limit the generalizability of the findings, but they demonstrate that psychologists with an understanding of the predictor instruments and the job performance measure are able to estimate with reasonable accuracy the appropriateness of the inferences drawn from test scores. Insofar as these judgments are based on a "theory" of test-performance relationships, they constitute further evidence that reliance on empirical relationships between measures of predictor and criterion relationships as support for inferences about test scores is not always the best approach. Of course, it is important to note that the experts' judgments should have been informed by the research literature, which consists of many hundreds of criterion-related studies about some test-performance relationships.

Landy (1988, 1989) describes a hybrid model that seems to include aspects of both content and construct designs. In a job analysis of the position of fire fighter, he was able to use fire fighter subject matter experts to identify the relevant KSAs for successful performance of fire-fighting tasks. He was then able to use I/O psychologist subject matter experts (SMEs) to identify the KSAs represented in various tests that could be used for selecting fire fighters. By comparing the KSAs derived from the tasks to the KSAs derived from the tests, he was able to create a battery that matched the test KSAs to the task KSAs, providing the all-important task-test link through the use of ability constructs.

Synthetic Validation

The use of traditional criterion-related validation as the primary means by which to validate test-criterion inferences meant that researchers often believed that small organizations were left with no alternative but content validation. Lawshe (1952) and Balma (1959) introduced the idea that one could infer validity by breaking jobs down logically into their basic elements, determining validity of tests for predicting performance on these elements, and then combining the elemental validities to estimate the overall validity of a set of tests. Guion (1965) presented an example of synthetic validation in a small organization.

Recently, Hollenbeck and Whitener (1988) revisited the concept of synthetic validity. Following job analyses using the Position Analysis Questionnaire, tests were chosen according to a priori theoretical judgments of their likely relationship to performance on a specific PAQ job element. Tests were then administered to those job incumbents whose jobs contained the element. Their predicted job performance was the average weighted (by the importance of the job element) sum of their predicted performance on elements relevant to their job. Performance evaluations were obtained on those elements relevant to each job. Overall performance was the average weighted sum of a person's performance on relevant job elements. The correlation of these two sums constituted the researchers' estimate of the relationship between a battery of tests and performance evaluations where each employee's test and performance measures may be unique in that they are the result of a different set of job elements.

Although proponents of this approach to validation insist on a type of empirical validation, a key element of this approach is an understanding of the different jobs; that is, the elements that are critical parts of the job performance domain and the ability constructs that underlie performance in these parts of the domain. Synthetic validity in one sense underscores the earlier argument that job analysis plays an important role in theory development and construct validation in personnel selection research.

Other Approaches to Construct Validation

Landy (1986) argues that if hypotheses about test–job performance relationships were approached as they are in doctoral or master's level research, we would not ask questions about the appropriate method of validation. Rather, we would be concerned about whether we should employ a lab or field study, what type of subjects should participate in the research, what conceptual and operational definitions of key variables would be appropriate, what statistical and empirical controls should be imposed, and to what degree we would be able to generalize beyond the results of a specific study.

Schmitt (1989) also argues that researchers ought to consider a wider variety of experimental and correlational approaches when evaluating inferences about predictor–job performance linkages. He provides some examples of the type of research studies that might be considered. A discussion of these studies follows.

Frederikson (1986) was interested in developing a test for admitting students to medical school. He was particularly interested in predicting applicants' performance in solving "patient management problems." Beginning with a theory of what was required of physicians as they analyzed medical problems, he developed job sample criteria simulating a situation that might be encountered by a resident on duty in the emergency ward of a hospital. In the simulation, examinees at first are given a small amount of information about a patient and asked for a diagnosis, after which they are allowed to seek further information. The requested information is provided, and they begin a new cycle of information gathering and hypothesis testing about the patient's problem.

Selection tests consisting of nonmedical problems requiring similar information-gathering and hypothesis-generation components were constructed. Data were then collected from fourth-year medical students on the job samples, the predictor tests, and a set of process variables (medical school grades and ratings, cognitive ability tests, and personality tests) that represented the researchers' hypotheses about what of an internal or process nature might be happening that would explain performance on either or both the job samples and predictors.

This design allowed for assessing predictor–job performance linkages in several ways. Correlations between process variables and predictor and criterion measures allowed for evaluation of linkages 2 and 4 in Figure 9.1. The similarity in the pattern of correlations for predictor and criterion measures allowed for indirect assessment of linkage 3. Correlations between criterion and predictor measures for the sample of fourth-year medical students provided a measure of traditional concurrent criterion-related validity (linkage 1). Also, longitudinal studies of the eventual job performance of incoming medical students provided evidence of predictive criterion-related validity.

Better and more systematic use of item analysis data may yield information about the construct validity of tests. Carroll (1979) describes comparisons of items of differing difficulties and evaluates inferences about the degree to which more difficult items require increased mental-processing or problem-solving ability. Careful analyses of scholastic aptitude tests allowed for inferences that the items in these tests measure vocabulary knowledge, the ability to notice relationships in verbal analogies, and the ability to perform various arithmetic, algebraic, and geometric manipulations. A similar approach should provide useful information about employment tests and test batteries as well. For example, a similar item analysis of tests such as the Bennett Mechanical Comprehension Test would yield information about those items that produce large gender and race differences and how such differences relate to various biographical information (such as hobbies, schools attended, classes taken, parental interests, occupations). Thus, information and hypotheses about the nature and potential causes of individual differences could be generated.

Experimental psychologists have correlated individuals' performance on traditional experimental tasks (for example, reaction time) with their performance on items on cognitive ability tests (Hunt, Frost, & Lunneborg, 1973). This cognitive correlates approach is similar to that used by Owens and his collaborators (Owens & Schoenfeldt, 1969) in their attempts to understand career decisions and success in terms of early-life experiences.

Since the 1970s, cognitive psychologists (for instance, Resnick, 1976; Sternberg, 1979) have used an information processing approach to study the patterns of performance on cognitive tasks with systematically varied attributes. Using methods such as content analyses of written or oral protocols, mathematical modeling of response time or error data, and computer simulation of cognitive processes, they have drawn inferences about the nature of mental ability.

Comparisons of the knowledge structures of experts and novices in a variety of different cognitive task domains (for example, Chi, Feltovich, & Glaser, 1981) suggest that the way information is stored and retrieved from long-term memory can largely account for differences between experts and novices. This has led to the hypothesis that the major difference between more and less intellectually able people derives from their ability to organize information in long-term memory in a way that makes it easily accessible. Most previous studies of differences between experts and novices have involved fairly complex mental tasks. Whether this research approach will be helpful in understanding simpler tasks or even physical tasks and skills would be an interesting research issue that may have implications for a broad range of work behavior.

Conclusion

In this chapter we trace the historical development of validity, beginning with early statements by Munsterberg (1913), Burtt (1929), Viteles (1932), and others, including Hull (1928) and Link (1919). We argue, like many other contemporary and early psychologists, that all evidence about predictor validation should be theory- or construct-based. Various methods of validation and some current research in I/O psychology are examined within this context. Moreover, we make strong arguments for the importance of theory at all stages of selection research, beginning with job analysis. Finally, we argue for the use of alternate paradigms for validation research as a means of producing greater understanding of both predictor and criterion constructs.

References

Ackerman, P. L. (1987). Individual differences in skill learning: An integration of psychometric and information processing perspectives. *Psychological Bulletin, 102*, 3–27.

Ackerman, P. L. (1989). Within-task intercorrelations of skilled performance: Implications for predicting individual differences? (A Comment on Henry & Hulin, 1987). *Journal of Applied Psychology, 74*, 360–364.

American Psychological Association. (1954). *Technical recommendations for psychological tests and diagnostic techniques.* Washington, DC: Author.

Anastasi, A. (1986). Evolving concepts of test validation. *Annual Review of Psychology, 37*, 1–15.

Arnold, J. D., Rauschenberger, J. M., Soubel, W. G., & Guion, R. M. (1982). Validation and utility of a strength test for selecting steelworkers. *Journal of Applied Psychology, 67*, 588–604.

Balma, M. J. (1959). The concept of synthetic validity. *Personnel Psychology, 12*, 395–396.

Barrett, G. V., Caldwell, M. S., & Alexander, R. A. (1989). The predictive stability of ability requirements for task performance: A critical reanalysis. *Human Performance, 2*, 167–181.

Bingham, W. V., & Freyd, M. (1926). *Procedures in employment psychology.* New York: Appleton.

Binning, J. F., & Barrett, G. V. (1989). Validity of personnel decisions: A conceptual analysis of the inferential and evidential bases. *Journal of Applied Psychology, 74*, 478–494.

Borman, W. C., Rosse, R. L., & Abrahams, N. M. (1980). An empirical construct validity approach to studying predictor–job performance links. *Journal of Applied Psychology, 65*, 662–671.

Borman, W. C., White, L. A., Pulakos, E. D., & Oppler, S. H. (1992). Models of supervisor job performance ratings: Evaluating the effects of ratee ability, technical knowledge and proficiency, temperament, awards and problem behavior on supervisor ratings. *Journal of Applied Psychology, 77,* 000–000.

Burke, M. J., & Pearlman, K. (1988). Recruiting, selecting, and matching people with jobs. In J. P. Campbell, R. J. Campbell, & Associates, *Productivity in organizations.* San Francisco: Jossey-Bass.

Burtt, H. E. (1917). Professor Munsterberg's vocational tests. *Journal of Applied Psychology, 1,* 201–213.

Burtt, H. E. (1929). *Psychology and industrial efficiency.* New York: Appleton.

Campbell, C. H., Ford, P., Rumsey, M. G., Pulakos, E. D., Borman, W. C., Felker, D. B., de Vera, M. V., & Riegelhaupt, B. J. (1990). Development of multiple job performance measures in a representative sample of jobs. *Personnel Psychology, 43,* 277–300.

Campbell, D. T., & Fiske, D. W. (1959). Convergent and discriminant validation by the multitrait-multimethod matrix. *Psychological Bulletin, 56,* 81–105.

Campbell, J. P., McHenry, J. J., & Wise, L. L. (1990). Modelling job performance in a population of jobs. *Personnel Psychology, 43,* 313–334.

Carroll, J. B. (1979). Measurement of ability constructs. In *Construct validity in psychological measurement: Proceedings of a colloquium on theory and application in education and employment.* Princeton, NJ: Educational Testing Service.

Chi, M. T. H., Feltovich, P. J., & Glaser, R. (1981). Representation of physics knowledge by experts and novices. *Cognitive Science, 5,* 121–152.

Conley, P. R., & Sackett, P. R. (1987). Effects of using high- versus low-performing job incumbents as sources of job analysis ratings. *Journal of Applied Psychology, 72,* 434–437.

Cook, T. D., & Campbell, D. T. (1979). *Quasi-experimentation: Design and analysis issues for field settings.* Skokie, IL: Rand McNally.

Cornelius, E. T., & Lyness, K. S. (1980). A comparison of holistic and decomposed judgment strategies in job analyses by job incumbents. *Journal of Applied Psychology, 65,* 155–163.

Cronbach, L. J. (1971). Test validation. In R. L. Thorndike (Ed.), *Educational measurement* (pp. 221–237). Washington, DC: American Council on Education.

Cronbach, L. J., & Meehl, P. E. (1955). Construct validity in psychological tests. *Psychological Bulletin, 52,* 281–302.

DeNisi, A. S., Cornelius, E. T., & Blencoe, A. G. (1987). Further investigation of common knowledge effects on job analysis ratings. *Journal of Applied Psychology, 72,* 262–268.

Dunnette, M. D. (1976). Aptitudes, abilities, and skills. In M. D. Dunnette (Ed.), *Handbook of industrial and organizational psychology.* Skokie, IL: Rand McNally.

Eder, B. W., & Ferris, G. R. (Eds.). (1989). *The employment interview: Theory, research, and practice.* Newbury Park, CA: Sage.

Fichman, M. (1988). Motivational consequences of absence and attendance: Proportional hazard estimation of a dynamic motivation model [Monograph]. *Journal of Applied Psychology, 73,* 119–134.

Fichman, M. (1989). Attendance makes the heart grow fonder: A hazard rate approach to modeling attendance. *Journal of Applied Psychology, 74,* 325–335.

Fine, S. A., & Wiley, W. W. (1974). An introduction to functional job analysis. In E. A. Fleishman & A. R. Bass (Eds.), *Studies in personnel and industrial psychology.* Homewood, IL: Irwin.

Fleishman, E. A., & Quaintance, M. K. (1984). *Taxonomies of human performance.* San Diego, CA: Academic Press.

Frederikson, N. (1986). Construct validity and construct similarity: Methods for use in test development and test validation. *Multivariate Behavioral Research, 21,* 3–28.

French, J. W., Ekstrom, R. B., & Price, L. A. (1963). *A kit of reference tests for cognitive factors.* Princeton, NJ: Educational Testing Service.

Gael, S. (1988). *The job analysis handbook for business, industry, and government.* New York: Wiley.

Goldman, H. (1918). The applied psychology of Hugo Munsterberg. *Journal of Applied Psychology, 2,* 116–127.

Goldstein, I. L., Zedeck, S., & Schneider, B. (1992). An exploration of the job analysis–content validity process. In N.

Schmitt & W. C. Borman (Eds.), *Personnel selection in organizations*. San Francisco: Jossey-Bass.

Gross, M. (1962). *The brain watchers*. New York: Signet Books.

Guilford, J. P. (1967). *The nature of human intelligence*. New York: McGraw-Hill.

Guion, R. M. (1965). Synthetic validity in a small company: A demonstration. *Personnel Psychology, 18,* 49–63.

Guion, R. M. (1980). On trinitarian doctrines of validity. *Professional Psychology, 11,* 385–398.

Guion, R. M. (1987). Changing views for personnel selection research. *Personnel Psychology, 40,* 199–213.

Harman, H. H. (1960). *Modern factor analysis*. Chicago: University of Chicago Press.

Harris, M. M., & Schaubroeck, J. (1988). A meta-analysis of self-supervisor, self-peer, and peer-supervisory ratings. *Personnel Psychology, 41,* 43–62.

Harrison, D. A., & Hulin, C. L. (1989). Investigations of absenteeism: Using event history models to study the absence-taking process. *Journal of Applied Psychology, 74,* 300–316.

Henry, R. A., & Hulin, C. L. (1987). Stability of skilled performance across time: Some generalizations and limitations on utilities. *Journal of Applied Psychology, 72,* 457–462.

Henry, R. A., & Hulin, C. L. (1989). Changing validities: Ability-performance relations and utilities. *Journal of Applied Psychology, 74,* 365–367.

Hirsh, H. R., Schmidt, F. L., & Hunter, J. E. (1986). Estimation of employment validities by less experienced judges. *Personnel Psychology, 39,* 337–344.

Hollenbeck, J. R., & Whitener, E. M. (1988). Criterion-related validation for small sample contexts: An integrated approach to synthetic validity. *Journal of Applied Psychology, 73,* 536–544.

Hull, C. L. (1928). *Aptitude Testing*. Orlando, FL: Harcourt Brace Jovanovich.

Hunt, E. B., Frost, N., & Lunneborg, C. L. (1973). Individual differences in cognition: A new approach to intelligence. In G. Bower (Ed.), *Advances in learning and motivation*. San Diego, CA: Academic Press.

Hunter, J. E., & Schmidt, F. L. (1990). *Methods of meta-analysis.* Newbury Park, CA: Sage.

Klimoski, R., & Brickner, M. (1987). Why do assessment centers work? The puzzle of assessment center validity. *Personnel Psychology, 40,* 243–260.

Landy, F. J. (1986). Stamp collecting versus science: Validation as hypothesis testing. *American Psychologist, 41,* 1183–1192.

Landy, F. J. (1988). Selection procedure development and usage. In S. Gael (Ed.), *The job analysis handbook for business, industry, and government* (pp. 271–286). New York: Wiley, 1988.

Landy, F. J. (1989). *The psychology of work behavior* (4th ed.). Pacific Grove, CA: Brooks/Cole.

Landy, F. J. (1991a). A conversation with Harold Burtt. *Industrial and Organizational Psychologist, 28,* 73–75.

Landy, F. J. (1991b, April). *Hugo Munsterberg: Victim, visionary or voyeur.* Paper presented at the meeting of the Society for Industrial and Organizational Psychology, St. Louis, MO.

Lawshe, C. H. (1952). Employee selection. *Personnel Psychology, 5,* 3–34.

Lawshe, C. H. (1985). Inferences from personnel tests and their validity. *Journal of Applied Psychology, 70,* 237–238.

Link, H. C. (1919). *Employment psychology.* New York: Macmillan.

Lippman, (1916). Zur psychologischen characteristik der "mittlern" berufe. *Zeitschrift für Angewandte Psychologie, 12,* 99–107. (Cited in Viteles, 1932.)

McCormick, E. J. (1979). *Job analysis.* New York: AMACOM.

McCormick, E. J., Jeanneret, P. R., & Meecham, R. C. (1972). A study of job dimensions as based on the Position Analysis Questionnaire. *Journal of Applied Psychology, 56,* 347–368.

Messick, S. (1980a). Meaning and values in measurement and education. *American Psychologist, 30,* 1012–1027.

Messick, S. (1980b). Test validity and ethics of assessment. *American Psychologist, 35,* 1012–1027.

Messick, S. (1988). The once and future issues of validity: Assessing the meaning and consequences of measurement. In H. Weiner & H. I. Braun (Eds.), *Test validity.* Hillsdale, NJ: Erlbaum.

Morita, J. G., Lee, T. W., & Mowday, R. T. (1989). Introducing survival analysis to organizational researchers: A selected
application to turnover research. *Journal of Applied Psychology,*
74, 280–292.

Mullins, W. C., & Kimbrough, W. W. (1988). Group composition as a determinant of job analysis outcomes. *Journal of*
Applied Psychology, 73, 657–664.

Mumford, M. D., & Owens, W. A. (1987). Methodology review: Principles, procedures, and findings in the application
of background data measures. *Applied Psychological Measure-*
ment, 11, 1–31.

Munsterberg, H. L. (1913). *Psychology and industrial efficiency.*
Boston: Houghton-Mifflin.

Munsterberg, H. L. (1915). *Business psychology.* Chicago: LaSalle
Extension University.

Nunnally, J. C. (1978). *Psychometric theory.* New York: McGraw-
Hill.

Organ, D. W. (1990). The motivational basis of organizational
citizenship behavior. In B. M. Staw & L. L. Cummings
(Eds.), *Research in organizational behavior* (Vol. 12). Greenwich,
CT: JAI Press.

Owens, W. A., & Schoenfeldt, L. F. (1969). Toward a classification of persons. *Journal of Applied Psychology, 53,* 569–
607.

Peterson, N. G., & Bownas, D. A. (1982). Skill, task structure,
and performance acquisition. In M. D. Dunnette & E. A.
Fleishman (Eds.), *Human performance and productivity: Human*
capability assessment. Hillsdale, NJ: Erlbaum.

Pritchard, R. D., Jones, S. D., Roth, P. L., Steubing, K. K.,
& Ekeberg, S. E. (1988). Effects of group feedback, goal setting, and incentives on organizational productivity. *Journal*
of Applied Psychology, 73, 337–358.

Pulakos, E. D., Borman, W. C., & Hough, L. M. (1988). Test
validation for scientific understanding: Two demonstrations
of an approach to studying predictor-criterion linkages. *Per-*
sonnel Psychology, 41, 703–716.

Rafaeli, A., & Sutton, R. I. (1990). Busy stores and demanding customers: How do they affect the display of positive emo-
tion? *Academy of Management Journal, 33,* 623–637.

Resnick, L. B. (Ed.). (1976). *The nature of intelligence.* Hillsdale, NJ: Erlbaum.

Roback, A. A. (1917). The moral issues involved in applied psychology. *Journal of Applied Psychology, 1,* 232-243.

Sackett, P. R. (1987). Assessment centers and content validity: Some neglected issues. *Personnel Psychology, 40,* 13-25.

Sackett, P. R., Zedeck, S., & Fogli, L. (1988). Relations between measures of typical and maximum job performance. *Journal of Applied Psychology, 73,* 482-486.

Sanchez, J. I., & Levine, E. L. (1989). Determining important tasks within jobs: A policy-capturing approach. *Journal of Applied Psychology, 74,* 336-342.

Schmidt, F. L., Hunter, J. E., Croll, P. R., & McKenzie, R. C. (1983). Estimation of employment test validities by expert judgment. *Journal of Applied Psychology, 68,* 590-601.

Schmidt, F. L., Hunter, J. E., & Outerbridge, A. N. (1986). Impact of job experience and ability on job knowledge, work sample performance, and supervisory ratings of job performance. *Journal of Applied Psychology, 71,* 432-439.

Schmidt, F. L., Hunter, J. E., Outerbridge, A. N., & Goff, S. (1988). Joint relation of experience and ability with job performance: Test of three hypotheses. *Journal of Applied Psychology, 73,* 46-57.

Schmitt, N. (1989). Construct validity in personnel selection. In B. J. Fullon, H. P. Pfister, & J. Brebner (Eds.), *Advances in industrial organizational psychology.* New York: Elsevier Science.

Schmitt, N., & Cohen, S. A. (1989). Internal analyses of task ratings by job incumbents. *Journal of Applied Psychology, 74,* 96-104.

Society for Industrial and Organizational Psychology. (1987). *Principles for the validation and use of personnel selection procedures* (3rd ed.). College Park, MD: Author.

Sternberg, R. J. (1979). The nature of mental abilities. *American Psychologist, 34,* 214-230.

Sulsky, L. M., & Balzer, W. K. (1988). Meaning and measurement of performance rating accuracy: Some methodological and theoretical concerns. *Journal of Applied Psychology, 73,* 497-506.

Tenopyr, M. L. (1977). Content-construct confusion. *Personnel Psychology, 30,* 47–54.

Thurstone, L. L. (1938). *The nature of human intelligence.* New York: McGraw-Hill.

Uniform Guidelines on Employee Selection Procedures. (1978). *Federal Register, 43,* 38290–38315.

Vance, R. J., Coovert, M. D., MacCallum, R. C., & Hedge, J. W. (1989). Construct models of job performance. *Journal of Applied Psychology, 74,* 447–455.

Viteles, M. (1932). *Industrial psychology.* New York: Norton.

Wilson, M. A., Harvey, R. J., & Macy, B. A. (1990). Repeating items to estimate the test-retest reliability of task inventory ratings. *Journal of Applied Psychology, 75,* 158–163.

Wise, L. L., McHenry, J., & Campbell, J. P. (1990). Identifying optimal predictor composites and testing for generalizability across jobs and performance factors. *Personnel Psychology, 43,* 355–366.

10

Assessing the Utility of Selection Decisions: Theoretical and Practical Considerations

Wayne F. Cascio

This chapter is a nontechnical review of theoretical and conceptual issues surrounding utility analysis. In the interest of focusing attention away from computational issues and toward broader conceptual ones, detailed formulas are not included.

Several authors (for example, Guion & Gibson, 1988; Vance & Colella, 1990) have noted the seemingly disjointed nature of much of the research conducted and published in the area of utility analysis, and they wonder where the area is going. Justifiably, in my opinion, they question the "utility" of utility analysis. They are not alone in their concern about the viability of this area. Ashe (1990) pointed out that dollar-based estimates of utility that dwarf the national debt eliminate the credible use of such information in management decision making and in arguments of the legal defensibility of selection techniques.

Yes, astronomical estimates of the economic value of selection methods abound in the literature. Yes, those who generate such numbers certainly strain credibility (their own as well as that of the profession of industrial and organizational [I/O] psychology). Rather than point an accusatory finger, however, a more rational approach is to examine carefully the underlying constructs purportedly being measured, and to identify important parameters that should be taken into account in deriving credible, relatively accurate utility estimates.

It has been said many times that there is nothing so practical as a good theory. Important theoretical and practical developments have occurred in utility analysis since the late 1970s, and there is a need to synthesize them in order to advance theory as well as practice in this area. In so doing, this chapter does not present a historical summary of developments or detailed derivations of alternative models; others have done this comprehensively (see, for example, Boudreau, 1991; Cascio, 1991a, 1991b; Zeidner, Johnson, Orlansky, Schmitz, & Nord, 1988). Rather, this chapter includes five major sections: (1) the role of utility analysis in strategic human resource management; (2) alternative utility metrics; (3) assumptions that underlie the use of utility analysis; (4) utility constructs and parameters; and (5) dealing with risk and uncertainty in utility analysis.

The Role of Utility Analysis in the Strategic Management of Human Resources

Strategic human resource management consists of three tasks (Dyer & Holder, 1988). The first arises during the formulation of general business strategies. The task is to ensure that human resource (HR) issues and the implications of various alternatives or proposals are considered fully. The second task is to establish HR goals or action plans — HR strategies — to support the general business strategies. The third and final task is to work with line managers as principal clients to ensure that action plans are implemented in the manner intended. These three tasks take place at three levels: the corporate (senior management) level, the middle management level, and the operating management level.

Utility analysis can play an important role at the corporate level, in identifying the economic implications of various human resource program alternatives or proposals *prior to their implementation* (ex ante). It also can play an important role at the middle management and operating management levels in assessing the outcomes of HR programs in financial terms *after their implementation* (ex post).

When strategy is an integral part of the human resource function, success is not defined in terms of measures that show

how busy the HR department has been (for example, the number of employees recruited, tested, or trained). Rather, success is defined in terms of the nature of the contribution to the achievement of HR objectives, and, in the longer run, in terms of the nature of the contribution to the success of the organization's business strategies (Dyer & Holder, 1988).

Alternative Competitive Strategies

The means that companies use to compete for business in the marketplace and to gain competitive advantage are known as *competitive strategies* (Porter, 1985). Competitive strategies may differ in several ways, including the extent to which companies emphasize innovation, quality enhancement, or cost reduction (Schuler & Jackson, 1987). Moreover, there is growing recognition that the different types of strategies require different types of HR management practices (Jackson & Schuler, 1990). Following are three common competitive strategies.

Innovation strategy is used to develop products or services that differ from those of competitors; its primary objective is to offer something new and different. Enhancing product or service quality is the objective of the *quality enhancement strategy*. Finally, the objective of a *cost reduction strategy* is to gain competitive advantage by being the lowest-cost producer of goods or provider of services. As Schuler and Jackson (1987) noted, an innovation strategy emphasizes managing people so that they work differently; a quality enhancement strategy emphasizes managing people so that they work smarter; and a cost reduction strategy emphasizes managing people so that they work harder.

Although it is convenient to think of each of these competitive strategies as pure types applied to entire organizations, business units, or even functional specialties, reality is more complex. Various combinations of these three strategies may be observed in the same organization or unit of an organization.

Because different types of human resource practices are important in different organizations or units of organizations, the assessment of outcomes associated with HR activities should focus on activities associated with the HR practices that are most crucial to implementing the competitive strategy chosen. HR practices, in turn, should be tailored to the desired role behaviors under each strategy. Later in this chapter, these points are considered in more detail.

Schuler and Jackson (1987) outlined the HR management implications of pursuing innovation, quality enhancement, and cost reduction strategies. An innovation strategy involves selecting highly skilled individuals, giving employees more discretion, using minimal controls, making a greater investment in human resources, providing resources for experimentation, allowing and even rewarding occasional failure, and appraising performance for its long-run implications.

Desired behaviors under a quality enhancement strategy include relatively repetitive and predictable behaviors, a longer-term focus, a modest amount of cooperative, interdependent behavior, a high concern for quality with a modest concern for quantity of output, a high concern for how goods are made or services are delivered, low risk-taking activity, and commitment to the goals of the organization. Because quality enhancement typically involves greater employee commitment and fuller use of each employee's abilities, fewer employees may be needed to produce the same level of output.

Finally, under a cost reduction strategy, organizations pursue tight fiscal and management controls, minimize overhead, make few if any investments in training, and search for economies of scale. Strategies for accomplishing these objectives include reducing the number of employees, reducing wage levels, using part-time workers, subcontractors, or automation, changing work rules, and permitting flexibility in job assignments.

The implications for utility analysis are straightforward. Companies most likely to invest in valid selection (or training) programs are those that pursue human resource strategies that emphasize innovation or quality enhancement. Such organizations seek to find and retain the best talent available, and they are more likely to address the long-term development needs of all employees through extensive investments in training activities. They do this because their perspective is long- rather than short-term in nature. Utility analyses that can enlighten managers about the expected economic consequences of alternative selection techniques or training programs are likely to be most useful in this context.

Alternative Metrics for Expressing Utility

Managers are frequently confronted with alternative courses of action, and decisions are made when one alternative is chosen in preference to others. Since different cost consequences are frequently associated with the various alternatives, principles are needed that will assist decision makers in choosing the most beneficial or most profitable alternatives. Utility theory provides such a vehicle, for it forces decision makers to consider the costs, consequences, and anticipated payoffs of all available courses of action. In short, utility theory is a tool that can help managers to organize information about decisions in a systematic manner and to communicate the results of their decisions in understandable terms to other interested parties. Cronbach and Gleser (1965, p. 121) noted these features almost thirty years ago when they wrote: "The unique feature of decision theory or utility theory is that it specifies evaluations by means of a payoff matrix or by conversion of the criterion to utility units. The values are thus plainly revealed and open to criticism. This is an asset rather than a defect of this system, as compared with systems where value judgments are embedded and often pass unrecognized."

The term *utility units* means that outcomes (criteria) may be expressed in different metrics, depending on the purpose for which the analysis is done. Some alternative metrics for expressing outcomes include financial terms (dollar-valued increases in sales or in output, or savings in payroll expenses), increases in output expressed in production-oriented terms, and reduction in the number of workers needed (see, for example, Eaton, Wing, & Mitchell, 1985; Sadacca & Campbell, 1985; Schmidt, Hunter, Outerbridge, & Trattner, 1986).

One example of an alternative utility metric is the Superior Equivalents Technique, developed by Eaton, Wing, & Mitchell (1985) for use in military contexts. Experienced U.S. Army tank commanders (TCs) were used as expert judges and asked to estimate how many tanks with superior (85th percentile) TCs it would take to perform the work of a specified number of tanks with average (50th percentile) TCs. The expert judges were more willing and able to make these estimates than they were estimates expressed in terms of dollars. In addition, the researchers found less variance among judges when they used this technique, compared to poor interrater agreement when they used dollar-based metrics.

Vance and Colella (1990) argue that users of utility analysis should reconsider the use of dollar metrics to express the outcomes of selection procedures. They should consider using alternative, non-market-driven metrics, such as units of production. Three reasons for doing this are (1) concerns have been raised about the accuracy and construct validity of dollar-based metrics, (2) non-market-driven metrics may be easier for managers to estimate and to comprehend, and (3) it is easier to assess the validity of utility estimates (that is, whether the gains predicted are actually realized) when they are expressed in production units rather than in terms of dollars. Different ways of operationalizing utility imply different conceptual definitions of the utility construct, and different conceptual definitions of the utility construct imply different ways of operationalizing utility.

Thinking about utility in terms other than dollars also refocuses attention on criteria (Bobko, Colella, & Russell, 1990). Questions such as the following must therefore be addressed: What criteria are most meaningful? What is the impact of a change (and the rate of change) in the criterion construct domain on assessments of utility? How can current procedures be modified to encompass multiple criteria?

The expression of outcomes in terms other than dollars has little impact on the application of the most popular utility analysis method, the Brogden-Cronbach-Gleser formula (Brogden, 1949; Cronbach & Gleser, 1965). In its simplest possible form, this formula expresses the following relationship:

$$\text{Utility} = \text{gains} - \text{costs}$$

Utility, as conceptualized by Brogden (1949) and Cronbach and Gleser (1965), refers to the net gain in economic terms over selecting people randomly for jobs. In the context of selection, gains are a multiplicative function of four parameters: (1) the number of individuals selected (N_s), (2) the validity coefficient that expresses the correlation between scores on a predictor and scores on a measure of job performance (r_{xy}), (3) the standard deviation of a dollar-valued measure of job performance or outcomes (SD_y), and (4) the average score on the predictor of those individuals selected (mean Z_x). Costs are a multiplicative function of the number of applicants times the fully loaded cost of recruiting, processing, and assessing each applicant.

If outcomes (SD_y in the formula above) are expressed in metrics other than dollars, the only implication is that gains and costs cannot be added together to derive a single utility estimate. Rather, projected gains must be treated separately from projected costs. Decisions then are based on judgments about the relative desirability of projected gains in performance or output, relative to projected costs. This is *cost-effectiveness analysis*. If both gains and costs are expressed in the same metric (in this case, dollars), then the procedure is termed *cost-benefit analysis*.

Few would argue with the proposition that criteria should be expressed in terms that are most meaningful to decision makers as they attempt to answer specific questions related to HR management. However, if the decision to be made involves comparing competing proposals for the use of an organization's resources, say, for an advertising campaign, for new construction, or for more valid selection procedures, then benefits should be expressed in financial terms so that capital budgeting methods can be used.

Capital Budgeting Analysis
Applied to Human Resource Programs

The purpose of capital budgeting is to facilitate comparison of competing proposals for the use of an organization's resources. In most organizations, resources for carrying out proposed programs are limited, and competing programs must be compared and evaluated. To be compared, all proposals should be presented in terms that measure the benefit of the program for the organization as a whole and that reflect the basic objectives of the organization. Comparisons among proposals are difficult if the expected outcomes of each one are expressed in terms of different yardsticks. Conversely, if the expected benefits of an HR program are presented in the same terms as competing proposals, comparisons among proposals are easier to make, and almost certainly are more valid.

There is general agreement, at least in the finance literature, that when different proposals for the use of an organization's funds are compared, discounting techniques must be used to facilitate comparison of costs and benefits that occur at different time periods (compare Brealey & Meyers, 1988; Brigham & Gapenski, 1988). It is also well established that the correct criterion for evaluating and comparing competing investment proposals is net present value (NPV) — not internal rate of return, not increment in sales, and not increment in profits. The NPV of a proposed investment in an HR program can be calculated as follows (Cascio & Morris, 1990):

$$\text{NPV} = \sum_{t=1}^{N} B_t (1/1 + k)^t - I_o,$$

where I_o is the initial cost outlay for the program, B_t denotes the incremental cash flows generated by the program in period t, k is the discount rate representing an organization's cost of capital or its minimum required rate of return, and N is the number of periods over which the program is expected to generate benefits. To be accepted, the NPV must be positive, which means that the present value of the benefits (incremental cash flows) exceeds the cost of the program. Alternatively, when the rate of return is defined, it means that the program's internal rate of return exceeds the required rate of return, k.

The correct application of NPV requires that the focus be on the incremental cash flow available after all expenses have been paid. Thus, calculating NPV on the basis of the increment in sales, the increment in profits, or the dollar-valued increment in performance may be incorrect if these measures differ from the incremental cash flow (net of all cash expenses) evaluated for the organization as a whole compared with the net cash flow that would be generated without the implementation of the proposed program. As we have seen, there are contexts in which it is appropriate to express utility in metrics other than dollars, but such metrics are not appropriate for a valid comparison of proposed organizational investments.

Using the Brogden-Cronbach-Gleser utility formula to analyze proposed HR programs as capital budgeting decisions requires that the variables be defined and measured in terms consistent with the cash flow definitions of capital budgeting. (See Boudreau, 1983a, for a more detailed discussion of incremental cash flow.)

When the utility formula is linked to NPV, the critical variable is the standard deviation of job performance (SD_y), expressed in dollars. When this variable is defined so that it measures the standard deviation of the incremental net cash flow, utility as conventionally calculated will be a valid input to the calculation of NPV.

To summarize, the central theme of this section is that to be useful, utility analyses should reflect the context in which management decisions are made. Is the task to choose among alternative selection procedures? If this is the case, then conceptually all that is needed to assess *relative gains* is the first term in the Brogden-Cronbach-Gleser formula: $N_s \, r_{xy} \, SD_y \, \bar{Z}_x$. Taking additional factors into account or changing the metric in which utility is expressed serves only to adjust the definition of utility. However, if the decision is to choose among alternative proposals for capital investments (for example, to fund a new selection program or to purchase new equipment), then it is necessary to use NPV analysis in order to make valid and systematic comparisons among the proposals.

Having examined the role of utility analysis in the strategic management of human resources and alternative metrics for expressing utility, we now examine the assumptions that underlie the use of utility analysis.

Utility Assumptions

A critical assumption in using the Brogden-Cronbach-Gleser formula is that the relationship between predictor and criterion is linear (that is, it is best described by a straight line). If the predictor-criterion relationship is not linear, then it is not appropriate to use this utility model. Fortunately, almost all ability-performance relations are linear, as shown by a large body of research (Coward & Sackett, 1990; Society for Industrial and Organizational Psychology, 1987).

A second assumption is that selection procedures are used optimally. That is, selection proceeds from the top-scoring applicant on down in rank order until the selection ratio (the percentage of applicants accepted) is reached. Any other use of valid test information will result in some loss in utility. For example, if a cutoff score was set at a point lower than that corresponding to the selection ratio (SR), and if applicants scoring above this minimum score were selected randomly or nonrandomly (for example, according to considerations of work force diversity), productivity gains, although still substantial, would be less than the maximum gains that could be achieved (Cascio, Outtz, Zedeck, & Goldstein, 1991; Schmidt, Mack, & Hunter, 1984).

A final assumption is that all applicants who are offered jobs accept and are hired. This is probably not realistic, because in practice, lower-scoring applicants must be accepted in place of higher-scoring applicants who decline offers of employment. Hence, the ability levels of those actually selected almost always will be lower than the ability levels of those who receive the initial offers (that is, $\bar{Z}_x$ in the general utility formula will decrease).

The same effect may be observed in a tight labor market, where the supply of available workers is low relative to the aggregate demand for them. Under these circumstances, unemployment is low, and, as Becker (1989) shows, companies may be forced to lower their minimum hiring requirements in order to fill vacancies. Lower hiring requirements mean higher SRs.

In practice, therefore, rejection of hiring offers and reduction in minimum hiring standards produce identical effects. They increase SRs and thus reduce the productivity gains from selection. For example, if an SR of .25 would provide the needed number of new employees given no rejections of job offers by applicants, and if half of all job offers are rejected, then the SR must be increased to .50 to yield the desired number of new hires. Murphy (1986) presents formulas for calculating the average ability of those actually selected when the proportion of initial offers accepted is less than 100 percent. He shows that under realistic circumstances, utility formulas currently used may over-estimate gains by 30 to 80 percent.

To summarize, predictor-criterion relationships are almost always linear, but if they are not, then use of the Brogden-Cronbach-Gleser continuous variable utility model is not ap-propriate. If selection decisions are not made in top-down fashion, if some applicants who are offered jobs reject them, or if tight labor markets force organizations to lower their hiring require-ments, then the actual payoffs associated with the use of valid selection procedures will be lower than predicted payoffs.

Utility Constructs and Parameters

In addition to the impact that changes in selection ratios have on estimates of utility, seven additional factors affect esti-mated payoffs: (1) employee tenure, (2) employee flows into and out of a workforce, (3) economic variables, (4) alternative de-finitions of the construct of dollar-valued criterion performance, (5) changes in performance levels over time, (6) predictor-cri-terion time lags, and (7) variations in labor market conditions on utility estimates.

Employee Tenure

Schmidt, Hunter, McKenzie, & Muldrow (1979) expand the basic Brogden-Cronbach-Gleser formula by multiplying the total economic gain for a cohort of new hires (N_s) by the aver-age tenure of new hires under the new selection system. In do-ing so, they argue that an organization will benefit from an in-dividual's increased productivity as long as the employee remains in the organization. For example, if the gain in individual productivity is $5,000 per year, and new employees stay an aver-age of ten years, then the total gain per new hire as a result of using the selection device is $50,000.

Multiplying the estimated economic gain for one year by the average tenure of employees assume two things: (1) the effect of inflation is zero, and, hence, dollars received at future time periods are equal in value to dollars received today, and (2) the effect of the intervention remains stable across all years of the employee's tenure.

Assumption (1) does not hold, because dollars received in the future must be worth less than dollars received today. Why? Because a dollar received today can be invested to earn interest. To account for this fact, dollars received in the future must be *discounted* (discounting is the reverse of compounding, as with interest accruals) to reflect their present value. As noted earlier, discounting is an integral part of NPV analysis.

With respect to assumption (2), and in the context of selection, it is assumed that performance levels *and* test validity remain constant over time. At present, this is a controversial issue, and is discussed further later in this chapter. Despite this controversy, however, we can say that to the extent that validity and variability of job performance do change over time (either increasing or decreasing), then estimates of utility will change, sometimes substantially (Cascio, 1991c).

Researchers who have applied utility analysis to assess the economic value of training programs generally acknowledge the existence of diminishing training effects over time (Cascio, 1989). For example, Schmidt, Hunter, and Pearlman (1982) address this issue by estimating marginal utility using the effect size (that is, the degree of departure from the null hypothesis that training had no effect, expressed in standard deviation units) at the midpoint of the period during which training effects are expected to last. Mathieu and Leonard (1987) refine this technique to account for turnover by calculating gains for each year, using a diminishing effect size, and summing the yearly estimates to obtain a total marginal utility.

Employee Flows Into and Out of a Workforce

Boudreau (1983b) expands the basic Brogden-Cronbach-Gleser formula by assessing the total marginal utility for the entire period that a selection test is used. Previous applications only assess utility for a single cohort of new hires — either for one year, or as with Schmidt, Hunter, McKenzie, and Muldrow (1979), over the expected tenure of a single cohort. This model takes into account the number of employees hired each year by means of the test, their tenure, and the number of years that the test will be used. Boudreau (1983b) demonstrates that incorporating the flow of multiple cohorts of employees into and out of a workforce during the period of time that a test is used greatly increases aggregate estimates of utility. Boudreau and Berger (1985) expand this model further by including the effects of employee separations. Examining the net number (accessions minus separations) of employees remaining each year that a test is used, computing yearly estimates of utility, and summing across years provide a more accurate estimate of the total economic value of a selection device over its entire life cycle. When the test is no longer used, yearly gains in utility will continue to be realized over the entire tenure of the last cohort hired using the test. However, yearly utility estimates will decrease owing to turnover and the failure to replace these employees by using the valid test.

Economic Variables

Boudreau (1983a, 1983b) introduces three important economic variables that generally serve to lower utility estimates. These are variable costs (costs that vary with changes in productivity, such as sales commissions), discounting (to account for the effects of inflation on cash flows received in future time periods), and corporate taxes. As profits increase (because of, at least in part, the use of more valid selection and training procedures), so do corporate taxes. Although selection costs will be reduced to the extent that they are tax-deductible, since the gains associated with the use of valid selection procedures are usually larger than the costs of those procedures, marginal utility will be lower when taxes are considered.

Cronshaw and Alexander (1985) add another economic consideration by separating costs into those that occur initially (start-up costs, as with assessment centers) and those that recur over time (for example, materials, administration, and scoring costs). Separating these costs into two categories allows utility to be defined in capital budgeting terms such as return on investment and payback period. As we noted earlier, the expression of utility in capital budgeting terms is most appropriate in contexts where decision makers must choose among alternative proposals regarding organizational investments (for instance, new construction, purchase of new equipment, or human resource interventions).

Dollar-Valued Criterion Performance

There has been debate in the literature about the meaning of the term *dollar-valued criterion performance.* It has been defined as the dollar value of output as sold (Hunter & Schmidt, 1982); the value of sales (Cascio & Silbey, 1979); service value (reflecting the benefit to the organization after accounting for variable costs, taxes, and discounting (Boudreau, 1983a); in cost-accounting terms as total contribution margin (Greer & Cascio, 1987); and in terms of the contribution of labor to individual productivity (Cascio & Ramos, 1986).

With the exception of the cost-accounting method (and direct work measurement methods that actually count outputs and then convert them into dollars), all other methods for estimating the dollar value of criterion performance (and its standard deviation, SD_y) rely on rational estimation procedures by supervisors of job incumbents. What do rational estimation procedures really measure? That is, what is the basis for supervisors' judgments of "overall worth"? Several studies now indicate that supervisors rely primarily on salary as an indicator of overall worth (for reviews, see Bobko, Colella, & Russell, 1990; Boudreau, 1991). There is both good news and bad news in this finding. The good news is that a review of thirty-four studies that included over one hundred estimates of SD_y found that differences among the methods for estimating the standard deviation of dollar-valued criterion performance are often less than 50 percent, and in many cases amount to less than $5,000 (Boudreau, 1991). The bad news comes in two parts.

First, from the perspective of the accuracy of utility estimates, salary-based methods consider only the contribution of labor to productivity; as such, they only estimate *partial productivity*. An estimate of *total productivity* must consider the combined contribution of labor, capital, and equipment. If it is any consolation, industrial engineers report that it is very difficult to develop measures of total productivity (Packer, 1983). Therefore, SD_y presumably refers to a total productivity measure, but since rational estimation techniques generally rely only on partial productivity measures, they tend to underestimate the "true" value of SD_y.

The second aspect of the bad news is that any given selection method or device may not have the same effect on all criteria, yet a "dollar criterion" assumes that it does. Thus Vance, Coovert, MacCallum, and Hedge (1989) demonstrated that an aptitude test predicted some criterion task domains for the job of jet engine mechanic better than others. In another study, Pulakos, Borman, and Hough (1988) studied the effectiveness of navy recruiters. They found that selling skills, human relations skills, and organizing skills all were important and related to success. They also found, however, that the three dimensions were unrelated to each other. Under these conditions, combining the measures leads to a composite that is psychologically nonsensical.

Where does this leave us—back at the old "composite versus multiple criteria" controversy? Yes, but let us not forget Schmidt and Kaplan's (1971) comments on this issue. They point out that combining the various elements into a composite does imply that there is a single underlying dimension in job performance but does not, in and of itself, imply that this single underlying dimension is behavioral or psychological in nature. A composite criterion may well represent an underlying economic dimension, while at the same time have essentially no meaning from a behavioral point of view.

The resolution of the composite versus multiple-criterion dilemma essentially depends on the objectives of the investigator. Both methods are legitimate for their own purposes. If the goal is increased understanding of predictor-criterion relationships, then the criterion elements are best kept separate. If managerial decision making is the objective, then the criterion elements should be weighted, regardless of their intercorrelations, into a composite representing an economic construct of overall worth to the organization. Bobko, Colella, and Russell (1990) have developed a "hybrid" utility model that accommodates multiple criteria in a single utility equation that also includes multiple predictors. Such an approach may go a long way toward helping us to improve our understanding of what we are measuring.

Changes in Performance Levels over Time

In most studies, the standard deviation of job performance (SD_y) has been treated as a static measure of performance variability across subjects. Yet a series of nine studies spanning over thirty years (Rothe, 1978) shows clearly that individual job performance is not stable over time. That is, the best performers at time 1 will not necessarily also be the best performers at time 2. Studies involving bank tellers (Mirvis & Lawler, 1977) and salespeople (Meyer & Raich, 1983) also found considerable variability in the month-to-month job performance of individuals.

Cascio and Silbey (1979) took such performance variability into account in their study of salespersons by assuming that the average stability of performance across years was .70, computing SD_y for year 1 (average tenure was five years), and then computing the standard deviation of a sum. If stable performance across years had been assumed, the five-year SD would have been \$47,500 (SD in year 1 of \$9,500 × 5). Taking performance unreliability into account, however, reduced the five-year SD to \$41,409, a difference of \$6,091 or 13 percent. Studies that have assumed longer average tenure or used a larger value of the one-year SD_y produce correspondingly larger overestimates of the aggregate SD_y.

Performance levels also may change as a function of the time lag from initial placement on a job to fully competent performance. To the extent that utility analyses do not incorporate adjustments for this phenomenon, then estimates of expected payoffs will be higher than is actually the case. Consider the familiar S-shaped learning curve that characterizes both knowledge and skill learning (Landy, 1987). The shape and steepness of the curve suggest that there is a lag from initial performance to fully competent performance. To illustrate this, let us consider the results of a study of jobs in a stockbrokerage firm. The firm reported the following number of weeks in the learning period in order to reach fully competent performance: office and clerical workers, 10 weeks; professionals and technicians, 16 weeks; managers and partners, 24 weeks; stockbroker trainees, 104 weeks (Cascio, 1983). The same study also reported the percentage loss in productivity during each third of the learning period. These losses ranged from 85 percent during the first third of the learning period for stockbroker trainees to 15 percent during the last third of the learning period for the other classes of jobs.

Unfortunately, most utility analyses assume that fully competent performance begins on the first day that a new employee is hired. That is, researchers simply multiply the payoff function $(r_{xy}SD_y)$ by the average tenure of employees in a job. At a broader level, we know from the literature on the socialization of new employees that it takes time for new employees (and even experienced employees who switch jobs) to get adjusted to their new jobs and to learn the organization and job-specific skills necessary to perform competently in a particular position (Schein, 1980). In practice, organizations frequently recognize this time lag in performance by establishing a probationary period for new employees. Completion of the probationary period usually indicates satisfactory progress toward some desired level of job performance.

Research on adjusting utility estimates (downward) to take account of the time lag between initial performance during the learning period and fully competent performance is much needed. Doing so would expand the traditional focus of utility research. In this newer approach, estimates of the utility of selection (or training) systems would consist of a forecast of expected utility *and* a forecast of how expected average performance will change over time. This suggests that criterion performance dimensions might be weighed and combined differently at different time periods, according to the strategic needs of an organization.

Bobko, Colella, and Russell (1990) have developed a hybrid utility model to permit such differential weighting over time. Although such an approach will add another layer of complexity to utility analysis, it also may make utility estimates more realistic.

Predictor-Criterion Time Lags

Many studies in applied psychology have assessed the relationship between performance in training and performance on the job (for example, Hunter & Hunter, 1984). As Bobko, Colella, and Russell (1990) note, in taking such sequential measures from the criterion domain, we are (at least implicitly) introducing the notion of *time* to any discussion of utility; we are assessing possible distinctions between early and late task performance. This distinction is important because it suggests that criterion-related validity coefficients as well as the variability of job performance (SD_y) may change over time.

Do validity coefficients and SD_y change as a function of predictor-criterion time lags? The question is not firmly resolved at this point. The work of Ackerman (1987, 1989), Barrett, Alexander, and Doverspike (1991), Fleishman and his colleagues (Fleishman & Quaintance, 1984), and Hulin, Henry, and Noon (1990) indicates considerable disagreement over the correct interpretations to be drawn from the empirical evidence that currently exists.

Nevertheless, we can infer from the early work of Fleishman, and from more recent reanalyses by Ackerman, that validity will be moderated by both the cognitive demands of a task and the way those cognitive demands change over repeated exposure to the task (that is, job experience). Predictors that measure cognitive skills and psychomotor skills are likely to demonstrate one level of predictive validity with criterion measures taken at one time and different predictive validities with criterion measures taken at later times. This further suggests that criterion measures taken over multiple time periods will not necessarily yield identical estimates of the mean and standard deviation of dollar-valued job performance.

Available evidence indicates that when utility estimates are adjusted for possible changes in validity and SD_y, the difference from unadjusted values may be more than 50 percent, depending on the magnitude of the adjustment (Cascio, 1991c). However, very little empirical evidence exists on the *actual rates of decay or increase* in validity coefficients over time. As examples of increasing validities, three longitudinal studies of assessment center results have found this pattern (Hinrichs, 1978; McEvoy & Beatty, 1989; Mitchel, 1975). Almost no evidence exists on possible changes in SD_y over time, and, as is the case with research on selection, almost no evidence exists on the duration of training effects or rates of decay or increase in them. These are fruitful areas for future research.

Effects of Labor Market Conditions on Utility Estimates

Most utility analyses focus on the economic impact of selection (or training) programs at the level of the individual organization. As Becker (1989) notes, there seems to be an implicit assumption that utilities do not vary across changing labor market conditions, and that current and prospective employees and employers will be unresponsive to these labor market dynamics. This assumption seems unrealistic. To illustrate, let us consider just three potential labor market effects on utility estimates.

First, if a company decides to invest in a more valid selection system, then it must enter the competition in the labor market for better workers. Higher validity should yield a higher average criterion score for new hires, but at a price. The price will be the wage premium required to be competitive with other companies currently using a similar selection strategy with this level of validity (Becker, 1989). Hence, any estimate of the gains in utility associated with the adoption of such a strategy should include the variable cost of higher wages. Failure to do so will result in a consistent overestimation of economic gains for the company.

Another labor market dynamic may affect the length of the learning period from initial to fully competent performance. For example, in tight labor markets (low supply, high demand for workers), where firms cannot recruit fully competent personnel, the time lag to fully competent performance among new hires will probably be much longer, due to training time, than in loose labor markets (high supply, low demand for workers), where fully competent personnel are readily available.

A third labor market effect on utility estimates is recruitment costs. Recruitment costs are important components in selection systems, and variations in such costs may affect utility estimates significantly (Boudreau & Rynes, 1985). The fully loaded per applicant cost of selection is an important parameter in the Brogden-Cronbach-Gleser utility model. To consider only the direct costs of testing in the selection process underspecifies the true cost of selection per applicant.

To be sure, the costs of recruitment are highly variable over labor market conditions, seasons, and sources. Thus, it is well known that in order to maintain relatively favorable (low) selection ratios, companies must often widen their recruitment efforts. The effect of increased recruitment, in turn, is well known: costs escalate considerably (Sands, 1973). Recruitment costs also vary by source (Lord, 1989). For example, consider that the cheapest source of applicants is walk-ins, while the most expensive generally is employment agencies, whose fees can be as high as 35 percent of a new hire's first-year salary. In many companies it may be the case that the full cost of recruiting a given cohort of applicants is unknown because data that show variations in recruitment costs as a function of source and labor market conditions are unavailable. However, to leave such costs out of utility analyses is to overestimate the expected benefits of a selection method.

It should be clear by now, given the number of factors we have discussed (and probably more that we have not discussed), that to date we have oversimplified utility analyses enormously. A summary of these factors, along with their likely effect on utility estimates, is presented in Table 10.1.

Dealing with Risk and Uncertainty in Utility Analysis

In conducting utility analyses, we have tended to assume away or not even consider many of the factors shown in Table 10.1. However, even if we could develop a more complete (and

**Table 10.1. Some Key Factors That Affect
Economic Payoffs from Selection Programs.**

Generally Increase Payoffs	Generally Decrease Payoffs	May Increase or Decrease Payoffs
Low selection ratios	High selection ratios	Changes in the definition of the criterion construct
Multiple employee cohorts	Discounting	
Start-up costs[a]	Variable costs (materials + wages)	Changes in validity
Employee tenure	Taxes	Changes in the variability of job performance
Loose labor markets	Tight labor markets	
	Time lags to fully competent performance	
	Unreliability in performance across time periods	
	Recruitment costs	

[a]Start-up costs decrease payoffs in the period incurred, but they act to increase payoffs thereafter, because only recurring costs remain.

admittedly more complex) utility model, we probably never will develop a model that captures *all* of the factors that influence the dollar payoff associated with the use of one intervention over another. In other words, estimates of economic utility will always be somewhat deficient. There will always be uncertainty in our estimates.

Researchers have developed three techniques to deal with such uncertainty. Alexander and Barrick (1987) developed a procedure for estimating the standard error of utility estimates. This is important because researchers (and managers) tend to view utilities as point rather than interval estimates. Given the uncertainty of many of the parameters in the utility model, interval estimates are probably more appropriate. Rich and Boudreau (1987) extended this work by using Monte Carlo simulation of a wide range of parameter estimates and assessing the impact of such changes on estimated payoffs.

The third approach is by far the simplest: break-even analysis (Boudreau, 1984). This approach seems most appropriate in situations where the task is to estimate the relative gains associated with using one selection method in preference to another (for example, multiple interviews versus assessment centers). Instead of estimating the *level* of expected utility for each alternative selection method, decision makers focus instead on determining the *break-even values* that are critical to making the decision. In other words, after setting the expected payoff equal to zero, and holding all other parameters in the utility equation constant, they try to determine the smallest value of any given parameter (for example, validity, SD_y, $\bar{Z}_x$, or cost of selection) that will permit gains to be offset exactly against costs.

Break-even analysis has been used most often to estimate the minimum value of SD_y necessary before valid selection methods begin to pay dividends. Although there may be considerable disagreement over the exact point value of SD_y (given different ways of estimating it), break-even analysis allows practicing managers to appreciate how little variability in job performance is necessary to generate positive economic gains in productivity. Whatever the estimated value of SD_y is, decision makers can probably agree that it is higher than the break-even value, and, therefore, that valid selection methods are worth using.

Conclusion

Utility analysis is simply a tool for decision making. It may be applied ex ante, to estimate expected payoffs before a decision is made, or ex post, to assess actual payoffs after a decision is made. Several emerging theoretical and practical issues should be considered carefully when assessing the utility of selection decisions.

At a broad level, researchers and practitioners need to understand the role that utility analysis plays in the context of alternative competitive strategies such as innovation, quality enhancement, and cost reduction. They then need to consider carefully the type of utility metric, financial or nonfinancial, that would be most meaningful to decision makers as they grapple with specific questions related to human resource management. However, if the purpose of the decision in question is to compare competing proposals for the use of an organization's resources (one of which happens to be for improved selection methods), then benefits must be expressed in financial terms so that capital budgeting methods (specifically, net present value analysis) can be used.

Many researchers and practitioners are uneasy when confronted with projections of huge economic returns from the use of valid selection programs. Such numbers seem "too good to be true." Indeed, one may logically ask, if the return on investment associated with such programs is so high, then why do not all companies invest substantial amounts of resources in them? The answer is that the actual returns are likely to be considerably lower than the estimated returns, because researchers have tended to make simplifying assumptions with regard to certain variables, and to omit others that add to an already complex mix of factors.

Two such assumptions are that selection procedures are used optimally (that is, in top-down fashion) and that all applicants who are offered jobs accept them and are hired. In practice, labor market conditions may force organizations to deviate from these assumptions. As a result, selection ratios increase and actual payoffs decrease. Another practice commonly used by analysts is to multiply estimated economic gains for one year by the average tenure of employees. This practice is based on two other assumptions, neither of which may be tenable: the effect of inflation is zero, and the effect of the intervention remains stable across all years of an employee's tenure (that is, performance levels and test validity remain constant over time). Not only has empirical research raised serious questions about these assumptions, it also has shown three things: (1) the effect of discounting future returns to account for inflation is to reduce estimated payoffs (the higher the discount rate and the longer the time period in question, the lower the estimated payoffs), (2) changes in validity over time (positively or negatively) may produce considerable changes in estimated payoffs, and (3) changes in performance over time generally serve to lower SD_y, and therefore also to lower estimated payoffs. With regard to the last two points, we still know very little regarding why these phenomena occur or the magnitude of their effects. Longitudinal research is sorely needed on these issues.

To develop more accurate and credible estimates of payoffs, ex ante or ex post, requires considering the effects of variables that often are omitted from utility analyses. Two such variables are employee flows into or out of a workforce (additions and separations) and multiple-cohort effects. Further, it is important to consider the potential impact on payoffs of four economic variables that may be relevant in any given situation: start-up costs, variable costs, corporate taxes, and discounting.

The definition of *dollar-valued criterion performance* should be made very clear when communicating the results of utility analyses to decision makers. It is critically important to recognize that the specific way in which this construct is operationalized (for example, as a partial versus a total measure of productivity) has a direct impact on the meaning and interpretation of any utility analysis. Interpretation of utility analysis results by decision makers can be enhanced further by acknowledging the risk and uncertainty inherent in such results. This can be done by computing standard errors of utility estimates, by using Monte Carlo simulation to assess the impact of changes in parameter estimates on payoffs, or by using break-even analysis.

The results of utility analyses are also affected by *when* criterion measurement is performed. In the case of new employees, it simply is not realistic to expect fully competent performance on day 1. Research is needed to further our understanding of the size of the decrement on estimated payoff from time lags between initial performance during the learning period and fully competent performance. At present, there is very little empirical research on this issue.

Additionally, I/O psychology has tended to focus on individual performance and ignore broader economic factors, such as labor market conditions, that have important effects on individual performance. More accurate and credible utility analyses require that we take such information into account, yet our research base for doing so is extremely limited. Questions such as the following need to be addressed systematically: What is the variable cost of higher wages associated with competition for "the best and the brightest"? How do labor market dynamics (tight versus loose) affect time lags from initial performance to fully competent performance? How do such dynamics affect variable and total recruitment costs across different cohorts of employees?

Although research can clarify many of these issues, we also need to be realistic about what utility analysis can and cannot accomplish. We need to recognize that it probably will never be possible to capture precisely *all* the factors that affect the economic returns associated with valid selection programs. Other issues, such as the *interactions* of the utilities associated with alternative human resource management interventions (recruitment, selection, training, goal setting and feedback, job design, incentives, job safety and health, labor-management cooperative efforts, and so on), impose a level of complexity on our analyses that seems impossible to deal with, given the current stage of development of the field.

At a broader level, it may also be appropriate to ask whether organizations that adopt progressive human resource management practices that are consistent with their strategic objectives (for example, innovation, quality enhancement, or cost reduction) outperform their counterparts in the same industry. Does the adoption of progressive HR practices represent a source of sustained competitive advantage? This kind of research is likely to be particularly difficult to conduct because it requires the use of entire organizations as subjects. Nevertheless, it is important at least to raise the issue, for it represents a new and different focus of utility analysis. From a general management perspective, it is an eminently relevant application of this technology.

Finally, many criticisms of utility analysis seem understandable. In many cases we have enormously oversimplified our analyses by omitting key variables and making questionable assumptions about others. Doing so has produced astronomical estimated payoffs for valid selection programs. Also, research in this area does appear fragmented and disjointed, and it is logical to ask where it is leading. The answer requires that we return to the fundamental objective of utility analysis, that is, to improve the quality of management decisions.

Questions from decision makers about the economic impact of valid selection procedures are reasonable and eminently justifiable. They will not go away. Meaningful answers require the use of information from several disciplines: I/O psychology, corporate finance, accounting, and labor economics. As long as utility analysis research is cast in a systematic framework that identifies and clarifies factors that affect estimated payoffs associated with alternative human resource management interventions, then this area will endure, and perhaps even flourish.

References

Ackerman, P. L. (1987). Individual differences in skill learning: An integration of psychometric and information processing perspectives. *Psychological Bulletin, 102,* 3–27.

Ackerman, P. L. (1989). Within-task intercorrelations of skilled performance: Implications for predicting individual differences? (A comment on Henry & Hulin, 1987). *Journal of Applied Psychology, 74,* 360–364.

Alexander, R. A., & Barrick, M. R. (1987). Estimating the standard error of projected dollar gains in utility analysis. *Journal of Applied Psychology, 72,* 475–479.

Ashe, R. L., Jr. (1990, April). *The legal defensibility of assessment centers and in-basket exercises.* Paper presented at the meeting of the Society for Industrial and Organizational Psychology, Miami Beach, FL.

Barrett, G. V., Alexander, R. A., & Doverspike, D. (1991). *A critique of Hulin, Henry, and Noon's "Adding a dimension: Time as a factor in the generalizability of predictive relationships."* Manuscript submitted for publication.

Becker, B. E. (1989). The influence of labor markets on human resources utility estimates. *Personnel Psychology, 42,* 531–546.

Bobko, P., Colella, A., & Russell, C. J. (1990, July). *Estimation of selection utility with multiple predictors in the presence of multiple performance criteria, differential validity through time, and strategic goals* (Contract No. DAAL03-86-D-0001). San Diego, CA: Navy Personnel Research and Development Center.

Boudreau, J. W. (1983a). Economic considerations in estimating the utility of human resource productivity improvement programs. *Personnel Psychology, 36,* 551–557.

Boudreau, J. W. (1983b). Effects of employee flows on utility analysis of human resource productivity improvement programs. *Journal of Applied Psychology, 68,* 396–407.

Boudreau, J. W. (1984). Decision theory contributions to HRM research and practice. *Industrial Relations, 23,* 198–217.

Boudreau, J. W. (1991). Utility analysis for decisions in human resource management. In M. D. Dunnette & L. M. Hough (Eds.), *Handbook of industrial and organizational psychology* (2nd ed., Vol. 2). Palo Alto, CA: Consulting Psychologists Press.

Boudreau, J. W., & Berger, C. J. (1985). Decision-theoretic utility analysis applied to external employee movement [Monograph]. *Journal of Applied Psychology, 70,* 581–612.

Boudreau, J. W., & Rynes, S. L. (1985). Role of recruitment in staffing utility analysis. *Journal of Applied Psychology, 70,* 354–366.

Brealey, R., & Meyers, S. (1988). *Principles of corporate finance* (3rd ed.). New York: McGraw-Hill.

Brigham, E., & Gapenski, L. (1988). *Financial management: Theory and practice* (5th ed.). New York: Dryden.

Brogden, H. E. (1949). When testing pays off. *Personnel Psychology, 2,* 171–183.

Cascio, W. F. (1983, August). *One year's turnover costs in a major brokerage firm.* Paper presented at the meeting of the American Psychological Association, Anaheim, CA.

Cascio, W. F. (1989). Utility analysis as an evaluation tool. In I. L. Goldstein (Ed.), *Training and development in organizations* (pp. 63–88). San Francisco: Jossey-Bass.

Cascio, W. F. (1991a). *Applied psychology in personnel management* (4th ed.). Englewood Cliffs, NJ: Prentice-Hall.

Cascio, W. F. (1991b). *Costing human resources: The financial impact of behavior in organizations* (3rd ed.). Boston: PWS-Kent.

Cascio, W. F. (1991c, April). *The impact of dynamic criteria on the assessment of the outcomes of selection and training programs.* Paper presented at the meeting of the Society for Industrial and Organizational Psychology, St. Louis, MO.

Cascio, W. F., & Morris, J. W. (1990). A critical reanalysis of Hunter, Schmidt, and Coggin's (1988) "Problems and pitfalls in using capital budgeting and financial accounting techniques in assessing the utility of personnel programs." *Journal of Applied Psychology, 75,* 410–417.

Cascio, W. F., Outtz, J., Zedeck, S., & Goldstein, I. L. (1991). Statistical implications of six methods of test score use in personnel selection. *Human Performance, 4,* 233–264.

Cascio, W. F., & Ramos, R. A. (1986). Development and application of a new method for assessing job performance in behavioral/economic terms. *Journal of Applied Psychology, 71,* 20–28.

Cascio, W. F., & Silbey, V. (1979). Utility of the assessment center as a selection device. *Journal of Applied Psychology, 64,* 107–118.

Coward, W. M., & Sackett, P. R. (1990). Linearity of ability-performance relationships: A reconfirmation. *Journal of Applied Psychology, 75,* 297–300.

Cronbach, L. J., & Gleser, G. C. (1965). *Psychological tests and personnel decisions* (2nd ed.). Urbana: University of Illinois Press.

Cronshaw, S. F., & Alexander, R. A. (1985). One answer to the demand for accountability: Selection utility as an investment decision. *Organizational Behavior and Human Decision Processes, 35,* 102–118.

Dyer, L., & Holder, G. W. (1988). A strategic perspective of human resource management. In L. Dyer and G. W. Holder (Eds.), *Human resource management: Evolving roles and responsibilities.* Washington, DC: Bureau of National Affairs.

Eaton, N. K., Wing, H., & Mitchell, K. J. (1985). Alternative methods of estimating the dollar value of performance. *Personnel Psychology, 38,* 27–40.

Fleishman, E. A., & Quaintance, M. K. (1984). *Taxonomies of human performance.* Orlando, FL: Academic Press.

Greer, O. L., & Cascio, W. F. (1987). Is cost accounting the answer? Comparison of two behaviorally-based methods for estimating the standard deviation of job performance in dollars with a cost-accounting-based approach. *Journal of Applied Psychology, 72,* 588–595.

Guion, R. M., & Gibson, W. M. (1988). Personnel selection and placement. *Annual Review of Psychology, 39,* 349–374.

Hinrichs, J. R. (1978). An eight-year follow-up of a management assessment center. *Journal of Applied Psychology, 63,* 596–601.

Hulin, C. L., Henry, R. A., & Noon, S. L. (1990). Adding a dimension: Time as a factor in the generalizability of predictive relationships. *Psychological Bulletin, 107,* 328–340.

Hunter, J. E., & Hunter, R. E. (1984). Validity and utility of alternative predictors of job performance. *Psychological Bulletin, 96,* 72–98.

Hunter, J. E., & Schmidt, F. L. (1982). Fitting people to jobs: The impact of personnel selection on national productivity. In M. D. Dunnette & E. A. Fleishman (Eds.), *Human performance and productivity.* Hillsdale, NJ: Erlbaum.

Jackson, S. E., & Schuler, R. S. (1990). Human resource planning. *American Psychologist, 45,* 223–239.

Landy, F. J. (1987). *Psychology: The science of people* (2nd ed.). Englewood Cliffs, NJ: Prentice-Hall.

Lord, J. S. (1989). External and internal recruitment. In W. F. Cascio (Ed.), *Human resource planning, employment, and placement.* Washington, DC: Bureau of National Affairs.

Mathieu, J. E., & Leonard, R. L., Jr. (1987). Applying utility concepts to a training program in supervisory skills: A time-based approach. *Academy of Management Journal, 30,* 316–335.

McEvoy, G. M., & Beatty, R. W. (1989). Assessment centers and subordinate appraisals of managers: A seven-year examination of predictive validity. *Personnel Psychology, 42,* 37–41.

Meyer, H. H., & Raich, M. S. (1983). An objective evaluation of a behavior modeling training program. *Personnel Psychology, 36,* 755–761.

Mirvis, P. H., & Lawler, E. E., III. (1977). Measuring the financial impact of employee attitudes. *Journal of Applied Psychology, 62,* 1–8.

Mitchel, J. O. (1975). Assessment center validity: A longitudinal study. *Journal of Applied Psychology, 60,* 573–579.

Murphy, K. M. (1986). When your top choice turns you down: The effect of rejected offers on the utility of selection tests. *Psychological Bulletin, 99,* 133–138.

Packer, M. B. (1983). Measuring the intangible in productivity. *Technology Review, 86,* 48–57.

Porter, M. E. (1985). *Competitive strategy.* New York: Free Press.

Pulakos, E. D., Borman, W. C., & Hough, L. M. (1988). Test validation for scientific understanding: Two demonstrations of an approach to studying predictor-criterion linkages. *Personnel Psychology, 41,* 703–716.

Rich, J. R., & Boudreau, J. W. (1987). The effects of variability and risk on selection utility analysis: An empirical simulation and comparison. *Personnel Psychology, 40,* 55–84.

Rothe, H. F. (1978). Output rates among industrial employees. *Journal of Applied Psychology, 63,* 40–46.

Sadacca, R., & Campbell, J. P. (1985, April). *Assessing the utility of personnel/classification systems.* Paper presented at the meeting of the Southern Psychological Association, Atlanta, GA.

Sands, W. A. (1973). A method for evaluating alternative recruiting-selection strategies. *Journal of Applied Psychology, 57,* 222–227.

Schein, E. H. (1980). *Organizational psychology* (3rd ed.). Englewood Cliffs, NJ: Prentice-Hall.

Schmidt, F. L., Hunter, J. E., McKenzie, R. C., & Muldrow, T. W. (1979). Impact of valid selection procedures on workforce productivity. *Journal of Applied Psychology, 64,* 609–626.

Schmidt, F. L., Hunter, J. E., Outerbridge, A. N., & Trattner, M. H. (1986). The economic impact of job selection methods on size, productivity, and payroll costs of the federal workforce: An empirically-based demonstration. *Personnel Psychology, 39,* 1–29.

Schmidt, F. L., Hunter, J. E., & Pearlman, K. (1982). Assessing the economic impact of personnel programs on workforce productivity. *Personnel Psychology, 35,* 333–347.

Schmidt, F. L., & Kaplan, L. B. (1971). Composite vs. multiple criteria: A review and resolution of the controversy. *Personnel Psychology, 24,* 419–434.

Schmidt, F. L., Mack, M. J., & Hunter, J. E. (1984). Selection utility in the occupation of U.S. park ranger for three modes of test use. *Journal of Applied Psychology, 69,* 490–497.

Schuler, R. S., & Jackson, S. E. (1987). Linking competitive strategies with human resource management practices. *Academy of Management Executive, 1*(3), 207–219.

Society for Industrial and Organizational Psychology. (1987).

Principles for the validation and use of personnel selection procedures (3rd ed.). College Park, MD: Author.

Vance, R. J., & Colella, A. (1990). The utility of utility analysis. *Human Performance, 3*(2), 123–139.

Vance, R. J., Coovert, M. D., MacCallum, R. C., & Hedge, J. W. (1989). Construct models of task performance. *Journal of Applied Psychology, 74,* 447–455.

Zeidner, J., Johnson, C., Orlansky, J., Schmitz, E., & Nord, R. (1988, December). *The economic benefits of predicting job performance.* Alexandria, VA: Institute for Defense Analyses.

11

Selection Out:
Firings, Layoffs, and Retirement

Stephen M. Colarelli, Terry A. Beehr

Why are people "selected out" of organizations? How do managers decide who to select out? What is the best way to select people out? What happens to people when they are selected out? If we were to ask these questions about selection *in,* we would find a wealth of research addressing them. By comparison, research on selection out is scarce. Why is this? Firings, layoffs, and retirements are part of organizational life. In fact, practitioner industrial and organizational (I/O) psychologists spend *more* time on job loss than on employee selection (Howard, 1990). Yet researchers spend virtually no time studying selection out (Howard, 1990).

Perhaps research on selection out has not become commonplace because selection out has not been a problem that affected managers' careers. Managers often stimulate research by asking I/O psychologists to help solve problems. However, managers may not see a problem as important if it has little effect on their own careers. With selection out, managers might see the problem as solved once they dismiss people, and there have been few rewards given to managers for doing a good job of

Note: We thank Walter Borman, Kirk O'Hara, and Bob Sinclair for helpful comments on earlier versions of this chapter.

terminating employees. Therefore, managers have had little incentive to ask I/O psychologists how to select people out effectively and humanely. Another possibility is that selection out is part of the darker side of organizational life that people prefer to ignore. It is an aversive, emotional experience that affects a person's whole being. Finally, its emotional character is inconsistent with the mechanistic techniques that have dominated industrial psychology since Frederick Taylor, and its aversive nature is at odds with the humanistic outlook of organizational psychology. Firing people exposes a cruel reality of organizational life: when all is said and done, employees work at the pleasure of top management.

Now, however, is an appropriate time for systematic theory and research on selection out. Newspaper articles appear almost daily about layoffs, firings, or early retirement incentive programs to trim an employer's workforce. Over the past decade, organizations have been doing an increasing amount of selection out. This has been stimulated by global competition, mergers and acquisitions, recessions, and a trend toward flatter organizational structures. Selection out has also become management's problem. In the past, layoffs were blue-collar workers' problems; but now, many of those being selected out are middle managers ("White-Collar Layoffs," 1991). Therefore, self-interest, if nothing else, may be prompting managers to think about implementing effective and humane policies for terminating employees. Another reason for managers' increased interest in selection out is the changing interpretation of the employment-at-will doctrine. The traditional interpretation of employment at will was that an employer could fire an employee for a good reason, for a bad reason, or for no reason at all. Recent court rulings and state statutes are beginning to change this interpretation. Organizations are increasingly susceptible to lawsuits and punitive damages from disgruntled former employees who believe they were wrongly terminated (Ledvinka & Scarpello, 1991).

Similarly, interest in retirement is growing. An aging workforce, earlier retirements, and laws protecting older workers have heightened managers' and policy makers' interest in retirement. We know that there will be a more aged population at the beginning of the twenty-first century. This, in conjunction with laws banning mandatory retirement, portends an older workforce. Therefore, management may want to encourage larger numbers of retirements or selective retirements. These are selection out issues.

Although selection out is a new topic in I/O psychology, a chapter on selection out should not seem foreign in a book on personnel selection. Selection *out* of organizations and selection *into* organizations both concern events that lead to a decision about who gets — or who gets to keep — a job. In selecting *in,* organizations are simultaneously selecting out by not hiring some applicants. In selecting *out,* they are simultaneously selecting in by not firing, laying off, or retiring some employees.

The purpose of this chapter is to develop ideas to guide future research and practice. We begin by defining the three types of selection out — firings, layoffs, and retirements — and argue that functionalism and systems theory are useful frameworks for conceptualizing selection out. Next we discuss the organizational functions of selection out, the influence of culture on selection out practices, and the organizational and psychological processes related to selection out. The chapter concludes with a discussion of the outcomes of selection out and suggestions for future research and practice.

Definitions and Conceptual Framework

Selection out is the termination of an employee's employment with an organization. Organizations select people out in three ways: firings, layoffs, and retirements. Firing is terminating an employee because he or she displeased a superior to such an extent that the employee's presence can no longer be tolerated. Layoffs are terminating employees because managers consider them or their jobs superfluous to the needs of the organization. Layoffs may or may not be permanent. Retirement is somewhat more complicated than the other two, because it is less at the discretion of the organization. Definitions of retirement can vary depending on whether one approaches the topic from the viewpoint of society, the organization, or the individual.

We adopt the organization's viewpoint because this chapter is primarily concerned with what happens when organizations select people out. In the United States, retirement involves employees' leaving an organization (and usually full-time employment) voluntarily and permanently. In most cases, employees who retire are older and have longer tenure than other employees. Also, the organization often continues to pay former employees from a retirement pension fund, and the amount is based on a contractual agreement.

Two theoretical bases that are useful for understanding selection out are functionalism and open systems theory. Functionalism implies that it is important to study human resource (HR) activities from the perspective of how they contribute to organizational adaptation and survival. Thus, while not opposed to normative prescriptions, a functional orientation results in approaching an HR activity (or any organizational phenomenon) with an attitude of curiosity — asking why does it exist and persist? What purpose does it serve? And what would happen to the organization if the activity were eliminated or replaced? Moreover, a functional approach suggests that any HR activity can serve *multiple* functions (Colarelli, 1992) and have intended *and* unintended consequences (Merton, 1957). Open systems theory emphasizes the organization's dependency on its environment and views organizations as being composed of interrelated subsystems (Katz & Kahn, 1978). Thus, an open systems orientation suggests that HR programs — once adopted — become integral components of the systems in which they are embedded (Colarelli & Stumpf, 1990).

Finally, we believe that HR policies and practices are not installed in organizations in the same way that new parts are installed in machines. Rather, HR practices pass through cultural screening mechanisms. The history of technological innovation and diffusion makes a strong case that *cultural values* play a major, perhaps even the key, role in determining whether organizations will or will not adopt and use a technology, including HR technologies (Landes, 1969; Rogers, 1983). Therefore, we argue that cultural values play a critical role in influencing the choices that managers make about selection out.

The Functions of Selection Out

What is the purpose of selecting people out of an organization? The intended purpose is the same as the intended purpose of any other HR effort: to improve the enterprise. A traditional view is that the purpose of selection out is to identify and terminate incumbents who are, or who are likely to be, superfluous or unsuccessful. However, selection out involves more than just firing incompetent employees. Selection out serves at least four functions (Colarelli & Beehr, 1991): adaptation to the environment, goal attainment, integration, and cultural pattern maintenance.

Adaptation to the Environment

Adaptation to the environment involves defining, monitoring, exploiting, interacting with, and adjusting to the environment. Selection out influences adaptation to the environment primarily by influencing the attitudes of people in the environment toward the organization. Because gainful employment is most adults' economic lifeline and source of identity, how an organization deals with job security should influence how people think about that organization. Selection out is a means of communicating organizational values, and an organization's values influence people's decisions about what organization they want to work for (Tom, 1971).

Consider how stories about executives firing or refusing to fire people communicate an organization's values. The way that Henry Ford II of the Ford Motor Company is said to have fired his heir apparent, Lee Iacocca, has become automobile industry folklore. Apparently Ford called Iacocca into his office and said, "Clean out your desk, Lee, you're fired." Taken by surprise, Iacocca asked Ford why he was being fired. Ford responded, "Because I don't like you." Contrast Ford's behavior with that of Thomas Watson, Jr., the former CEO of IBM, when confronted with an executive who made a $10 million mistake. The story goes that the manager who made the mistake came into Watson's office to offer him his resignation. After listening to the manager, Watson said, "How could I accept your resignation now? I just spent ten million dollars educating you." Stories like these become part of an organization's mythology, which in turn communicates an organization's values and enhances or detracts from its reputation.

Selection out practices can attract media attention. For example, Susan C. Faludi, a reporter for the *Wall Street Journal*, won the 1991 Pulitzer Prize in journalism for an article she wrote on the human costs of the leveraged buy-out (LBO) of Safeway Stores ("Journal's Faludi Wins Pulitzer," 1991). Faludi argued that Kroger (another supermarket chain that underwent a management LBO at about the same time) achieved the same objective as Safeway (fending off a hostile takeover) but with less human cost (Faludi, 1990). Safeway came across as ruthless, while Kroger projected a businesslike and humane image. One cannot say precisely how such media attention will affect a company's fortunes and its reputation with lawmakers, investors, prospective employees, and customers. With the increasing concern over corporate ethics, however, the net effect of media attention on ruthless selection out policies is likely to be harmful.

Finally, the way an organization deals with selection out is likely to influence how former employees, their friends, and relatives feel and act toward the organization. Involuntary job loss can be devastating to the individual who loses the job and to his or her family, as well as to a community if job loss is widespread. Organizations that deal callously with employees whom they let go may create lifelong enemies — people who are unlikely to buy the organization's products and who may speak ill of the organization. Although humane termination may be an oxymoron, organizations that let employees go in a humane way probably minimize ill will.

Goal Attainment

Goal attainment involves the development of goals and strategy and the organization of resources necessary to attain desired results. Selection out can affect goal attainment in several ways. It can improve productivity by removing individuals who are not meeting expectations. The threat of selecting people out may also enhance productivity because the fear of losing one's job can rejuvenate motivation. It may also serve as a goad to keep people who are performing well on track. Laying off portions of their workforce can also help organizations reduce costs when the economy softens. Finally, selection out can eliminate employees who, after a merger, acquisition, or reorganization, become redundant or unnecessary.

Reducing head count will increase productivity *if* the organization had been using people inefficiently and *if* layoffs eliminated the most inefficient jobs and workers. (Productivity is the ratio of outputs to inputs — that is, the efficiency with which inputs are transformed into outputs [Mahoney, 1988].) On the other hand, *if* an organization has no excess manpower, then reducing head count will lower output, and no productivity gains will be realized. One recent survey found that layoffs do not necessarily bring productivity or profitability (Bennett, 1991). Fewer than half the companies surveyed said that downsizing resulted in meeting expense-reduction targets. Across-the-board or seniority-based cutbacks apparently do not help. Layoffs are most likely to result in increased productivity when *low-value* work is eliminated.

Productivity may also be enhanced by selecting out people who do not have values congruent with the organization's culture. It is basic to organizational survival that members behave in reasonable accordance with the directives of authorities and with generally accepted norms. These are the minimum necessary for the coordinated action that distinguishes an organization from a collection of individuals (Sampson, 1963). Because of goal or value incongruence, an employee may refuse to perform aspects of the job, be obstructionist, or engage in behavior that is antithetical to the norms and values of the organization. Selecting out such people would be a reasonable course of action. Although a *moderate* amount of heterogeneity in personality, outlook, and opinion is necessary for effective organizational decision making (Janis, 1989), excessive heterogeneity is likely to cause problems.

Selection out can also be a part of a human resource strategy to enhance productivity. Such strategies include "up or out" mobility, retirement policies, and permanent employment. Up-or-out mobility is an HR policy in which employees can remain with an organization only if they are promoted at specific career junctures. For example, at many accounting and law firms, junior associates' jobs are on the line each time they come up for a promotion. It is not until they have been promoted to partner that they have tenure with the firm. Up-or-out mobility is based on a pyramidal organization structure, fixed and vertical career paths, and regular and rapid career movement. The up-or-out strategy helps to improve productivity by maintaining a pool of young, energetic employees at the bottom, basing promotions on merit, and having a continuous supply of job openings at higher levels. Job openings at higher levels are visible rewards and also ensure a flow of new talent into top positions.

Like up-or-out practices, retirement policies affect job openings, the flow of people through an organization, career paths, career development, and opportunities for advancement. For example, the ages at which people retire can influence the number of entry-level job openings and employment tenure policies. Many Japanese corporations require managers to retire at age 55; some even have earlier mandatory retirement ages (Sasaki, 1981). Early mandatory retirement is one factor that makes it feasible for Japanese corporations to have lifetime employment policies. Also, early mandatory retirement makes human resource planning more efficient by injecting more certainty into the HR flows and by shortening the number of years in the HR planning horizon. The trends in the United States have been toward earlier retirements for at least thirty or forty years (Talaga & Beehr, 1989). Even though mandatory retirement policies may not be possible in the United States due to federal laws, various inducements can encourage employees to retire early. For example, companies can increase employees' projected retirement finances (and therefore the likelihood of choosing early retirement) with retirement incentive plans. Early-retirement incentives, as a means of accelerating retirement rates, also have the advantage of leading to a separation in which the former employees are likely to leave with good attitudes toward the company (contrasted with negative attitudes likely to be created by firings or layoffs).

Permanent employment may also increase productivity, and permanent employment practices usually require specific selection out policies. One version of permanent employment refers to a policy of no layoffs. When employees' jobs become redundant, companies will place employees in other jobs within the organization. Such a policy means that management can count on its employees to be around for the long haul, and therefore can invest more in training. Better-trained employees are more skillful and more productive. Porter (1990) suggests that permanent employment pressures organizations to develop new products and to diversify as ways to redeploy people. Moreover, the ongoing training that is associated with permanent employment creates an ethos of careful hiring, human resource development, efficiency, and continuous improvement (Porter, 1990).

No-layoff policies often require structural arrangements that allow an organization flexibility in redeploying people. Common practices are flexible job descriptions, employing temporary workers, and contracting work out. Flexible job descriptions allow employees to be assigned to a variety of tasks and jobs as the need arises. Temporary workers are not considered regular employees of the organization, and therefore can be laid off when the economy softens. Similarly, contracts cannot be renewed with small suppliers or service providers when an organization faces lean times. All these strategies provide flexibility and slack, and they serve as mechanisms to protect the job security of permanent employees.

Another variant of permanent employment refers to no "at-will" employment. No at-will employment may involve tenure for all or certain groups of employees; it may also involve due process procedures that must be followed should a supervisor want to fire a subordinate. Employees who are not fearful of losing their job for peccadillos, independent thinking, disagreeing with the boss, making a mistake, or taking a risk are more likely to innovate. And the ability of organizations to innovate is a key factor in how well they compete in the global marketplace (Porter, 1990). When companies view employees "as permanent instead of to be hired and fired at will, pressures are created to upgrade and sustain competitive advantage" (Porter, 1990, p. 586).

Yet permanent employment policies have the unintentional consequence of making it difficult for organizations to get rid of deadwood. Consider the following example from academia: A university administrator asked an unproductive, tenured faculty member to take early retirement. The administrator said that he would give the professor a generous lump sum for retiring and a monthly stipend of half of his current salary. The professor thanked the administrator, smiled, and politely declined (Wiener, 1990, p. 1). "Why," he said "should I take early retirement at half salary, when I am already retired on the job at full salary?"

Integration

Integration is the process by which collaboration, cooperation, and communication take place among diverse organizational components. It involves creating solidarity despite the inevitable strain and conflict involved in struggling for goal attainment. Selection out contributes to integration by providing organizations with a means of removing people who do not get along with other employees. Such people may rub others the wrong way, interject unpleasantness into interactions, and foment unproductive conflict. This impedes organizational integration. Although organizations have a tendency to publicly proclaim that people are fired for poor performance, at least one study suggests that people are usually fired or derailed because they cannot get along with others (McCall & Lombardo, 1983). The courts may view this as an unacceptable reason for terminating employees (Ledvinka & Scarpello, 1991). As a result, it may be hard to get accurate information regarding the reasons for firing people, especially if the reasons are not socially or legally acceptable.

Cultural Pattern Maintenance

Cultural pattern maintenance involves the development, transmission, and maintenance of a coherent system of organizational values. A system of values guides the decisions and actions of organizational members. Just as organizations can maintain or change a culture by the type of people they select in, they can also maintain or change their culture by whom they select out.

Judicious selection out (and in) of an executive's staff and lieutenants plays a critical role in the ability of an executive to lead and to infuse an organization with values. It is not uncommon for people who report to chief executives to submit their resignations when a new executive takes office, or for a new executive to "clean house" at the top and install his or her own people. This is typical with high-level elected officials in government and in organizations that acquire other companies. Work at the top is nonroutine, involves ambiguity and long time horizons, and requires discretion and image management. Therefore, it is important that an executive's direct subordinates not only be competent men and women but also share the executive's values and goals. This is particularly important when the accession of a new executive involves considerable cultural change — as would be the case with a new political regime or new business ownership. Therefore, it is important that the people who represent the chief executive be able to communicate his or her values with clarity and conviction.

Why people are selected out can also influence an organization's values. Despite the tendency for organizations to keep terminations private, word quickly gets out when people lose their jobs. What employees *perceive* to be the facts (whether true or not) will affect their perceptions of the organization and of top management's values. For example, if an organization has a no-exception policy of firing employees who use drugs, it sends a clear message about the type of behavior it values. Similarly, when employees engage in behavior that is officially prohibited and they are *not* fired, top management is also sending a message — albeit a more subtle one — about what it values. As noted earlier, *how* people are selected out influences an organization's values and people's perceptions of its values. If an organization selects out employees in a ruthless or capricious manner, it is sending a signal about how it views employees.

The Role of Culture

Whenever a manager faces the prospect of selecting people out, he or she makes a choice: to select out or to do something else to solve the problem. Choices are informed by values, that is, by what one perceives as desirable. That some organizations select people out in response to an economic downturn while others take alternative measures (for example, reduced hours) suggests that organizational culture plays a role in selection out. Similarly, the fact that layoffs and firings are more prevalent in the United States than in Germany and Japan suggests that national culture also plays an important role in how decision makers think about and deal with selection out. For example, when Chase Manhattan Bank executives in New York ordered worldwide layoffs during the 1990–92 recession, managers in its Tokyo offices did not institute staff cutbacks. Because of Japan's traditional lifetime employment practices, bank officers there achieved cost savings by requiring some employees to take pay cuts ("Nice Try," 1991).

Perhaps the most important way in which culture influences selection out is through beliefs and values about human resources (Haire, Ghiselli, & Porter, 1966). Consider management beliefs about the employer-employee relationship. In the United States, the employer-employee relationship tends to be associative, based primarily on contractual and legal foundations (Cornfield, 1981). In other countries, such as Japan and Germany, the relationship is more communitarian, based more on emotional and cultural ties. When the relationship is communitarian, there tends to be an emotional bond between employer and employees, and thus a reluctance to fire or lay off employees.

Another cultural belief that is likely to influence selection out policies is whether management perceives labor as a variable or fixed cost. American management perceives it as a variable cost—something that can be cut when times get rough. Japanese management, on the other hand, tends to perceive labor as a fixed cost, something that cannot be cut during economic downturns (Dertouzos, Lestor, & Solow, 1989; McCraw, 1986). When management views employees as fixed costs, employees' job security gets priority over other costs, such as executive perks and stock dividends.

The way that managers view organizations is also likely to influence selection out policies. Many American managers view organizations as machines (Morgan, 1986). Such managers see employees as cogs, replaceable parts. Those with such a view may be more likely to look at selection out as a mechanical operation to solve a problem. For example, the layoffs following the Safeway LBO reflected this orientation. Layoffs were done quickly, and with little notice given to employees, in order, as Safeway's CEO said, "to put this whole unpleasant matter behind us as soon as possible" (Faludi, 1990, p. A8). Managers who view organizations as social systems, however, are more likely to see employees as sentient actors in a web of relationships, both within and outside of the organization. Rather than viewing selection out only in terms of incompetent or superfluous individuals, systems-oriented managers are more likely to be sensitive to its wider implications.

There are at least four reasons why an understanding of culture is useful when determining selection out policies. First, by understanding organizational and national culture, we get a clearer picture of what an I/O psychologist or manager can and cannot expect to accomplish regarding selection out practices and processes. Second, we can better understand an organizational culture by analyzing selection out practices as reflections of culture. Third, when culture is malleable (as is often the case in new organizations, organizations in a crisis, or organizations undergoing a change in regime), knowledge of culture can help managers and consultants alter and improve selection out practices. And finally, opinion leaders influence culture. If we can convince opinion leaders of the merits of effective selection out policies, they may support them.

Organizational Processes in Selection Out

Research in personnel selection—and other areas of personnel psychology—has focused on technologies. Technology is a design to reduce uncertainty in cause-effect relationships involved in achieving an intended effect (Rogers, 1983). Unfortunately, little research has focused on the *processes* by which personnel psychology technologies are implemented and used (Colarelli, in press). Process is the series of events involved in the utilization of a technology and which lead to its anticipated (and unanticipated) outcomes. Part of the series of events is the manner in which people relate to one another when deciding upon, implementing, and using a personnel psychology intervention. The process by which psychological technologies are implemented and used is important for several reasons. First, because people attribute meaning to the events that they perceive, the same technology is likely to evoke different reactions if it is used in different ways. For example, subordinates are more likely to accept managers' explanations for layoffs when managerial accounts of the reasons for the layoffs are clear than when they are unclear (Brockner, DeWitt, Grover, & Reed, 1990). Process also influences the way in which a behavioral science intervention is accepted and understood. Employees tend to resist interventions that are forced upon them by I/O psychologists or management. They tend to understand and accept an intervention when they have had an opportunity to participate in the decision making that leads to the use of the intervention (Maier, 1963). A third reason for the importance of process is that it can improve the fit between the intervention and the organization. Process sensitizes us to the idiosyncracies of an organization and thus helps us tailor interventions so that they fit the context. Finally, it is through process that ideas are sharpened, perspectives understood, needs identified, values clarified, and goals formulated and sharpened. Simply focusing on installing a technology assumes that problems, needs, and goals are known and shared. However, this is rarely the case in organizations. Crucial components of process are interaction and dialogue, and it is through interaction and dialogue that clear conceptions of problems, needs, values, and goals become articulated (Colarelli, in press). Five organizational processes relevant to selection out are communication, participation, control, planning, and support.

Communication

Communication of accurate information is crucial for employees about to be laid off, fired, or retired. Layoffs and most firings are unpleasant, and more so when they are a surprise. Accurate and timely communication about impending selection out plans is likely to reduce employees' anxiety and help them develop realistic expectations and coping strategies (Sutton & Kahn, 1987). Employees who receive accurate and timely information should also be less suspicious and hostile toward management. The burden falls on management to communicate its intentions to employees and to initiate programs where other useful information is communicated. For example, organizations can provide employees with a "realistic preview" of selection out. Talking to people who have been selected out is a credible method of communicating information (Colarelli, 1984). In addition to providing employees with information, it may be helpful to engage them in dialogue and to listen to their ideas about how to handle the selection out process.

Participation

Employee participation in selection out policies can benefit employers and employees. Employees can generate creative alternatives that may be more beneficial to an organization than the traditional selection out policies. Employee participation also provides feedback to management on the options it has generated, and it helps provide new options. For example, rather than being laid off during a recession, employees may suggest that they take a wage cut, or work one fewer day per week, or take voluntary, unpaid sabbaticals. Overall, participation creates a sense of involvement and commitment, and it enhances understanding.

Control

The more control an employee has over important outcomes related to selection out, the better he or she will fare.

The most critical area of control for U.S. employees is financial resources, since Americans save little money. Americans have among the lowest rates of personal savings of advanced industrial countries — about 4 percent of income ("The Squirrel's Curse," 1991). This compares with 18 percent for the Japanese and 14.5 percent for the Germans. Americans also have high debt (19 percent of disposable income, *excluding* mortgages ("Borrowers All," 1991). Without financial reserves, the loss of a job can be devastating. *If* the economic consequences were not devastating, however, then management and employees might be able to work together more constructively on selection out issues. Therefore, the first way to improve the selection out process is to help the employee be financially secure, or at least not destitute, if selection out occurs. This is already done on a regular basis for retirement, through pension plans and annuities. There is some help for involuntary job loss through unemployment insurance, and termination policies in *some* companies provide financial assistance (for example, severance payments). Unfortunately, unemployment insurance benefits vary from state to state, and they tend to be short-lived and less than an employee's regular earnings (Blaustein, 1981). And not a'l companies provide a separation allowance. Therefore, to enhance individuals' sense of financial control, more creative solutions are needed.

A step in this direction is the "income security" plan negotiated between General Motors (GM) and the United Auto Workers (UAW). Under this plan, GM supplements unemployment benefits. GM's income security agreement, however, only applies to unionized workers, and it came about through the pressure of a strong union. Furthermore, the UAW was able to negotiate the agreement with GM because of the company's strong financial position at the time of negotiations. GM makes contributions to the income security payments out of its cash reserves. The viability of this type of program rests on a company's cash reserves. When cash reserves run low, the program is in jeopardy (Patterson, 1991). Also, such an agreement seems unlikely to occur with nonunionized employees or with smaller and less profitable organizations.

An approach we recommend is a federally sponsored unemployment trust fund. People would be required to enroll in a restricted savings plan as soon as they start working. They could withdraw principal or interest from their unemployment savings only in the event of being fired or laid off. The organization and the employee would each be required to contribute a percentage of the employee's annual salary to the fund. If an employee were never laid off or fired, the fund would be transferred to the individual's retirement fund. This would differ from unemployment insurance in that it would be an *individual trust*. The money contributed by the employer and employee would be in an individual account for the employee. Employees (or employers) could also contribute more than the required minimum. However, the money could only be used in the event of involuntary job loss (or retirement). An individualized unemployment trust fund would provide more of an incentive for the unemployed to find work than traditional unemployment benefits; payments from such a trust fund come from an *individual's own money*. The longer an individual stays out of the job market, the smaller his or her trust fund becomes. The longer he or she works, the larger the trust fund becomes.

Employees could also gain more financial control by moonlighting. Organizations might encourage employees to take on (within reasonable parameters) part-time jobs. For example, it is not uncommon for universities to allow faculty members to engage in outside consulting one day a week during the academic year, and moonlighting appears to be a common practice in some occupations (for instance, fire fighters). Most organizations, however, seem to discourage the practice. Many managers believe that moonlighting is disloyal and distracts employees from their work, resulting in absenteeism and poor job performance. A recent study of moonlighting employees (Jamal, 1988), however, found that moonlighters did not differ from nonmoonlighters in job performance and absenteeism. In addition, moonlighters were more emotionally stable and practical, had higher levels of self-esteem, and suffered less anxiety. We believe moonlighting can offer advantages to organizations, if it is managed well. Moonlighting may make employees less fearful of layoffs, since they become less dependent on their full-time jobs for their income. It may be a source of innovations for large organizations, because employees moonlighting in skilled work may improve their own skills and develop new ideas.

Traditionally, American management has limited employees' control; giving them financial control over their lives would seem to leave management with less leverage over employees. Numerous surveys show, however, that modern workers work for more than a paycheck. Therefore, loss of financial control does not necessarily imply that they will be less loyal or committed or motivated. For example, top management typically has "golden parachutes" (generous severance awards) built into their employment contracts, and these agreements do not appear to have reduced top managers' motivation. Furthermore, the old notion that managers' power would be increased by taking away power from employees has been largely discredited. Years ago Tannenbaum (1968) discovered that all employees report experiencing more control when lower-level employees receive more of it. Therefore, it appears that managers' power should increase as they empower their subordinates.

Control is also enhanced by the *organization's* financial security. When organizations have minimal financial reserves set aside for difficult times, they are likely to select people out in a hasty manner when difficult times come. Management in a failing organization does not have the time, resources, or presence of mind to act in a thoughtful manner.

Another area that would enhance employee control over involuntary job loss is skill training. The unemployed are better able to compete for jobs, and to weather the vicissitudes of economic cycles, if they have skills that employers want. Government and private organization policies, as well as individual development efforts, that equip people with marketable skills should enhance people's "employability security." Such a policy has contributed to Sweden's recent low unemployment rate of 3.1 percent (Layard, Jackman, & Nickell, 1991).

Planning

Being laid off or fired is not something that regularly happens to most employees. They are, therefore, unlikely to have the knowledge or skills to cope effectively with job loss and finding another job. One way to help employees acquire the skills and knowledge to cope with the loss of a job is to give them the time to plan *before* a job loss occurs. Employees who have time to plan their future are likely to experience more positive outcomes than those who are given no time to plan (Earley, Wojnaroski, & Prest, 1987).

Public interest in giving employees advance notice of layoffs due to plant closings has been sufficiently high to result in passage of legislation. Although opposed by many business lobbies, Congress passed the Worker Adjustment and Retraining Notification (WARN) Act in 1988 (Cooper & Holmes, 1990). WARN is a federal statute that requires companies with one hundred or more employees to give their employees sixty days' advance warning of plant closings. Since WARN was enacted into law, it seems to have had none of the dire economic consequences that its foes predicted. Moreover, it seems to have accelerated the rate at which state agencies reach displaced workers (Cooper & Holmes, 1990).

Support

A number of organizations make available support for laid-off or fired employees by providing them with the services of a consulting outplacement counselor. Outplacement counseling involves providing terminated employees with career and psychological counseling, training in job search skills, moral support, and administrative support for conducting a job search. Because the quality of outplacement services varies from company to company, it is important that organizations do their homework and select outplacement counselors that provide a full range of services and that have a good track record of helping clients find jobs (Challenger, 1989).

Although outplacement for terminated employees provides some support, it cuts all ties with the employer. Terminated employees and organizations, however, may benefit by working together for their mutual benefit before the marriage is dissolved. To be sure, layoffs and firings are emotionally charged. Nevertheless, a calm and reasoned dialogue between the employer and the soon-to-be-terminated employee is possible. For example, an organization may be able to help laid-off employees, or even some fired employees, get jobs in companies with which it does business or hopes to do business. By doing this, an organization could—if it dealt effectively with the emotional issues of selecting out employees—put a loyal alumnus inside an element of its environment, someone who could be the company's advocate. Certainly, a former employee whose company helped him or her get a good job would be less likely to work against the company. This is a practice that some large accounting firms have followed for years. Of course, this policy's success depends on the quality of the people the company lets go. Obviously, the selected out employees need to meet functional and interpersonal competencies before an organization would feel comfortable helping them get a job with a client or supplier.

Psychological Processes in Selection Out

Selection out also involves *psychological* processes, which are the psychological and behavioral events that influence outcomes related to selection out. These events include attributions, emotions, and decisions. They can occur both in people who select people out and in people who are selected out. We focus first on the psychological processes that are likely to occur in managers when they fire an employee. We then examine some commonalities in processes that are likely to occur in people who are fired, who are laid off, and who retire.

Selecting People Out

We propose that, in deciding to fire an employee, managers engage in a multistage process. Initially, the manager must be dissatisfied with the organization's or subunit's functioning. Dissatisfaction is likely to arise because the manager's values are not being realized (Locke, 1976), particularly with respect to some aspect of the unit's task or socioemotional functions. At this point the manager is likely to engage in problem definition, which involves identifying a starting state (that is, knowledge of the situation), a goal state, and a means (Gilhooly, 1982). To the extent that any one of these three elements is missing or unclear, the problem is ill defined and a favorable resolution is less likely.

In appraising the starting state, the manager is likely to look for causes of the dissatisfaction. In social systems, determining the cause is no easy task. There is usually no *one* cause, although some factors may be more important than others. If the individual is the problem, is the problem due to lack of ability or lack of motivation? Is the problem chronic or acute? If the problem is situational, where is it: is it in the technology, the organizational or job design, or the reward system? At this point, perceptual accuracy is critical. Can the manager maintain enough emotional distance to accurately assess causes? Because people tend to focus on behavior itself rather than its causes (Heider, 1958), and because a problem residing in the situation suggests that the manager is responsible, managers probably attribute the cause of the majority of problems they face to individuals. This is consistent with the "fundamental attribution error" (Ross, 1977): people tend to attribute the cause of events to the person rather than to the situation. They are, however, more prone to attribute the causes of *their own* outcomes to the situation. This tendency is especially strong regarding attribution for failures. People tend to avoid attributing causes of failure to themselves and attribute these causes to situations; but the failures of other people are more usually interpreted as failures of the person (Miller & Ross, 1975). Work by Mitchell and his colleagues on performance attributions, however, suggests that experienced supervisors tend to make situational attributions for poor performance, whereas less experienced supervisors tend to make personal attributions (Mitchell & Kalb, 1982).

The goal state involves specific, expected future outcomes. Does the manager know what he or she expects from an employee, or is there a vague sense that things are not right? When goals are clear, and if the starting situation has been accurately appraised, the manager is more likely to select an appropriate means to achieve the goal. When the goal is missing or ill defined, the manager is likely to become frustrated. Frustration involves responding to emotional tensions rather than to a goal (Maier & Verser, 1982). To the extent that this occurs, the manager is likely to react negatively toward people who irritate him or her. This may be why people with poor interpersonal skills seem to be disproportionately fired or passed over for promotions (McCall & Lombardo, 1983). Even though he or she may not be the cause of the problem, a frustrated manager is more likely to lash out at people who make him or her uncomfortable.

Finally, the manager is faced with the choice of a means to reach the goal. The choice of means will be influenced by the manager's assessment of the starting state (particularly the cause) and the goal state. If the cause of the problem resides in the situation, the manager is likely to modify the situation — and has a variety of options. On the other hand, if the cause of the problem is an individual, the manager has four options: remediation (training, counseling), motivation (setting up rewards), disciplinary action (for example, demotion), or firing the employee. What the manager decides to do with the individual is likely to depend on the manager's values and personality, perception of the problem, decision-making ability, and organizational and social constraints. Research by Mitchell and his colleagues suggests that disciplinary action or firing is more likely to occur if the manager perceives the employee's poor performance as a result of internal rather than external causes, and if the manager attributes the internal cause to lack of motivation (Mitchell & Kalb, 1982). After the manager fires an employee, he or she is also likely to undergo a process of rationalization and justification. He or she is also likely to dehumanize the selected out people, that is, to see them more as inanimate objects.

It appears that many terminations in the United States are handled poorly (Sweet, 1989). Why is this? For one thing, ter-

minations are rare in many organizations, so managers get little opportunity to practice how to conduct them well. Terminations are also unpleasant, and they might imply that the manager made a mistake in hiring or training. Thus, managers have
reasons to avoid terminating employees and to avoid careful
analysis and deliberation about termination situations. However, as noted earlier, when firing cannot be avoided, managers
may act hastily to try to eliminate this "unpleasantness" as quickly
as possible, rather than approach it in a thoughtful manner.

Being Selected Out

Stages of unemployment are a common description of the
psychological processes in selection out. The loss of a job has
multiple psychological and behavioral consequences, and these
seem to occur in stages. Each stage tends to be associated
with somewhat different cognitive, emotional, and behavioral
processes.

There are at least five stages of involuntary unemployment.
The first is "anticipatory job loss." Employees may have a sense
that they will lose their jobs even before a layoff occurs. People
who are not performing well or who are not getting along with
their bosses may also fear that they will be fired. Rumors of
layoffs can create widespread anxiety about job security. The
degree of fear of losing a job, or the degree of denial, may depend on company history, policies, and communication regarding the employee's future with the company. Personal history
may also play a role. Individuals who have never been laid off
(or fired), or individuals in jobs that have traditionally been im-
mune from layoffs, probably would deny that it could happen
to them. The next four stages of unemployment, which begin
after an individual has been fired or laid off (Kaufman, 1982),
are shock, relief, and relaxation; concerted effort; vacillation,
self-doubt, and anger; and resignation and withdrawal. Kaufman (1982) reports some empirical evidence for the existence
of these four stages. A summary of the psychological processes
and behavioral and physical outcomes is presented in Table 11.1.

Table 11.1. Stages of Unemployment.

	Stage 1: Shock, Relief, and Relaxation (approximately 1–2 months)	Stage 2: Concerted Effort (approximately 3 months)	Stage 3: Vacillation, Self-Doubt, and Anger (approximately 1½ months)	Stage 4: Resignation and Withdrawal (indefinite duration)
Psychological processes	1. Initial shock; reduction in stress following period of anticipation and uncertainty	1. Stress depends on financial security and social support; those in midcareer most affected	1. Frustration and questioning of ability to find a job	1. Resignation to being in a jobless state
	2. Low need to return to work to attain security	2. High motivation to work, including a. High initiative b. High occupational aspirations	2. Lower motivation to work, including a. Low initiative b. Low occupational aspirations c. Occupational identity problems	2. Work inhibition accompanied by a. Low initiative b. Low occupational aspirations c. Occupational rigidity d. Professional obsolescence
	3. Positive mental state in terms of a. Self-esteem b. Life satisfaction c. Hopefulness d. Low anomie	3. Mental state improved in terms of a. Low anxiety b. Personal control	3. Some hope still remains	3. Mental state improves in terms of reduced feelings of a. Anxiety b. Desperation c. Being burdened with responsibility

4. Some negative reactions in terms of
  a. Resentment of employer
  b. Anxiety
	4. Mental state begins to deteriorate in terms of
	  a. Anomie
	  b. Life dissatisfaction
	  c. Being burdened with responsibility
		4. Mental state deteriorates in terms of
		  a. High anxiety
		  b. Extreme anger
			4. Mental state deteriorates in terms of
			  a. Low motivation
			  b. Low self-esteem
			  c. Loss of control
			  d. Helplessness
			  e. Hopelessness

Possible behavioral and physical outcomes 1. Behaves as if on vacation 2. Normal social relationships; lack of openness about job loss 3. Hostility against employer	1. Concentrates almost totally on finding work 2. Receives social support 3. Attempts to be in control	1. Job search becomes erratic; attempts to change career or occupation 2. Conflicts with family and friends 3. Psychosomatic disorders and suicide proneness begin	1. Avoidance of searching for a job 2. Social relations limited to a few close relatives and friends with activities centered at home 3. Increase in psychosomatic disorders, suicide proneness, and susceptibility to premature death

Source: Adapted from Kaufman, 1982, pp. 118–119. Used by permission of John Wiley & Sons, Inc.

During the first stage of involuntary unemployment, the individual initially feels some shock, followed by a reduction of anxiety related to the uncertainty and anticipation that might have preceded the job loss. People are fairly optimistic about the future at this point, and some may even take a vacation. Stage 2, concerted effort, occurs after one or two months and generally lasts for about three months. During this stage energy is focused on finding a job. However, if a job is not found, the person's mental state begins to deteriorate. After approximately five months of unemployment, people enter Stage 3 — vacillation, self-doubt, and anger — which last for approximately one and one-half months. Although there is still some hope left for finding another job, people have lower motivation to work and to look for work, and their mental state continues to deteriorate. Anxiety and anger increase. Finally, those who remain unemployed enter Stage 4, resignation and withdrawal. People become resigned to being unemployed, and their motivation for work (and looking for work) continues to decrease, as does their self-esteem.

An individual's career stage is likely to influence the way the person experiences involuntary job loss. People at early and late career stages tend to have the least severe and least debilitating reactions to job loss (Feldman, 1988). Individuals at the early, establishment phase of a career tend to have fewer family and financial obligations and can more easily move into jobs at entry-level positions, which are typically more abundant than middle-level or senior positions (Colarelli & Bishop, 1990). Also, less of their ego is likely to be invested in their careers at an early stage. At the other end of the spectrum, individuals at late career stages also have fewer family and financial responsibilities (children are grown and educated, houses paid for, and a retirement nest egg built up). Late-career individuals are more likely to have a flexible range of career options if they lose their job. For example, they can retire, do volunteer work, start a small business, or engage in consulting or public service. However, individuals during their middle career years are hit hardest by the loss of a job. People in their thirties and forties are most likely raising children, saving for college educations, and paying for homes. Their earning power and responsibilities tend to be high, and finding jobs with equivalent financial remuneration and responsibility tends to be difficult.

Atchley, a longtime writer on retirement, has proposed three stages of retirement. Similar to Kaufman's (1982) stages of unemployment, these retirement stages focus on the individual's point of view rather than on the organization's. Atchley's phases of retirement are labeled according to the time of their occurrence: preretirement, retirement transition, and postretirement (Atchley, 1982). Kaufman's stages of unemployment tend to focus on aversive effects; Atchley's retirement phases do not. Retirement, as opposed to layoffs and firings, has a large voluntary component. Unlike layoffs and firings, retirement is not necessarily aversive. In fact, reviews of research on the stressful effects of retirement often conclude that retirement is not stressful for most people (for example, Kasl, 1980; Beehr, 1986). It is easy to conclude that, aside from problems associated with aging, retirement is probably not aversive to most people the way that layoffs and firings are.

During the preretirement phase, for example, people usually have the time to plan for retirement. Planning, anticipation, and simply getting used to the idea can probably make the transition easier than most firing and layoff situations. Research on the retirement transition phase has focused on the employee's decision to retire and on what factors led to this decision. Not surprisingly, finances are one of the most important factors in this decision, although there are probably many other determinants of the decision to retire for most people. Research on the postretirement phase has focused on the effects that retirement and adjustment to retirement have on retirees. There are a number of theories claiming that retirement has positive effects on people, negative effects on people, or no effects at all (Beehr, 1986; Talaga & Beehr, 1989). Whatever the effects, retirement phases nearly always occur in the later stages of people's careers. Under typical circumstances, career stage has little impact on retirement, because most retiring people are in the last stage of their working careers. An exception may be retirement from occupations in which people tend to retire quite young (for instance, the military). It seems likely that such people often retire with the intention of finding another full-time position.

Outcomes of Selecting People Out

Selection out, like all human resource management technologies, has multiple outcomes and outcomes at multiple levels of analysis — societal, organizational, and individual. Some outcomes are intended, others are unintended; and some are positive, others are negative. Because some outcomes will be incompatible with one another, selection out will involve some degree of conflict.

Outcomes to Society

Societies in which layoffs and firings occur widely, often, and at all levels have difficulty developing skilled employees. Skills are behaviors that are instrumental to accomplishing a specific task or set of tasks, and thus are best learned with training and experience on the tasks specific to the job and organization. Despite the rhetoric about teaching skills in secondary schools, colleges, and professional schools, the skills that are most valuable to organizations are those that are learned at work (Porter, 1990). The more complex the job, the longer it takes to become skillful at it. The transmission of these skills is the essence of training, and not of education — which is more general and works best in the school setting. When individuals lose their jobs, learning job skills normally stops. Employees are most likely to become skillful when they remain with an organization long enough to become well trained. The training investment pays dividends: a more skilled workforce means more productive organizations and a more productive society (Dertouzos, Lester, & Solow, 1989).

Extensive firings and layoffs may also contribute to a high level of cynicism among a nation's workforce. Because layoffs signal a lack of commitment from employers, employees are unlikely to trust them, will work solely for their own advantage, and will be less committed to the effectiveness of the organization (Kanter & Mirvis, 1989). Similarly, large-scale layoffs concentrated in single towns or communities are likely to result in economic dislocation and an upsurge in social and emotional problems.

Massive layoffs and firings, or widespread fear of job loss, can also have recessionary effects on the economy. Since the modern American economy is primarily fueled by consumer spending, drops in consumer spending can send the economy into recession. When consumers lose their jobs, or fear that they may lose them, they spend less money, and this weakens the economy.

Large-scale, earlier retirements may also have some negative effects on society as a whole, although there is little evidence for it one way or another. Financially, if employers and governments are committed to a good standard of living for retirees (even at fairly young ages), then large-scale retirements place a heavy financial burden on those still working and producing. On the other hand, it should be recognized that official retirement does not necessarily mean the end of productive work. People can retire from one job or organization and still work elsewhere. Beehr and Nielson (1992a, 1992b) found that expecting to work for pay (either full- or part-time) is strongly predictive of the decision to retire. Expecting to have the opportunity to work for pay after retirement, but on a different job, is potentially an inducement for some people to retire. To the extent that these expectations are fulfilled, then the image of the nonproductive retiree is erroneous. The same data, however, also indicate that retirees may not actually work for pay as much as they expected to before retirement.

Selection out can have positive outcomes to society. When industries that traditionally attract talented people (for example, investment banking) lay employees off, this increases *and improves* the applicant pools for less prestigious industries. A recent article in the *Wall Street Journal* (Salwen, 1990) entitled "U.S. Agencies Get Dividends from Wall Street as Hordes of Yuppies Look for Government Jobs" illustrates the point. The 1990–1992 recession caused over fifty thousand firings from brokerage houses and Wall Street law firms. As a result, federal agencies received many applications from former investment bankers and lawyers. When massive firings or a poor job market inject critical masses of talented people into laggard organizations, they are likely to become dissatisfied. Since dissatisfaction can stimulate change, these individuals may become a vanguard for change (Hirschman, 1970) and may improve mediocre organizations.

People who have lost their jobs involuntarily *and* survived the psychological fallout may become valuable assets to society. The experience of having lost a job may motivate them to forgo the life of a wage earner and start their own business. Indeed, a characteristic of entrepreneurs is that they do not like working for other people. Entrepreneurs, of course, are valuable to society because they create companies, jobs, and innovations. In addition, people who have experienced job loss are likely to be more conscientious about saving for the future. Such individuals may help society by saving and investing at higher than average rates.

Retirement may also have positive effects on organizations and society. Organizations offering successful early retirement incentives may benefit financially by being relieved of some higher-paid employees. Indeed, this is probably a reason for many of the early retirement offers described in recent newspaper articles. Other companies, however, may benefit from having these reliable and skilled retirees willing to work part-time for lower pay. Society also may benefit from retirees' volunteer labor for social causes. The crux of the issue is what the retirees do after they retire. Organizations could even help their retirees plan second careers or community service projects (for example, engineers teaching math or science in high schools, executives lending management expertise to nonprofit organizations). Activities of this sort can boost an organization's public reputation.

Outcomes to Organizations

The idea of permanent employment has a certain appeal. Permanent employment appeals to our humane instincts and ideas of good management. As mentioned earlier, permanent employment is conducive to long-term training and skill development; it also seems to be associated with a better organizational image (which helps in recruiting and public relations) and may be associated with higher morale. On the other hand, permanent employment may also be associated with stagnation, inefficiency, lack of creativity, and poor productivity (Shaw, Fisher, & Randolph, 1991).

Thus, permanent employment, per se, is not necessarily good or bad. Permanent employment, like virtually all human resource strategies, is likely to produce positive organizational outcomes under certain types of conditions and negative outcomes under other conditions. Permanent employment is likely to result in the most positive outcomes in well-managed companies, where employees and managers have high internal motivation and work standards, and where there are cohesive groups and high productivity norms. In such circumstances, employees do not need the threat of losing a job to motivate hard work and productivity. Such companies, for instance, some major Japanese corporations, rely heavily on selective hiring practices and intense socialization. For most other organizations, it may be better if managers and employees are less secure. The potential of losing one's job if performance slips may motivate employees to continue working hard. In a recent meeting of top managers at IBM, for example, the chairman, Robert Akers, suggested that too much job security might have been a cause of the organization's recent poor performance. According to one manager's notes, Mr. Akers said, "The fact that we're losing market share makes me God-damn mad. I used to think my job as a [sales] rep was at risk if I lost a sale. Tell [the sales reps that] theirs is at risk if they lose one. . . . If the people in the labs and plants miss deadlines . . . tell them their job is on the line, too. . . . The tension level is not high enough in the business — everyone is too damn comfortable at a time when the business is in crisis" (Carroll, 1991, p. B1).

While the threat of being fired may motivate laggard individuals, the threat of layoffs for poor company performance may inspire superior effort and performance throughout an organization. For example, Buick's major plant in Flint, Michigan, was in jeopardy of closing owing to low sales and poor quality. As a result, managers and employees started working together. They devised new management and production techniques and improved old ones, with the objective of improving sales by producing automobiles of top quality. By some accounts, Buick has succeeded in meeting its objective ("Making Them," 1991).

The threat of losing a job is likely to be an effective motivator if employees *believe* that the threat is real. They must also believe that their jobs become more secure by working productively. In addition, employees must be sufficiently skilled and sufficiently thick-skinned so that they can perform under pressure. Fiedler and his colleagues (for example, Fiedler & Garcia, 1987) suggest that experienced employees seem to perform effectively under such pressure. The general climate of the organization should be sufficiently supportive so that employees believe that, although poor performance has harsh consequences, the organization will help people succeed and managers will deal with people fairly. Employees need to perceive management as credible and fair. Finally, managers must be able to articulate desired behaviors, results, and consequences.

There is an increasing amount of theoretical work and empirical research on the effects of layoffs on survivors (employees who remain employed in an organization that has recently laid off a portion of its workforce). Much of this work has been done by Brockner and his colleagues, and it has applied ideas from social psychology to the reactions of survivors to layoffs. Layoffs are likely to affect survivors' psychological reactions (for instance, anger, grief), behaviors (working harder or working less), and attitudes (attitudes toward management; sympathy for layoff victims or derogation of them) (Brockner, 1988). Unfortunately, the empirical work in this area has yielded few substantive results. This appears to be the case for at least three reasons: many factors influence survivors' reactions; survivors have a variety of reactions, many simultaneously and some contradictory; and numerous conditions moderate the relationships between antecedent conditions and outcomes.

Perhaps the most parsimonious way to view survivor reactions is in relation to occupational stress. Since layoffs and firings (but probably not retirements) are stressful, we may want to conceptualize survivor reactions in broad categories of reactions to stress. Jick (1985) notes that layoffs are one of the expected and actual effects of budget cuts. He proposes that the objective characteristics of the situation (especially the severity and immediacy of the cuts) lead to the experience of "demand." The experience of demand is typical of stressful situations. Survivors' stress occurs because of employees' uncertainty about their abilities to do much about the situation and their uncertainty over performance and reward outcomes. This type of uncertainty may be the essence of stress for survivors.

Aside from financial outcomes, which were mentioned previously, retirements may affect organizations in other ways. Too many retirements in an organization, especially among employees in critical positions, may weaken an organization's culture. Senior organization members are often the strongest carriers of the organization's culture. If they have long tenure in the organization, they have seen events occur, have accepted them over time, and might even have helped to create those events. This probably breeds conservatism in them. For better or for worse, it may become easier to change the culture of an organization when many people retire. "Survivors" of retirement may even perceive better opportunities for advancement and for taking on new responsibilities. Alternatively, massive retirements may present more uncertainty to employees, because the people with the most experience and knowledge about the organization and its industry are no longer present. Most of these effects of retirement on organizations have not been the focus of intensive study (Talaga & Beehr, 1989).

Outcomes to Individuals

Being fired or laid off has unpleasant psychological and physiological consequences — as well as unhealthy consequences for family relations (for overviews see Kaufman, 1982; Leana & Ivancevich, 1987). Involuntary job loss tends to be associated with depression, hostility, anxiety, unhappiness, and loss of self-esteem and pleasure in life. People who are laid off or fired report more strain and sleeplessness and have higher incidences of hospitalization, self-reported disability, hypertension, and cardiovascular diseases. Involuntary job loss increases the risk of suicide. Cobb and Kasl (1977) report the suicide rates in their sample of unemployed workers to be *thirty* times higher than expected. Brenner (1973) reports that a 1 percent rise in unemployment in society is associated with about a 4 percent rise in suicide.

The families of individuals also suffer when a male bread-winner loses his job. When male employees lose their jobs, there is an increase in marital discord, family violence, aggression toward children, and child abuse. The father's authority and status in the family — especially in middle-class families — slips after he loses his job (again, for reviews see Kaufman, 1982; Leana & Ivancevich, 1987). Coopersmith (1967) reports that only 7 percent of children with fathers who were occasionally out of work had high self-esteem, whereas 44 percent of children whose fathers were rarely out of work had high self-esteem.

Although most of the research on the effects of involuntary job loss on individuals has focused on the unpleasant side, it is possible that being fired or laid off may have positive effects. Although we were unable to find much empirical work in the area, we offer the following speculations about the positive effects of involuntary job loss. Losing a job may "season" a person. That is, a person who loses a job is less likely to have a naive view of organizations and the world. He or she may be more motivated, hardworking, cautious in judgment, politically astute, and sensitive in interpersonal relationships after he or she finds another job. Having been fired or laid off may also provide a shock which forces a person to think deeply about his or her career and life. When things are going well, people tend to take things for granted, not questioning institutions, goals, and values. The shock of involuntary loss of a job may stimulate questioning and reassessment of values and goals. It may also stimulate serious, proactive career and life planning. Being fired or laid off may also increase an individual's sense of personal responsibility.

In fact, it may be that experiencing, surviving, and profiting from such traumas are important in the development of leaders (Zaleznik, 1977). The trauma of being fired or laid off might provide the shock that opens the individual up to other perspectives. The time away from work can provide the opportunity for solitude and reflection. It is during this reflective period that the individual crystallizes goals and a vision for the future. Surviving the experience may instill the sense of personal mastery and confidence that is necessary for leadership.

Retirement as a form of selection out, as noted earlier, is likely to have far fewer adverse effects than layoffs or firings. Most people react fairly well to retirement. When they are doing poorly in retirement, it is as likely due to aging or other normal problems as to retirement itself. There is no doubt that for some individuals retirement is more adverse than not retiring, but no research exists which identifies individual differences that may help to predict these varied reactions (Talaga & Beehr, 1989).

Future Research and Practice

The field of selection out is broad, and comparatively little research or theory exists in the area. Thus, there are many avenues for future research and practice. Because the purpose of this chapter is to stimulate theory and research, we offer more general than specific suggestions. At this early stage, the field will benefit more from good theories and broad research programs than from fine-tuning technologies.

Future Research

We have little information on organizations' actual selection out practices. Therefore, it would be beneficial to conduct descriptive, ethnographic, and taxonomic research on these practices. Given the global economy, we would also encourage cross-cultural research. Once we have an idea of *what* organizations do, it is important to answer the question of why they do what they do. The more we know about the conditions under which certain techniques are likely to be used, the more likely it is that our ideas will be used and will contribute to organizational effectiveness.

We need more research on structural and cultural factors that influence the use of selection out (and other human resource) practices. Environmental, structural (Greenhalgh, Lawrence, & Sutton, 1988), and cultural (Schein, 1985) factors appear to have a strong influence on whether organizations use particular selection out practices. For example, the structure of financial markets and the motivations of owners and debtors can affect the way organizations treat employees. In publicly owned corporations in the United States, investors are concerned about short-term profits and managers tend to be motivated by short-term incentives (Porter, 1990). Thus, the financial structures and motivations in the United States support cyclical mass hirings and layoffs in response to short-term business cycles. In Germany, on the other hand, shares of public corporations are often owned by large institutions (for example, banks) and are rarely traded. German financial, accounting, and regulatory structures encourage management to take a long-term perspective and accumulate large cash reserves to provide a cushion to help weather hard times (Porter, 1990). As a result, German organizations have less pressure to lay off employees when the economy softens.

We also need research on the possible transformational outcomes of selection out. How might selection out influence major psychological transformations—such as changes in values, goals, ego development, or identity? Are major changes in identity associated with painful and profound events? What are the conditions that determine when selection out has positive outcomes, and what are the conditions when it has negative outcomes?

Although the profession of I/O psychology has been enamored with methods since its founding, we urge going slowly on standardizing selection out methods. As the principle of equifinality from open systems theory suggests, there are multiple paths to a given outcome (Katz & Kahn, 1978). Organizations can therefore use a variety of methods to achieve an outcome. Although we want to develop and validate methods for selection out, this should not be the primary focus of selection out research and theory. It may be useful to shift our focus to outcomes (Colarelli, Dean, & Konstans, 1987). Instead of doing things better, we might attend to doing better things—that is, keeping the overall goals in mind rather than focusing only on methods to reach a goal.

Regardless of the area of research in selection out, we strongly urge that research be informed by a systems perspective. Given that the antecedents, processes, and consequences of selection out are multifaceted, research that focuses on isolated variables and ignores context will miss important aspects of the process.

Practice

Greenhalgh, Lawrence, and Sutton (1988, p. 243) suggest several selection out practices. They categorize them according to both the short-term cost savings they afford organizations as well as the level of protection they provide for employee well-being. We suggest that selection out practices can also be categorized by their degree of communication, participation, control, planning, and support. We suggest that organizations utilize selection out techniques that maximize these processes. We have included some suggestions on how this might be done in Table 11.2.

One novel method that maximizes these processes is voluntary (unpaid) sabbaticals. They are likely to involve more communication, participation, control, planning, and support than traditional layoffs. Moreover, voluntary sabbaticals have a number of other advantages over layoffs. First, since sabbaticals are for specified time periods, employers that provide sabbaticals during recessions will have a pool of experienced and trained workers they can count on when the economy improves. Because a sabbatical implies self-development, employees who take sabbaticals are expected to engage in developmental experiences. Therefore, sabbaticals provide organizations with an excellent way of upgrading their human resources (organizations may want to pay for some developmental experiences). Also, a sabbatical policy is philosophically more compatible with the knowledge-based, technologically sophisticated economy of the twenty-first century than a layoff policy is — sabbaticals give employees time to think. Finally, sabbaticals send a different signal to employees. Sabbaticals signal to employees that they are important, that it is important that they think, and that it is important that they improve their skills. Layoffs, on the other hand, signal to employees that they are excess baggage.

Table 11.2. Techniques to Enhance the Practice of Selection Out.

Processes	Firings	Layoffs	Retirements
Communication	Warnings Due process	Advance notification Frequent and accurate information	Clear policies
Participation	Warnings Due Process	Employee participation in policy making	Employee participation in policy making
Control	Severance pay Enhanced financial control	Severance pay Enhanced financial control	Financial security
Planning	Orderly termination	Time to plan while still employed	Time to plan while still employed
Support	Quality outplacement Organizational assistance in finding another job	Quality outplacement Organizational assistance in finding another job	Help in preparing for transition

If there are any universals to guide selection out practices, we recommend decency and civility, while pursuing organizational effectiveness. The more that these three factors can be structurally and culturally ingrained in organizations, the better. Likert's principle of supportive relationships holds true as a rule of thumb for selection out: "The leadership and other processes of the organization must be such as to ensure a maximum probability that in all interactions and in all relationships within the organization, each member, in the light of his background, values, desires, and expectations, will view the experience as supportive and one which builds and maintains his sense of personal worth and importance" (Likert, 1961, p. 103). By using selection out methods that treat employees with dignity, organizations are more likely to minimize the negative emotional and social consequences of selection out, while enhancing organizational effectiveness. Although there is no one sure method to terminate employees without anguish, reasoned and supportive methods are likely to minimize the damage.

Finally, we offer a caveat for designing selection out practices and policy. Despite the fascination with participation, and despite American culture's value on equality, human groups involve *dominance hierarchies* — a small number of dominant, alpha males and females at the top, and a majority of followers at the middle and bottom (Davis & Moore, 1945; Etkin, 1971). Those at the top have the most resources and accumulate the most rewards — including job (and financial) security. As a result, the people at the middle and bottom will usually go first when an organization reduces the size of its workforce. This is unlikely to change.

References

Atchley, R. C. (1982). Retirement: Leaving the world of work. In F. Berardo (Ed.), Middle and later life transitions. *Annals of the American Academy of Political and Social Science, 464,* 120–131.

Beehr, T. A. (1986). The process of retirement. *Personnel Psychology, 39,* 31–55.

Beehr, T. A., & Nielson, N. L. (1992a). *On the usefulness of prospective and retrospective reports in retirement research.* Paper presented at the annual meeting of the Midwestern Psychological Association, Chicago.

Beehr, T. A., & Nielson, N. L. (1992b). *Predicting the decision to retire.* Paper presented at the annual meeting of the Midwestern Psychological Association, Chicago.

Bennett, A. (1991, June 6). Downsizing doesn't necessarily bring an upswing in corporate profitability. *The Wall Street Journal,* p. B-1.

Blaustein, S. J. (1981). *Job and income security for unemployed workers.* Kalamazoo, MI: W. E. Upjohn Institute.

Borrowers all. (1991, March 9). *Economist,* p. 81.

Brenner, M. H. (1973). *Mental illness and the economy.* Cambridge, MA: Harvard University Press.

Brockner, J. (1988). The effects of work layoffs on survivors: Research, theory, and practice. In B. M. Staw and L. L. Cummings (Eds.), *Research in organizational behavior* (Vol. 10, pp. 213–255). Greenwich, CT: JAI Press.

Brockner, J., DeWitt, R. L., Grover, S., & Reed, T. (1990). When it is especially important to explain why: Factors affecting the relationship between managers' explanations of a layoff and survivors' reactions to the layoff. *Journal of Experimental Social Psychology, 26,* 389–407.

Carroll, P. B. (1991, May 29). Akers to IBM employees: Wake up! *The Wall Street Journal,* pp. B1–B2.

Challenger, J. E. (1989, February). When outplacement is a sham. *Personnel Journal,* pp. 27–30.

Cobb, S., & Kasl, S. V. (1977). *Termination: The consequences of job loss* (Report No. 76-1261). Washington, DC: National Institute for Safety and Health.

Colarelli, S. M. (1984). Methods of communication and mediating processes in realistic job previews. *Journal of Applied Psychology, 69,* 633–642.

Colarelli, S. M. (1992). *The context of hiring practices.* Manuscript submitted for publication.

Colarelli, S. M. (in press). Organization development and personnel psychology: Issues and integration. In F. Massarik (Ed.), *Advances in Organization Development* (Vol. 2). Norwood, NJ: Ablex.

Colarelli, S. M., & Beehr, T. A. (1991). Effective organizations in the twenty-first century. In J. W. Jones, B. D. Steffy, & D. W. Bray (Eds.), *Applying psychology in business: The handbook for managers and human resource professionals.* New York: Lexington Books.

Colarelli, S. M., & Bishop, R. C. (1990). Career commitment: Functions, correlates, and management. *Group & Organization Studies, 15,* 158–176.

Colarelli, S. M., Dean, R. A., & Konstans, C. (1987). Comparative effects of personal and situational influences on job outcomes of new professionals. *Journal of Applied Psychology, 72,* 558–567.

Colarelli, S. M., & Stumpf, S. A. (1990). Compatibility and conflict among organizational entry strategies: Mechanistic and social system perspectives. *Behavioral Science, 35,* 1–10.

Cooper, M., & Holmes, A. (1990, February 26). The disaster that never happened. *U.S. News and World Report,* p. 47.

Coopersmith, S. (1967). *The antecedents of self-esteem.* San Francisco: Freeman.

Cornfield, D. B. (1981). Industrial social organizations and layoffs in American manufacturing industry. In I. Berg (Ed.). *Sociological Perspectives in Labor Markets.* New York: Academic Press.

Davis, K., & Moore, W. (1945). Some principles of stratification. *American Sociological Review, 2,* 242–249.

Dertouzos, M. L., Lestor, R. K., & Solow, R. M. (1989). *Made in America: Regaining the productive edge.* Cambridge, MA: MIT Press.

Earley, P. C., Wojnaroski, P., & Prest, W. (1987). Task planning and energy expended: Exploration of how goals influence performance. *Journal of Applied Psychology, 72,* 107–114.

Etkin, W. (1971). *Social behavior from fish to man.* Chicago: University of Chicago Press.

Faludi, S. C. (1990, May 16). Safeway LBO yields vast profits but exacts a heavy human toll. *The Wall Street Journal,* pp. A1, A8–A9.

Feldman, D. C. (1988). *Managing careers in organizations.* Glenview, IL: Scott, Foresman.

Fiedler, F. E., & Garcia, J. E. (1987). *New approaches to effective leadership — cognitive resources and organizational performance.* New York: Wiley.

Gilhooly, K. S. (1982). *Thinking.* London: Academic Press.

Greenhalgh, L., Lawrence, A. T., & Sutton, R. I. (1988). Determinants of work force reduction strategies in declining organizations. *Academy of Management Review, 13,* 241–254.

Haire, M., Ghiselli, E. E., & Porter, L. W. (1966). *Managerial thinking: An international study.* New York: Wiley.

Heider, F. (1958). *The psychology of interpersonal relations.* New York: Wiley.

Hirschman, A. O. (1970). *Exit, voice, and loyalty.* Cambridge, MA: Harvard University Press.

Howard, A. (1990). *The multiple facets of industrial-organizational psychology.* Arlington Heights, IL: Society for Industrial and Organizational Psychology.

Jamal, M. (1988, May). Is moonlighting mired in myth? *Personnel Journal,* pp. 49–55.

Janis, I. L. (1989). *Crucial decisions.* New York: Free Press.

Jick, T. D. (1985). As the ax falls: Budget cuts and the experience of stress in organizations. In T. A. Beehr & R. S. Bhagat (Eds.), *Human stress and cognition in organizations: An integrated perspective* (pp. 83–114). New York: Wiley.

Journal's Faludi wins Pulitzer for story on human costs of Safeway buy-out. (1991, April 10). *The Wall Street Journal,* p. A2.

Kanter, D. L., & Mirvis, P. H. (1989). *The cynical Americans.* San Francisco: Jossey-Bass.

Kasl, S. V. (1980). The impact of retirement. In C. L. Cooper & R. Payne (Eds.), *Current concerns in occupational stress.* Chichester, England: Wiley.

Katz, D., & Kahn, R. L. (1978). *The social psychology of organizations* (2nd ed.). New York: Wiley.

Kaufman, H. G. (1982). *Professionals in search of work: Coping with the stress of job loss and underemployment.* New York: Wiley.

Landes, D. S. (1969). *The unbound Prometheus.* New York: Cambridge University Press.

Layard, R., Jackman, R., & Nickell, S. (1991). *Unemployment: Macroeconomic performance and the labor market.* New York: Oxford University Press.

Leana, C. R., & Ivancevich, J. M. (1987). Involuntary job loss:

Institutional interventions and a research agenda. *Academy of Management Review, 12,* 301–312.

Ledvinka, J., & Scarpello, V. G. (1991). *Federal regulation of personnel and human resource management.* Boston: PWS-Kent.

Likert, R. (1961). *New Patterns of Management.* New York: McGraw-Hill.

Locke, E. A. (1976). The nature and causes of job satisfaction. In M. D. Dunnette (Ed.), *Handbook of industrial and organizational psychology* (pp. 1297–1349). Skokie, IL: Rand McNally.

Mahoney, T. A. (1988). Productivity defined: The relativity of efficiency, effectiveness, and change. In J. P. Campbell, R. J. Campbell, & Associates (Eds.), *Productivity in organizations* (pp. 13–39). San Francisco: Jossey-Bass.

Maier, N. R. F. (1963). *Problem-solving discussions and conferences.* New York: McGraw-Hill.

Maier, N. R. F., & Verser, G. C. (1982). *Psychology in industrial organizations* (5th ed.). Boston: Houghton Mifflin.

Making them like they used to. (1991, April 27). *Economist,* p. 70.

McCall, M. W., & Lombardo, M. M. (1983). *Off the track: Why and how successful executives get derailed.* Greensboro, NC: Center for Creative Leadership.

McCraw, T. K. (Ed.). (1986). *America versus Japan.* Boston: Harvard Business School Press.

Merton, R. K. (1957). *Social theory and social structure* (rev. ed.). New York: Free Press.

Miller, D. T., & Ross, M. (1975). Self-serving biases in the attribution of causality: Fact or fiction? *Psychological Bulletin, 82,* 213–225.

Mitchell, T. R., & Kalb, L. S. (1982). Effects of job experience on supervisor attributions for a subordinate's poor performance. *Journal of Applied Psychology, 67,* 181–188.

Morgan, G. (1986). *Images of organization.* Newbury Park, CA: Sage.

Nice try. (1991, April 23). *The Wall Street Journal,* p. A1.

Patterson, G. A. (1991, March 22). GM plans retirement deal for its blue-collar workers. *The Wall Street Journal,* p. A-3.

Porter, M. E. (1990). *The competitive advantage of nations.* New York: Free Press.

Rogers, E. M. (1983). *The diffusion of innovations* (3rd ed.). New York: Free Press.

Ross, L. (1977). The intuitive psychologist and his shortcomings: Distortions in the attribution process. *Advances in Experimental Social Psychology, 10,* 173–220.

Salwen, K. G. (1990, December 21). U.S. agencies get dividends from Wall Street as hordes of yuppies look for government jobs. *The Wall Street Journal,* p. A-14.

Sampson, E. E. (1963). Status congruence and cognitive consistency. *Sociometry, 26,* 146–162.

Sasaki, N. (1981). *Management and industrial structure in Japan.* Oxford, England: Pergamon.

Schein, E. H. (1985). *Leadership and organizational culture.* San Francisco: Jossey-Bass.

Shaw, J. B., Fisher, C. D., & Randolph, W. A. (1991). From maternalism to accountability: The changing cultures of Ma Bell and Mother Russia. *The Executive, 5,* 7–20.

The squirrel's curse. (1991, February 9). *Economist,* p. 69.

Sutton, R. I., & Kahn, R. L. (1987). Prediction, understanding, and control as antidotes to organizational stress. In J. Lorsch (Ed.), *Handbook of organizational behavior* (pp. 272–285). Englewood Cliffs, NJ: Prentice-Hall.

Sweet, D. H. (1989). *A manager's guide to conducting terminations.* Lexington, MA: Lexington Books.

Talaga, J., & Beehr, T. A. (1989). Retirement: A psychological perspective. In C. L. Cooper & I. T. Robertson (Eds.), *International review of industrial and organizational psychology 1989.* Chichester, England: Wiley.

Tannenbaum, A. S. (1968). *Control in organizations.* New York: McGraw-Hill.

Tom, V. R. (1971). The role of personality and organizational images in the recruiting process. *Organizational Behavior and Human Performance, 6,* 573–592.

White-collar layoffs in America—a lot more than you would think. (1991, February 2). *Economist,* p. 66.

Wiener, J. (1990, December). Dealing with deadwood. *Lingua Franca,* pp. 1, 14–17, 29.

Zaleznik, A. (1977, May–June). Managers and leaders: Are they different? *Harvard Business Review, 73,* 67–78.

12

Personnel Selection in the Future: The Impact of Changing Demographics and the Nature of Work

Lynn R. Offermann, Marilyn K. Gowing

Widespread societal change is radically altering employment in the United States. The nature of work, the workforce, and the workplace have all undergone and will continue to undergo tremendous change, bringing new challenges and opportunities to those interested in personnel selection issues (Offermann & Gowing, 1990). With these changes comes the realization that traditional selection practices will no longer serve the best interests of organizations wishing to be globally competitive. In this chapter, we address the current and future impact of these work changes on personnel selection. We begin by briefly summarizing the major demographic changes affecting organizations today and into the future as well as the changing demands created by the nature of work itself. We then discuss the implications of change for new or modified constructs of job performance, and examine the effects of projected changes on recruitment, selection, and promotion of the new workforce. For many organizations, that "future" is already here, and we present their experiences and solutions as instructive to those concerned about maintaining organizational competitiveness into the next century.

Changing Workers, Changing Work

Demographic changes in the composition of the workforce as well as changes in the nature and structure of work organizations present an important challenge to those charged with maintaining the effective use of human resources. Some future trends in workforce composition can be foreseen with relative accuracy. For example, over two-thirds of the individuals who will be members of the workforce in the year 2000 are working today. While prognostications about the nature of organizations are more speculative than those about demographic changes in the domestic workforce, several clear trends can still be identified that pose significant challenges for personnel selection.

Changing Demographics

Recently, we attempted to summarize the best prognostications about the nature of the U.S. workforce in coming years (Offermann & Gowing, 1990). We found that most scenarios about future workforce changes included four areas of concern: (1) the age distribution of the workforce, (2) the sexual, cultural, and ethnic composition of the workforce, (3) worker skills, and (4) job attitudes possessed by workers.

Age Distribution of the Workforce. Significantly fewer young people will enter the job market than in the recent past. The so-called baby bust will produce a small pool of entry-level talent, with greater organizational competition for their services. At the same time, the escalating number of middle-aged individuals in the workforce (products of the baby boom) will result in increasingly limited promotion opportunities. A large-scale motivational problem may develop as many workers reach career plateaus. One traditional solution to this problem has been early retirement — a solution based on the assumption of available, recently trained, less expensive, and more motivated young workers. This assumption will become increasingly questionable with the small incoming cohort of new workers. Yet, programs to keep older workers or delay retirement have often not been enthusiastically endorsed by organizations (Towers Perrin, 1990). Older workers still face age bias, despite consistent evidence that age is typically unrelated to job performance for most jobs (for example, McEvoy & Cascio, 1989).

Sexual, Ethnic, and Cultural Composition of the Workforce. The increasing diversification of the workforce will continue unabated. White males will make up only 15 percent of the net increase in the workforce during the next ten years. Increasingly, the U.S. workplace is populated by women, minorities, and immigrants. Organizations that never really mastered affirmative action are now scrambling somehow to "manage diversity." Prior attempts to force diverse groups to meld into a homogeneous organization were never totally successful. The extent of the diversity challenge will be affected by immigration patterns and organizational policies. Reich (1991) and others have charged that rather than training local entry-level talent, many U.S. organizations merely export work abroad. New approaches to training and managing resident individuals from diverse backgrounds will be ever more necessary as we approach the century's end if the United States is to realize both economic productivity and a developed native workforce.

Worker Skills. The skill level of new workers is expected to be far less than desirable. Talk is rampant about a "skills gap" wherein the organizational need for increasing skills in a technologically advanced world far outstrips the skill level of the applicant group. In fact, current concerns about skills often focus on lack of even the basic literacy skills that were assumed to be possessed by previous cohorts of new workers on organizational entry. A recent study at Nynex found that only 4 percent of 57,000 entry-level job seekers passed its rudimentary employment test (Fuchsberg, 1991). Current workers face three to four career changes in their lifetime, making the need for skill retraining and flexibility critical.

Job Attitudes. Job attitudes are also changing. Increased desire for autonomy, self-development, and balance between work and family life is surfacing among many workers (Hall & Richter, 1990). Attracting and keeping employees with these desires will force organizations to consider new programs for worker involvement and motivation, as well as options such as flextime, job sharing, and work at home to allow workers to coordinate the work and nonwork aspects of their lives.

Many organizations are already very concerned about these projected workforce changes, and some have instituted programs to deal with them. In 1990, Towers Perrin reported data from 645 organizations across the United States designed to represent a cross section of both industry and location. Of their respondents, the majority are concerned about the increasing diversity in their workforce, the needs of women employees, and future labor shortages. Currently, 70 percent report difficulty in recruiting technical personnel, 63 percent in hiring professionals, and 55 percent in finding secretarial and clerical staff. Table 12.1 summarizes some of the key findings about employer concerns as well as actions being taken. It can be seen that the level of action is not keeping up with the level of concern expressed.

Changing Organizations

Just as the people composing the workforce are changing, so too are organizations. Among the more dramatic changes we have noted (Offermann & Gowing, 1990) are (1) changes in organizational size and structure, (2) a shift to a service economy, (3) globalization, (4) increasing importance of work teams, and (5) increasing technology.

Changing Size and Structure. Companies are failing at a substantial rate; many of those surviving are reducing the size of their workforce. It is ironic that well-educated white male workers are being laid off in record numbers at a time when organizations are forecasting their shortage in future supply (Fuchsberg, 1991). Companies are restructuring along flatter, leaner lines, with fewer layers of management and fewer people at upper levels. This is occurring at the same time that large numbers of baby boomers are ready to take their places in those positions. Mergers, acquisitions, and buy-outs are creating new corporate cultures virtually overnight, with great attendant stress.

The Service Economy. The focus of today's organizations has shifted from manufacturing to service. The service sector

Table 12.1. Employer Responses to Demographic Changes.

What they are concerned about	Percentage
Managing diversity	74
Needs of women	68
Labor shortage	65
Skills gap	42
Aging workforce	40

What they are current doing

Managing diversity

Formal harassment policy	81
Supervisory training for women	57
Minority recruiting programs	42
Manager diversity training	29
Specific hiring for women	15
Supervisory training for minorities	12
Minority support groups	11
Immigration assistance	11
Mentor programs—minorities	10
English as a second language	9
Mentor programs—women	8
Women's support groups	8

Work/family issues

Flexible spending accounts	36
Extended maternity leave	32
Sick days for kids	31
Child-care information	27
Paternity leave	20
Gradual return to work	13
On-site day care	8
Sick child care	6

Source: Data compiled from Towers Perrin, 1990.

continues to grow, unaccompanied by comparable gains in productivity. Future concerns about national productivity will inevitably emphasize performance in the service sector. The challenge for employers is to identify those factors contributing to top-quality service, including human, material, and technological resources.

Globalization. The increasing globalization of U.S. businesses is forcing a new consideration of the skills needed for successful performance. The sun now sets on the British Empire, but, as Brown points out, not on IBM, Hitachi, or Volkswagen (Toffler, 1980, p. 320). Becoming truly global means not only understanding one's foreign clients and suppliers, but managing the diverse elements within the company as well. As more companies become global, "what once was 'nice to understand' becomes imperative for survival, let alone success" (Adler, 1991, p. 121).

Work Teams. There is considerable agreement that team structures will play an increasingly key role in organizations in the future (for example, Tuttle, 1988). Some have gone so far as to advocate that all functions be organized into largely self-managing teams (Peters, 1988). As such work teams gain in popularity, new employee skills in performing as a member of a group will be required. Can the demand for selection systems to predict this performance be far behind?

Increasing Technology. Increasing use of technology theoretically allows organizations to maximize performance through the optimal combination of human and automated capabilities. Practically, however, increased technology may require an increasingly skilled workforce to utilize it effectively. It is feared that technology is expanding the skills gap faster than organizations can find ways to span it. Further, although ideally technology should be used in place of workers whom the organization cannot find, in practice advanced technologies currently are replacing those employees available in greatest numbers (Greller, 1990).

Construct Issues

The changes in the nature of workers and their work detailed above suggest the need to reexamine some of the core constructs used in personnel selection. New methods of job and organizational analysis need to be considered, as well as expanded predictor measures of individual capabilities that go beyond the assessment of knowledge, skills, and abilities to include motivation, attitudes, and values. Criterion measures will also require expansion to broader organizational concerns about commitment, retention, teamwork, and quality service.

What Are We Selecting For?

This new organizational complexity demands new selection methodologies, including revised procedures for occupational analysis to determine present and future work requirements. Molecular job analytic methods are too narrow in their focus, even those designed as multipurpose procedures to provide job data for all human resource (HR) management systems (Bemis, Belenky, & Soder, 1983; Schmidt, Hunter, & Pearlman, 1981).

Occupational Analyses. Job analytic procedures must be undertaken, but at a higher level of abstraction, such as analyses of occupations or occupational groups. Researchers must use these procedures to search for underlying commonalities in the work and for the personal dimensions or constructs contributing to effective performance across occupations. Such procedures will enable organizations to maximize the use of their human resources through skills transferability. Skills transferability helps organizations to adapt to changing environmental conditions and to retrain their employees as necessary to fill openings when they encounter labor shortages. Several studies have successfully identified such generalized work and worker characteristics for use in defining occupational families (O'Leary, Rheinstein, & McCauley, 1989, 1990; Outerbridge, 1981; Pearlman, 1980).

Organizational Analysis. It is not sufficient for occupational analysis systems to identify generalized work requirements. They must also capture the situational or organizational factors within which the work is carried out. Examples of organizational factors include the nature of the organization's leadership or the support from top management (for example, for the development of quality cultures or environments), the degree of strategic planning conducted by management, the focus on the customer and customer satisfaction, the opportunity for employee training and recognition, the type of information systems and measurement procedures available, the type of quality assurance program, and the emphasis on quality and productivity improvement. These situational factors underlie both the Malcolm Baldrige National Quality Award and its public-sector counterpart, the President's Award for Quality and Productivity Improvement. Recent winners have included Motorola, Federal Express, and the U.S. Air Force (Logistics). There is increasing recognition that many of these factors shape corporate culture and that corporate culture dramatically influences immediate and long-term profitability of organizations (Petrock, 1990).

Future selection procedures will need to identify those persons who can function effectively in such total-quality environments, by using such criteria as pride in one's work, a value for quality, and a commitment to the pursuit of excellence. Selection procedures designed to assess need for achievement and need for self-actualization may have relevance here, and new measures will need to be developed.

Outcome Assessment. Similarly, the occupational analysis systems of the future must describe individual, team, and organizational outcomes. These outcomes include products and services delivered and indices of productivity, defined as the efficiency of transformation of inputs into outputs (Mahoney, 1988). B. F. Skinner argued forcefully for behavior analysis of individual outcome measures to identify the reinforcement contingencies that would make it possible "to design better environments—personal environments that would solve existing problems and larger environments or cultures in which there would be fewer problems" (1990, p. 1210). However, as Guzzo (1988) points out, individual output is but one component of productivity. Only by analyzing the entire organizational environment (the situational or process factors) and all outputs (outcome variables) will accurate predictions be made regarding the individual attributes required for effective functioning within organizations.

Some new methodologies have already been conceptualized and implemented to capture such occupational information, including MOSAIC (Multipurpose Occupational Systems Analysis Inventory—Closed-End; see U.S. Office of Personnel Management, 1991) and the Air Force's CODAP ASCII. The Department of Labor has appointed an advisory panel for the *Dictionary of Occupational Titles (DOT)* to advise on the appropriateness of such methodologies of occupational analysis for identifying, classifying, defining, and describing jobs in the *DOT*.

Whole-Person Measurement

Numerous reviews (for example, Corts & Gowing, 1992; Fleishman & Quaintance, 1984; Hough, Eaton, Dunnette, Kamp, & McCloy, 1990; Mumford, Fleishman, Levin, Korotkin, & Hein, 1988; Northrop, 1989) suggest that many individual attributes contribute to effective individual performance at the professional, supervisory, managerial, and executive levels. What is needed is emphasis on "whole-person" measurement, whereby motivation, attitudes, values, and interests as well as knowledge, skills, and abilities are assessed. Such evaluation of the whole person can maximize prediction of performance.

For example, in 1990, the U.S. Department of Labor appointed the Secretary's Commission on Achieving Necessary Skills (SCANS) to develop a preliminary list of core proficiencies needed for entry-level work. These include the ability to use resources such as time, money, and staff; interpersonal abilities such as teaching or serving others, working on teams, leading, and working with culturally diverse individuals; the ability to use social, organizational, or technological systems and performance monitoring; and the ability to use technology. Each of these core proficiencies can be viewed as a part of the whole person. Three underlying dimensions to these competencies were also identified: basic skills such as reading, writing, and mathematics; thinking skills such as problem solving and knowing how to learn; and personal qualities such as individual responsibility, self-management, and sociability. These dimensions are another way of viewing whole-person measurement. Future se-

lection systems may be used to develop generic work samples
for occupational groups that assess core proficiencies necessary
for entry-level work or to focus directly on the assessment of
the three foundation skills through objective marker tests.

Administrative Careers with America. A recent example
of an attempt at measurement of the whole person is the new
Administrative Careers with America examination of the U.S.
Office of Personnel Management (OPM). This test battery,
which is used to assess applicants for entry-level administrative
and professional occupations in the federal government, consists of an ability test and a structured biodata questionnaire.
The ability test contains items constructed according to the principle of logic-based measurement (Colberg, Nester, & Trattner, 1985). It is complemented by a biodata instrument, the
Individual Achievement Record (IAR), which is supported by
evidence of both criterion-related validity (Gandy, Outerbridge,
Sharf, & Dye, 1989) and construct validity (Dye, 1990). Preliminary results suggest the IAR is measuring several constructs,
including cognitive ability, self-esteem, and motivation or willingness to achieve (Dye, 1990).

Building Composite Batteries. Literature reviews on the
criterion-related validity of alternative selection procedures (for
example, Hunter & Hunter, 1984; MacLane, 1988; Reilly &
Chao, 1982; Tenopyr, 1981) are useful in identifying possible instruments to augment the validity of composite batteries, as are
studies of validity generalization (Pearlman, Schmidt, & Hunter,
1980; Rothstein, Schmidt, Erwin, Owens, & Sparks, 1990). Similarly, research investigations focusing on the construct validity
of such alternatives are also useful (for example, Reilly, Henry,
& Smither, 1990; Shore, Thornton, & Shore, 1990).

Changing Definitions of Success

Just as definitions of individual attributes are expanding
to include new dimensions for selection batteries, so too are definitions of criteria evolving. The measurement focus is shifting from consideration of individual criterion measures to variables including team and organizational performance.

Individual Outcomes

Traditionally, industrial and organizational psychologists have sought criterion measures that included measures of the quality of individual behavior, such as performance appraisal ratings. Although criterion measures have traditionally focused on job performance, the need to maintain competitiveness and service quality may increase the use of other types of criterion measures, such as commitment and organizational citizenship behaviors. Research will be needed to identify and validate such measures. Projected shortages in the workforce have also brought renewed attention to retention and turnover as key outcome vari-- ables. If organizations are going to make large investments in their human resources, then they will expect those personnel to stay for a reasonable period of time to maximize their return on investment.

Individual outcome measures of the future will undoubtedly include composite measures of the quality of individual performance on multiple dimensions as well as measures of individual retention. For example, the OPM is currently experimenting with the development of biographical data profiles to select those individuals who will both perform effectively and stay on the job for several years. These profiles are designed for government occupations with traditionally high turnover rates.

Team Outcomes

Organizations are increasingly relying on teams of workers to perform complex work assignments. The restructuring of work into team assignments mandates new evaluation criteria that accurately reflect the group's contribution to meeting organizational objectives and to enhancing organizational productivity. Although research findings indicate that self-managing teams can positively affect productivity, the magnitude of the effect is not well known owing to the scarcity of well-designed evaluations (Goodman, Devadas, & Hughson, 1988).

As noted earlier, the projected popularity of work teams in the future will also require the development of more sophisticated measurement methods to select individuals capable of performing effectively in team environments. Traditional methods of individual performance prediction must be expanded to include skills such as supporting and building on the work of others, getting along with others, and managing conflict. Future selection procedures can replicate work team settings. Simulations similar to leaderless group discussion exercises found in assessment centers can easily be adapted to evaluate potential effectiveness in team environments. As an alternative, biographical questionnaire items designed to assess past success in team activities in school, volunteer work, or prior jobs may well be found to be predictive of team effectiveness in future work situations.

Organizational Outcomes

Traditionally, organizations have viewed financial figures as the foundation for measuring organizational performance (Eccles, 1991). Although other measures, such as quality, market share, and other nonfinancial measures, have been tracked for years, they have only recently been given equal (or even greater) status in determining strategy, promotions, bonuses, and other rewards. Recently, in some companies earnings per share have been placed last on the list when evaluating organizational performance, being preceded by customer satisfaction, cash flow, manufacturing effectiveness, and innovation.

The total quality management (TQM) revolution has certainly contributed to this phenomenon. The *Federal Total Quality Management Handbook* defines quality as "meeting customer's requirements, needs, and expectations, the first time and every time" (Federal Quality Institute, 1990, p. 2). In the last ten years, TQM has caught on very fast in both the public and private sectors. Inspired by the work of Deming and others, TQM has caused measures of productivity improvement, cost reduction, and performance management to be deemphasized in favor of a new commitment to work quality (Hyde, 1990).

We project that future organizational outcome measures will use composites to reflect multiple interests. The composites will include measures of (1) bottom-line productivity, (2) success in meeting customer expectations under a TQM system, and (3) organizational processes (such as strategic planning and employee empowerment) that result in products or the delivery of services.

Implications for Recruitment

Elizabeth Dole, former secretary of the U.S. Department of Labor, has predicted that organizations of the future will "need to utilize all possible workers to make up for the shrinking labor pool of the 1990s" (Dole, 1990, p. 17). Although traditional selection practices have focused on the organization (who should we choose from the wide array of available candidates?), those practices are now becoming more focused on the individual (how can we get those we want to accept our offers?). This change in focus places increasing emphasis on good recruitment practices.

Attracting Applicants

Now that employers have been placed in a competitive position for talent, increased attention is being given to examining what will attract members of the future workforce. According to surveys by the University of California, Los Angeles, and the American Council on Education, the percentage of college freshmen who said that it is "important to be well-off financially" rose from 41 percent in 1966 to 76 percent in 1987 (National Commission on the Public Service, 1989). At the same time, average starting salaries are increasing in both the private and the public sectors. The National Commission on the Public Service reported that the average starting salary for careers in private-sector consulting and research rose 15 percent in real terms over the past decade, while pay for careers in banking, finance, and insurance increased 18 percent. Although the future workforce values pay to attain an acceptable standard of living, many future employees also value altruism. The number of college freshmen who see helping others as an essential or very important objective in life has remained steady at almost 60 percent over the past twenty years (National Commission on the Public Service, 1989). Organizations have recognized the need to publicize career opportunities satisfying such values.

Introducing Flexible Human Resource Management Programs. Organizations are also initiating a variety of HR management programs to attract and retain a quality workforce. Some companies are taking steps to accommodate the needs of dual-career couples, especially when both individuals have strong identification with their chosen professions (Quaintance, 1989). Two working partners may have problems arranging both work and family obligations. Such couples affect the organization's ability to move people geographically and often require dual-career management (Schein, 1981).

The increasing number of women in the workforce has led some companies to take a critical look at their family-directed policies. In analyzing the work patterns of nine thousand women, the Census Bureau found that 71 percent of the women with maternity benefits returned to work within six months of childbirth, compared with 43 percent of those without benefits (De-Loux, 1990). General Dynamics has implemented a part-time program for mothers returning from maternity leave, has made unpaid leave available before and after delivery, and is currently addressing the issue of child care (DeLoux, 1990). Apple Computer pays women two-thirds of their full pay during maternity leave, with the remainder made up through accrued sick leave. Apple also gives a $500 bonus to any employee who has a baby or adopts a child, allows unpaid personal leave of up to six months, and provides on-site child care and a resource referral network to help employees find child-care providers. Apple's turnover rate of 5 percent is very low for high-technology companies (DeLoux, 1990), and this may reflect the company's innovative programs.

The care of preschool children of working parents is likely to remain a major issue for the coming decades. Abraham and Bowdidge (1990) note that the issue has similarities to other "revolutions," such as civil rights, occupational safety, and age discrimination, which have since been legislated into public policy. Until legislation is enacted, employers who are voluntarily progressive in establishing policies in this area may well find themselves in a more competitive position for attracting the 56 percent of married couples composed of two working parents.

Numerous organizations are experimenting with programs such as job sharing, alternative work schedules, and flexiplace or telecommuting, in which employees are allowed to work at least part of their workweek at their own homes. LINK Resources Corporation has collected survey data from twenty-five hundred randomly selected households that suggest that a total of 32.8 million Americans currently work at home, compared with 26.8 million a year ago (U.S. Office of Personnel Management, 1990). Companies with telecommuting efforts in the private sector include Pacific Bell, J. C. Penney, Digital Equipment Corporation, Du Pont, Traveler's Insurance, Control Data, IBM, Johnson & Johnson, Blue Cross/Blue Shield, and American Express (Joice, 1989). Public-sector flexiplace initiatives have been undertaken by the states of Washington, Florida, California, and Arizona.

Professionalizing Recruiters. Renewed emphasis has been placed on the importance of recruiters and interviewers, who serve as the organization's representatives to those in the labor force. We are seeing increased attention and resources dedicated to recruitment efforts (Ingraham, 1990) as well as to enhancing the quality of preemployment interactions with potential employees (Byham, 1990). Recruiters need to become more sensitive to diversity issues in order to attract needed talent to their organizations.

Expanding Traditional and Nontraditional Sources of Recruitment

Some organizations already are facing staff shortages for entry-level positions, with projections indicating more hiring difficulty to come. As a result, organizations have been forced to develop new mechanisms for securing needed staff while reaching out to underrepresented groups. The result has been creative interfaces with the country's educational system at several levels as well as reconsideration of recruiting efforts directed at segments of the population previously hired in more limited numbers.

Partnerships with Colleges and Universities. Projections of increasing numbers of minorities in the future workforce have led employers to seek new partnerships with colleges and universities having large minority populations. For example, the OPM announced Project Partnership, a memorandum of understanding with the presidents of the Hispanic Association of Colleges and Universities (HACU) and National IMAGE, Inc. The intent of the project is for the combined resources of HACU, IMAGE, and OPM to work with federal agencies to promote the additional use of federal student employment programs as an avenue to increase representation of Hispanics in the federal workforce. Similarly, in 1991 OPM hosted a meeting between federal agencies and the nation's historically black colleges and universities. The meeting established avenues for continuing partnerships to bring the best and brightest students from outstanding black institutions of learning into government service. Private-sector organizations are likewise pursuing relationships with traditionally minority colleges and universities.

Partnerships with Junior and Senior High Schools. In light of the predicted "skills gap" and the lack of a structured transition from school to the workplace, there have been many partnerships between businesses and schools operating for years at both the junior high and high school levels. American Express led the way with its Academy of Finance, offering a special two-year curriculum for public high school juniors and seniors, on-the-job internships with businesses in the summer, and training for public high school teachers to instruct the academy courses. In 1990, the first Academy of Public Service was begun in Washington, D.C., under the sponsorship of the National Academy Foundation.

Many other such partnerships are under way throughout the country. These are documented by the National Association of Partners in Education, a nonprofit association sponsoring symposia, conferences, and training academies throughout the country. Among the partnerships under way are adopt-a-school programs by 3M, Citibank, and the Travelers Corporation. Such programs vary dramatically. The 3M program encourages young women to pursue careers in the fields of science and engineering. The Citibank branches each adopted a school and created a fund to award cash grants to local educators who devise ways to cut Miami's dropout rate ("Adopt a School," 1990).

Recruiting People with Disabilities. Shortages in the labor pool are leading employers to be more creative in tapping nontraditional recruitment sources. The recent passage of the Americans with Disabilities Act (ADA) is encouraging employers to reevaluate their hiring practices and to seek qualified workers with disabilities. For example, Kreonite, Inc., a small business based in Kansas that manufactures photographic and graphic arts film, reported that its annual turnover rate was reduced from 32 percent to 10–12 percent after increasing the number of employees with disabilities (Martinez, 1990). These employees are totally integrated into the workforce, holding positions such as machine operator, electronics assembler, and fiberglass trimmer. Recruiting resources for these workers include municipal and state rehabilitation services, Gallaudet University, the Epilepsy Foundation, the Bridges Program funded by Marriott, and the Lighthouse for the Blind. Employer resources to accommodate their workplace to those with disabilities are available from the President's Committee on Employment of People with Disabilities.

Future assessment procedures for persons with disabilities are likely to be power, rather than speeded, tests to ensure the measurement of the individual's full capacity. Depending on the disability, some modifications may have to be made in the media used to assess a given applicant. As with many nontraditional groups, the overall focus needs to be on what individuals *can* do rather than cannot, and matching their abilities with job requirements identified through careful job analysis.

Recruiting Older Workers. With an aging population, some employers are turning to those who have retired to fill their workforce needs. The American Association of Retired Persons offers a job counseling service to its members attempting to match their skills with organizational job requirements. Assessment practices appropriate for selecting older workers have been well documented by Hunt and Lindley (1989), and again include the avoidance of speeded tests as well as sensitivity to declines in visual and auditory skills necessary for effective test performance but unnecessary for job performance. Oddly enough, according to the Towers Perrin (1990) survey, only 40 percent of companies expressed concern about aging workers, with 30 percent of companies using retirees on special projects or as consultants. Few companies (3 percent) had gradual retirement programs or retrained older workers. Despite increasing health and longevity, the current trend toward early retirement shows no sign of abating. Given future projections, it is surprising that organizations have not shown more concern about keeping workers on the job longer. A valuable human resource seems to be going untapped.

Although societal pressures and civil rights legislation have attempted to create a workforce representative of the nation's diversity at every level of the organization, this goal has not been fully achieved. The shifting demographics will help ensure that those who have been denied fair and open competition for employment opportunities in the past will now be actively sought after by organizations in the public and private sectors. Research is needed to determine effective recruiting strategies for diverse groups. At present, favorable ratings as an employer of minorities or women as published by popular magazines are touted by Xerox and Hewlett-Packard to prospective applicants from those groups (Dreyfuss, 1990). It may be that the best future recruiting strategy is a reputation for fair, unbiased personnel practices. To accomplish this, effective human resource systems will undoubtedly consider some or all of the selection options discussed below.

Further Implications for Selection

The changes to recruitment just described present additional challenges for selection procedures. Good recruitment practices are designed to generate a sizable pool of talent from which the organization can make judicious selections. However, the size of the talent pool is already shrinking for many occupations. As fewer new workers enter into the workforce, higher selection ratios for many positions have resulted, with still higher selection ratios likely to exist in years to come. And as selection ratios rise, the utility of traditional selection testing may decrease. For many companies already facing personnel shortages, the idea of selection already seems a fond memory. For them, the traditional selection focus on exclusion has already changed to a recruitment, placement, and retention model.

Broadening Selection. Despite these changes, selection is hardly a dying field. In fact, as organizations downsize and select fewer applicants, each new selection will have greater potential impact on productive potential (Greller & Nee, 1989). Rather, the field of personnel selection needs to be broadened to emphasize the assessment of individual talents and abilities in relation to organizational needs. We believe that the traditional focus on exclusion on the basis of talents lacked will change to a focus on inclusion on the basis of talents possessed or that could be developed. Testing may be used less as a screen than as a diagnostic for placement and development. The notion of whole-person measurement already discussed is an example of attempts to more completely profile individuals with an eye toward matching individual profiles with occupational responsibilities. Given the rampant changes in organizational needs over time, selection becomes the initial point of measurement in a comprehensive system of evaluation that could be updated regularly to continue matching future jobs with the developing profiles of incumbent workers. General Foods' Professional Development Program (Courtney, 1986) is an example of a successful application of a system that continually updates both employee qualifications and job-performance standards.

Selecting Generalists. The likelihood of organizational change and the need for periodic retraining over the course of a career may increase the demand to hire generalists rather than specialists in order to maximize adaptability. Organizations such as AT&T have already found liberal arts graduates to be as successful or more so in general management positions as business graduates in terms of performance and promotions (Howard, 1986). The capacity to learn, rather than the skills possessed, may become more critical as a selection target under conditions of great change. The projected lack of necessary applicant skills makes this trainability a doubly important selection criterion. In addition, testing for generic skills such as reading, writing, and mathematics will also continue to increase. The demand for team functioning by diverse individuals may increase testing for basic communication skills such as the ability to interact successfully with people of different backgrounds and origins.

Computer-Adaptive Testing. Another possible option to deal with increasingly diverse applicants is the use of computer-adaptive testing. Such individually tailored testing has been shown to have equal or better reliability than conventional tests while providing more accurate estimates of the ability levels of those of high or low ability (Anastasi, 1988). Given the projected differences in worker ability levels and the projected number of low-skilled applicants, these techniques may prove particularly useful. It is also possible that some groups may be differentially sensitive to test length and exposure to many items beyond their ability level. If so, the capability of adaptive tests to estimate ability levels with 50 percent fewer items and with more positive examinee responses (Green, 1991) by routing questions by ability level may limit such sensitivity problems. Some of these tests will increasingly be at the level of basic literacy assessment.

Compensatory and Provisional Selection. Another approach to deal with the projected lack of adequately skilled applicants is the greater use of compensatory models of selection (Steinhaus & Morris, 1990). Such models would need to identify strengths in some areas of performance that offset weaknesses in other areas. Compensatory selection systems may also help to minimize adverse impact and improve prediction (see Chapter Six). Provisional selection may also be used more extensively, where individuals are selected despite some deficit provided they reach minimum training requirements within a given amount of time.

Sensitivity to Diversity. Specific selection techniques will need to be far more sensitive to the increasing diversity of the new workforce. The potential for differential performance may increase along with the diversity of job applicants and needs to be carefully considered. In addition to traditional concerns about the performance of different groups on predictive tests, recent work is addressing the issue of test bias and fairness from the level of the test item. Differential item functioning (DIF) occurs when a test question itself produces group differences rather than reflecting real differences between groups of similar ability taking the test. Early results from research examining federal tests indicate that although few items show potential bias, placement of the item within the test and certain item characteristics such as abstractness or the amount of verbal information may affect the amount of DIF found (Harris, 1989). Because DIF analyses take into account differences in applicant ability, they may prove even more appropriate than traditional assessments of adverse impact in the future. Far more research will be needed to understand group differences in individual item performance.

More work also needs to be done addressing different subgroup characteristics that may affect performance on the predictors used for selection. Some selection techniques may be considered inappropriate or offensive by some groups, thereby driving away potential applicants. In other cases, the process of test-taking itself is unfamiliar to some groups, such as the elderly, for whom test formats and directions may need restructuring. Some cultures consider it unseemly to discuss one's accomplishments, and thus may behave more modestly in interview situations. These possibilities present opportunities for increased error of measurement with diverse applicants, error that could be controlled by greater information about the effects of selection techniques themselves on different subgroups.

What most of these options in selection methodologies have in common is an increasing focus on the individual applicant in selection as opposed to traditional group-oriented strategies. It has long been argued that individual profiles on a variety of measures are most critical when labor is scarce (Dunnette, 1966). As more organizations find themselves in situations of diverse applicants and scarce labor supply, we should not be surprised to see targeted selection strategies increase.

Implications for Promotion

Changes in workers and their organizations warrant reconsideration not only of the job entry process but also of the way individuals are treated once they have joined the organization. Although progress has been made in getting members of traditionally underrepresented groups into organizations, there is growing concern about their prospects for advancement. Indeed, future opportunities for advancement are likely to be more limited for everyone. While one person in twenty was promoted to a top management position in 1987, that ratio is expected to be one in fifty by the year 2001 (Arnett, 1989). What will be required is a reexamination of career paths and motivating opportunities other than vertical advancement, as well as HR systems that fairly promote individuals of diverse backgrounds.

Career Ladders/Lattices

Traditionally, employees have spent their careers aspiring for vertical progression up the career ladders in their occupations. More recently, organizations have begun to use the term *career lattice* to suggest a variety of paths for individual development across occupations and organizations. Career lattices will become increasingly frequent as organizations streamline their managerial positions, leaving fewer top career opportunities, and struggle to find ways to deal with career plateaus. Ingraham (1990) noted that those organizations offering such diversity of experience to young workers and others who are undecided about long-term career objectives will be more competitive in their recruitment efforts.

The idea of a career lattice allows for lateral career moves. Several organizations, such as IBM, Hartford Insurance Group, Atlantic Richfield, and the Sheraton Hotel chain, have set up separate equivalent career ladders for high-technology nonmanagement employees so that grade levels, pay ranges, recognition, and rewards for these people correspond with positions in the management hierarchy (Goddard, 1990). These positions promote technical and professional excellence. Lombardo and Eichinger (1989) present eighty-eight different assignments that can be used for "development in place," that is, increasing the challenge of one's existing job without promotion.

One of the key provisions of the career lattice is the need for skills transferability. The occupational analysis methodology used to establish the career lattice requires gathering information on the level of difficulty of various knowledge, skills, abilities, and other individual attributes required to perform the occupational responsibilities. In some companies, these skills transferability linkages are made by using the organization's point factor job evaluation system (Wellback, Hall, Morgan, & Hamner, 1983). Quaintance (1989) reported that prior to a job transfer in Sears the new position is compared to the individual's current position. The transfer is made if the new position requires at least one additional skill area for effective performance, a 10 percent increase in work demands as evidenced by the total number of job evaluation points, and some assignments in different functional areas.

The advisory panel on the *Dictionary of Occupational Titles* is attempting to use an occupational analysis methodology to study all occupations in the U.S. economy and to address their commonality in terms of skills transferability. Once completed, it will provide an invaluable data base to assist organizations wishing to develop career lattices for their employees.

Advancing Women and Minorities

Advancement and retention of women and minorities is still a problem in many organizations. Although the percentage of minority and women managers has grown, most are still in positions with little authority and relatively low pay (Morrison & Von Glinow, 1990). Organizations maximizing their ability to promote as well as attract and retain diverse individuals will have a competitive advantage in the future. Companies that have already been actively recruiting minorities and women have often been discouraged to find that those hired have not progressed as far in the organization as was hoped. For example, Corning and Digital Equipment both found it easier to attract women and minorities than to keep them (Dreyfuss, 1990). According to Thomas (1990), many companies faced with this pattern blamed selection strategies for failing to bring in the "right" people and proceeded to try again — still searching for women and minorities to bring into the pipeline, only to fail once more. What they fail to realize is that affirmative action alone is not enough to achieve management diversity at all levels. The goal can no longer be assimilation, but management and affirmation of unassimilated diversity.

Persons brought to the organization by competent selection must be provided with environments allowing diverse individuals to thrive. According to Thomas (1990), "So long as racial and gender equality is something we grant to minorities and women, there will be no racial and gender equality. What we must do is create an environment where no one is advantaged or disadvantaged, an environment where 'we' is everyone" (p. 109). Thomas (1990) likens the situation to a car engine designed to run on regular fuel: changing to a mixed fuel does not just require pumping the new gas in, but requires basic changes to the engine itself to allow it to run effectively on the new fuel. Organizations have tried — and often failed — to assimilate different types of people by hiring without changing the basic assumptions and behaviors driving the organization. Small wonder that many persons with different backgrounds found such organizations to be inhospitable places in which to build their career. Future selection practices may play a role in creating more agreeable environments by identifying applicants who, in addition to other credentials, score high on measures of interpersonal sensitivity or who have successfully worked in diverse environments in previous jobs.

Identifying Leaders Who Can Manage Diversity

Successful management of a diverse workforce is now a key issue for organizations. Research suggests that increasing differences in supervisor-subordinate demographics in terms of age, gender, race, education, and job and company tenure are associated with lower supervisor perceptions of subordinate effectiveness, less liking for the subordinate, and greater subordinate role ambiguity (Tsui & O'Reilly, 1989). If diverse employees are to have equal chances of success on the job, the first line of needed action is with supervisors and managers. Although no one expects to eliminate lifelong attitudes over the course of a few days' training, current managers are being sent for training in managing diversity in large numbers as a way of developing awareness. For example, Wang Laboratories has sent more than one thousand managers through their diversity-training program (Braham, 1989), and Mobil has been using such programs since 1986 (Kleeb, 1989). The Towers Perrin (1990) survey reports that about 29 percent of companies are currently doing something to train managers to deal with diversity.

Although typically lacking in clear evaluation data indicating objective measures of program success, the experiences of some companies (for example, Digital Equipment) that have increased retention of minorities since program implementation are encouraging. The number of initiatives being undertaken is enormous, and organizations go about it quite differently and for different reasons. The second Society for Industrial and Organizational Psychology Practice Series book presents in-depth case analyses of different organizational experiences with managing diversity (Jackson, 1992). These cases demonstrate that the strategies proposed to manage diversity are as diverse as the workforce itself.

Future challenges for managerial selection and promotion will include the identification of individuals capable of working with diverse individuals rather than solely training existing managers. As with the selection of workers at all levels, skills and abilities related to interpersonal sensitivity, cultural awareness, and acceptance of differences may take on new prominence. Further research in selection is critically needed, first to identify the requisite skills for working with diversity and then to develop appropriate selection strategies to assess it. Given the present and projected demographic changes, such research should be a high priority in personnel selection.

Conclusion

The changes in workers and work itself pose numerous challenges for organizations. Some organizations are already facing staffing shortages and are devising new solutions to their selection problems. Other organizations have chosen not to respond to the changes predicted, perhaps in the hope of riding out the current trends until conditions similar to those of the past are restored. Those organizations should recognize that in terms of demographics, it was the baby boom that was the anomaly (Greller, 1990). The present so-called bust is actually a reestablishment of more typical birth patterns. A return to past conditions of wide choices within a limited demographic group is considered very unlikely. The organizations that make changes now will be the ones that will have the resilience to accommodate workers of many backgrounds, use their diverse talents, and make themselves strong market forces.

As the costs of recruitment and selection escalate, retaining trained employees becomes ever more critical. As selection prospects are found lacking in basic skills, placement models combined with organizational training will gain in prominence. The increased importance of training and retraining does not substitute for good selection, but rather supplements it. The best HR management systems will integrate the traditional personnel functions of recruitment, selection, placement, and training into a coordinated total effort. It will not be enough to select people for the skills they currently possess, but rather for their potential to learn and adapt through training as conditions change. It will not be enough to recruit and select diverse individuals, but rather consideration must be given to changing organizational culture, procedures, and practices to use effectively the skills provided by this diversity. This indicates a need for training not only for those entering the organization but also for present employees.

The trends described in this chapter indicate that those of us working with organizations on selection issues will see many changes in the years ahead. Although the projections described in this chapter provide a reasonable future scenario, changes in economic, social, and organizational conditions can all affect the future reality. Changes made by organizations today can have tremendous impact on the choices made by current and potential workers. In keeping with the change in the U.S. economy from products to services, Bowen and Greiner (1986) suggest that it is we ourselves who need a change from the traditional selection "product orientation" of stamping persons as qualified or unqualified to a greater "service orientation" whereby we provide individuals matched to different client needs. That service orientation should continue once individuals are selected and placed to permit them an environment in which they can thrive and contribute. Only then will we have achieved the dual objectives of fully using the nation's diverse human resources and improving organizational performance.

References

Abraham, Y. T., & Bowdidge, J. S. (1990). Work-place child care act: A prototypical portrayal of potential public policies. *Public Personnel Management, 19,* 411–418.

Adler, N. J. (1991). *International dimensions of organizational behavior* (2nd ed.). Boston: PWS-Kent.

Adopt a school. (1990, September). *The Atlantic,* p. 23.

Anastasi, A. (1988). *Psychological testing* (6th ed.). New York: Macmillan.

Arnett, E. C. (1989, July 20). Futurists gaze into business's crystal ball. *Washington Post,* pp. F1–F2.

Bemis, S. E., Belenky, A. H., & Soder, D. A. (1983). *Job analysis: An effective management tool.* Washington, DC: Bureau of National Affairs.

Bowen, D. E., & Greiner, L. E. (1986). Moving from production to service in human resources management. *Organizational Dynamics, 15,* 34–53.

Braham, J. (1989). No, you don't manage everyone the same. *Industry Week, 238,* 28–35.

Byham, W. C. (1990). Keep job candidates from becoming lost hires. *HR Magazine, 35*(12), 52–54.

Colberg, M., Nester, M. A., & Trattner, M. H. (1985). Convergence of the inductive and deductive models in the measurement of reasoning abilities. *Journal of Applied Psychology, 70,* 681–694.

Corts, D. B., & Gowing, M. K. (1992). *Dimensions of effective behavior: Executives, managers, and supervisors* (PRD-92-05). Washington, DC: U.S. Office of Personnel Management.

Courtney, R. S. (1986). A human resources program that helps management and employees prepare for the future. *Personnel, 65,* 32–40.

DeLoux, G. (1990). Is your maternity policy ready for the 90's? *HR Magazine, 35*(11), 61–62.

Dole, E. (1990). Four by four: "Ready, set, work," says labor secretary. *Training & Development Journal, 44,* 17–22.

Dreyfuss, J. (1990). Get ready for the new work force. *Fortune, 121,* 165–181.

Dunnette, M. D. (1966). *Personnel selection and placement.* Belmont, CA: Wadsworth.

Dye, D. A. (1990). An explication of a model for assessing the quality of the federal work force. Washington, DC: U.S. Office of Personnel Management.

Eccles, R. (1991, January–February). The performance measurement manifesto. *Harvard Business Review, 69,* 131–137.

Federal Quality Institute. (1990). *Federal total quality management handbook: How to get started.* Washington, DC: Author.

Fleishman, E. A., & Quaintance, M. K. (1984). *Taxonomies of human performance: The description of human tasks.* San Diego, CA: Academic Press.

Fuchsberg, G. (1991, January 22). Despite layoffs, firms find some jobs hard to fill. *The Wall Street Journal,* pp. B1, B3.

Gandy, J. A., Outerbridge, A. N., Sharf, J. C., & Dye, D. A. (1989). *Development and initial validation of the individual achievement record (IAR).* Washington, DC: U.S. Office of Personnel Management.

Goddard, R. (1990). Lateral moves enhance careers. *HR Magazine, 35*(12), 69–70.

Goodman, P. S., Devadas, R., & Hughson, T.L.G. (1988). Groups and productivity: Analyzing the effectiveness of self-managing teams. In J. P. Campbell, R. J. Campbell, & Associates, *Productivity in organizations: New perspectives from industrial and organizational psychology* (pp. 295–327). San Francisco: Jossey-Bass.

Green, B. F. (1991). Guidelines for computer testing. In T. B. Gutkin & S. L. Wise (Eds.), *The computer and the decisionmaking process*. Hillsdale, NJ: Erlbaum.

Greller, M. M. (1990). The changing work force and organisation effectiveness: An agenda for change. *Journal of Organizational Change Management, 3*, 4–15.

Greller, M. M., & Nee, D. M. (1989). *From baby boom to baby bust: How business can meet the demographic challenge*. Reading, MA: Addison-Wesley.

Guzzo, R. A. (1988). Productivity research: Reviewing psychological and economic perspectives. In J. P. Campbell, R. J. Campbell, & Associates, *Productivity in organizations: New perspectives from industrial and organizational psychology* (pp. 63–81). San Francisco: Jossey-Bass.

Hall, D. T., & Richter, J. (1990). Career gridlock: Baby boomers hit the wall. *Academy of Management Executive, 4*, 7–22.

Harris, P. A. (1989). *A summary report on differential item functioning on a written ability test: An application of the Mantel-Haentzel procedure*. Unpublished manuscript, U.S. Office of Personnel Management, Washington, DC.

Hough, L. M., Eaton, N. K., Dunnette, M. D., Kamp, J. D., & McCloy, R. A. (1990). Criterion-related validities of personality constructs and the effect of response distortion on those validities. *Journal of Applied Psychology, 75*, 581–595.

Howard, A. (1986). College experiences and managerial performance. *Journal of Applied Psychology, 71*, 530–552.

Hunt, T., & Lindley, C. (1989). *Testing older adults: A reference guide to geropsychological assessments*. Austin, TX: Pro Ed.

Hunter, J. E., & Hunter, R. S. (1984). The validity and utility of alternative predictors of job performance. *Psychological Bulletin, 95*, 72–98.

Hyde, A. C. (1990). Quality measurement and TQM. *The Bureaucrat, 19*(4), 16–20.

Ingraham, P. W. (1990). Federal recruitment revisited. *The Bureaucrat, 19*(3), 13–17.

Jackson, S. E. (1992). *Diversity in the workplace: Human resource initiatives.* New York: Guilford Publications.

Joice, W. (1989). Home based employment: A consideration for public personnel management. *Public Personnel Management, 20,* 49–60.

Kleeb, R. (1989). Mobil drills holes through the color barrier. *Business & Society Review, 70,* 55–57.

Lombardo, M. M., & Eichinger, R. W. (1989). *Eighty-eight assignments for development in place: Enhancing the developmental challenge of existing jobs.* Greensboro, NC: Center for Creative Leadership.

MacLane, C. N. (1988, May). *After the PACE: A summary of alternatives research under the Luevano consent decree* (OED Report No. 88-16). Washington, DC: U.S. Office of Personnel Management.

Mahoney, T. A. (1988). Productivity defined: The relativity of efficiency, effectiveness, and change. In J. P. Campbell, R. J. Campbell, & Associates, *Productivity in organizations: New perspectives from industrial and organizational psychology.* (pp. 13–39). San Francisco: Jossey-Bass.

Martinez, M. (1990). Creative ways to employ people with disabilities. *HR Magazine, 35*(11), 40–44, 101.

McEvoy, G. M., & Cascio, W. F. (1989). Cumulative evidence of the relationship between employee age and job performance. *Journal of Applied Psychology, 74,* 11–17.

Morrison, A. M., & Von Glinow, M. A. (1990). Women and minorities in management. *American Psychologist, 45,* 200–208.

Mumford, M. D., Fleishman, E. A., Levin, K. Y., Korotkin, A., & Hein, M. B. (1988). *Taxonomic efforts in the description of leadership behavior: A synthesis and cognitive interpretation.* Unpublished manuscript, George Mason University, Fairfax, VA.

National Commission of the Public Service. (1989). Leadership for America: Rebuilding the public service. Washington, DC: Author.

Northrop, L. C. (1989). *The psychometric history of selected ability constructs.* Washington, DC: U.S. Office of Personnel Management.

Offermann, L. R., & Gowing, M. K. (1990). Organizations of the future: Changes and challenges. *American Psychologist, 45,* 95–108.

O'Leary, B. S., Rheinstein, J., & McCauley, D. E., Jr. (1989, November). *Developing a taxonomy of generalized work behaviors.* Paper presented at the annual conference of the Military Testing Association, San Antonio, TX.

O'Leary, B. S., Rheinstein, J., & McCauley, D. E., Jr. (1990, November). *Developing job families using generalized work behaviors.* Paper presented at the annual conference of the Military Testing Association, Orange Beach, AL.

Outerbridge, A. N. (1981). *The development of generalizable work behavior categories for a synthetic validity model* (Report No. PRR-81-1). Washington, DC: U.S. Office of Personnel Management.

Pearlman, K. (1980). Job families: A review and discussion of their implications for personnel selection. *Psychological Bulletin, 87,* 1–27.

Pearlman, K., Schmidt, F. L., & Hunter, J. E. (1980). Validity generalization results for tests used to predict job proficiency and training success in clerical occupations. *Journal of Applied Psychology, 65,* 373–406.

Peters, T. J. (1988). *Thriving on chaos.* New York: Knopf.

Petrock, F. (1990). Corporate culture enhances profits. *HR Magazine, 35*(11), 64–66.

Quaintance, M. K. (1989). Internal placement and career management. In W. F. Cascio & D. H. Sweet (Eds.), *Human resource planning employment and placement.* Washington, DC: Bureau of National Affairs.

Reich, R. B. (1991). *The work of nations: Preparing ourselves for 21st century capitalism.* New York: Knopf.

Reilly, R. R., & Chao, G. T. (1982). Validity and fairness of some alternative employee selection procedures. *Personnel Psychology, 35,* 1–62.

Reilly, R. R., Henry, S., & Smither, J. W. (1990). An examination of the effects of using behavior checklists on the construct validity of assessment center dimensions. *Personnel Psychology, 43,* 71–84.

Rothstein, H. R., Schmidt, F. L., Erwin, F. W., Owens, W. A., & Sparks, C. P. (1990). Biographical data in employment selection: Can validities be made generalizable? *Journal of Applied Psychology, 75,* 175–184.

Schein, E. H. (1981). Increasing organizational effectiveness through better human resource planning and development. In D. E. Klinger (Ed.), *Public personnel management: Readings in context and strategies.* Palo Alto, CA: Mayfield.

Schmidt, F. L., Hunter, J. E., & Pearlman, K. (1981). Task differences as moderators of aptitude test validity in selection: A red herring. *Journal of Applied Psychology, 66,* 166–185.

Shore, T. H., Thornton, G. C., III, & Shore, L. M. (1990). Construct validity of two categories of assessment center dimension ratings. *Personnel Psychology, 43,* 105–116.

Skinner, B. F. (1990). Can psychology be a science of mind? *American Psychologist, 45,* 1206–1210.

Steinhaus, S. D., & Morris, G. W. (1990). Human resource evaluation for the 1990s and the workforce 2000. *Journal of Organization Change Management, 3,* 80–94.

Tenopyr, M. L. (1981). The realities of employment testing. *American Psychologist, 36,* 1120–1127.

Thomas, R. R., Jr. (1990, March–April). From affirmative action to affirming diversity. *Howard Business Review,* 107–117.

Toffler, A. (1980). The third wave. New York: Morrow.

Towers Perrin. (1990). *Work force 2000: Competing in a seller's market.* New York: Author.

Tsui, A. S., & O'Reilly, C. A., III (1989). Beyond simple demographic effects: The importance of relational demography in superior-subordinate dyads. *Academy of Management Journal, 32,* 402–423.

Tuttle, T. C. (1988). Technology, organizations of the future, and non-management roles. In J. Huge (Ed.), *Futures of organizations* (pp. 163–180). Lexington, MA: Lexington Books.

U.S. Office of Personnel Management. (1990, September). Survey indicates 22% increase in working at home. *Flexiplace Focus, 4.*

U.S. Office of Personnel Management. (1991). A proposal for multipurpose occupational systems analysis inventory— closed-end (MOSAIC). Washington, DC: Author.

Wellback, H. C., Hall, D. T., Morgan, M. A., & Hamner, W. C. (1983). Planning job progression for effective career development and human resources management. In K. M. Rowland, G. R. Ferris, & J. L. Sherman (Eds.), *Current issues in personnel management* (2nd ed.). Needham Heights, MA: Allyn & Bacon.

13

Selection in Small *N* Settings

Paul R. Sackett, Richard D. Arvey

We were initially asked to write a chapter on "Selection in Small Organizations." Implicitly, the focus is on settings in which selection researchers and practitioners face situational constraints which force them into a different mode of thought and action than is reflected in the rest of this book.

As we began working on the chapter, we realized that many of the issues that we were dealing with were driven by the number of incumbents in a job at least as much as by organization size. Thus, we broadened our focus to what we will label "small *N* jobs." We define a small *N* job as one with insufficient incumbents for a traditional criterion-related validity study to be technically feasible. The figure below outlines the types of situations to be covered. While number of incumbents in a job and number of employees in an organization represent continuous variables, both the figure below and subsequent text refer to imprecise dichotomies (for example, small versus large organizations) for ease of discussion.

Thus, what we will call "small *N* settings" range from the single-incumbent job in a small organization to the multiple-incumbent job in a large organization with the number of incumbents just shy of that deemed necessary for a meaningful criterion-related validity study. What all situations in this domain

	Single-incumbent job	Multiple-incumbent job
Small organization		
Large organization		

have in common is that all preclude the classic textbook approach to the validation process. While the inability to conduct a traditional local criterion-related validity study is the defining characteristic of this domain, other aspects of the selection system development and evaluation process also are unfeasible in these situations. Traditional fairness analyses, involving the examination of slope and intercept differences by subgroup, cannot be conducted. Criterion reliability cannot be estimated with confidence. Adverse impact computations are suspect due to the small sample size. Using the test performance of current incumbents as an aid in setting cutoffs may not be possible.

However, despite these similarities, there are some meaningful differences between the various combinations of single-incumbent versus multiple-incumbent jobs in small versus large organizations. Unlike the commonalities, which tend to involve technical issues, many of these differences are contextual issues. Consider the following examples:

- A large organization may be more receptive to the concept of formal systematic selection systems, as managers in such organizations may have exposure to formal selection systems if such systems are used for large *N* jobs in the organization.
- In a large organization, there is more flexibility for reassignment if a person does not perform well in the position for which he or she was selected.
- The impact of a hiring error may be greater in a small organization. Robinson (1981) describes a small construction company considering essentially doubling its size by adding a second construction crew. Hiring an effective versus an ineffective construction foreman may mean the dif-

ference between the company's thriving and failing to survive.
- Psychologists know that no selection system is perfectly valid; errors are made with all currently
available predictors. We commonly think about
selection problems in probability terms (for instance, improving the proportion of high performers over the base rate). When small numbers are
hired, though, managers tend to evaluate selection systems in more absolute terms: "the psychologist recommended that we hire Joe; we did and
he didn't work out; therefore the psychologist is
no good." Explanations that Joe is a "false positive" and that in the long run the selection system
would produce higher numbers of successful employees are not likely to be of much consolation
to the small organization.

We also note that certain jobs that are small N jobs in particular organizations have a large N counterpart in other organizations (for example, a fledgling real estate firm may have
two salespeople while an established firm in the same market
has hundreds). In this case it is not unlikely that selection systems for such jobs have been developed and validated elsewhere.
On the other hand, there are some jobs that are inherently small
N jobs: no other company will have large numbers of incumbents in the same job. Perhaps the most common instance involves high-level managerial jobs: regardless of size, a company
will have but one CEO, or one vice president of human resources. However, one can conceive of nonmanagerial examples as well: bullpen catcher for a professional baseball team,
or school mascot, for example. For jobs such as these, selection
systems and validity evidence will not be available from large
organizations.

Also worthy of some discussion is the hypothesis that organizational size may moderate selection system validity. Note
that this hypothesis is difficult to test as traditional local validity studies cannot be conducted in small organizations. We

would, however, speculate along the following lines: researchers have distinguished between "strong" and "weak" situations (for example, Davis-Blake & Pfeffer, 1990), with a strong situation defined as one where situational factors strongly influence behavior. Individual difference variables are expected to have more influence on job behavior in weak situations. An example of this is the observation that selection system validities are typically lower in military settings than in civilian settings. Factors such as extensive training, close supervision, and military discipline may reduce the potential for individual difference factors to influence job behavior. To the extent that small organizations are characterized by an absence of rigidity and bureaucracy, one might see them as relatively "weak" situations, and thus as situations where individual difference variables would have greater impact. Thus, we argue that careful attention to selection issues is even more important in small organizations.

In the sections to follow we examine various components of the selection process as reflected in the general outline for the book: job analysis, validation models, predictor selection and construction, fairness and legal issues, and utility. Cost issues are addressed in the section on utility analysis. In our discussion of job analysis and predictor selection and construction we focus on whether one _could_ make use of various approaches and techniques; the issue of whether these techniques are cost-effective is set aside until the utility section.

Job Analysis

We see three primary purposes for which job analysis data are used in the selection context. The first is criterion development: the determination of what the important components of the job performance domain are and the development of measures of these components. This is an issue only when a criterion-related validity study is being undertaken, and to the extent that this validation strategy is unfeasible in small _N_ settings, criterion development will be less of an issue. Only when data are being pooled across jobs, across organizations, or both to make empirical validation feasible does criterion development enter the picture.

The second purpose for job analysis data is predictor development. Locally constructed predictors, such as structured interviews, job knowledge tests, work sample tests, and assessment center exercises, all are built to sample aspects of a job domain, and all use job analysis to specify that domain. The same job analytic information is needed regardless of the size of the organization or the number of job incumbents.

The third purpose is to determine job similarity. This is needed for one of two purposes: (1) to determine whether jobs are similar enough to be pooled for the development of a common selection system or for conducting a criterion-related validity study, or (2) to determine whether a job is similar enough to another job or group of other jobs for which validity evidence is available such that validity evidence can be transported. While industrial and organizational (I/O) psychology has not clearly answered the question "how different do jobs have to be for validity to be affected?" for the range of possible predictors, the same job analytic data are needed regardless of the size of the organization or the number of incumbents.

The number of job incumbents can influence aspects of the job analysis process. One potential problem is that it becomes more difficult to separate the incumbent and the position with a single-incumbent job. With multiple incumbents, data can be gathered from many incumbents, and a clear picture emerges of both the most frequent job activities and the variability in time spent on various tasks or variability in the reliance on various knowledge, skills, and abilities dimensions (KSAs).

Another issue is that some job analysis technologies either require or are enhanced by access to large numbers of subject matter experts (SMEs). The critical incident technique, for example, is based on asking large numbers of individuals to each provide a handful of incidents of effective or ineffective job behavior. The single-incumbent job in a small organization seems to preclude use of this technique.

Other techniques are feasible, but in a scaled-down fashion. Task-oriented and KSA-oriented approaches to job analysis commonly involve meeting with multiple panels of SMEs to generate a preliminary task or KSA list; the multiple panels are used to ensure completeness. Conceivably, such a task could be generated in a small organization from a single meeting with a two-person panel: the incumbent and the immediate supervisor. The adequacy of the resulting list may be questionable, given the lack of checks and balances provided by use of large numbers of informants. Standardized job analysis questionnaires, such as the Position Analysis Questionnaire (PAQ), may be used effectively in small *N* settings, as they can be completed by a single job analyst with an understanding of the job gained from observation, interviews, and other sources. However, we add the caveat that ease of use should not supplant conceptual appropriateness in selecting a job analysis technique: only if the question at hand can be answered with worker-oriented data would an approach like the PAQ make sense.

In short, the type of job analysis data needed for selection problems is not greatly influenced by the number of incumbents or the size of the organization. Job analysis techniques can generally be applied to the small *N* situation, though the resulting profile of task or ability requirements will be based on the input of a considerably smaller number of SMEs.

Approaches to Validation

We opened this chapter by defining a small *N* job as one for which traditional local criterion-related validation was not technically feasible. In this section we examine various potential bases for supporting the inference of a relationship between scores on a selection device and job behaviors. We discuss two approaches to empirical validation that do involve local data, which we will term "whole job" and "job component" approaches. We then discuss approaches that do not involve local data, but instead rely on transporting validity evidence gathered elsewhere. Finally, we discuss the role of content sampling approaches.

Whole Job Approaches to Empirical Validation

We see four possible ways of building a sufficient data base to conduct a criterion-related validity study in a small *N* setting.

The first is to combine similar jobs within the organization to build a sufficient sample size. This is not a viable option in small organizations. In some large organizations, though, job titles may proliferate, and a job analytic study may reveal that jobs can be combined for a common validation study.

The second way to build a data base is to combine similar jobs across organizations. Both large and small organizations can make use of this strategy. Conceivably, a validity study could be conducted in which every data point comes from a different organization (for instance, a study of CEOs). A key issue when working in multiple organizations is criterion comparability. This is of particular concern when rating data are used as criteria. In nationwide consortium studies we have encountered, regional differences in the labor pool for a particular job are such that there is virtually no overlap in the predictor distributions between organizations in different parts of the country. Yet in each one, the criterion distributions are essentially the same: the ratings are made in a relative manner, and the top performers in each situation receive ratings at the top of the scale. When the multiple companies in such a study each contribute a substantial number of participants, predictor and criterion data are sometimes standardized within company before pooling data in order to deal with this problem; this option is not available when companies are contributing a single data point or a small number of data points to a study.

The third data base construction method is a combination of the first two: combine across jobs both within and across organizations. Comments about the first two approaches apply similarly to this approach.

The fourth method involves accumulating data over time. Although unfeasible for the single-incumbent job, a job with, say, fifty incumbents and a relatively high turnover rate may produce predictor and criterion data for a substantially larger sample if data are systematically gathered over a several-year period. Such an approach is clearly not suited to a situation in which a decision whether or not to put a predictor into operational use is needed quickly. Note that this approach can conceivably be combined with the three earlier approaches, thus combining data across jobs, across organizations, and across time. Considerable judgment would be required as to whether the results of such an exercise are meaningful, or whether issues such as the criterion problems discussed earlier and job change over time render the data uninterpretable.

Job Component Approaches to Empirical Validation

The preceding approaches pool data across job titles, organizations, and/or time. The approaches in this section are conceptually very similar: the only difference is that the basis for pooling data is not that entire jobs are judged sufficiently similar, but that job components across different jobs are quite similar. For example, if a wide variety of jobs all include the task "verify accuracy of arithmetic computations," and a measure of this component of job performance is available, data can be pooled across job titles, across organizations, and over time in order to estimate the relationship between various predictors and this component of job performance. Thus, job components do not require separate treatment here: all the whole job approaches can be applied at the level of the job component rather than the whole job. Technical treatments of combining estimates of relationships between predictors and job components can be found in the literature on synthetic validity (for example, Guion, 1965; Mossholder & Arvey, 1984).

Approaches Involving Transporting Validity Evidence

Two approaches focus on inferring predictor-criterion relationships for a particular job solely from data gathered outside the target organization. The first involves reliance on meta-analysis-based validity generalization models in which existing data about predictor-criterion relationships for a given job or job class are gathered, effect size measures are corrected to produce as accurate an estimate of operational predictive validity as possible, distributions of effect sizes are compiled and separated into subdistributions if evidence of moderator effects is found, and conclusions are drawn about expected values and lower-tail "worst case" values. The inference made is that if the job in question is similar to the jobs making up this prior distribution, the predictor-criterion relationship for the target job can be expected to be at least the lower-tail value of the prior distribution.

The second approach involving transporting validity evidence relies on a single-criterion-related validity study done at another location. Solely from job analytic evidence of job similarity, one infers a similar predictor-criterion relationship for the target job. The quality of the existing validity study and the degree of job similarity are the main sources of disputes about the appropriateness of this inference.

Note that the inference process with either of these approaches is independent of the number of incumbents or the size of the organization. Thus, these approaches are as viable for small N jobs as they are for large ones.

Worthy of discussion is the implicit belief that validation strategies involving local data are superior to those involving sole reliance on data from other settings. However, in the approaches to empirical validation in small N settings discussed earlier, the contribution of data from the target small N job to the validation effort is very small—potentially as small as data on a single individual. The situation in which a company contributes 1 percent of the data for a validity study does not seem markedly different from the situation in which one relies solely on validity evidence gathered elsewhere (for example, 99 percent versus 100 percent of the data comes from other settings). Thus, we reject the notion that contributing data to a validity study inherently permits a stronger inference than reliance on the transporting of validity evidence.

Content Sampling Approaches

These approaches involve using expert judgments of the relationship between selection system content and job content as the basis for a conclusion about the job-relatedness of a selection system. These approaches seem well suited to the small N setting, as they are not dependent on obtaining predictor and criterion data from large samples of people. However, the judgment processes that make up content sampling approaches are affected by the number of expert judges available, thus requiring some modification in the small *N* setting. We see these expert judgments as falling into five areas; we describe each and then comment on the effects of a small *N* setting.

The first area involving expert judgment is the specification of important job tasks and important KSAs. This is the job analysis process, which was described earlier. Job experts are used to generate initial lists of tasks and KSAs, to rate the tasks and KSAs on various scales, and to establish links between tasks and KSAs.

The second area involves item writing and review. The term *item* is used loosely here to reflect anything from multiple-choice test items to interview questions to assessment center exercises. Unless an existing item pool is being used, experts are needed to write items. Although the item writing function may be taken on by the psychologist in some settings, reviewing items for clarity and for subtle shades of meaning specific to the organizational context of necessity involves individuals with intimate knowledge of the organization, such as incumbents or supervisors.

The third area involving expert judgment entails linking selection system content to KSAs. Job experts are asked to rate the linkage between each KSA and each item to determine whether items are tapping the intended KSAs. One outcome of this process is an assessment of how adequately the job content domain has been sampled (that is, whether certain KSAs have been over- or underemphasized).

The fourth area involves an evaluation of the relationship between successful item performance and job success. Lawshe's (1975) content validity ratio exemplifies this approach. Job experts rate the degree to which successful performance on each item is essential, helpful, or not needed for effective job performance.

Use of expert judgment in the fifth area involves creation of a scoring system for the selection device. Expert judgment plays differing roles depending on the type of selection device. In the case of multiple-choice tests asking an applicant to select the most appropriate course of action from an array of choices, expert consensus as to appropriateness is commonly obtained. In the case of open-ended written exams or interview questions, experts may be asked to rate answers to create behavioral anchors for a rating scale.

Each of these five areas may involve making numerical ratings to reflect job experts' judgments. For each of these sets of ratings, the more raters the better: the greater the number of raters, the less likelihood that idiosyncratic perspectives will affect the decisions made on the basis of the ratings. As the number of potential raters decreases, the process shifts from a somewhat mechanical one, based on the averaging of input from large numbers of raters, to one where every judgment made by every rater is of great importance. At the extreme, consider a single incumbent job that is currently vacant. A single supervisor may be the primary informant, with supplemental information obtained from nontraditional sources of job analytic information, such as co-workers, subordinates, and customers. As the number of potential raters decreases, it becomes more and more important to ensure high rating quality, via rater training, attempts to get the raters to buy into the importance of the rating process, and the like.

In this section we have outlined a variety of approaches to gathering evidence to support the inference of a relationship between scores on a selection device and job behaviors. One thing that strikes us is the role played by professional judgment in these approaches. Whether jobs are similar enough to pool for empirical validation, whether jobs are similar enough to transport validity evidence from one setting to another, and whether linkages between selection system content and job content are strong enough to support the use of a selection system all involve exercising considerable judgment.

Predictor Selection and Construction

In this section we discuss a variety of predictor types, highlighting ways in which a small number of incumbents influences the selection or construction of predictors.

Cognitive Ability Testing

Cognitive ability testing, more than any other type of selection device, has been influenced most heavily by developments in validity generalization theory. Combining the enormous amount of evidence for consistently positive nonzero validities of general cognitive ability tests across jobs (for example, Hunter & Hunter, 1984; Hartigan & Wigdor, 1989) with evidence for the linearity of ability-performance relationships (for example, Coward & Sackett, 1990), one can argue that general cognitive ability tests can be used in small *N* settings.

What does not follow from the above is how to identify an optimal set of specific ability tests for a particular setting. Among the more counterintuitive findings of recent years is the failure of specific ability tests carefully chosen for the job in question to exhibit higher criterion-related validities (after cross-validation) than measures of general cognitive ability (Hunter, 1986; Thorndike, 1986). Thus, in a large *N* situation a researcher may compare the relative efficacy of general and specific ability measures and find an optimal combination of tests for that setting. However, this strategy is not available to the researcher in the small *N* setting. Without a data base showing lawful relationships between job content and the validity of specific ability tests, and despite the face validity and public relations advantages of specific ability tests, general cognitive ability tests would seem to be the defensible approach in a small *N* setting.

Personality Testing

The applicability of personality testing to the small *N* setting presents a particularly interesting case. Some of the alternatives to local criterion-related validation discussed earlier are not appropriate for personality tests, and others may only be available in select settings. First, unlike the domain of cognitive ability testing discussed above, examination of the cumulative data base on personality testing produces a less consistent pattern of findings. Only in recent years has there been movement toward a commonly used and shared taxonomy of personality constructs (that is, research on the "Big 5" personality dimensions; Digman, 1990). A recent attempt to organize the cumulative data base in terms of these dimensions finds consistent support for only one dimension—conscientiousness—as a generalizable predictor across jobs (Barrick & Mount, 1991). A meta-analysis focusing on one specific type of test, namely, integrity tests, also shows consistent positive nonzero validity (Ones, Viswesvaran, & Schmidt, 1991). Thus, at the present time only in the related domains of conscientiousness and integrity can validity generalization arguments be used to support personality test use in small N settings.

Second, content sampling approaches to establishing job-relatedness are commonly acknowledged as not applicable to personality tests. Personality tests are perhaps the prototype of the "sign" end of the classic Wernimont and Campbell (1968) sign-sample continuum. The content of the test is not intended as a sample of job content; rather, the test is intended as a measure of a construct, the relationship of which to job performance must be established. Both professional and regulatory documents (for example, the 1987 Society for Industrial and Organizational Psychology's (SIOP) *Principles for the Validation and Use of Personnel Selection Procedures* and the 1978 *Uniform Guidelines on Employee Selection Procedures*) recognize this distinction.

Third, skepticism about personality tests among I/O psychologists over the last two decades, together with the large number of available tests and the lack of a common vocabulary for describing the personality domain, decreases the likelihood that a researcher in a small N setting will find an existing high-quality validity study for the job and construct combination of interest. Thus, transporting validity evidence may not be a viable strategy in many settings.

Fourth, although pooling resources across organizations for a cooperative study is always a possibility, the opportunity for such studies must be acknowledged as rare. The studies of this sort that we have been involved in have been initiated in one of two ways: either by an industry association or by a test publisher. Even though all participating organizations share the costs of data collection, the up-front costs of organizing a cooperative study are often substantial. We do not consider it reasonable to tell a small organization wishing to fill an opening in a single-incumbent job that it should organize a consortium study in order to build a convincing argument for the job-relatedness of the methods used to place an applicant in a single opening.

If the above alternatives are not available, what options remain? Construct validation strategies, that is, establishing that the test measures the intended construct and that the construct is related to job performance, have not yet been discussed. Are such approaches viable? In this area there remains a great deal of ambiguity: both the SIOP _Principles_ (1987) and the _Uniform Guidelines_ (1978) acknowledge that the concept of construct validity is evolving and that the standards for establishing construct validity are not as well developed as for criterion-related validity. The _Principles_ and the _Guidelines_ differ markedly in their treatment of construct validity. The _Guidelines_ indicate that establishing construct validity requires a series of research studies, including providing criterion-related validity evidence. As we have defined a small _N_ setting as one where criterion-related validity is not technically feasible, under the _Guidelines_ construct validity must be rejected as a viable approach in the small _N_ setting.

Under the _Principles,_ construct validity is established through essentially two processes: first, the documentation that the test measures the intended construct, and second, the articulation of the rationale for the linkage between the construct and the job in question. The _Principles_ reject simply asking SMEs to list constructs required for job performance as a sufficient basis for establishing construct validity. They call for judgments "based on knowledge of worker characteristics required for adequate job performance and how they are measured by the proposed selection procedure" (p. 26). We interpret this as an indication that a construct validity strategy is a viable approach to establishing the job-relatedness of personality tests in small _N_ settings, and that what emerges again as critical is careful professional judgment. The psychologist must develop a thorough understanding of both the job in question and the construct domain in question, and/or ensure the possession of this understanding among key informants; having done so, the psychologist's judgment about the job-construct linkage can justify use of the test.

Construct validity as the informed judgment of a psychologist is a far cry from the *Guidelines'* view of construct validity as "an extensive and arduous effort." We do want to explicitly reject the notions that (1) the various approaches to establishing job-relatedness are to be viewed as alternatives from which a single approach is selected, (2) all forms of evidence are equally informative, and (3) the easiest, least demanding approach in any setting is the approach of choice. We share Landy's (1986) rejection of the notion of validation as "stamp collecting" (that is, finding the one right approach for a particular setting) and endorse Landy's view that the psychologist's task is to gather evidence from whatever sources are appropriate to build a case for the relationship between scores on a selection device and job performance. Relying solely on the informed judgment of a psychologist to establish the job-relatedness of a personality test in a small N setting clearly involves more uncertainty and more potential for error than would be the case if more sources of evidence were available. However, we do regard the selection of such a test solely on the basis of informed judgment to be a marked improvement over shrugging your shoulders and telling an organization that since a criterion-related validity study is unfeasible, you cannot assist it, or, alternatively, that you can only assist it in developing or selecting measures of other attributes for which other forms of validity evidence are available.

In sum, to the extent that precedence is given to quasi-legal standards over professional standards, it seems clear that personality testing will often be unavailable as part of a selection system in small N settings. Giving precedence to professional standards leads to the conclusion that professional judgment about the adequacy of construct measurement and job-construct linkage is sufficient to justify test use.

Biodata

Formal scoring of biographical data can be seen as offering three advantages over informal judgmental evaluation: large numbers of applicants can be processed, scoring schemes can be empirically validated, and candidates are treated consistently. The first may not be a concern in the small *N* setting, and the second is precluded by the definition of a small *N* setting. The third may be reason enough for considering a formal approach to biodata screening.

Although empirically developed biodata keys are perhaps the ultimate in raw empiricism, there exists a long history in the public sector of developing rational keying approaches (see Ash, Johnson, Levine, & McDaniel, 1989, for a detailed treatment). These focus on training and experience evaluation, but the judgment techniques used can be applied in the same way to biodata items that go beyond these content domains. There has also been a call in recent years to abandon the raw empiricism of empirical keying methods. The Pace and Schoenfeldt (1977) "hand of reason" is often appealed to in support of limiting a biodata key to items for which a rational explanation for the relationship between the keyed response and job success can be offered. Thus, the development of scored biodata in small *N* settings seems quite feasible.

Assessment Centers

In most cases development of an assessment center for use in a small *N* setting is possible. However, in several circumstances there would be reasons to question the viability of an assessment center approach.

In developing an assessment center, major activities include job analysis, exercise development or selection, and assessor selection and training. Regarding job analysis in small *N* settings, all the previously discussed issues apply here. Exercise development or selection is not affected significantly by a small *N* setting, although we speculate that cost considerations make use of existing exercises, perhaps with some minor modification, more likely than the development of exercises unique to the situation.

Assessor selection and training may pose some problems in a small *N* setting. First, it is common to use current or former incumbents of the target position as assessors, because of their unique insight into the nature of the job. This would not be possible where only one incumbent is available to serve as assessor or where only a few are. Second, it is common to avoid assessor teams consisting of individuals markedly different in status in the organization. In very small organizations, the only way to use current managers rather than outsiders as assessors is to include assessors quite different in status. Third, larger organizations commonly take great pains to ensure that assessors are not assigned to evaluate candidates with whom they have had extensive on-the-job contact. Whereas this can be avoided in large organizations, it may be impossible in many small N settings. Hiring outside assessors is a possibility, though such assessors may lack the insight into job requirements possessed by current or former incumbents.

There are other logistic issues as well. For example, to the extent that a center involves group exercises, running it requires a group of candidates. In some small N settings, an organization may have only, say, two or three candidates for a single-incumbent job. These issues may not prove a problem in some small N settings. For example, external assesssors may be used to avoid the problem of prior knowledge of the candidates, although recent research suggests higher validity in a school principal assessment center using principals as assessors than with professors of education as assessors (Schmitt, Schneider, & Cohen, 1990). In some settings, though, problems such as too few candidates to mount an assessment center may force the organization to consider other alternatives.

Considerable evidence may be introduced to support the job-relatedness of assessment center evaluations. Meta-analytic evidence of the criterion-related validity of assessment centers is available (Gaugler, Rosenthal, Thornton, & Bentson, 1987). We do offer three cautionary notes, however. First, Schmitt, Schneider, and Cohen (1990) report regional variation in the validity of what is nominally the same assessment center. Second, one can question whether the meta-analytic data base is representative of the range of assessment center practices. The question is whether empirical validity evidence is only available for particularly well developed and well administered assessment centers. This hypothesis is plausible if the skills needed to recognize the value of empirical validation, the skills needed to carry out empirical validation, and the willingness of an organization to devote resources to empirical validation covary positively with the quality of the assessment center process. Third, there is the possibility of some unique dynamics in small *N* settings. Specifically, in the case of the single-incumbent job, candidates are in more explicit competition with one another than in the case of assessment centers in large *N* settings. In large *N* settings candidates are commonly told that while all of them are being evaluated in terms of their potential for, say, a middle management position, there are many middle management positions in the organization, and in any group of candidates being assessed at the same time, it is possible that all will be evaluated as having high potential. When it is clear that there is a single available position, and thus that there can only be one "winner" among a group of candidates, a markedly different set of dynamics are created. Even though assessors are commonly trained to evaluate candidates not in relationship to one another but against a performance standard, when both assessors and candidates know that only a single position is available, the effects on candidate performance or assessors' evaluation of that performance are not clear. We see this as an interesting research question.

A content sampling rationale also can contribute to evidence of job-relatedness. However, because of the subjective judgments typically made about how candidates respond to the exercise materials presented to them, the fact that the exercises are developed on the basis of sampling job content does not ensure that candidates' responses are evaluated in a meaningful way (Sackett, 1987). Thus, evidence about underlying constructs must also come into play. That assessment center judgments predict subsequent behavior is in our opinion a conclusion that rests on a firmer foundation than conclusions about the constructs underlying assessor judgments. Discussion continues about factor analytic evidence of dimension factors versus exercise factors, and about the implications of this factor analytic evidence for the construct validity of assessment centers (for example, Sackett and Dreher, 1982; Bycio, Alvares, & Hahn, 1987). Given the variety of possible explanations for the failure to find strong evidence of dimension factors, other forms of evidence for construct validity, such as evidence of interassessor consistency in assigning behavior samples to dimensions, also deserve attention.

Individual Assessment

Individual assessment is probably the area in which I/O psychologists have the greatest degree of contact with small N settings. The single-incumbent managerial job is the prototypical setting for conducting individual assessment, though the individual assessment process is used for nonmanagerial and multi-incumbent jobs as well. The typical individual assessment involves a single psychologist integrating data from personality tests, ability tests, biodata forms, an in-depth interview, and possibly one or more simulation exercises (for instance, an in-basket) to form an overall evaluation of a candidate's suitability for a specific position and also to identify specific strengths and weaknesses (Ryan & Sackett, 1987).

Although each of the components of the individual assessment process have already been discussed separately, the integration of data from these sources into an overall decision brings an additional set of concerns to bear. The SIOP *Principles* (1987) state that "decision makers who interpret and act upon predictor data interject something of themselves into the interpretive or decision making process. The judgments or decisions thus become at least an additional predictor, or, at the most, the only predictor. For example, if the decision strategy is to combine test and non-test data . . . into a subjective judgment, the actual predictor is the judgment reached by the person who weights and summarizes all the information. It is this decision that should be validated in addition to the information which was available to the decision maker" (p. 12).

Thus, in a small N setting the organization wants the psychologist conducting individual assessments to offer evidence both that the individual components of the process are appropriate and that the psychologist's integration of the information represents valid inference. Evidence about the individual components of the process is the focus of previous sections of this chapter. Evidence about the psychologist's integration of information is discussed here.

As local validation of the psychologist's inference is by definition not feasible in a small _N_ setting, the psychologist can potentially offer at least the following three types of evidence from other settings:

1. _Validation of a single assessor's inferences for a single job._ Such empirical validation is feasible in only two situations. The first is the situation in which individual assessment is done for a large _N_ job. The most common example here is protective service jobs, where individual assessment is common. However, the focus in protective service assessment is most commonly on identifying individuals unsuited for the job in question, rather than on attempting to predict who will be the most successful performer on the job. The second is the instance in which a single assessor has a long-term relationship with an organization and over time a large number of assessments can be aggregated.

2. _Validation of a single assessor's inferences aggregated across jobs and organizations._ A meaningful across job–across organization criterion is a major obstacle.

3. _Validation aggregated across assessors and across jobs and organizations._ Here the focus shifts from validating an assessor to validating a process common to a group of assessors (for example, a consulting firm that trains all its assessors in its particular approach to assessment). This approach depends on comparability of assessors; evidence to that effect, such as interassessor agreement when evaluating the same candidate, is called for.

As one moves from 1 to 2 to 3 in the above list, the sample size component of technical feasibility is eliminated as a problem. However, other significant problems remain, the most critical of which is criterion contamination. If organization level is used as a criterion, a positive correlation can be viewed simply as evidence that the psychologist's recommendations are being followed. If performance in the target job is used as a criterion, a correlation between a go/no-go recommendation by a psychologist and a criterion can be computed only if some "no-go's" are promoted despite the negative recommendation of the psychologist. It seems likely that "promoted no-go's" and "non-promoted no-go's" may differ in any number of important ways, making the interpretation of a validity coefficient troublesome at best.

As a result of factors such as these, we would expect it to be the exception rather than the rule for a psychologist practicing individual assessment to be able to produce criterion-related validity evidence for his or her assessment practices. Transporting criterion-related validity evidence from studies of the validity of individual assessment practices conducted elsewhere is also troublesome. First, that other assessors elsewhere produce evidence of the validity of their judgments says little about the validity of the judgments of other assessors without evidence that the assessors share common information integration strategies. Ryan and Sackett (1989) produce striking evidence that different individual assessment practitioners can produce markedly different assessments of the same candidates. Second, there simply is not much evidence in the literature about the criterion-related validity of individual assessment practices. Ryan (1987) summarizes this limited literature; her review located a set of studies of one assessment program in 1962, and a handful of additional studies, none more recent than 1970. Thus, neither local, cooperative, nor transported criterion-related validity evidence is available for most applications of individual assessment in small N settings.

What about other forms of evidence of job-relatedness? Although some components of individual assessment programs, such as in-baskets, may be categorized as job samples, other components are clearly aimed at construct measurement. Thus, job content sampling is not a viable approach to establishing the job-relatedness of the assessor's information integration strategy.

For us, the bottom line is that the psychologist is making a judgment about a construct labeled something like "job suitability." Absent compelling empirical evidence for the predictive power of the psychologist's judgment, the psychologist needs to justify rationally three components of the assessment process: the constructs to be assessed, the linkage between the measuring tools used and these constructs, and a causal model relating the constructs to the overall decision (for example, Which constructs are most important? Which are compensatory? Which, if any, are knock-out factors?). All of these, and their rationale, should be made explicit. In essence, the assessor is being asked to articulate a model of job performance, as a model that cannot be articulated cannot be critiqued. The assessor who either cannot or will not articulate his or her model of information integration cannot, in our opinion, claim to be making valid inferences.

Job Sampling

In job sampling, we typically follow a process something like the following: (1) conduct a job analysis, (2) develop a structured set of questions or stimulus materials (or collect a sample of the applicant's existing work product, as in the case of a portfolio submitted by an artist or copywriter), (3) develop behavioral scales for scoring the interview or work sample, and (4) train the interviewers or raters. This process is clearly applicable in both small and large *N* settings.

What if the small *N* organization thinks it cannot afford to do all of this? What do we say? Is our implicit model of the way these aspects of selection system development contribute to validity additive or multiplicative? If it is additive, we believe that each of the components of the process contributes to its validity. A system that incorporates all four components is better than one that incorporates two of the four; but a system that incorporates two is better than one that incorporates one. If it is multiplicative, then lack of any one makes the value of an incomplete system zero. We would put our money on a modified version of the additive model: each component adds to validity *if* the components are applied in order. An interviewer armed with a job analysis should do better than one without.

If both have a job analysis, the one with a structured set of questions should do better than the one without. If both have a structured set of questions, the one with a behavioral scoring guide should do better than the one without. Each of these steps contributes to systematic, thoughtful hiring decisions; each is readily applied in small N settings.

Legal and Fairness Issues

In light of the uncertainties at this time regarding possible changes in civil rights laws, we do not detail here legal issues in showing job-relatedness in small N settings. We simply offer a few overall observations.

Challenges to selection procedures are based on one of two theories of discrimination, commonly labeled *disparate impact* and *disparate treatment*. Disparate impact is inherently restricted to at least moderate N settings, as it is based on a comparison of selection rates for majority and minority groups. As recognized in documents like the *Uniform Guidelines,* as one approaches the extreme of the single-incumbent job, computation of selection rates by group becomes meaningless. Thus, in small N settings, a company's focus can be on preventing disparate treatment discrimination.

Disparate treatment discrimination is one area where differences may be found between small N jobs in large organizations and in small organizations. Large organizations are more likely to be sensitive to fair-employment issues, and to have policies such as a requirement that any manager with hiring responsibilities attend training dealing with fair-hiring practices. Managers in small organizations are less likely to have been sensitized to these concerns, and thus we suspect that disparate treatment may occur more commonly in small organizations.

Like disparate impact computations, quantitative approaches to selection system fairness, such as testing for differential prediction, are also not possible in small N settings, other than in settings where data are being pooled within or across organizations in order to make criterion-related validation feasible.

Because pooling data across jobs has been introduced as a means of building an adequate sample size for criterion-related validation, one could by analogy consider pooling data for purposes of disparate impact computations. If the scenario is the pooling of data from very similar jobs that are to be filled from the same applicant pool, this may make sense. But pooling markedly different jobs simply to get a large enough sample to compute selection rates can lead to some paradoxical conclusions. Consider the following simple example.

A company has two jobs, A and B. For job A they select fifteen of twenty majority group applicants and three of four minority group applicants — an identical selection rate for both groups. For job B they select five of twenty majority group applicants and five of twenty minority group applicants — again, an identical selection rate for both groups. If the data are pooled across jobs, one finds that twenty of forty majority group applicants have been selected (a selection ratio of 50 percent) and that eight of twenty-four minority group applicants have been selected (a selection ratio of 33 percent). The ratio of minority group selection to majority group selection is 67 percent, which is less than the four-fifths ratio established by the 1978 *Uniform Guidelines*. Thus, the 67 percent ratio suggests discrimination. If larger numbers of minority group members apply for jobs with lower selection ratios than for jobs with higher selection ratios, strange outcomes such as this are possible. Thus, we advise against pooling data for disparate jobs for purposes of disparate impact computation.

Utility Issues

Most of the discussion to this point has focused on whether various selection devices can be implemented and on how their job relatedness can be examined in small *N* settings. We turn now to the issue of the cost-effectiveness of various selection devices.

Boudreau (1989) offers the following as a conceptually straightforward approach to utility analysis:

$$\text{Utility} = \text{Quantity} \times \text{Quality} - \text{Cost}$$

We consider each of these components in turn.

Quantity is typically a measure of the number of "person years" of productivity that will be achieved as a result of the selection system (that is, the number of people hired times the mean tenure per employee). In large N settings, this parameter contributes greatly to total utility. If large numbers of individuals are selected per year, if average tenure is fairly long, and if the selection system is used repeatedly for a number of years, even a small increment in value per person hired results in a very large total utility figure. However, in small N settings, one does not have this advantage: at the extreme, the selection system will result in a single hire over its lifetime.

Quality is typically expressed as a multiplicative function of three factors: the criterion-related validity of the selection system, the mean predictor score of selected individuals in standard score terms (essentially a reflection of the selection ratio), and the standard deviation of performance in dollar terms. In small N settings, the validity estimate used is not derived locally, but rather obtained using one of the methods discussed earlier. The selection ratio term may prove to be harder to estimate in advance in small N settings. In large N settings, organizations should be able to continuously monitor applicant to opening ratios, as openings arise regularly. In small N settings, a company may simply have no idea whether an announcement of a job opening will produce a single application or hundreds. Thus, this parameter of the utility function may be estimated with more uncertainty in a small N setting. Regarding estimating the standard deviation of performance in dollar terms, rough rules of thumb, such as using a certain percentage of salary as an SD_y estimate, can be applied in either large or small N settings. Approaches based on expert estimate can also be used, though the availability of a smaller number of raters in the small N setting would increase the effect of idiosyncratic raters on the final SD_y estimate.

The cost component can be divided into two parts: development costs and administration costs. In absolute terms, for many types of selection procedures development costs are lower in small N settings. For example, job analytic efforts in large N settings are often very extensive: multiple task and KSA generation panels are used, and task and KSA lists may be rated for importance by hundreds, if not thousands, of incumbents and supervisors. Of necessity, these activities are done on a smaller scale in the small *N* setting.

Administrative costs may or may not differ between small and large *N* settings. For some selection devices there may be economies of scale enjoyed in large *N* settings. The cost of a test monitor is the same whether there are three or thirty applicants. Purchased tests may be less expensive in bulk. For other selection devices, such as an interview, per applicant costs are identical in small and large *N* settings.

Although development costs may be lower in absolute terms in small *N* settings, they will typically make up a far higher proportion of the total cost per selectee in a small *N* setting, the net result being a higher cost per selectee in small *N* settings.

Utility models also give either average utility per hire or total utility across hires. These are expected values: the organization that implements a new selection system and hires a single individual may be the victim or the beneficiary of the standard error of estimate in the selection system, and may react to the system accordingly.

In sum, utility analysis is likely to be critical in determining the extent of involvement by psychologists in small *N* settings. Three features emerge as especially important when considering utility analysis in small *N* settings. First, several parameters of the utility model may be estimated with more uncertainty in small *N* settings, including the validity coefficient, the selection ratio, and the standard deviation of performance in dollars. Second, even if the parameters of the model were precisely known, the model gives the expected value across large numbers of hires, and thus in small *N* settings there is considerably more risk of failing to obtain the expected benefits than in large *N* settings. Third, due primarily to the inability to spread development costs over large numbers of hires, costs per selectee are likely to be higher in small *N* settings. All of this is not to say that selection systems may not prove to have considerable positive utility in small *N* settings; these concerns simply mean that it is likely to be more difficult to convince decision makers in small *N* settings that the potentially hard-to-grasp future benefits outweigh the very concrete and real present costs.

Conclusion

In this chapter we focus on three issues: (1) are the central selection techniques of I/O psychology applicable only to settings with large numbers of applicants and openings, or can these techniques also be applied in small N settings; (2) are the techniques used to establish job-relatedness of selection devices in large N settings also applicable to small N settings; and (3) do cost considerations preclude applying our selection techniques to small N settings?

We indicate that with limited exceptions the same selection techniques used in large N settings can be used in small ones. However, the types of evidence of job-relatedness that can be obtained are often quite different. In small N settings job-relatedness is less dependent on quantitative analysis and empirical forms of evidence; rather, far more weight is placed on judgment and rationality. There is no doubt that decisions about the job-relatedness of selection systems are made with less certainty in small N settings. The more forms of evidence available to support a claim of job-relatedness, the better; in large N settings more forms of evidence are technically feasible, and more are affordable. If all that is available is the rational informed judgment of a psychologist regarding job content–selection system content linkages, we endorse that rational judgment as evidence of job-relatedness. The alternative is singularly unattractive: if that rational, informed judgment is not adequate evidence of job-relatedness, then we are in effect endorsing whatever haphazard selection procedures a company may use instead.

The utility question is harder to answer. As our discussion of the topic noted, utility may be estimated with greater uncertainty in small N settings. As development costs cannot be spread over large number of hires, selection systems that may have considerable positive utility in large N settings may not pay off in small organizations. The result may be scaled-down efforts in small N settings: assessment centers may give way to structured interviews and homegrown work samples.

We conclude with the point of view that has driven this chapter. Graduate training often leaves a student feeling that "if you can't do it by the book, don't do it at all." We prefer to frame the issue as one of incremental improvement over the haphazard selection done in many organizations. The issue often is not "can we design the ideal selection system," but "given resource constraints, can we produce a system preferable to what has been used previously?" We believe I/O psychology can contribute to better selection in any setting, regardless of size.

References

Ash, R. A., Johnson, J. C., Levine, E. L., & McDaniel, M. A. (1989). Job applicant training and work experience evaluation in personnel selection. In K. Rowland and G. Ferris (Eds.), *Research in personnel and human resources management* (Vol. 7). Greenwich, CT: JAI Press.

Barrick, M. R., & Mount, M. K. (1991). The big five personality dimensions and job performance: A meta-analysis. *Personnel Psychology, 44,* 1–26.

Boudreau, J. (1989). Selection utility analysis: A review and agenda for future research. In M. Smith and I. Robertson (Eds.), *Advances in selection and assessment.* West Sussex, England: Wiley.

Bycio, P., Alvares, K. M., & Hahn, J. (1987). Situational specificity in assessment center ratings: A confirmatory factor analysis. *Journal of Applied Psychology, 72,* 463–474.

Coward, W. M., & Sackett, P. R. (1990). Linearity in ability-performance relationships: A reconfirmation. *Journal of Applied Psychology, 75,* 297–300.

Davis-Blake, A., & Pfeffer, J. (1990). Just a mirage: The search for dispositional effects in organizational research. *Academy of Management Review, 14,* 385–400.

Digman, J. M. (1990). Personality structure: Emergence of the five-factor model. In M. Rosenzweig and L. Porter (Eds.), *Annual Review of Psychology, 41,* 417–440.

Gaugler, B. B., Rosenthal, D. B., Thornton, G. C. III, & Bentson, C. (1987). Meta-analysis of assessment center validity. *Journal of Applied Psychology, 72,* 493–511.

Guion, R. (1965). *Personnel testing.* New York: McGraw-Hill.

Hartigan, J., & Wigdor, A. K. (1989). *Fairness in employment testing: Validity generalization, minority issues, and the General Aptitude Test Battery.* Washington, DC: National Academy Press.

Hunter, J. E. (1986). Cognitive ability, cognitive aptitudes, job knowledge, and job performance. *Journal of Vocational Behavior, 29,* 340–362.

Hunter, J. E., & Hunter, R. F. (1984). Validity and utility of alternative predictors of job performance. *Psychological Bulletin, 96,* 72–98.

Landy, F. J. (1986). Stamp collecting vs. science: Validation as hypothesis testing. *American Psychologist, 41,* 1183–1192.

Lawshe, C. H. (1975). A quantitative approach to content validity. *Personnel Psychology, 28,* 563–575.

Mossholder, K., & Arvey, R. (1984). Synthetic validity: A conceptual and comparative review. *Journal of Applied Psychology, 69,* 322–333.

Ones, D. S., Viswesvaran, C., & Schmidt, F. L. (1991). *Integrity test validities: Meta-analytic tests of moderator hypotheses.* Paper presented at the meeting of the Society for Industrial and Organizational Psychology, St. Louis, MO.

Pace, L. A., & Schoenfeldt, L. F. (1977). Legal concerns in the use of weighted applications. *Personnel Psychology, 30,* 159–166.

Robinson, D. D. (1981). Content-oriented personnel selection in a small business setting. *Personnel Psychology, 34,* 77–87.

Ryan, A. M. (1987). *An exploratory study of individual assessment practices: Interrater reliability and judgments of assessor effectiveness.* Unpublished doctoral dissertation, University of Illinois, Chicago.

Ryan, A. M., & Sackett, P. R. (1987). A survey of individual assessment practices by industrial/organizational psychologists. *Personnel Psychology, 40,* 455–488.

Ryan, A. M., & Sackett, P. R. (1989). An exploratory study of individual assessment practices: Interrater reliability and judgments of assessor effectiveness. *Journal of Applied Psychology, 74,* 568–579.

Sackett, P. R. (1987). Assessment centers and content validity: Some neglected issues. *Personnel Psychology, 40,* 13–25.

Sackett, P. R., & Dreher, G. F. (1982). Constructs and assessment center dimensions: Some troubling empirical findings. *Journal of Applied Psychology, 67,* 401–410.

Schmitt, N., Schneider, J. R., & Cohen, S. A. (1990). Factors affecting validity of a regionally administered assessment center. *Personnel Psychology, 43,* 1–12.

Society for Industrial and Organizational Psychology. (1987). *Principles for the validation and use of personnel selection procedures* (3rd ed.). College Park, MD.

Thorndike, R. L. (1986). The role of general ability in prediction. *Journal of Vocational Behavior, 29,* 332–339.

Uniform guidelines on employee selection procedures. (1978). *Federal Register, 43,* 38290–38315.

Wernimont, P. F., & Campbell, J. P. (1968). Signs, samples, and criteria. *Journal of Applied Psychology, 52,* 372–376.

14

Staffing as Strategy

Charles C. Snow, Scott A. Snell

Staffing—the act of recruiting, selecting, appraising, and promoting individuals—is an important ingredient in the success of every organization. However, there are trends in today's workplace that indicate that staffing will become even more important to organizational success in the future. Included among these trends are the changing demographics of the American workforce, the increasing importance of intellectual capital as a competitive advantage, growth of the service economy, and the need for rapid resource deployment due to globalization. Companies that respond quickly and appropriately to the staffing challenges presented by these trends will find that they can outperform competitors who are slower to develop a strong human resource planning and management function.

This chapter characterizes the staffing process according to three conceptual models. Model 1, whose use dates to World War I, seeks to match individuals to specific, well-defined jobs. Model 1 essentially ignores the company's competitive strategy. Model 2, which began to be used in the early 1980s, views staffing as part of the overall process of implementing a business strategy. In model 2, staffing is tied explicitly to business strategy and is concerned with more broadly defined jobs than model 1, as well as with the linkages between jobs. Model 3, presently more theoretical than applied, reverses the logic of model 2. Model 3 focuses on the recruitment, assessment, and selection of high-caliber individuals as the foundation of strategy. Thus, in model 3 staffing drives the formation of competitive strategy.

In the following sections, each of these models is discussed in order of its historical appearance. Then, the implications of each model for management practice and research are drawn. Last, the chapter concludes with a call for research that examines the value of each model in different organizational contexts. All three models are likely to be used by organizations in the future; the critical issue is understanding where and how each model should be implemented.

Model 1: Staffing as Matching Individuals to Jobs

In preindustrialized America, there was no explicit notion of staffing. Work was performed in family units or craft guilds, neither of which relied on the hiring of employees. Staffing became important only when organizations became so large and complex that jobs had to be clearly defined and employees hired to fill those jobs.

Origins of Model 1

In industries such as railroads, automobile manufacturing, and steelmaking, the U.S. industrial revolution was marked by company strategies of vertical integration and expanded volume to achieve scale economies that lowered costs and prices (Chandler, 1962). The overriding organizational challenge in these companies was the transformation from a simple agency form to a functional structure that could be used to maximize efficiency. Division of labor, specialization, and job design were used as basic means of control — that is, methods for reducing uncertainty in the system. During this period, labor came to be viewed as one of the most costly and uncontrollable resources in the production equation. Consequently, it was logical to expect that if jobs could be clearly defined, and if individuals could be found whose attributes met job requirements, then the overall efficiency of operations could be maximized.

Characteristics of Model 1

From its origin in early industrial organizations, the traditional staffing model evolved as an analytical process of matching the attributes of individuals to the requirements of jobs. Through job analysis, the tasks, duties, and responsibilities (TDRs) of a job are specified, and tests are developed to measure individual differences in relevant knowledge, skills, abilities, and other characteristics (KSAOs). The process of matching individuals to jobs is facilitated when a large number of candidates with varying attributes are available. In turn, validation studies are conducted to assess the relationship between test results and subsequent performance on previously determined criteria of job success (see Table 14.1).

Applications of Model 1

The first large-scale use of the traditional staffing model occurred in World War I. The U.S. Army, as well as the armies of England and France, used cognitive abilities tests to select soldiers. After the war, similar testing procedures were used by companies to select and place employees. Today, after many decades of research, there is ample evidence to indicate that the proper use of model 1 improves the quality of staffing decisions. Indeed, it may be fair to say that model 1 staffing influenced personnel management almost as much as mass production revolutionized business in general. The systematic analysis of jobs, individuals, and performance added logic and precision to what previously had been a haphazard approach to personnel decision making, thereby moving staffing closer to the level of a science. The kind of rigor evidenced in well-done validation studies, for example, allowed model 1 to hold up under scrutiny by the courts (*Uniform Guidelines on Employee Selection Procedures,* 1978).

Table 14.1. Three Models of the Staffing Process.

	Model 1: Staffing as Person-Job Match	Model 2: Staffing as Strategy Implementation	Model 3: Staffing as Strategy Formation
Characteristics	Staffing based on job analysis	Staffing based on competitive strategy (part of implementation)	Staffing based on strategy formation
	Many candidates available per job	Role descriptions	Broad skill base
	Tests to measure individual differences	Interdepartmental team synergies	Rapid deployment of resources
	Validation studies	Open-system perspective	Open-system perspective
	Closed-system perspective		
Assumptions	Organizations and jobs can be separated into individual components	Deductive logic	Inductive logic
		Reactive staffing	Proactive staffing
	People and jobs are stable	Tight fit between strategy and staffing	Loose fit between strategy and staffing (slack)
	Job performance can be measured validly and reliably		
Applications	Organizations with stable, definable jobs	Organizations with clear strategies and known competencies	Organizations that need the ability to develop or change strategy quickly

Staffing decisions made according to the model 1 matching process have occurred in countless companies and jobs. Some knowledgeable observers have noted that, by increasing the validity of staffing decisions, the traditional model may potentially help organizations realize "hundreds of millions of dollars in increased productivity" (Schmidt, Hunter, McKenzie, & Muldrow, 1979, p. 609).

Assumptions and Limitations of Model 1

As with any model, the underlying assumptions of the traditional staffing model define the parameters of its application. First, the traditional model is an analytic process. Model 1 assumes that it is meaningful to separate organizations and jobs into individual components. Doing so makes it easier to understand the complexity of organizations and to systematize work processes. However, there may be instances when an analytic perspective is overrestrictive. When organizations are configured in such a way that interdependence and mutual adjustment are imperative, perhaps the most important aspects of performance are those that occur at the interface between jobs. Important information about organizational effectiveness may be omitted by looking only at each job in isolation. In such circumstances, a strictly analytic staffing model may be insufficient (Schmitt & Schneider, 1983).

A second assumption of the traditional model is that individuals, jobs, and the match between them are stable over time. Schneider and Konz (1989), for example, note that job analysis techniques treat jobs as static rather than dynamic entities. This is acceptable for a job "as it currently exists and/or has existed in the past" (Schneider & Konz, 1989, p. 51). However, the more jobs change because of technological advances or organizational innovations, the less accurate a given job analysis becomes. Schneider and Konz (1989, p. 51) argue that in cases where jobs change over time, staffing experts should gather information about the future and develop job analyses (and staffing procedures) for the job "as it will be." However, even this approach assumes that change is predictable and that job requirements can be projected into the future. If change is unpredictable, this may not be possible (Snell, 1992).

Third, the traditional model is based on the assumption that valid and reliable criteria can be identified to measure employee performance. Researchers have long acknowledged that the ultimate performance criterion — the long-term contribution of an employee to the company — is an abstraction (Cascio, 1991; Thorndike, 1949). Also, the more dynamic and multidimensional a job, the more difficult it is to specify valid or reliable performance criteria. Last, people themselves may change, making a stable person-job fit often unlikely. Addressing these concerns, researchers such as Dunnette (1963) and Prien (1966) have pointed out that reliance on short-term or unidimensional measures of job performance may not adequately capture the complexities of an employee's overall contribution to an organization.

In sum, the traditional staffing model is designed to measure jobs and individuals systematically and to maximize person-job fit. The underlying assumptions of analyzability and stability suggest that the traditional model is best suited for staffing decisions that take place in predictable organizational environments. In cases where these assumptions do not hold, the value of the traditional staffing model may be limited. As the limitations of model 1 became apparent, researchers began to develop additional frameworks for making staffing decisions.

Model 2: Staffing as Strategy Implementation

In efforts to develop a broader and more integrated perspective of staffing, several researchers have argued that human resource planning (including staffing) should be linked to strategic planning (Alpander & Botter, 1981; Miles & Snow, 1984; Smith, 1982a, 1982b; Tichy, Fombrun, & DeVanna, 1982; Walker, 1980). As Mason and Mitroff (1981, p. 15) note, organizational problems "must be dealt with in a holistic or synthetic way as well as in an analytic way." This requires jobs to not only be subdivided into their main elements but also to be reassembled in order to understand both the linkages between jobs and the organization as a whole. The concept of strategy helps to describe the overall orientation of the organization and, in this way, provides a more comprehensive notion of staffing requirements than is obtained from job analysis alone. Thus, the basic purpose of staffing in model 2 is to implement competitive strategy.

Origins of Model 2

By the middle of the twentieth century, many companies had begun to pursue diversification strategies. Based on the pioneering efforts of such companies as General Motors, Sears, Du Pont, and Exxon, the availability of the divisional structure beginning in the late 1940s made diversification feasible for a wide cross section of American organizations (Chandler, 1962). Companies that adopted the divisional structure established separate divisions or business units that focused on their respective markets. This organizational innovation allowed a single corporation to operate multiple businesses.

One of the biggest personnel challenges of diversified companies was the selection of general managers to head up the various divisions (Leontiades, 1982). Not surprisingly, the bulk of the initial research linking staffing to strategy concentrated on the division or general manager's job (Chaganti & Sambharya, 1987; Gerstein & Reisman, 1983; Gupta, 1984; Kerr & Jackofsky, 1989; Sonnenfeld & Peiperl, 1988; Stumpf & Hanrahan, 1984; Szilagyi & Schweiger, 1984). Because each division in a diversified company operated as a largely independent business unit, the staffing requirements for an individual division manager's job tended to be unique. For example, some managers were charged with cutting costs and improving efficiency, while others were asked to develop new products and build market share. Without a set of standardized job requirements—indeed there appeared to be no "typical" general manager's job—a modification of the traditional staffing model was needed. As a consequence, model 2 arose from the recognition that staffing requirements hinge largely on the demands of competitive strategy.

From their work with Canadian Pacific, a highly diversified company with over eighty subsidiaries, Miles and Snow

(1984) extended the logic linking strategy and staffing to incorporate all aspects of human resource management. They argued that a fit between strategy and the division manager's job was desirable but incomplete. What was needed was a total integration of the company's competitive strategy and its human resource management function. Achieving a complete fit required heavy involvement of human resource specialists in the strategic planning process.

Characteristics of Model 2

Staffing, according to model 2, is a systemic process. It is a key implementation device, taking a place alongside factors such as organization structure, reward systems, and shared values in support of competitive strategy (Peters & Waterman, 1982). Thus, the effectiveness of staffing in model 2 is defined not only by a person-job match but also in terms of whether the company accomplishes its strategic goals (Butler, Ferris, & Napier, 1991).

In model 2, strategy supplements job analysis as the basis of staffing. Gerstein and Reisman (1983), for example, note that as environmental uncertainty increases, jobs tend to become more oriented toward goals than procedures. They suggest that job descriptions, which standardize and formalize behavior, be broadened into role descriptions that reflect the broader and more changeable strategic requirements of the company. Similarly, Butler, Ferris, and Napier (1991) argue that a company's strategy suggests an additional set of criteria, above and beyond job analysis, to which staffing can be linked. These KSAOs derive from both technological and cultural requirements of the company's strategy, and they change the mix and weight of selection criteria. Role descriptions may grow in use as organizations incorporate more contextual factors into decisions about staffing and job performance (Borman & Motowidlo, 1992).

A third characteristic of model 2 staffing is its emphasis on the relationships among jobs and larger organizational units. This emphasis reflects a synergistic view of staffing—the whole is greater than the sum of its parts. Just as corporations can achieve financial and operating synergies across business units (Pitts & Snow, 1986), staffing procedures can be designed to obtain synergies across individuals and jobs. For example, Susman and Dean (1992) found that the single best predictor of high-technology companies' success in new product development was the ability of interdepartmental teams to work together. As a top executive at Polaroid put it, "Our researchers are not any smarter, but by working together they get the value of each other's intelligence almost instantaneously" (Stewart, 1991a, p. 44).

Last, model 2 staffing takes into account a company's relationship to the environment. In contrast to model 1 staffing, which is based on a closed-system view of the organization, model 2 staffing reflects the market posture a company establishes in its industry. Some companies, such as White Consolidated Industries and Lincoln Electric, try to insulate themselves from environmental disturbances and may, therefore, stabilize staffing by hiring at entry levels and promoting from within using narrow career paths. Conversely, companies such as Merck and Citibank continually launch new ventures in order to capitalize quickly on emerging opportunities. To maximize responsiveness, these companies are much more likely to staff positions at all levels with people hired from outside the company. "Acquiring" external human resources rather than "growing" them internally allows firms to change or add to their traditional businesses (Miles & Snow, 1984).

Applications of Model 2

The results of efforts to improve upon model 1 staffing began to appear in the early 1980s. Most of these efforts focused on higher management levels. For example, Kerr (1982) described how general managers could be selected or placed according to where a business was in its life cycle (growing, mature, and so on). Gupta and Govindarajan (1983) examined relationships among managerial characteristics, business unit strategy, and unit effectiveness. In general, they found that managerial characteristics should be fitted to business strategy to obtain high performance. Olian and Rynes (1984) echoed Miles and Snow

(1978) in suggesting that "defender" companies (efficiency-oriented organizations with narrow product or service lines) are likely to have top management teams dominated by production and accounting specialists. In contrast, management teams of first-to-market "prospector" companies are dominated by research and product development specialists.

The search for a better fit between strategy and staffing was later extended below the general manager level. For example, Borucki and Lafley (1984) described a program at Chase Manhattan Bank that expanded staffing practices to emphasize marketing and managerial skills in addition to financial skills. At about the same time, Corning Glass began to assess qualities such as entrepreneurial flair and creativity in an attempt to align managers with new strategic profiles (Tichy, Fombrun, & DeVanna, 1984). More recently, Polaroid revamped its selection system to reflect its new strategy in digital photography. Among other things, the company must forecast whether to replace departing chemists with other chemists or with electronics engineers (Stewart, 1991a). In all these companies, staffing practices have been modified to better accommodate new strategic directions.

In addition to the link with strategy, staffing practices have been connected with corporate culture (Kerr & Slocum, 1987; Ouchi, 1980). Some companies, such as IBM and Procter & Gamble, have a strong marketing orientation, and staffing decisions conform, at least to some extent, with marketing values. Other companies, such as Hewlett-Packard, are oriented toward R&D and engineering, while still others, such as McDonalds, concentrate on sheer consistency and efficiency. By linking staffing decisions to cultural factors, companies try to ensure that employees have internalized the enterprise's strategic intent and core values (Hamel & Prahalad, 1989). In this way, they will be more likely to act in the interest of the company and as dedicated members of the team, regardless of their formal job duties.

The pursuit of synergy through model 2 staffing can be seen in several companies which rely on teamwork. At the Campbell Soup plant in Maxton, North Carolina, self-managed work teams meet with vendors and set their own schedules. They even propose capital expenditures, including calculations of the internal rates of return on projects (Stewart, 1991a). Other companies, such as Cincinnati Milacron, Digital Equipment, and Hewlett-Packard, have used staffing to enhance productivity among work team members rather than to maximize the fit between individuals and jobs.

The most recent model 2 staffing applications include forming teams through computerized information systems. Apple Computer has a system called Spider that combines a network of personal computers with a video-conferencing system and a data base of employee characteristics. This system allows managers who are considering various business ventures to determine rapidly whether an employee in the company is available to join the project team, what the employee's skills are, and where he or she is located in the company (Dumaine, 1991). It will probably soon be possible for these types of data bases to include information about individuals outside the company who are available for assignment to a business venture on a contractual basis.

Assumptions and Limitations of Model 2

Model 2, staffing as strategy implementation, is becoming increasingly popular. As is true of the traditional staffing model (model 1), model 2 is based on certain underlying assumptions. These assumptions should be examined in order to understand the conditions under which the model is most useful.

First, the model portrays staffing as having a deductive logic—strategy is the premise and staffing is the consequence. This assumption is based on a rational and comprehensive perspective of organizations in which there is clear agreement on, and articulation of, strategy (Kerr & Jackofsky, 1989). However, in some instances, top managers may have different views of strategy and may not communicate their views in detail to lower management levels (Bourgeois, 1980; Hambrick, 1981). Therefore, the success of model 2 staffing is contingent on strategic directions and goals being communicated throughout the organization.

Second, model 2 is a reactive approach to staffing. Staffing as strategy implementation assumes that a company can formulate a strategy to take advantage of opportunities and then harness the necessary human resources to accomplish its goals. However, in rapidly changing industries, it may be difficult to achieve this kind of responsiveness (Bourgeois & Brodwin, 1984; Eisenhardt & Bourgeois, 1988). Consequently, use of model 2 for staffing purposes may be most appropriate when there is sufficient time to position human resources in reaction to environmental changes and opportunities.

Finally, model 2 embraces the assumption that job-person-strategy fit is a desired state of affairs. Although this is certainly true in many circumstances, it has been noted that the fit between strategy and human resources may result in an inability to adapt to changing business environments (Lengnick-Hall & Lengnick-Hall, 1988). In companies where rapid adaptability is essential to success, it may be unwise to tightly couple staffing to the company's current strategy. If it becomes necessary to alter substantially the company's market or technology base, the current pool of human resources may be a source of organizational inertia (Dean & Snell, 1991).

In sum, model 2 characterizes the staffing process as one major aspect of implementing a company's chosen strategy. The alignment between strategy and staffing can be viewed in terms of technological and cultural requirements, broad role descriptions rather than narrow job descriptions, the synergistic relationship among interdepartmental teams, and the company's relationship to its environment. Based on the underlying assumptions that strategy is well defined and stable, that human resources can be quickly deployed after a strategic decision has been made, and that the fit between strategy and human resources is desirable, model 2 may be best suited for organizations that intend to maintain their current strategy over time.

Model 3: Staffing as Strategy Formation

Staffing, as defined in model 2, seems unlikely to evolve as systematically as it did under model 1, nor does it appear that model 2 staffing will enjoy the heyday that its predecessor experienced during the two decades after World War II. This is because some very powerful forces are pushing organizations to consider yet another way of thinking about the staffing process. These forces include changes in workforce demographics, growth of the service sector, and increasingly intense global competition.

Origins of Model 3

The origin of model 3 staffing cannot be pinpointed in time or place. Probably the biggest stimulus of model 3 is coming from demographic changes in both the American and global workforce. Broadly speaking, the domestic workforce in the last years of the twentieth century will grow slowly, become older, more female and ethnically diverse, and more educationally disadvantaged (Johnston & Packer, 1987). Globally, workforces will become much more mobile as legal, economic, and cultural barriers to employment come down (Johnston, 1991). Because all staffing decisions are intimately tied to labor market conditions, the model 2 assumption that staffing can be used to implement a chosen strategy may be called into question. Instead, it may be more prudent to assume that the workforce is essentially fixed and that competitive strategy is a more adjustable element of the company.

Another stimulus of model 3 staffing is the growth of the service sector (Johnston & Packer, 1987). Manufacturing will be a much smaller part of the economy in the year 2000 than it is today. Service industries will create most of the new jobs and wealth during the remainder of this decade. Further, many of the new service jobs will demand much higher skill levels than the jobs of today. Couple this fact with the declining educational levels of the workforce, and the inevitable conclusion is that companies will not be able to implement all the competitive strategies they would like to pursue.

A third factor that has altered the staffing patterns of many companies is global competition. For most U.S. companies, competition during the last two decades has been fierce. Estimates vary widely, but approximately 70–85 percent of the U.S.

economy today is affected by foreign competitors. There is simply more competition in the world marketplace these days. Global competitors reduce profit margins to the barest minimum for low-end goods, and they innovate high-end products and services at ever-increasing rates. Thus, in many industries, American companies have been forced to decide just exactly where they can compete on a world-class basis.

Many companies have decided to meet the challenges posed by global competition by forming network organizations (Miles & Snow, 1986; Snow, Miles, & Coleman, 1992). Unlike a traditional hierarchy, a network organization is a configuration of independent business units linked together by contracts. For example, a single company may research and design a product, while a second assembles finished products from components produced by a third company, and so on. Network organizations thus rely heavily on managers who act as brokers, putting together the resources needed to offer a particular product or service. Staffing a network organization may involve identifying, locating, and organizing human resources across companies and international borders, and the resultant pool of human assets may be used only temporarily.

Characteristics of Model 3

The central feature of model 3 is that staffing propels strategy formation (Dyer, 1983, 1984; Golden & Ramanujam, 1985; Lengnick-Hall & Lengnick-Hall, 1988). Traditionally, competitive strategies have been formed around products, markets, or technologies. However, as business cycles shorten and technological advances accelerate, it is increasingly difficult to build a sustainable strategy around the exploitation of a protected market position (Ohmae, 1982). As the competitive environment becomes more transitory, perhaps the most sustainable source of competitive advantage in the future will be people (Pucik, 1988; Reich, 1991; Schuler & MacMillan, 1984). Because people can learn and adapt, potentially they are a self-renewing resource. Consequently, many companies are beginning to realize that the foundation of their competitive strategy is the quality of their human capital.

Another characteristic of model 3 staffing is its focus on strategic capability (Lenz, 1980; Prahalad, 1983), which refers to a company's potential to simultaneously conceive and implement a wide range of strategies with minimal response time. Instead of staffing to develop a single set of core competencies, strategic capability is enhanced by developing a broad skill base for value creation. A broad skill base helps to prepare for an unpredictable or unknowable future. In sports jargon, model 3 staffing has been referred to as selecting "the best available athlete." Rather than hire for a predefined position, model 3 suggests that companies hire on a value-added basis—locating and solidifying relationships with individuals who offer something unique or different from the company's current stock of talent. Perhaps, too, those individuals with broad knowledge and skills would be more valued than those with narrow skills (though an organization with a broad base of specialists may be more adaptive than one full of generalists). Staffing an organization with diverse skills essentially means that strategic capability is valued more highly than short-term efficiency in the use of human resources. Managers and academics are only beginning to appreciate the need to measure and increase the value of a company's intellectual capital (Stewart, 1991a).

In volatile environments especially, strategic capability requires that organizations rapidly acquire and allocate resources in order to adapt to whatever circumstances arise. In some instances, this involves use of temporary cross-functional teams to handle special projects. Team Taurus at Ford Motor Company is often cited in this regard. In other cases, the solution is a network organization in which independent parties pursue their respective specialties but form more or less permanent relationships to offer a product, conduct a project, and so on. Networks typically allow a wider range of resources to be tapped and frequently at greater speed.

Applications of Model 3

An example of model 3 staffing occurred inadvertently at a start-up company called Heritage Guitars. In 1984, when

Gibson Guitar Company closed its Kalamazoo, Michigan, plant, some of the former employees decided to start their own company. Since Gibson had operated in Michigan for nearly a hundred years, developing a highly skilled workforce, Heritage managers could be unusually selective in their hiring decisions. The overall competence of its employees allowed Heritage to develop a new competitive strategy based on a dedication to craftsmanship. This successful niche strategy thus emerged entirely from the reconstituted employee group.

Alternatively, model 3 staffing can be used by a going concern. For example, at Becton Dickinson, maker of medical diagnostic equipment, corporate executives lay out broad guidelines and let product market strategies emerge "bottom up" from employees in its fifteen divisions. Within each division, the process is spearheaded by a cross-functional team that includes not only division members but also vendors, suppliers, and people from other divisions. The team conceives the strategy and then carries it out (Dumaine, 1991).

Last, in some situations model 3 staffing extends across companies—challenging the notion that staffing is only concerned with the internal accumulation of human assets. For example, at Lewis Galoob Toys (San Francisco), just a hundred or so employees run the core enterprise. Other needed resources are contracted for through an ongoing network. Independent inventors and entertainment companies conceive most of Galoob's products, while outside specialists do most of the design and engineering. Galoob contracts for manufacturing and packaging with a handful of companies in Hong Kong, and they, in turn, pass on the most labor-intensive work to factories in China. When the toys arrive in the United States, they are distributed by commissioned manufacturers' representatives. Galoob does not even collect its accounts. It sells its receivables to Commercial Credit Corporation, a factoring company that also sets Galoob's credit policy. Because the participants in Galoob's network may change with each product cycle, its use of model 3 staffing involves identifying and nurturing potential relationships with outsiders year after year. As one top executive at Galoob describes the approach, "Our business is one of relationships" ("And Now," 1986, p. 64).

Assumptions and Limitations of Model 3

At the moment, model 3, or staffing as strategy formation, is more of a philosophy than a practice. Indeed, in today's economic environment, it would be a farsighted and courageous company that deliberately set out to use the model 3 approach heavily. And yet, because of the trends in workforce demographics and global competition discussed earlier, major competitive advantages may accrue to those companies that move first toward a "staffing as strategy" policy.

Companies considering model 3 staffing face a very different set of assumptions in their decision making. First, staffing follows an inductive logic — staffing is the premise and competitive strategy is the consequence. There is no way to forecast the particular strategy that will evolve from a specific configuration of human resources. Those companies that choose to create a broad skill base through their staffing decisions potentially must be prepared to evaluate large numbers of quite different business strategies. This goes against the conventional wisdom in strategic planning to "stick to the knitting."

Second, model 3 is a proactive approach to staffing. Staffing assumes an equal status with, perhaps even takes priority over, all other resource acquisition and allocation decisions. For most companies, this would require major changes in philosophy and practice. Traditionally, in business circles the human resource function has not enjoyed the status of finance, marketing, manufacturing, and so on. Moreover, companies frequently do not allow their human resource professionals to play an influential role in the strategic planning process (Miles & Snow, 1984). To elevate staffing to a position of preeminence may be a step many companies are unwilling to take. In such cases, the proactive nature of model 3 staffing may be the primary factor inhibiting its adoption.

Last, model 3 is based on the notion of a loose fit between staffing and strategy. Whereas in model 2 strategy and staffing are tightly coupled, staffing in model 3 is intended to generate some amount of organizational slack. That is, at any point in time a portion of a model 3 company is likely to have excess capacity—more ideas and tools in its kit than are being used. Presumably, the excess human resources are working on new strategies that subsequently will be implemented. Thus, slack is both a necessary and desirable by-product of strategic capability, suggesting that model 3 staffing is most appropriate under conditions of continuous change.

In sum, model 3 represents a process in which staffing is a precursor of competitive strategy. The process begins with a search for the "best" people. However, *best* is not defined as those individuals who are needed to implement a chosen strategy; *best* refers to people who possess value-added KSAOs. Companies that rely heavily on model 3 staffing acquire a broad skill base that can be used to rapidly develop strategies for dealing with coming competitive realities. These companies are not efficient users of human resources. Rather, they possess the capacity to deploy resources quickly to take advantage of shifting pockets of opportunity. It seems likely that small companies (or particular units of large companies) will adopt a model 3 approach.

Implications for Staffing Practice and Research

Each of the three conceptual models discussed above has direct implications for staffing practice and research. In general, both managers and researchers need to focus greater attention on the issues associated with the newer model 2 and model 3 approaches.

Practical Implications

The basic components of the staffing process according to models 1, 2, and 3 are shown in Table 14.2. By comparing and contrasting each component, one can see how the major staffing goals and implementation activities vary across the three models. For example, the goal of recruitment under model 1 conditions (a largely stable organizational environment and little consideration given to competitive strategy) is designed to fill open positions. The availability of jobs is broadcast widely in order to generate a large number of applicants. Casting a wide net for applicants increases the probability of selection mechanisms being effective.

By contrast, recruiting under model 2 (implementing a business strategy that may persist for some time) is much more targeted. The goal here is to identify and attract individuals whose talents support the desired strategy. Rather than advertising widely for applicants, recruiting may take the form of hiring specific individuals away from competitors, using headhunter firms to locate candidates, and so on.

Last, under model 3, recruiting may not even be designed to bring new individuals into the company. Instead, the purpose of recruiting may be to identify potentially useful human resources and to build preliminary relationships with them. Recruiting, for example, may involve offering small projects to these individuals, not only to assess their competence but also to familiarize them with the company's operations. The same recruiting logic could be extended to include alliances with schools, ventures with potential upstream and downstream partners, and so on. For example, at Imcera Group, which makes drugs and health care products for humans and animals, recruiters maintain ongoing relationships with colleges and vocational and technical schools as well as with small companies that need investors. Each of these relationships is a potential conduit through which the company may acquire intellectual capital (Stewart, 1991b).

Just as recruitment varies considerably across the three models, so does selection. Because model 1 is oriented toward maximizing person-job fit, selection decisions are based on a rational process of weeding out unqualified applicants from those that fit the job requirements. Given the structured nature of jobs, selection decisions tend to be embedded in the testing process itself. For example, using either a multiple hurdle or a compensatory decision formula, managers compare test scores to differentiate acceptable from unacceptable candidates. To the extent possible, the testing procedures eliminate subjectivity, and the highest-scoring individuals are the most desirable candidates.

In contrast, selection decisions under model 2 may be less systematic. Since the goal here is to select a configuration of

Table 14.2. Basic Components of the Staffing Process.

	Model 1: *Staffing as* *Person-Job Match*	Model 2: *Staffing as* *Strategy Implementation*	Model 3: *Staffing as* *Strategy Formation*
Recruitment	Expand pool of job applicants	Attract targeted individuals to enhance core competencies	Build relationships with potentially useful human resources
Selection	Achieve person-job fit by rejecting less desirable applicants	Develop a configuration of individuals that meets synergistic needs of strategy	Enhance strategic capability by choosing individuals who bring new skills to the company
Appraisal	Based on job performance	Based on strategy implementation	Based on strategy formation
Promotion	Reward is upward movement within a hierarchy	Reward is increased centrality to current strategy	Reward is greater inclusion in strategy-formation process

individuals who can best work with one another and who, as a group, meet the strategy requirements, selection criteria would extend beyond the technical requirements of jobs to include such factors as interpersonal compatibility among team members and fit with corporate culture. Consequently, selection decisions might involve debate and negotiation among managers, with each one providing his or her rationale for selecting certain individuals. Along these lines, there has been a trend among companies to move away from paper-and-pencil tests (American Society for Personnel Administration, 1983). Instead, methods such as leaderless group discussions and business simulations, typically found in assessment centers, provide both the forum for observing dynamics among individuals and the opportunity for debate among managers about whom to select. Not surprisingly, companies such as Motorola, Saturn, and Hewlett-Packard, which rely heavily on teamwork, also invest heavily in the development of assessment centers.

Last, selection decisions under model 3 are designed to bring into the organization's sphere of operations individuals who add value by broadening the skill base and enhancing flexibility. At the extreme, selection decisions may not be based on a preconceived definition of the job. Instead, decision makers consider who among available candidates offers the highest marginal (value-added) contribution to the firm. In addition, selection decisions under model 3 may include contracting for an individual's services rather than absorbing that individual into the company. The idea is to enhance strategic capability rather than fill a position.

Performance appraisal, the third major component of staffing, also varies across the three models. Each model contains a different set of assumptions about the role that employees play in contributing to the company's success. In model 1, individuals are viewed as executors of jobs, and jobs in turn are aggregated to form the organization as a whole. Therefore, according to this model, managers assess an individual's contribution by evaluating the quality and quantity of performance on the job.

Alternatively, model 2 staffing views employees as the source of distinctive competencies needed to implement company strategy. Consequently, the appropriate criterion for evaluating performance under model 2 is the degree of success achieved in strategy implementation. Individuals are evaluated not only according to job performance but also in terms of the role they play in strategy implementation. The criteria of role performance, compared to job performance, are likely to be longer-term, more subjective, and more closely related to overall business unit performance. Of course, there is an implicit trade-off between criterion deficiency and contamination. Broader performance criteria may reflect the impact that individuals have on strategy implementation, but they also may be affected by factors outside the individual's control. To balance the appraisal between individual job performance and strategy implementation, companies need to include input from (in addition to superiors) peers, subordinates, the job holder, and other internal stakeholders.

Last, employee contribution under model 3 staffing concerns the extent to which a person adds strategic value to the company, an understandably difficult assessment to make. Economists have made some progress in measuring intellectual capital at the organizational level. For example, Tobin's Q (the ratio of a company's market value to the replacement value of physical assets) indicates the value of intangible assets, part of which is intellectual capital (Stewart, 1991a). However, this index only refers to the value of the employee group as a whole. To appraise the contribution of an individual under model 3, managers must balance the need for future organizational adaptability with the requirements of current performance. Managers must attempt to ascertain whether an individual's ideas and skills (which represent potential) have actually led to the creation of successful strategies. While a certain amount of organizational slack is expected in model 3 companies, in those cases where an individual has not regularly contributed to strategy formation, he or she would represent dysfunctional slack. Over time, as in all organizations, managers must find ways of making such individuals more productive.

The last component of staffing, promotion, can be viewed as both a reward for good performance and a way of solidifying the employment relationship. Just as recruiting, selecting, and appraising vary across the three staffing models, so does promotion. In model 1, for example, the employment relationship occurs inside a hierarchical organization. Consequently, promotion involves some form of vertical advancement (higher status, pay, benefits, and so on compared to others in the hierarchy).

In contrast, model 2 staffing depicts the employment relationship in systemic terms based on strategy implementation. Although vertical advancements are used in model 2 companies, promotions also may take the form of increased centrality to strategy. Over time, top management tends to rely more on individuals (and functions) whose efforts are instrumental to successful strategy implementation. For example, at Polaroid, certain types of scientists and engineers have moved from peripheral roles in strategy implementation to become mainstays of the company's competitive advantage (Stewart, 1991a). In addition to enjoying greater prominence within the organization, these individuals are also assured of greater employment security (for example, their budgets might be the last to be cut during retrenchment or they might be the last to be laid off in the event of downsizing).

Last, under model 3 staffing, the concept of employment may extend beyond traditional organizational boundaries. Therefore, a promotion need not be constrained to a position within the company (although it could). Rather, in these situations, a promotion may be increased inclusion in the strategy-formation process. Either to reward valuable contributions, or to ensure continued relations, the company can make certain individuals a more permanent part of the decision-making process that determines where and how the company will position itself in the future.

Research Implications

If the characterizations of models 1, 2, and 3 are valid, what do they suggest about future research in the staffing area? In our view, the research issues associated with model 1, which has undergone decades of development, need no further articulation. Conversely, model 2, though buttressed by a limited amount of empirical evidence, needs much additional work before it will become useful to practitioners. Last, model 3 is a revolutionary staffing approach that requires further conceptual as well as empirical development. Therefore, our recommendations about future research will address only models 2 and 3.

First, both staffing models require contingency studies to determine where they are most effective. For example, several aspects of model 2 have been investigated empirically: (1) the matching of general managers with business strategies (Gupta and Govindarajan, 1983), (2) the integration of business strategy with human resource management practices (Miles & Snow, 1984; Snell, 1992), and (3) the role and process of the human resource function with respect to strategy (Golden & Ramanujam, 1985). However, there have been relatively few studies of the synergies within and across work teams required by competitive strategy and, in turn, the requirements of team composition on staffing practice (Snell & Dean, 1990). In all likelihood, as the form of interdependencies changes, so too will the requirements for staffing. For example, as companies such as Ford, Boeing, and Carrier attempt to integrate design and manufacturing, they require that their employees understand and contribute to each other's work (Susman & Dean, 1992).

With regard to model 3, contingency studies first must identify where this approach is likely to be used. In particular, research should focus on those factors in the organization and environment that make the value of flexibility high enough to outweigh the carrying costs of slack. Because of the expense needed to achieve capacity, model 3 may not be used for the entire company but rather in special pockets or at higher organizational levels. Also, the philosophy of model 3 may be employed to guide staffing in dynamic network organizations that are regularly reconfigured to pursue shifting market opportunities. Here, contingency studies should determine which network elements (designers, producers, marketers, suppliers) require the most excess capacity to achieve flexibility.

Second, both newer models require longitudinal field studies to closely monitor staffing decisions and processes. The dynamics of models 2 and 3 are substantially different. Staffing under model 2 is a logical, derivative process, whereas in model 3 it is proactive and anticipatory. The intricacies of these two different approaches perhaps can be uncovered best by conducting case studies that trace staffing decisions. Such studies also are able to place staffing decisions in the broader context of human resource planning as it relates to competitive strategy. These types of field studies are necessary to determine the effectiveness of as well as the interplay between models 2 and 3 when they are used simultaneously in a particular organization.

Third, since the nature of predictors and criteria differs under models 2 and 3, the appropriate approach to studying validity should be examined. Although the concept of individual differences is important to each model, the capacity to specify desired attributes is reduced. Job analysis, which clarifies KSAOs under model 1, may be less useful under models 2 and 3. However, without the specificity of job analysis, companies may have problems demonstrating content validity in their selection procedures. Under model 2, for example, KSAOs must be inferred from strategy or broad role descriptions. As discussed earlier, translating the selection requirements of these concepts is a difficult task. Similarly, model 3 staffing may be conducted with minimal preconception of desired applicant attributes since requirements cannot be completely forecast. Perhaps general tests of cognitive ability (such as the General Aptitude Test Battery or Differential Aptitude Tests) may be the most valuable since these selection techniques demonstrate useful validity for a wide variety of jobs, especially when task complexity is high (Hunter & Hunter, 1984).

Just as the nature of predictors differs, staffing outcomes also differ under the three models, suggesting that the criteria for validation studies must be defined carefully in each case. Broadly speaking, staffing effectiveness under model 2 concerns the ability to implement strategy; effectiveness under model 3 refers to the capability of formulating strategy. However, as noted earlier, if the criteria used to judge performance are expanded to include strategy implementation (model 2) or strategy formation (model 3), it becomes more difficult to isolate the extent to which these organizational outcomes are due to an individual's contribution. Clearly, demonstrating criterion-related validity becomes more problematic in these cases. Therefore, research on dynamic criteria and criterion dimensionality should continue, with a special focus on the influence of strategy.

In sum, the research implications indicate that both models 2 and 3 should be examined in light of their different organizational contexts. This includes both content and process issues as well as the validity and effectiveness of each model over time. In the future, organizations are likely to rely on all three of the staffing models discussed here in their human resource planning and management activities. Since none of the models is inherently better than the others, future research should examine when, where, and how each would most effectively be used.

Conclusion

As companies increasingly depend on intellectual capital as the basis for competitive advantage, human resources in general, and staffing practices in particular, move toward the top of the organizational agenda. The assumptions and parameters underlying model 1 make it an appropriate staffing approach for organizations that continue to operate in industries characterized by stability and certainty. However, an increasing number of companies must learn how to integrate strategy and staffing in order to cope with rapid change and fierce competition in the global marketplace. Model 2 helps them implement strategy through staffing, whereas model 3 helps conceive strategy through staffing. Each of these models has its place within and across organizations, and each, used appropriately, may help companies outperform those which are slower to link staffing to the priorities of competition.

References

Alpander, G. C., & Botter, C. H. (1981). An integrated model of strategic human resource planning and utilization. *Human Resource Planning, 4,* 189–203.

American Society for Personnel Administration. (1983). *Employee selection procedures* (ASPA-BNA Survey No. 45). Washington, DC: Bureau of National Affairs.

And now, the post-industrial corporation. (1986, March 3). *Business Week,* pp. 64–71.

Borman, W. C., & Motowidlo, S. J. (1992). Expanding the criterion domain to include elements of contextual performance. In N. Schmitt & W. C. Borman (Eds.), *Personnel selection* (Vol. 4). San Francisco: Jossey-Bass.

Borucki, C. C., & Lafley, A. F. (1984). Strategic staffing at Chase Manhattan Bank. In C. J. Fombrun, N. M. Tichy, & M. A. DeVanna (Eds.), *Strategic human resource management.* New York: Wiley.

Bourgeois, L. J., III. (1980). Performance and consensus. *Strategic Management Journal, 1,* 227–248.

Bourgeois, L. J., III, & Brodwin, D. R. (1984). Strategic implementation: Five approaches to an elusive phenomenon. *Strategic Management Journal, 5,* 241–264.

Butler, J. E., Ferris, G. R., & Napier, N. K. (1991). *Strategy and human resources management.* Cincinnati, OH: South-Western.

Cascio, W. F. (1991). *Applied psychology in personnel management.* Englewood Cliffs, NJ: Prentice-Hall.

Chaganti, R., & Sambharya, R. (1987). Strategic orientation and characteristics of upper management. *Strategic Management Journal, 8,* 393–401.

Chandler, A. D., Jr. (1962). *Strategy and structure: Chapters in the history of the American industrial enterprise.* Cambridge, MA: MIT Press.

Dean, J. W., Jr., & Snell, S. A. (1991). Integrated manufacturing and job design: The moderating effect of organizational inertia. *Academy of Management Journal, 34,* 776–804.

Dumaine, B. (1991, June 17). The bureaucracy busters. *Fortune,* pp. 36–50.

Dunnette, M. D. (1963). A note on the criterion. *Journal of Applied Psychology, 47,* 251–253.

Dyer, L. (1983). Bringing human resources into the strategy formulation process. *Human Resource Management, 22,* 257–271.

Dyer, L. (1984). Linking human resource and business strategies. *Human Resource Planning, 7,* 79–84.

Eisenhardt, K. M., & Bourgeois, L. J,. III. (1988). Politics of strategic decision making in high velocity environments: Toward a mid-range theory. *Academy of Management Journal, 31,* 737–770.

Gerstein, M., & Reisman, H. (1983). Strategic selection: Matching executives to business conditions. *Sloan Management Review, 24,* 33–49.

Golden, K. A., & Ramanujam, V. (1985). Between a dream and a nightmare: On the integration of the human resource management and strategic business planning processes. *Human Resource Management, 24,* 429–452.

Gupta, A. K. (1984). Contingency linkages between strategy and general manager characteristics: A conceptual examination. *Academy of Management Review, 9,* 399–412.

Gupta, A. K., & Govindarajan, V. (1983). Business unit strategy, managerial characteristics, and business unit effectiveness at strategy implementation. *Academy of Management Journal, 27,* 25–41.

Hambrick, D. C. (1981). Strategic awareness within top management teams. *Strategic Management Journal, 2,* 263–279.

Hamel, G., & Prahalad, C. K. (1989, May–June). Strategic intent. *Harvard Business Review,* pp. 63–76.

Hunter, J. E., & Hunter, R. F. (1984). Validity and utility of alternative predictors of job performance. *Psychological Bulletin, 96,* 72–95.

Johnston, W. B. (1991, March–April). Global work force 2000: The new world labor market. *Harvard Business Review,* pp. 115–127.

Johnston, W. B., & Packer, A. E. (1987). *Workforce 2000.* Indianapolis, IN: Hudson Institute.

Kerr, J. L. (1982). Assigning managers on the basis of the life cycle. *Journal of Business Strategy, 2,* 58–65.

Kerr, J. L., & Jackofsky, E. F. (1989). Aligning managers with strategies: Management development versus selection. *Strategic Management Journal, 10* [Special issue], 157–170.

Kerr, J. L., & Slocum, J. W., Jr. (1987). Managing corporate culture through reward systems. *Academy of Management Executive, 1,* 99–108.

Lengnick-Hall, C. A., & Lengnick-Hall, M. A. (1988). Strategic human resources management: A review of the literature and a proposed typology. *Academy of Management Review, 13,* 454–470.

Lenz, R. T. (1980). Strategic capability: A concept and framework for analysis. *Academy of Management Review, 5,* 225–234.

Leontiades, M. (1982). Choosing the right manager to fit the strategy. *Journal of Business Strategy, 3,* 58–69.

Mason, R. O., & Mitroff, I. I. (1981). *Challenging strategic planning assumptions.* New York: Wiley.

Miles, R. E., & Snow, C. C. (1978). *Organizational strategy, structure, and process.* New York: McGraw-Hill.

Miles, R. E., & Snow, C. C. (1984, Summer). Designing strategic human resource systems. *Organizational Dynamics,* pp. 36–52.

Miles, R. E., & Snow, C. C. (1986). Network organizations: New concepts for new forms. *California Management Review, 28,* 62–73.

Ohmae, K. (1982). *The mind of the strategist.* New York: McGraw-Hill.

Olian, J. D., & Rynes, S. L. (1984). Organizational staffing: Integrating practice with strategy. *Industrial Relations, 23,* 170–181.

Ouchi, W. (1980). Markets, hierarchies, and clans. *Administrative Science Quarterly, 20,* 129–141.

Peters, T. J., & Waterman, R. H., Jr. (1982). *In search of excellence.* New York: HarperCollins.

Pitts, R. A., & Snow, C. C. (1986). *Strategies for competitive success.* New York: Wiley.

Prahalad, C. K. (1983). Developing strategic capability: An agenda for top management. *Human Resource Management, 22,* 237–254.

Prien, E. P. (1966). Dynamic character of criteria: Organizational change. *Journal of Applied Psychology, 50,* 501–504.

Pucik, V. (1988). Strategic alliances, organizational learning, and competitive advantage: The HRM agenda. *Human Resource Management, 27,* 77–94.

Reich, R. (1991). *The work of nations.* New York: Knopf.

Schmidt, F. L., Hunter, J. E., McKenzie, R. C., & Muldrow, T. W. (1979). Impact of valid selection procedures on workforce productivity. *Journal of Applied Psychology, 64,* 609–626.

Schmitt, N., & Schneider, B. (1983). Current issues in personnel selection. In K. M. Rowland & G. R. Ferris (Eds.), *Research in personnel and human resource management.* Greenwich, CT: JAI Press.

Schneider, B., & Konz, A. M. (1989). Strategic job analysis. *Human Resource Management, 28,* 51–64.

Schuler, R. S., & MacMillan, I. C. (1984). Gaining competitive advantage through human resource management practices. *Human Resource Management, 23,* 241–255.

Smith, E. C. (1982a). Strategic business and human resources: Part I. *Personnel Journal, 61,* 606–610.

Smith, E. C. (1982b). Strategic business and human resources: Part II. *Personnel Journal, 61,* 680–683.

Snell, S. A. (1992). A test of control theory in strategic human resource management: The mediating effect of administrative information. *Academy of Management Journal, 35,* 292–327.

Snell, S. A., & Dean, J. W., Jr. (1990). The match between human resources management and advanced manufacturing. Academy of Management *Proceedings, 41,* 294–298.

Snow, C. C., Miles, R. E., & Coleman, H. J., Jr. (1992, Winter). Managing 21st century network organizations. *Organizational Dynamics,* pp. 5–20.

Sonnenfeld, J. A., & Peiperl, M. A. (1988). Staffing policy as a strategic response: A typology of career systems. *Academy of Management Review, 13,* 588–600.

Stewart, T. A. (1991a, June 3). Brainpower. *Fortune,* pp. 44–60.

Stewart, T. A. (1991b, Spring–Summer). The new American century: Where we stand. *Fortune,* pp. 12–23.

Stumpf, S. A., & Hanrahan, N. M. (1984). Designing organizational career management practices to fit strategic management objectives. In R. S. Schuler & S. A. Youngblood (Eds.), *Readings in personnel and human resource management* (2nd ed.). St. Paul, MN: West.

Susman, G. I., & Dean, J. W., Jr. (1992). Development of a model for predicting design for manufacturability effectiveness. In G. I. Susman (Ed.), *Design for manufacturing.* Cambridge, MA: Harvard University Press.

Szilagyi, A. D., & Schweiger, D. M. (1984). Matching managers to strategies: A review and suggested framework. *Academy of Management Review, 9,* 626–637.

Thorndike, R. L. (1949). *Personnel selection: Test and measurement techniques.* New York: Wiley.

Tichy, N. M., Fombrun, C. J., & DeVanna, M. A. (1982). Strategic human resource management. *Sloan Management Review, 23,* 47–61.

Tichy, N. M., Fombrun, C. J., & DeVanna, M. A. (1984). The organizational context of strategic human resource management. In C. J. Fombrun, N. M. Tichy, & M. A. DeVanna (Eds.), *Strategic human resource management.* New York: Wiley.

Uniform guidelines on employee selection procedures. (1978). *Federal Register, 43,* 38290–38315.

Walker, J. W. (1980). *Human resource planning.* New York: McGraw-Hill.

Part Two

COMMENTARIES

15

The Need for Change:
Six Persistent Themes

Robert M. Guion

I have chosen to comment on six overlapping themes that recur in this book. They are persistent and important, and after one reads these chapters, clearer in focus. They are (1) enlarged units of analysis, (2) mutations of the perennial criterion problem, (3) the symbiosis of science and application, (4) additional predictor constructs, (5) evaluating selection practices, and (6) revisiting moderators.

Another theme, arching over all six, is the compelling need for change. People in organizations must become smarter in hiring, placing, transferring, and "selecting out" other people if they want to be competitive now and in the years ahead, domestically and internationally. Agreeing with Offermann and Gowing (Chapter Twelve), I would say that traditional selection practices alone will no longer serve adequately the interests of organizations wishing to be globally competitive.

Change is demanded. In the process of change, however, we should be careful not to throw out methods that have a proven record of usefulness. The proven record supports the Snow and Snell (Chapter Fourteen) model 1 approach to staffing; we know the most about it, we have the most evidence that it is likely to work, and we know how to find out if it does not. An analogy in educational measurement is the popularity of bashing

481

multiple-choice examinations; Frechtling (1991) and Mehrens (1992) have shown that most of the criticisms are unwarranted and that the rush to a new form of performance assessment that wholly rejects traditional testing is a disservice. Change is demanded, but, to follow the old cliché, let's change the bath water and keep the baby.

These six themes are my personal choices. Others might have included the ubiquitous legal theme, but I chose to set it aside. Changing laws will, of course, require changes in selection practices. Nevertheless, there were a couple of reasons for passing up the opportunity to comment on legal matters. First, the new laws (the Americans with Disabilities Act and the 1991 revisions of the Civil Rights Act) have yet to be interpreted by federal courts, so we do not yet know their real implications. Second, current regulations, such as the *Uniform Guidelines,* tend to freeze the status quo of a couple of decades ago. Interestingly, and disturbingly, they tend to call for the old concept of excluding people "on the basis of talents lacked" (see Chapter Twelve, p. 403) instead of looking for new and better ways to do things. In a Frontiers series book, we should be looking for improvements.

Units of Analysis

Several of these chapters require us to expand our notion of the proper unit of analysis in designing and evaluating selection procedures or systems. Traditionally (and into the foreseeable future), the individual job applicant has been the unit of analysis. The traditional approach—model 1 for Snow and Snell (Chapter Fourteen)—considers one applicant at a time for one job at a time, despite occasional lip service to placement. (The psychometrically oriented among us like to think the consideration is typically based on reliable measures predicting an important criterion demonstrably well, but we need not explore personnel offices widely to discover that psychometric ideals often have little to do with actual decisions.)

The traditional approach involves some implicit assumptions, made explicit by Snow and Snell (Chapter Fourteen): that jobs exist and function independently, that people and jobs (and job-person matches) are stable over time, and that meaningful individual criteria can be specified. These do not always hold. Some jobs are so inextricably linked that it makes no sense to talk about the performance of a person on one such job as if it were independent of the performance of those on linked jobs. Technological change, or simple drift of job duties over time, or transfers to new or different responsibilities can mean that personal resources — the familiar knowledge, skills, abilities, and other characteristics (KSAOs) — originally required are replaced by demands for different resources in the changed conditions. Appropriate criteria can be conceptualized more often than measured. Where one or more of these assumptions do not hold, it is reasonable to seek alternative ways of doing things.

There are others, but one alternative inferred from several of these chapters is to consider more inclusive units of analysis, at least for the criterion predicted. Although Campbell, McCloy, and Oppler (Chapter Two) explicitly describe a theory of individual performance, they acknowledge that performance can be an attribute of groups, organizations, or larger entities. The contextual criteria described by Borman and Motowidlo (Chapter Three) clearly call for a level of analysis cutting across different jobs and job families. In the Snow and Snell (Chapter Fourteen) models 2 and 3, criteria (if sought) would be organizationwide, or at least in organizational units. As a matter of fact, in these models and in references to selection "systems" in other chapters, the outcomes might not even be called criteria; they would be described as the dependent variables of quasiexperimental research. Perhaps the word *criterion* has itself unduly restricted our thinking about what is to be accomplished through changed selection procedures.

Expanding criterion units to measures of team or group or organizational unit outcomes does not change the fact that decisions are still made about individual candidates. We still ask, for example, Which candidate will contribute more to the performance (or the stability, or the cohesiveness, or some other outcome) of the work group to which he or she is to be assigned? or, Which candidates make the organization more vulnerable to inventory shrinkage? It is not uncommon to work at an individual unit of analysis with individual predictor data and collective (team, group, or work unit) common criterion data across cases in a larger unit of criterion analysis. It is not a practice with which I am comfortable, perhaps because of its slavishness to a traditional selection model.

There are situations where larger units of analysis are appropriate, for example, the initial formation of teams. A group ability profile, group mean ability, or the standard deviation of ability measures might be hypothesized predictors of a measure of group performance. If there are enough candidates, trying different rules for team formation to maximize a team criterion is desirable; unfortunately, the domination of our thinking by the individual approach leaves us with little guidance either for methods of team formation or for evaluating the methods once developed.

We probably need to put experimental and quasiexperimental research methods into our battery of techniques for evaluating the success of selection systems in producing intended outcomes. A study done several decades ago (to which I can no longer find a reference) was said to find that merely having a testing program resulted in superior candidates. Replication of the study today would require testing in some organizational units but not others and measuring some form of organizational unit performance as a dependent variable. Much of the integrity-testing literature has used such a research design (Goldberg, Grenier, Guion, Sechrest, & Wing, 1991). The Snow and Snell (Chapter Fourteen) synergistic models 2 and 3 are organizational gestalts. Such models offer approaches to selection decisions that, for some kinds of jobs at least, are badly needed. Allegiance to tradition must not prevent us from evaluating what we have accomplished in terms of broader objectives.

Outcomes

We should specify more clearly what we want to accomplish through selection. When we propose or install new selection procedures, we do so (presumably) to seek some sort of organizational change. Do we seek improved mean performance? If so, how will we define it? Is our aim to cut costs, to improve quality, to develop a more stable and committed workforce, to reduce employee stress, to facilitate achievement of community or social goals, to promote safety, or all of the above and more? Answers to such questions specify the results or outcomes of selection or staffing decisions at an organizational level.

They are typically achieved by hiring people who can contribute to these results. If we seek improved quality of products or services, we try to hire people who have or will promptly acquire high skill levels and who will be motivated to do better than merely good enough. The organizational outcomes are achieved by hiring people whose individual performance is predicted to be of high quality.

It sounds so easy. The cup-to-lip slippage is often attributable to the hoary "criterion problem." In part, the criterion problem is a measurement problem. In more serious part, it is a conceptual problem. We have so much trouble defining the individual outcomes leading to intended organizational results, and in seeing the linkage between individual and organizational outcomes, that it is necessarily hard to determine the utility of our efforts to achieve them (see Chapter Ten). Many of the chapters in this book require expanded thinking about the outcomes to be achieved.

Expanded Criterion Constructs

Job performance is one such outcome, but it is not the only one. Nor do the contextual criteria listed by Borman and Motowidlo (Chapter Three) exhaust the possibilities. Some criteria worthy of greater consideration include extraorganizational considerations such as public perceptions of organizational fairness and basic humanity (see Chapters Six, Eleven, and Twelve). Chapter Eleven, in particular, requires expanding our views about the organizational values affected by selection procedures of all kinds. Selection is not simply a matter of bringing people from outside into the organization. It is also a matter of "selecting out" and also of transferring people, promoting people, choosing a few people for special opportunities, and making many other decisions about people already in one organizational role and being considered for another.

When we consider the extent of the kinds of personnel decisions a selection paradigm encompasses, we need a broader identification of relevant criteria. As Offermann and Gowing (Chapter Twelve) make clear, there are vital changes in the values and attitudes — and circumstances — in the larger society. As just one example, the forefathers who developed the traditional selection paradigm rarely found it necessary to think about spouses or other family members in making selection decisions; it is simply foolish, in this era of dual-earner and dual-career families, to ignore these very human, personal considerations in making decisions. In this book I see new concern for outcomes such as perceptions of basic fairness and consideration of people as people. In short, I see more humane considerations being included in the outcomes to be influenced by selection decisions. I think that is not merely wishful thinking.

Clearly, personnel decisions are driven by organizational values and policies. There seems to be some movement in American industry toward policies and practices that guarantee greater job security; such movement surely requires changes in the way people are selected. If employees have assurance of continued employment with an organization, then criteria such as flexibility in accepting and performing task responsibilities, or sustained motivation, will be far more important to consider in initial hiring — and "selecting out" will be far more difficult (see Chapter Eleven).

Dimensions of Performance

The traditional criterion is performance, but that is another excessively simplistic statement, as is made clear in Chapter Two. Performance is not likely to be unidimensional; for example, in Chapter Two the authors argue for eight, not one, general factors in performance. Moreover, in each general factor distinctions can be made according to the three "parameters" they propose (speed versus accuracy, for example). Concomitant with the growing acceptance of validity generalization has been a growing belief in a single general factor of performance; obviously, Campbell and his associates (Chapter Two) do not share that belief. How are we to determine which view is more tenable? The one-factor and the eight-factor camps *could* set up forts and (metaphorically, of course) throw snowballs at each other; systematic research is a more profitable alternative. Metaphorical snowballs aside, such research should get under way as soon as possible; it is long overdue.

Whatever the dimensionality, a more important but also more troublesome theme may be the insistence that a theory of performance is a theory of behavior, of activity — not of the results of that activity. In this sense, the theory posited by Campbell and colleagues (Chapter Two) is a systematically coherent response to the "criteria for what?" question posed so long ago by S. R. Wallace (1965), who insisted on behavioral criteria for the sake of understanding utilitarian predictions. A similar view was expressed by Borman and Motowidlo (Chapter Three), who define task performance as proficiency in carrying out task activities and "contextual criteria" as activities establishing the environment in which tasks are performed. More frequently, however, performance is still treated mainly as a general criterion concept without much distinction between the results of doing something and the act of doing it.

Even Campbell and colleagues (Chapter Two) are not totally consistent. To me, at least, there is something not quite consistent in saying at one point that performance and behavior are synonyms, and at another that performance is what an organization hires someone to do — well. It seems to me that organizations usually hire people to produce outcomes, not simply to behave. There is no necessarily "one best way" to produce those outcomes; we must entertain the idea that different kinds of performance may be equally effective (or equally ineffective). Consider a sales example. An organization hires salespeople to sell its product, and it defines performance not in terms of persuasive behavior but in terms of the volume or of the dollar value of goods or services sold. Activities producing such *results* may be different for equally successful salespeople. One person may sell high dollar value by carefully selecting clients likely to make very large purchases; another may do so by getting out of the office and canvassing widely.

What is to be predicted? We may predict any of three things in this example: sales level in dollars, client screening, or aggressive canvassing. What do we want to predict? Probably all three. Sales level is important to the organization, but finding out whether those who behave in one way sell more, less, or about the same as those who behave in another will help us refine and understand the relationship between predictor and outcome and thereby, it is to be hoped, improve our predictions.

Campbell and associates (Chapter Two) say further that performance consists of "goal-relevant actions" the individual controls. Is client screening goal relevant? Is canvassing goal relevant? In both cases, the intuitive answer is yes, if the technique works for the individual using it. The distinction between performance as activity and performance as a consequence of activity is important, but it imposes the burden of determining which goal-relevant actions are more useful to the organization. Sometimes we know. Sometimes we do not, and we should be finding out.

Job Analysis and More

How will we find out? The traditional answer is to analyze jobs. Here again the authors of the preceding chapters give us a recurring theme: job analysis could do with some new thinking. Arvey and Sackett (see Chapter Six) said we have an "incredible obsession" with job analysis; resources expended on job analysis sometimes beggar those devoted to developing and understanding predictor and criterion measures. Job analysis, especially through task inventories, seems to focus as much on minutiae as on grander themes of job responsibilities, and it is not always easy to tell the difference. As Offermann and Gowing (Chapter Twelve) say, too much job analysis is too narrow in intent; they argue that analysis of larger groups—occupations or occupational groups—is probably more fruitful. A narrow job analysis inventory can tell us the many things people on the job do; it can even tell us how important people think it is to do each of these things. It cannot, however, give us evidence that these opinions are correct, and it ordinarily does not try to find out how the job may be improved. (That may require more detailed research, maybe experimental research or the use of structural equations, to test hypotheses that certain kinds of actions lead to the outcomes incumbents are hired to produce.) Further, it cannot tell us much about long-range contributions of the job to the business strategies of the organization.

Job analysis, as we generally know it, suffers from a couple of serious plagues, at least for inferring performance requirements. One of these is its emphasis on the status quo. Hiring bookkeepers today to do what they did thirty years ago would be obviously crazy; they simply do not perform the same tasks. They do, however, have the same outcomes from their differing tasks: summary reports of debits and credits.

We need further kinds of analysis to avoid the static nature of conventional job analyses. We need organizational forecasting information, strategic plans, and both current information and plans related to the interactions between different organizational entities (Chapter Fourteen). When we learn what information and plans we need, and how to get them, we can move to strategic staffing.

Symbiosis of Research and Practice

It is worth pointing out that much of what seems implied by these first two themes will require research, much of it extensive. Who will do the research: the academic scientific community? Probably not; except for some aspects of the theory by Campbell and colleagues (Chapter Two), the required research is too closely tied to mundane, practical matters with little theoretical interest and too large in scope for tenure-ensuring little papers. Will the community of psychologists full time in industry do the research? Probably not; the payoffs are not immediate enough. Will the community of consulting research psychologists do it? Maybe; but only if other communities can provide the essential funding.

Instead of looking for the right party, we need to acknowledge that all of these communities have a stake in finding answers to the questions raised in these themes and those yet to be discussed. We all — academicians, psychologists in organizations, and consultants — share a need to consider larger units of analysis, expanded and clarified constructs defining the outcomes of work and of personnel decisions, and analyses of needs going beyond conventional job analysis.

This, too, is a recurring theme in this book. The phrase "research and practice" occurs often, and I think it is generally used in implicit recognition of the symbiotic relationship of the two. The practical art of making personnel decisions needs to be informed by research, both straightforward validation research and more basic theoretical, explanatory research. The more basic research needs to be responsive to the realistic objectives of selection systems in developing its efforts to improve the foundations of the decision maker's art. And it needs to recognize that these are efforts to *improve,* not to reach perfection. I was pleased at the practical comments of Sackett and Arvey (Chapter Thirteen) to the effect that we seek processes that can contribute to better selection procedures, even when they are less than ideal, and that use of all components of the process is better than the use of only a couple — and that using a couple may contribute more than using only one.

Snow and Snell (Chapter Fourteen) noted that "there have been relatively few studies of the synergies within and across work teams required by competitive strategy and, in turn, the requirements of team composition on staffing practice." The gifted understatement aside, "studies of the synergies" are not likely to be feasible in single organizations; the research *may* start with some delimiting laboratory studies, but eventually it will require studies of long-term groups across varying kinds of organizations and competitive strategies; such research will be done by academicians, consultants, or leaders of consortiums of interested organizations. When such studies have shown clearly how people can become the major self-renewing resource of organizations, more companies will, as Snow and Snell conclude, reach the practical realization that getting good human capital from good staffing practices will be the foundation of a truly competitive strategy.

It is easy for academics to ignore the practical needs of decision makers. Consider the statement by Goldstein, Zedeck, and Schneider (Chapter One, p. 3) "that the central interest in the selection context is the demonstration of the linkage between the construct underlying test measurement and the construct underlying performance measurement." It is, to me, academic. Surely it is the central *scientific* interest. But within employing organizations, the central interest in selection is the improvement of organizational functioning. Knowledge of the construct linkages may serve that interest better than ignorance can. Nevertheless, a linkage of measures that works, even without knowledge of the underlying constructs, still serves the basic purpose. Moreover, scientific investigations of construct linkages are more likely to be fruitful if they examine things that work empirically and try to understand why they do.

Expanding Predictor Constructs

Some discussions in the last decade or so have seemed to suggest that we have a surplus of predictors, that mental ability is the only really well-established and important predictor, and that measures of general mental ability may prove sufficient for many jobs (for example, Gottfredson, 1986). Others have questioned this view (for instance, Prediger, 1989), and it certainly finds little support in this book. Indeed, a recurring theme is that further predictors are needed, including further approaches to mental or cognitive abilities.

There seems to be a rebirth of interest in personality variables as predictors. Borman and Motowidlo (see Chapter Three) identify them as the most likely predictors of contextual criteria, and Klimoski (see Chapter Four) seems to give major attention to motivation and related constructs. Campbell and colleagues (Chapter Two) attribute about as much importance to motivation as to knowledge. Social skills and motivation, both commonly considered personality variables, may be constructs most likely to be measured by structured interviews (see Chapter Five).

When personality measures are discussed, the question of faking typically appears, but Rynes (see Chapter Eight) adds the tantalizing suggestion that we ought to be investigating the *ability to fake*. Maybe other personality traits should be investigated largely as abilities or behavioral capacities (Dawes, 1991; Wallace, 1966). Not do you fake, but can you? Not are you jovial (or conscientious, or whatever), but do you have the capacity to be jovial (or whatever)? Two persons may both habitually or characteristically be pretty gloomy, yet one of them may be *able* to behave in a cheerful way when circumstances call for it. Some contextual criteria may call for consistent cheerfulness, but others may be satisfied equally well by cheerfulness on demand. I suspect that Rynes (see Chapter Eight) has put her finger on an important way of thinking about the behaviors usually associated with personality traits — abilities to behave as situations demand. Maybe this is a kind of situational empathy — an awareness of the demands of jobs or of situations faced in jobs — somewhat analogous to the interpersonal empathy stressed by Borman and Motowidlo (see Chapter Three).

Even within more conventional concepts of ability, these chapters call for some expansion of thinking. Burke (see Chapter Seven), of course, identifies lots of new constructs for testing with computers, such as time sharing, divided attention, working under severe time pressures, and so on. Snow and Snell (see Chapter Fourteen) require cognitive predictors for their models 2 and 3, but not the usual employment test factors. Abilities required in planning, or in identifying different possible consequences from a course of action, or in changing strategies in response to changed circumstances — these are cognitive abilities that have so far had little influence on conventional personnel selection assessments. I am not sure that models 2 and 3 are necessarily different from model 1, but I *am* sure that their virtue lies in calling attention to these less familiar but perhaps more necessary intellectual abilities.

In short, the identification and measurement of predictor constructs give us no reason for complacency. Expanded concepts of predictors will require expanded concepts of recruiting, of job and organizational need analysis, of criteria or outcomes of selection and individual performance, of validation research—in short, the entire field of personnel selection research and practice.

Beyond Validation: Evaluation of Selection Practices

Some of the ideas contributed in these chapters call for something a bit different from the usual concepts of validity in evaluating how well the proposed selection procedures actually work. I have already mentioned that consideration of work and organizational outcomes beyond criteria of individual performance or success—outcomes at the group, unit, or organizational level—may call for quasiexperimental research designs. Consideration of noncognitive predictors, especially those emphasizing motivation, may well call into question our traditional allegiance to linearity and the investigation of nonlinear, even discontinuous functions. Dipboye and Gaugler (see Chapter Five) say that research on interviewing processes must go beyond criterion-related validation, perhaps to basic kinds of judgment research such as the policy-capturing model used by Dougherty, Ebert, and Callender (1986).

Borman and Motowidlo (see Chapter Three) point out the difference between *expecting* or wanting contextual behaviors and *requiring* them. When a job requires specific behaviors or outcomes, they can (perhaps) be measured as criteria, predictor data can be (perhaps) correlated with them, and selection can be based on the predicted criteria. However, if employees are not required to do more than their jobs specifically require, what selection practices, and what evaluations of those practices, will be deemed appropriate? The same sort of criterion-related validation is a plausible evaluation, but how are the predictions of these merely desired behaviors to be handled along with predictions of genuinely required behavior?

If these are two independent predictions, what are decision makers to do if the people predicted to perform tasks well are not predicted to do very well contextually—or vice versa? Indeed, if independent predictions of *required* criteria—for example, task outcomes of high quality and dependability of being at the workplace at specified times — are predicted with contradictory implications, what are the decision makers to do? These questions, I think, are what Cascio (see Chapter Ten) had in mind when he asked how current procedures could be modified or supplemented to take multiple criteria into account.

My answer — as it was for interviews — is (1) to do policy-capturing research among an organization's decision makers to determine how various leaders weigh different predictions in different patterns, (2) to negotiate among the various policies to choose an organizational policy, and then (3) to train decision makers in the use of that policy. So far as I know, this has never been done, but the background research on judgment suggests that it is plausible. To do it, however, we may need to change the habits of the cut score psychologists who believe that organizational decision makers are incapable of anything other than single go/no-go decisions.

Moderators and Other Reasons for Humility

A quarter of a century ago, the moderator concept was the great new hope in personnel selection research. Demographic moderators were expected to produce fairness in employment decisions, and sweeping searches of whatever data might be around were supposed to find other moderators. Neither worked very well. Validity generalization searches for moderators have turned up a few, but in general that research has not been very fertile. In conventional wisdom, moderators have been out.

However, authors of these chapters have not been constrained by such conventions. Borman and Motowidlo (see Chapter Three) point out that the contextual criteria contribute to the general environment in which the "technical core" must operate, and that the operation of that core may not be the same across different contexts. Almost these same words appear in the Klimoski chapter (see Chapter Four); he predicts that efforts to build his anticipated theories of effectiveness will be developed with reference to specified contexts. Can contextual activities be cast as potential moderators? I should think so. Rynes (see Chapter Eight), in her consideration of faking, suggests a range of variables, such as labor market differences, that may interact with personal motivation to fake; if so, then these broader contextual variables would also be cast as moderators worth investigating. The old song has it that the times are "a-changin'"; Rynes says that the changing times constitute moderators in that research conducted at one time, under one zeitgeist, cannot be assumed to generalize to others. Sackett and Arvey (Chapter Thirteen) explicitly identify levels of organizational rigidity and bureaucracy as examples of situational strength in organizations and suggest that the individual differences among people entering organizations characterized as "weak situations" will have stronger influence on subsequent outcomes than in those considered "strong situations." This seems an example of what is often called organizational climate or culture, a collection of constructs investigated rather widely, and all of them potential moderators.

The field of industrial and organizational psychology is a broad one, probably too broad to be wholly within the vision of any one of its adherents. In this whole field, there are many activities and concepts intended to influence performance and the consequences of performance, or the contexts in which task performance occurs, or to determine the influences from outside on the organizations themselves. In this array of activities and ideas, surely there are potential moderators far more worthy of investigation than demographics or the variables found serendipitously among the scree of what is available for trial. That the moderator concept has not been systematically approached from such a broad perspective should make us humble.

There is ample room for humility in the chapters of this book. The authors have generally gone beyond conventional or traditional thinking and practice, and they have encouraged us to expand our thinking in many ways in these times of rapid change. I hope I have hit upon the most useful themes of the many that are here.

References

Dawes, R. M. (1991, June). *Discovering "human nature" versus discovering how people cope with the task of getting through college: An extension of Sears's argument.* Paper presented at the annual meeting of the American Psychological Society, Washington, DC.

Dougherty, T. W., Ebert, R. J., & Callender, J. C. (1986). Policy capturing in the employment interview. *Journal of Applied Psychology, 71,* 9–15.

Frechtling, J.A. (1991). Performance assessment: Moonstruck or the real thing? *Educational Measurement: Issues and Practice, 10*(4), 23–25.

Goldberg, L. R., Grenier, J. R., Guion, R. M., Sechrest, L. B., & Wing, H. (1991). *Questionnaires used in the prediction of trustworthiness in pre-employment selection decisions.* Washington, DC: American Psychological Association.

Gottfredson, L. S. (Ed.). (1986). The *g* factor in employment [Special issue]. *Journal of Vocational Behavior, 29*(3).

Mehrens, W. A. (1992). Using performance assessment for accountability purposes. *Educational Measurement: Issues and Practice, 11,* 3–9, 20.

Prediger, D. J. (1989). Ability differences across occupations: More than *g. Journal of Vocational Behavior, 34,* 1–27.

Wallace, J. (1966). An abilities conception of personality: Some implications for personality measurement. *American Psychologist, 21,* 132–138.

Wallace, S. R. (Ed.). (1965). Criteria for what? *American Psychologist, 20,* 411–417.

16

Personnel Psychology at the Cutting Edge

Frank L. Schmidt

This book is intended to be about personnel selection at the cutting edge of new developments. Does it measure up to this intention? By and large, I believe it does. My assigned task is to present a *critical* evaluation of the chapters in this book. Space limitations do not permit me to commend or comment on much that I agree with and find encouraging in these pages.

General Comments

By and large the chapters in this book present a fairly accurate picture of mainstream thinking about personnel selection in industrial and organizational (I/O) psychology, and there is much to be commended in this thinking. But mainstream thinking, I believe, falls short in several respects. Some critical issues are either not addressed or inadequately addressed.

One key problem hobbling personnel selection is the dilemma created by the conflict between productivity and the need to increase minority representation. Chapter Six, by Arvey and Sackett, discusses this dilemma but does not fully explore it.

Note: I thank John Hunter, Deniz Ones, and C. Viswesvaran for their helpful comments on an earlier version of this manuscript.

Measures of ability (especially general mental ability), achievement, and knowledge are among the most valid and useful predictors of performance in most jobs. Yet blacks, and to a lesser extent Hispanics, have lower average scores, and hence lower hiring rates. But these differences are not due to any bias in the tests as predictors of job performance; research evidence is strong that tests are predictively fair for minorities (and that validity coefficients are comparable, too). Failure to use such tests would cause great productivity losses to employers and the economy, losses we can ill afford in today's competitive international economy. But increasing use of such tests could mean fewer minorities hired in the more desirable jobs, or at least could make it difficult to increase current minority representation. A similar dilemma exists in Israel (Zeidner, 1988) and many other countries (Klitgaard, 1986), but not in ethnically homogeneous countries such as Japan. Most economic gains (utility) from testing can be maintained by hiring top-down within white, black, and Hispanic groups, while still eliminating hiring rate differences. However, this approach can be criticized as reverse discrimination. Further, this possibility for escape from the dilemma has recently been taken away: the Civil Rights Act of 1991 specifically makes it illegal to use separate within-group test norms to eliminate adverse impact while retaining most of the (substantial) productivity gains from selection. Also, another approach to attaining this same goal — use of score-banding procedures (Cascio, Outtz, Zedeck, & Goldstein, 1991) — has been shown to be based on a rationale that is internally logically contradictory (Schmidt, 1991).

This leaves us in the following troubling position. The American economy needs major improvements in efficiency and productivity to be competitive internationally and to prevent loss of American jobs and reduction in our standard of living. Research has established the wide applicability and economic importance of personnel selection. We now know how to improve productivity substantially and at relatively low monetary cost to organizations. Yet research has not — and cannot — resolve the conflict between the competing American values of individual efficiency and international competitiveness, on the one hand,

and economic opportunity and equality for minorities, on the other. This is a serious conflict, and there appears to be no clear way to resolve it. This problem is of such importance that it should be a major theme in a book of this sort. The critical question is: Will it be politically and legally possible to employ valid selection methods (with or without adjustments or mechanisms to reduce adverse impact) to improve the efficiency and productivity of our economy in our litigious, multicultural society? The stakes here are enormous. This is a key issue.

The next issue is related but would exist without the first one. Homogeneous Japan has found it necessary to develop a two-tier economy to compete effectively. Intentionally or not, Japan has developed what amounts to a national human resources (HR) policy that puts the most able people in the companies that compete in the international export market while assigning the less able to sectors of the economy that do not compete internationally. This is accomplished through a rigorous educational system that assigns students to schools differentially according to ability. This sorting is accomplished by repeatedly administered academic achievement tests — which we know correlate very highly with general mental ability (particularly so when effort and motivation are almost uniformly high). The best and brightest go to schools such as the University of Tokyo, and the large, high-paying companies that dominate the export sector of the economy recruit almost exclusively from such schools. Sectors that compete only domestically, such as retail distribution, recruit lower-ability employees from the lower-ranked schools. Thus, the country systematically assigns its best and its brightest to the competition with the rest of the world.

If a relatively low-variance country like Japan requires such a system, how much more so a high-variance country like the United States? A recent report of the National Educational Progress Study found that although American students as a whole were below international averages, our top 10 percent were above the top 10 percent in most other countries — indicating the United States has a relatively low mean but a large standard deviation. To successfully compete internationally, we may need an HR policy that puts our most able people in the

export-oriented companies that compete globally—and the rest
into areas of the economy not so exposed to foreign competition
(for example, food, transportation, services of various kinds).
This includes such service areas as law, which currently drains
large numbers of highly talented people from industry. (The
United States, with 5 percent of the world's people, has 70 percent of the world's lawyers.) To compete, we need a two-tiered
economy in terms of human resources. To achieve this, we need
to resolve the value conflict between productivity and equality.
Among other things, this may require different affirmative action burdens for the export segment in comparison to other segments of the economy (Hunter & Schmidt, 1991). What can
we, as I/O psychologists, contribute to the question of a two-
tiered economy? This is perhaps the ultimate megaissue in personnel selection, and it may appear daunting. But we should
not forget that we are the experts in human resources. No other
group has as much to offer. During my eleven years in Washington, I was repeatedly struck by the fact that, in comparison
to other groups intervening in HR issues and policy debates,
we have much more solid usable knowledge than they do. We
have the wherewithal and the obligation to tackle really big questions like this on which the future of the country depends. This
book contains no mention of this question.

A third problem is the fact that traditional I/O approaches
to personnel selection were developed for, and are geared to,
large, stable, bureaucratic organizations, but such organizations
are decreasing in number and importance and smaller organizations are becoming more important. In addition, independent of size, many organizations are more loosely organized today, with boundaries between jobs constantly shifting, resulting
in enhanced need for very general capacities, abilities, and skills.
Chapter Fourteen by Snow and Snell does a good job of describing this development. The methods of detailed job analysis
described in Chapter One by Goldstein, Zedeck, and Schneider,
which lead to content-valid tests to be used in connection with
stable, unchanging jobs, are suited to the disappearing stable
bureaucratic organizations. Such organizations are still represented today (so far, anyway) by state and local governments,

the area of application emphasized in Chapter One. But in smaller organizations with limited resources, and in dynamic midsize organizations with shifting goals and constantly changing job duties, such approaches appear archaic. These important points are developed in more detail by Offermann and Gowing in Chapter Twelve and by Snow and Snell in Chapter Fourteen.

Can I/O psychology adjust to these changes? So far, the mainstream I/O response does not appear promising. Chapter Thirteen is entitled "Selection in Small N Settings," and one might expect it to present an appropriate response. However, the chapter is not about *selection* in small-sample settings — it is mostly about *conducting validation studies* in small-sample settings. Validation studies — whether done in the traditional manner or using synthetic validity methods or other methods discussed in this chapter — are expensive and time-consuming. Small, struggling organizations are not looking for an opportunity to finance research. Neither are the dynamic, rapidly changing organizations described in Chapter Fourteen. Their question to us (and it is a legitimate question) is: what can you do to improve our selection quickly and at low cost? And we can answer that question: we know from meta-analytic studies that there are several procedures that can be introduced almost immediately that have demonstrated generalizable validity. We also know from utility research that the gains in productivity will be substantial. Complex, expensive, time-consuming studies are *not necessary*. If we truly want to improve selection in substantial numbers of such organizations, this should be our first response — it should not merely be mentioned as one item in a long list of possibilities as is done in Chapter Thirteen. It is true that research is desirable for the advancement of our field. But we should not try to induce every small company to conduct expensive, involved research studies when major improvements in their current selection can be effected quickly and without much research. To do so is to reflect a guild orientation and perhaps an unwillingness to make use of our cumulative research knowledge to improve the efficiency of our industries and our economy.

Chapter Thirteen defines a small N job as "one with insufficient incumbents for a traditional criterion-related validity study to be technically feasible." This definition *implies* that whenever there *are* sufficient incumbents to make a traditional criterion-related validity study feasible, such a study should probably be conducted — or at least advocated by the I/O psychologist. This is not the case. Even in such circumstances, the cumulative research on the validity of ability tests, assessment centers, interviews, integrity tests, evaluations of training and experience, and so on, is sufficient that such studies are often not necessary. Further, even if they are conducted, they yield very little information about validity in comparison to the information already in the cumulative literature. That is, such studies are incapable — except in the rarest of megasample studies — of overturning (or even modifying) the conclusions already in the literature.

There is a heavy emphasis throughout this book — starting with the Preface by the editors — on the importance of understanding constructs (that is, the importance of construct validity) and the relations among constructs. This emphasis is especially strong in Chapters Two, Four, Five, and Nine. And indeed this is important. It is essential to the construction of theories — and the development and testing of theory are the major task of any science. However, we may have slipped into the habit of beating a dead horse. Few, if any, in I/O psychology today would argue with the importance of constructs, construct validity, and theory development. Calls for increased emphasis on constructs and construct validity have been numerous in I/O psychology for about fifteen years and sometimes appear to have taken on a ritual quality. Also, there appears to be an important omission: discussion of the critical role of corrections of correlations for the effects of artifacts.

Consider, for example, the correction of correlations between measures of constructs for measurement error. There can be no unbiased estimates of relations among constructs without such corrections; uncorrected correlations do not and cannot estimate relations among constructs — only relations among imperfect *measures* of constructs. Accurate estimates of construct relations require correction for measurement error — and for other artifacts, too. This omission is important because there has been and still is resistance to the need for and use of such corrections. My work in meta-analysis has exposed me to the extent of such attitudes. There are some who argue that research should focus on measures, not on constructs, and who therefore hold that no corrections should ever be made. There are some who hold that since perfectly reliable measurement is unattainable, there is no point in knowing what the correlation wou'd be if we used perfectly reliable measures. There are still others who accept the correction in principle but think one should not actually make the correction unless one has an almost perfectly precise estimate of the scale reliabilities — even though the result is a far more erroneous estimate of construct relations than even an imperfect correction would yield.

Similar attitudes prevail in connection with corrections for other artifacts, such as range restriction and dichotomization of measures. All reflect an unwillingness or inability to think theoretically. Campbell's (1990) recent defense and advocacy of such corrections, one would hope, will have a positive effect. The key point is that virtually all articles issuing calls for increased emphasis on constructs *fail to even mention this question.* This book is a case in point. None of the chapters in this book, despite the emphasis on the importance of constructs, mentions that without careful attention to corrections for artifacts we can never get accurate estimates of relations among constructs. And such relations are the essence of construct validity evidence — and are an indispensable foundation for theory construction.

Specific Comments

In Chapter Two, Campbell, McCloy, and Oppler present something long needed in I/O psychology — a clear, specific theory of the nature of job performance. They do so in a direct and forthright manner that does not hide the hard questions behind vague and abstract language (as so often happens). This chapter is a major contribution. Ironically, their success in being detailed and specific makes it easier to see some unsolved practical problems. One such problem may lie in their definition of performance: "Performance is *not* the consequence or result of action, it is the action itself" (p. 40). This distinction is made for the very good reason that the consequences or results are often not under the control of the individual — and thus appear to be dubious measures of performance. The authors go on to say: "Admittedly, this distinction is troublesome in at least one major respect — behavior is not always observable (for example, cognitive behavior, as in solving a math problem) and can be known only by its effects (for example, producing a solution after much 'thought'). However, 'solutions,' 'statements,' or 'answers' produced *as a result of covert cognitive behavior* and totally under the control of the individual are included as actions that can be defined as performance" (p. 40; emphasis added). This is designed to take care of behavior that is not "observable." But the real problem is not behavior that is not observable — it is behavior that *is* observable but may not be *evaluatable* by the observer. It is not enough to observe and record behavior; we must be able to evaluate it. That is, we must know *what it means.* The problem is that behavior is often subtle enough that its meaning can be inferred only from its consequences; it cannot be inferred from observations of the behavior.

For example, consider the behaviors expected from door-to-door salespeople. If we carefully observe two saleswomen, we may find they have both shown ostensibly the same behaviors — both have called on the same number of comparable homes, both have given the same sales pitch, and so on. Yet we may find the consequences (results) are very different: one has sold twice as much as the other. The same is true for the observable behaviors that make up most jobs — from auto mechanics to trapeze artists. The point is that there are thousands of subtle differences in *how* people "emit" the same observable behaviors that determine how successful they will be, but these differences are very difficult to observe or cannot be observed — they are just not visible to most people. This is another example of the fact that behaviorism simply does not work (Schmidt, Hunter, & Pearlman, 1981). We may often have to look to consequences or results to evaluate, assess, and measure performance. We may not have the luxury of declaring that results and consequences will not be used as indicants of performance.

Campbell, McCloy, and Oppler (Chapter Two) correctly state that consequences and results are often not fully under the control of the individual. That is true. But we may have to use results and consequences anyway; we may have no choice. In many cases, the best we can do is try to make intelligent judgments about the extent to which specific individuals are responsible for observed outcomes.

Chapter Three, by Borman and Motowidlo, is thought-provoking. They argue for expansion of our traditional concepts of job performance to include what they call "contextual performance"—which includes such things as helping co-workers, volunteering for tasks unrelated to one's job, representing the organization favorably to outsiders, and so forth. The emphasis on such behaviors meshes nicely with the current increased emphasis on personality variables—especially conscientiousness—in selection and with the increased use by employers of personality-based integrity tests designed to predict a wide variety of "counterproductive behaviors" (Schmidt, Ones, & Hunter, 1992).

The kinds of behaviors that are the focus of Borman and Motowidlo are clearly important to employers. However, there is a problem with creating a new performance construct called "contextual performance." Contextual performance is *defined* by the fact of being absent from the job description. As soon as a behavior is included in the job description, it ceases being part of contextual performance. Some of the behaviors discussed in this chapter may be included in a job description (for example, employees may be expected to help co-workers learn their jobs), while other, similar behaviors are not. Thus, even though they are very similar, they are considered different categories of performance. Even where no changes are made in formal job descriptions, organizations may informally communicate increased expectations for an expanding range of "contextual performances." These behaviors are important and, in my judgment, are likely to become increasingly important because of heightened competition and emphasis on quality and service. However, we should think twice before we create a new construct to describe them. Perhaps it would be preferable to state that traditional job analysis and position description methods have failed to identify behaviors that are often important at the extreme high end of job performance, behaviors that are part of "excellence" in job performance.

Like personality and personality tests, the employment interview has received increased attention recently. Dipboye and Gaugler (Chapter Five) present a well-crafted and thoroughly thought out discussion of what research has revealed about the psychological processes underlying the interview. Much good research has been done in this area recently, and Dipboye and his associates have been responsible for a lot of it. One striking aspect of this chapter is the focus on theoretical (construct-based) explanations for the meta-analytic finding that structured interviews are more valid than unstructured interviews. A few short years ago, most of us were reasonably convinced (myself among them) that unstructured interviews generally had zero or nearly zero validity. Now it is widely accepted (as reflected in this chapter) that, if conducted reasonably carefully, unstructured interviews have an average validity of about .40 against supervisory ratings of job performance. This is not an insubstantial figure. We have undergone a sea change in our assessment of the unstructured interview—even more so than in the case of the structured interview, which was traditionally thought by many to be capable of yielding decent validity. Unstructured interviews were for decades the whipping boy of personnel psychologists.

We need to think about the meaning of the validity findings for the unstructured interview. If unstructured interviews can produce validities of .40, what does this say about the validity of our other selection predictors? The average validity for assessment centers is about .37 (Gaugler, Rosenthal, Thornton, & Bentson, 1987). Although the average validity for general mental ability tests is somewhat higher (about .50), the average validity for measures of single aptitudes—such as verbal, quantitative, or spatial ability—is about .40. The unstructured interview is seemingly an unsophisticated instrument, yet it does about as well (McDaniel, Whetzel, Schmidt, & Russell, 1991). One obvious hypothesis is that the unstructured interviews on which validity studies have been conducted are more carefully planned, more thorough, and perhaps longer than the short conversational unstructured interviews that are commonly used in business and industry. It seems unlikely that the latter type of interview could have an average validity as high as .40.

The topic of fairness in selection has preoccupied personnel psychologists since the 1964 Civil Rights Act was passed. After years of discussion and debate, most purely statistical definitions of fairness have been rejected on various logical grounds. The exception has been the regression (or Cleary) model of predictive bias, which has been widely accepted. But it has become apparent that what lay people mean by "fairness" is potentially much broader than predictive fairness. In Chapter Six, Arvey and Sackett explore a wide variety of potential popular meanings for the term *selection fairness*. It *is* important what applicants and the general public think of our selection methods, and we should study these reactions. But this chapter has broadened the scope to such a degree that it has essentially made the term *fairness* scientifically useless. First, early in their chapter *fairness* is defined as a mere "perception." Any perception of unfairness, no matter how baseless or self-serving, is defined as an instance of unfairness. Second, later in the chapter, we see that the perception does not even have to be one of unfairness. If someone objects to a selection method, not because it is unfair, but on grounds that it is invasive, or falsifiable, or has some other flaw, this is defined as unfairness. The upshot is that we have an all-inclusive definition: anything that anybody does not like about any selection method for any reason is unfairness. This chapter has essentially defined the meaning out of the construct of fairness. A fair selection procedure becomes one that no one anywhere objects to on any grounds. It is hard to see how this is a step forward in the conceptualization and treatment of fairness in I/O psychology.

That it is not necessary to subsume all objections to selection methods under the construct of fairness is illustrated in Chapter Eight, in which Rynes discusses research on the effects of selection methods on applicant attitudes and behaviors. Rynes makes a good case that we need more research on the reactions of applicants to commonly employed selection methods and practices. These reactions are sometimes surprising—and can have major effects on the success of organizational recruitment and hiring. Research on applicant reactions has been under way for some time in Israel and Germany (Nevo & Jager, 1987). It is time we caught up. Also, the implicit antibehaviorist stance in this chapter is refreshing and commendable: researchers in this area learn about reactions by *asking applicants* to describe their reactions. There was a time in I/O psychology, during the heyday of behaviorist influence (still evident in parts of the Campbell, McCloy, and Oppler chapter), when this would have been considered "unscientific." Some may still hold that attitude. But apparently people do know what their reactions are — and by and large can provide useful and informative explanations of them.

Computerized testing — and especially computer-adaptive testing (CAT) — has a twenty-year history of being the wave of the future that will sweep all before it, and then failing to live up to its promise. From 1975 to 1985, there was a wave of enthusiasm for CAT (in which I admittedly participated; see, for example, Schmidt, Urry, and Gugal, 1978). Today only one major CAT program is still in existence — that of the military — and it is in imminent danger of termination. What I like about Burke's chapter on computerized testing (Chapter Seven) is that it does not fall into the trap of promising the sky. Burke presents a thoughtful, realistic, and sober assessment of what computerized testing has achieved after almost twenty-two years and what it is likely to achieve in the future. CAT is an important element in what we have to offer organizations, but it has turned out to have more limitations than we initially realized.

In a book touted as being on the "cutting edge" of new research, it seems a little odd to find one-third of a chapter devoted to the history of personnel selection during the early part of this century. But this is what is done in Chapter Nine, on "The Concept of Validity." Nevertheless, the history can be informative. We find, for example, that in 1919 an early I/O psychologist was conducting criterion-related validity studies on sample sizes of twelve! Early I/O psychologists apparently had *even less* understanding of sampling error and statistical power than we did until recently. Inexplicably, the chapter states of these studies, "Nevertheless, the standards were high" (p. 283). Elsewhere, this chapter states that validity generalization findings seem to suggest that combinations of predictors would yield "near perfect validity," on grounds that interviews, cognitive ability tests, and biodata "are often uncorrelated" (p. 296). This assumption is erroneous: they *are* correlated. For example, the average correlation between one biodata scale (from the Supervisory Profile Record; Rothstein, Schmidt, Erwin, Owens, & Sparks, 1990) and tests of mental ability is .50. And the correlation between interview evaluations and ability tests is also substantial (McDaniel, Whetzel, Schmidt, & Russell, 1991). We are not on the verge of obtaining a multiple correlation of 1.00.

Chapter Nine presents much useful information on the meaning of constructs. This chapter would have been an ideal place to clarify the distinction between construct validity and construct validity *evidence*. The construct validity of a measure x is the correlation (in any defined population) between the true scores underlying that measure (that is, the construct it measures) and the construct θ that it is *intended* to measure. Thus construct validity is *defined* by a correlation, $r_{x_t\theta}$. But this correlation cannot be computed, because we have no perfect measures of θ. If we did, we would not need the measure x. Thus, we must attempt to assess $r_{x_t\theta}$ from a wide variety of pieces of research evidence that bear in one way or another on the likely general magnitude of $r_{x_t\theta}$. That body of information is construct validity *evidence* — not construct validity per se, as it is so often called. Construct validity evidence is complex, multifarious, and often confusing. But construct *validity* has a simple, straightforward definition. This distinction is helpful, I believe, in clarifying thinking about construct validity.

Selection utility — covered by Cascio in Chapter Ten — is not concerned with theory development. Its thrust is practical rather than scientific. One could, I suppose, argue that the question of whether valid selection has any substantial utility (practical value) at all is in some sense a scientific question. But that question has already been answered; we know that selection utility is often quite substantial. Remaining issues concern questions of how to make utility estimates more precise, what units to express utility in, how to communicate utility findings and figures to managers, and so forth. This chapter discusses a variety of such questions and issues in utility analysis.

The questions raised in this chapter all are relevant, but the specific opinions expressed often appear questionable. For example, the chapter questions the expression of selection utility gains in any metric other than dollars, a narrow and unjustified orientation. For example, organizations may be interested in reductions in accidents, turnover, or absenteeism. In addition, utility gains can usefully be expressed in terms of percentage increases in output (Hunter, Schmidt, and Judiesch, 1990), a metric that is surely meaningful to managers. Further, percentage increases in output can be more accurately estimated than can the dollar-value utility values (Schmidt, Ones, & Hunter, 1992; Hunter, Schmidt, & Judiesch, 1990). One reason that Cascio — and some others — avoid this metric may be that he judges the results to be less impressive. In my experience, psychologists are not very impressed with output gains of 6 percent to 15 percent, the typical range found in utility studies. However, economists are: they know that for all but the smallest organizations an output increase of even 6 percent represents a large amount of money — hundreds of thousands, perhaps millions, of dollars (Denison, 1985). Psychologists appear to be unaware of this. They often find the percentage increases in output from better selection unimpressive (and suspect they are probably underestimates), while at the same time they find the dollar-value figures — which are the same thing expressed in a different metric —"too large to be true." On the dollar end, many psychologists apparently have no idea how large employee payroll costs are in most organizations, and therefore no appreciation of the fact that even a small percentage payroll savings is a very large dollar figure. The same applies to sales figures. Chapter Ten accepts the currently popular criticism that dollar values presented in utility studies are too large to be credible. Credible to whom? The people to whom they are not credible are usually the psychologists making this criticism — and these are the people who do not understand the economics of organizations.

Chapter Ten argues that any instability in job performance across years will reduce selection utility. This is not necessarily the case. Less-than-perfect year-to-year performance correlations do *not* imply declining validities, as Ackerman (1989) has pointed out. Nor does it imply that SD_y declines over time. As long as SD_y and validity do not change (decline) over time, there is no change (decline) in utility. These questions are discussed in more detail in Schmidt, Ones, and Hunter (1992).

One of the most important areas of construct investigation for personnel selection is the conflict between specific aptitude theory and general mental ability theory (Thorndike, 1986; Hunter, 1986). Advocates of specific aptitude theory argue that different combinations of specific aptitude constructs lead to high job performance on different jobs. They hold that there are important real-world distinctions that must be made between and among such constructs as verbal ability, quantitative ability, mechanical ability, and so on. They maintain that these constructs should be measured separately and weighted optimally in regression equations specific to each job. The alternate theory holds that the only ability construct that matters in predicting real-life job performance is general mental ability (Hunter, 1986).

Even though most other construct validity questions have not even begun to be answered, this important question is well on its way to being answered by research. The evidence is clear that specific aptitudes contribute little or nothing to the prediction of job performance over and above general mental ability (for example, see Hunter, 1986; Thorndike, 1986; Ree & Earles, 1991; Ree & Earles, in press). The very small apparent observed incremental validities may be due to capitalization on chance (Schmidt, Ones, & Hunter, 1992). The validity of specific aptitudes appears to result almost entirely from the fact that such measures tap into general ability. The specific factors in aptitude tests do not appear to predict job performance. Nor can it be argued that these findings are not construct-relevant on grounds that we do not have complete construct validity evidence on the job performance measures—because the finding holds regardless of what kind of criterion measure is used (training performance, ratings of job performance, job sample measures, and so on). Who would argue that all these criterion measures are construct invalid—and construct invalid in very similar ways?

Yet in this book—ostensibly emphasizing the importance of construct-based research—this successful construct research effort is mentioned *only once* (in Chapter Thirteen [p. 429]), where it is referred to as being "among the more counterintuitive findings of recent years"). Further, the findings of this research area are apparently dismissed. The authors go on to state in the next sentence: "in a large N situation a researcher may compare the relative efficiency of general and specific ability measures and may find an optimal combination of tests for that setting" (p. 429). Why would a researcher do this, when it is known from cumulative research what the answer is? Even if the researcher believed that he or she saw a different answer in the data, the credibility of the cumulative literature would call into question the findings and conclusions from that single study. One study — even a large N study — cannot establish an exception to cumulative research findings based on many jobs over hundreds of thousands of cases. Another fact makes it even clearer that the authors of Chapter Thirteen have dismissed this research: they state that one thing that validity generalization does not do is "identify an optimal set of specific ability tests for a particular setting" (p. 429) — something that is, of course, unnecessary in light of the research findings on the validity of ability constructs and measures.

　　At present, the United States is in the grip of the longest recession since the Great Depression. Unemployment is high, and there are many more applicants than jobs. It is therefore strange to read in the Offermann and Gowing chapter (Chapter Twelve) that the future will be one of worker and applicant shortages — that organizations will be eager to hire every warm body, almost regardless of ability and skills. It may come to pass, but it just does not seem likely right now. Offermann and Gowing detail the projected demographic changes in new workforce entrants over the next decade — more women, more minorities, more older workers. Their presentation is so effective that it may be misleading to some: it may create the impression that we will see *abrupt* changes in the composition of the workforces and applicant pools. Actually, the changes they describe have been under way for fifteen to twenty years. They have proceeded gradually and will continue to proceed gradually, affording organizations and individuals a chance to adjust as best they can.

We are not in the midst of a sudden revolution. Another striking aspect of this chapter is the futuristically upbeat, positive tone it adopts in connection with changes that many would view as cause for concern. For example, an ever larger percentage of the workforce will be black, Hispanic, Puerto Rican, or from other groups with historically below-average levels of education, work skills, and measured abilities. Yet they seem to be blithely optimistic that everything will work out wonderfully, at least for organizations that successfully learn the techniques of "managing cultural diversity." I hope they are right. But this is not the view the Japanese—and much of the rest of the world— take of us and our future.

Chapter Twelve reflects the broadening concerns of I/O psychology. So does the chapter (Chapter Eleven) by Colarelli and Beehr on firings, layoffs, and retirements. These chapters describe the broad social context in which we must conduct our work. Major changes in the U.S. economy over the last ten years have made employee separations appear to be almost as frequent and numerous as the hiring of new employees. These changes have large and often devastating impacts on individuals, families, and organizations. Practitioner I/O psychologists have inevitably become involved with them. It is heartening to see that research has also focused on these problems. This research may be useful to organizations; let us hope it will also be taken into account by government policy makers—and those in industry. The cultural and national differences in handling employee redundancy—outlined in this chapter—suggest that there are alternatives to the often harsh way these matters have been handled in the United States in the past. This area is clearly an example of a much-broadened potential role for I/O psychology.

Conclusion

I/O psychology in general, and personnel psychology in particular, has made great strides in research and theory development in recent years (Schmidt, Ones, & Hunter, 1992). We have also expanded the scope of our concerns and research topics. As a science, we have become more mature. The timing of these advances has been good, for we are now in a position to make important contributions to the solution of some of the serious economic and social problems of the late-twentieth-century American economy. This book reflects these developments. A decade from now—in the year 2002—perhaps another book like this will be published. I hope it will be able to state that we seized these opportunities and that we made an important difference.

References

Ackerman, P. L. (1989). Within-task intercorrelations of skilled performance: Implications for predicting individual differences? A Comment on Henry and Hulin (1987). *Journal of Applied Psychology, 74*, 360–364.

Campbell, J. P. (1990). Modeling the performance prediction problem in industrial and organizational psychology. In M. D. Dunnette and L. M. Hough (Eds.), *Handbook of industrial and organizational psychology* (Vol. 1, 2nd ed.). Palo Alto, CA: Consulting Psychologists Press.

Cascio, W. F., Outtz, J., Zedeck, S., & Goldstein, I. L. (1991). Statistical implications of six methods of test score use in personnel selection. *Human Performance, 4*, 233–264.

Denison, E. F. (1985). *Trends in American economic growth.* Washington, DC: The Brookings Institution.

Gaugler, B. B., Rosenthal, D. B., Thornton, G. C., & Bentson, C. (1987). Meta-analysis of assessment center validity. *Journal of Applied Psychology, 72*, 493–511.

Hunter, J. E. (1986). Cognitive ability, cognitive aptitudes, job knowledge, and job performance. *Journal of Vocational Behavior, 29*, 340–362.

Hunter, J. E., & Schmidt, F. L. (1991). Fairness and bias in job testing. *Issues in Science and Technology, 7*(1), 27.

Hunter, J. E., Schmidt, F. L., & Judiesch, M. K. (1990). Individual differences in output as a function of job complexity. *Journal of Applied Psychology, 75*, 28–46.

Klitgaard, R. (1986). *Elitism and meritocracy in developing countries.* Baltimore, MD: Johns Hopkins University Press.

McDaniel, M. A., Whetzel, D. L., Schmidt, F. L., & Russell, J. (1991). *The validity of employment interviews: A review and meta-analysis.* Paper submitted for publication.

Nevo, B., & Jager, R. S. (Eds.). (1987). *Psychological test: The examinee perspective.* Frankfurt: German Institute for Pedagogical Studies.

Ree, J., & Earles, J.A. (1991). Predicting training success: Not much more than *g. Personnel Psychology, 44,* 321–332.

Ree, J., & Earles, J. A. (in press). Intelligence is the best predictor of job performance. *Current Directions in Psychological Science.*

Rothstein, H. R., Schmidt, F. L., Erwin, F. W., Owens, W. A., & Sparks, C. P. (1990). Biographical data in employment selection: Can validities be generalizable? *Journal of Applied Psychology, 75,* 175–184.

Schmidt, F. L. (1991). Why all banding procedures in personnel selection are logically flawed. *Human Performance, 4,* 265–277.

Schmidt, F. L., Hunter, J. E., & Pearlman, K. (1981). Task difference and the validity of aptitude tests in selection: A red herring. *Journal of Applied Psychology, 66,* 166–185.

Schmidt, F. L., Ones, D. S., & Hunter, J. E. (1992). Personnel selection. *Annual Review of Psychology, 43,* 627–670.

Schmidt, F. L., Urry, V. W., & Gugal, J. F. (1978). Computer assisted tailored testing: Examinee reactions and evaluations. *Educational and Psychological Measurement, 38,* 265–273.

Thorndike, R. L. (1986). The role of general ability in prediction. *Journal of Vocational Behavior, 29,* 332–339.

Zeidner, M. (1988). Cultural fairness in aptitude testing revisited: A cross cultural parallel. *Professional Psychology Research and Practice, 19,* 257–262.

NAME INDEX

517

Name Index

Weitzel, H., 120, 128
Wellback, H. C., 407, 417
Wernimont, P. F., 430, 447
Wetzel, C. D., 222, 223, 234
Whetzel, D. L., 168, 506, 509, 515
White, L. A., 42, 60, 65, 70, 292, 303
Whitener, E. M., 298, 305
Wiener, J., 350, 384
Wiener, Y., 140, 170
Wiesner, W. H., 122, 134, 136, 139-140, 142, 162-163, 170
Wigdor, A. K., 58, 67, 175, 182, 195, 201, 202, 429, 446
Wilcox, K. L., 213, 234
Wiley, W. W., 290, 304
Williams, R. L., 173, 202
Williams, W., 117, 127
Wilson, M. A., 289, 309
Wilson, S. L., 219, 238
Wing, H., 97, 132, 235, 241, 253, 256, 259, 260, 270, 314-315, 337, 484, 496
Wise, L. L., 49, 66, 92, 96, 211, 229, 238, 239, 293, 294, 303, 309
Wise, S. L., 214, 238
Wojnaroski, P., 359, 381

Wolfe, J., 218, 238-239
Woodward, J., 72, 98
Wright, P., 161, 170
Wroten, S. P., 6, 33
Wundt, W., 276
Wyer, R. S., Jr., 152, 170
Wylie, G., 219, 238

Y

Yarkin-Levin, K., 216, 234
Yen, W. M., 225, 239
Young, W. Y., 211, 239
Yu, L., 220, 232
Yukl, G., 49, 70

Z

Zaleznik, A., 374, 384
Zara, A. R., 212, 233
Zedeck, S., 3, 53, 56, 69, 122, 123, 134, 291, 292, 304-305, 308, 319, 337, 491, 498, 500, 514
Zeidner, J., 311, 340
Zeidner, M., 498, 515
Zeithaml, V. A., 89, 97
Zook, L. M., 49, 66
Zuckerman, M., 90, 91, 98

SUBJECT INDEX

A

Ability requirements model, and validation, 291. *See also* Knowledge, skills, and abilities
Academy of Public Service, 400
Accuracy, speed versus, 51
Adaptation to environment, as selection out function, 345–346
Administration: consistency of, 126; and fairness, 181–184; and performance, 48, 57, 83–87
Administrative Careers With America, 394
Age, workforce distribution of, 386
Airline personnel, and performance, 57–58
Allegiance, in contextual performance, 81
Alternative path models, for performance, 60
Alternative predictors, and fairness, 179–180
Altruism, in contextual performance, 76, 90
American Association of Retired Persons, 402
American Council on Education, 397

American Educational Research Association, 173, 200
American Express: Academy of Finance of, 400; and telecommuting, 399
American Psychological Association, 173, 200, 214, 228, 284, 302
American Society for Personnel Administration, 468, 474
Americans with Disabilities Act (ADA) of 1991, 126, 189–191, 219, 401, 482
Analogous tests, and validity, 283
Analytic tests, and validity, 277, 282–283
Apple Computer: family issues at, 398; Spider system at, 458
Applicants: affective reactions of, 243–253; attitudes and behaviors of, 240–274; attracting, 397–399; background on, 240–243; conclusion on, 268–269; deception by, 256–262; examples of, 242, 243–244, 254, 266; generalists among, 403–404; indirect research on, 263–265; issues of, 507–508; manipulative strategies of, 254–262, 267; research needed on, 248–253, 263–268;

and workforce characteristics,
251–252
Arizona, telecommuting in, 399
Armed Forces Qualification Test
(AFQT), 223
Armed Services Vocational Aptitude
Battery (ASVAB), 222, 223–224
Asians, discrimination against, 191
Assessment centers: and predictor
constructs, 122–124; in small set-
tings, 433–436; and staffing
models, 468
Assessment Systems Corporation,
206–207, 228
Assessors, selection and training of,
433–434
AT&T, liberal arts graduates at, 404
Atlantic Richfield, and career lattice,
406
At-will employment, impact of,
349–350
Attribute-job performance issues,
and computerized testing,
208–211
Attributional bias: in interviews,
151–152, 159; and selection out,
361
Automaticity, controlled processing
versus, 52

B

Becton Dickinson, staffing at, 463
Behavior sampling: in interviews,
148–149; issues of, 504, 505; for
predictor constructs, 126
Behaviorally Anchored Rating Scales
(BARS) technique, 49, 109, 141
Bennett Mechanical Comprehension
Test, 300
Biodata: on male and female stu-
dents, 118; for predictor con-
structs, 116–119; in small set-
tings, 432–433
Blue Cross/Blue Shield, and
telecommuting, 399
Boeing, and staffing, 471
Boston Railway Company, 277
Break-even analysis, of utility,
330–331

Bridges Program, recruiting from,
401
Brogden-Cronbach-Gleser formula,
315–316, 318, 320, 321, 329
Buick, and selection out, 371
Buros Institute of Mental Measurements, 220

C

California, telecommuting in, 399
California at Los Angeles, Univer-
sity of, surveys by, 397
California Psychological Inventory,
112
Campbell Soup, and staffing,
457–458
Canadian Pacific, and staffing, 454
Capital budgeting analysis, and utility, 316–318
Career ladders/lattices, and promotion, 406–407
Carrier, and staffing, 471
Chase Manhattan Bank: selection
out at, 352; and staffing, 457
China, work done in, 463
Cincinnati Milacron, and staffing,
458
Citibank: in school partnership, 401;
and staffing, 456
Citizenship, organizational, 75–76,
87–88, 93
Civil Rights Act of 1964 and
amendments, 176–177, 188, 482,
498, 507
Cognitive ability tests: attitudes
toward, 251; and construct validity, 301; and interviews,
143–147; in small settings, 429;
in staffing models, 450, 472; and
test bias, 192–193
Colleges and universities, partnerships with, 400
Commercial Credit Corporation,
and staffing, 463
Committee on Performance Measurement in the Military Services, 58
Commitment, in contextual performance, 78, 85–86, 91

ISBN 1-55542-475-9